High-Rise Manual
Typology and Design, Construction and Technology

High-Rise Manual

Typology and Design, Construction and Technology

Edited by Johann Eisele, Ellen Kloft

Birkhäuser – Publishers for Architecture
Basel · Boston · Berlin

Contents

Foreword

Johann Eisele, Ellen Kloft

Shanghai, Singapore, Kuala Lumpur, Sao Paulo, Chicago and New York: the major metropolitan centers around the world are unimaginable without high-rises. It isn't just that we have become accustomed to the skyline. The stacked area development in these megacities is inconceivable and would be impossible to organize in layers with only a few floor levels.

Warsaw and Moscow are two European examples of cities where the high-rise enjoys a positive image: residential density per square kilometer and urban density in terms of opportunities for working and leisure time go hand in hand and are appreciated.

In Western Europe, conversely, there is considerable resistance to the high-rise genre: the traditional, organically evolved European city is governed by urban planning directives that preclude an impartial treatment of this building form, and the type is unpopular for the residential function.

In recent years, however, high-rises have become more accepted. The city of Frankfurt am Main plays a leading role in bringing about this change in Europe: there are good reasons why it has been dubbed "Mainhattan" in analogy to Manhattan.

Increasing acceptance in Europe and especially the Asian boom in high-rise development provide the principal argument for publishing this high-rise manual. The complex task of planning high-rises can only be fully understood if not only the basic foundations but also the many interfaces between the individual disciplines are identified and considered. More than 20 authors offer an overview of the planning processes required for high-rise development and construction.

In response to the central theme of what is involved in the creation of a high-rise, the contributing authors address all the relevant issues surrounding this building task – from project development and controlling to permits and site supervision, from foundations to load-bearing structures and façade technologies, and finally from office organization to facility management.

Each contribution explores the relevant building task from the perspective of the various disciplines; the individual chapters present the basic principles and shed light on interactions with other disciplines. The featured examples illustrate that high-rise development cannot be motivated solely by the ambition to create extremely tall buildings. The taller a structure, the more limited the freedom in terms of form and design: the dominant themes are structural and constructional issues such as wind bracing, load transfer and fire protection. As fascinating as the race for the tallest high-rise in the world may be, the topic of the socially responsible, "sustainable high-rise", which meshes with the urban fabric, minimizes its impact on our environment and is designed to serve humankind, is no less interesting. In this regard, we still have a long way to go.

A Brief History of the High-rise

Johann Eisele

Excavations and many reconstruction attempts give us a fairly accurate image of the Tower of Babel. While the tower had some predecessors, it is the best-known and most fateful attempt to come closer to God using a structure built by human hands. Erected on a plan of roughly 92 by 92 meters and rising to the same height, nearness to God was surely not achieved: after all, high plateaus and mountains were regarded as sacred sites and the seat of gods in many cultures, and they soared to far greater heights by natural means.

Across all cultures, the soaring element reaching for the sky is always a semantic symbol of faith and nearness to God. Fundamentally, nothing has changed in this regard even today, although it is worth noting that the symbols of spiritual power have been transferred to worldly power.

USA: Chicago and New York

The first large office buildings were built towards the end of the 19th century in Chicago, sprouting like mushrooms from the ground. Increasing the building heights was the logical consequence of the enormous pressure on the building sector as a result of rapid population growth (1850: 30,000 inhabitants; 1870: 300,000; 1890: 1 million; end of the 19th century: 1.7 million), lack of space and speculation. Building high on the smallest possible footprint was not a demonstration of power but a reflection of economic necessity.

High-rises that were intended to demonstrate the economic success and hence the power of the clients they were built for would come later, especially in New York.

Europe

In Europe, the high-rise did not come into play as a building type until after the First World War, although the initial euphoria was quickly followed by skepticism: the organically grown European city was less suited for the American model. The spiritual symbols of power had become the yardstick for urban development and stood in the way, as they continue to do today, of impartial implementations of this building type. Frankfurt am Main was the only site where several high-rises were erected in the late 1960s on the western edge of the old city core. Inspiring hostility at the time, the pejorative catchword "Mainhattan" has become a positive attribute today and has sparked a current high-rise boom. Like no other European city, the silhouette is dominated by the juxtaposition of high-rises and the Frankfurt Cathedral, an unmistakable expression of the city's corporate image, which demonstrates progress, prosperity and economic power.

High – higher – highest

As early as 1896 Louis H. Sullivan answered his own question on the principal characteristic of a major office building: "It must be tall – every inch of it must be tall. The force and power of height must reside in it – the glamour and pride of enthusiasm." [Ada Louise Huxtable: Zeit für Wolkenkratzer]

Yet the high-rise is insufficiently characterized by height alone; it must be higher than all others, at least for a time. The Masonic Temple (1892/ 21 floors/ nearly 100 m high) was the first "tallest building in the world", the Empire State Building held the honor for more than 40 years (1931–1972/ 381 m), only to be surpassed by the World Trade Center (1972/ 415 m) and now the Petronas Towers (1998/ 452 m) – although the latter have "stolen" the title, so to speak, by installing the antenna as the official building peak, the only reason why they are measured as being taller than the Sears Tower (1974/ 442 m). But the intervals are growing ever shorter. The record has shifted from the United States to Asia, and Europe will hardly be able to play a role in this race.

Learning from the USA and Asia: Multifunctional High-rises

Skyscrapers have firmly established themselves in the United States and in Asia, where they are the natural focus of any metropolitan image. In the European city, the high-rise of the future could improve the immediate environment for people working, living and relaxing in the city by providing overlapping uses. This would mean both quantitative and qualitative (added) density in the urban environment. "West Ends" filled with office workers in the daytime and deserted at night, could be brought to life around the clock. This kind of added density, however, requires high-rises that differ from the familiar models. Uses such as theater, church, school, cinema or athletics facilities can be envisioned for high-rises; the Downtown Athletic Club in New York (architects: Starrett & van Vleck, Duncan Hunter Ass.) set an early example in 1931. In response to these unconventional uses and the increased space requirements per floor, the high-rise type will undergo a noticeable lateral expansion, which will, in turn, lead to high-rises of lower and medium height: "minimax" and "midimax houses". The structural and technical requirements will become less stringent and efforts can once again focus increasingly on form and design.

Even without taking these ideas of added density and the possible improvements to mixed use of urban areas into account, future high-rises must be planned and realized with mixed use in mind. In Europe this challenge is regarded as anywhere from undoable to difficult. Public uses for the bottom floors have become the norm, but even public

observation platforms and/or restaurants at the penthouse level often fail as a result of investor interests. But mixed use goes beyond such definitions. These problems do not seem to arise in Asia and North America, or at least they seem solvable: the high-rise is understood as a city within the city and thus makes an important contribution towards solving the structural and technical problems, as well as with regard to social problems and social responsibility.

Learning from Europe?: Energy-optimized High-rises

Many concepts and a few built examples demonstrate how the high-rise type can be used as an urban building block in large cities. Developments in Europe show that energy-conserving measures can produce high-rise types that offer new design opportunities.

Ken Yeang (Kuala Lumpur) takes his ideas a step further and formulates a fully integrated approach in his book "The Green Skyscraper": he defines important urban and regional criteria (orientation towards the sun and principal wind direction, shading for neighboring buildings, adaptation to daytime and changing temperatures, etc.) as the characteristics of future high-rise generations.

In addition to these energy-related and ecological ideas, the evolution of differentiated high-rise types in response to mixed use could also make an important contribution towards increased acceptance in some countries, and hence a more differentiated design of the external form as a reflection of internal content. Load-bearing structure and façades would no longer have to answer to the primary imperative of extreme conditions. Instead, there would be room for play: Sullivan's motto "form follows function" and the idea that underpins it, namely to design a building from the inside out, would be given another chance.

Typology

Ellen Kloft

1. When Does a Building Become a High-rise?

In everyday usage, the term high-rise commonly designates any tall building. The height at which a building is considered tall is, of course, relative and has undergone many changes at different times and places throughout all epochs of building history. A building is characterized as a high-rise when it is considerably higher than the surrounding structures and explodes their scale. For example, if buildings in an urban setting have an average height of two to three stories, a 5-story building that soars above them may be considered a high-rise. However, matters become more complicated if a building's neighbors are five to six stories high: now a building exceeding their height by a mere two to three stories will barely be perceived as a dominant structure. The town planners' definition of a high-rise as a building that rises above the skyline offers a relative but not absolute measure. Obviously it will scarcely serve as a basis for an unequivocal definition of a high-rise.

In Germany, consensus has been reached for the purposes of building supervision to define a high-rise in accordance with certain safety criteria. The dictates of fire protection and, above all, the effective use of fire escapes, have produced the following definition: "High-rises are buildings in which the floor of at least one occupied room is more than 22 m above the natural or a prescribed ground level."

Other countries also have building laws that define buildings exceeding specified heights (which can vary between 13 m and 50 m) as high-rises. This limit may even vary within a single country. It is therefore difficult to generalize about how high-rises are defined in international legislation. In their comparative surveys of high-rise buildings, international databases such as skyscrapers.com have chosen a building height of 35 m or 12 stories as a benchmark. From the standpoint of building typology, the category of height alone – whether for fire safety or for database considerations – is not satisfactory for determining whether or not a building should be classified as a high-rise. The construction of tall buildings also includes questions of form and design. These, in turn, are primarily related to the load-bearing structure, which must not only be designed to withstand the horizontal loads generated by the wind and earthquakes, but also take into account never-ending developments in building technology as well as the environmental and social compatibility of large structures.

The forms assumed by high-rise buildings have changed repeatedly over the course of time. Inventions and developments affecting structures and technologies, manifold influences exerted by prevailing legislation regulating the impact of high-rises on their immediate surroundings and urban surroundings, and last but not least, a wealth of architectural theories and styles have all left their mark on high-rise design. The following contains a survey, presenting typical examples, of the chronological development of this type of building and discusses the question: What are the characteristic features of the development of the high-rise as a specific type of building at a particular time and place?

We cannot consider the development of high-rise buildings in Europe and subsequently in Asia without first examining high-rise typologies in the USA. Tall buildings obviously existed long before the United States was founded: in Ancient Rome, for example, the timber-framed houses constructed to accommodate the lower classes in mass housing were around 35 m high. However, the progressive development of the high-rise proper begins in 19th-century Chicago, and its continual typological evolution can be followed there and in New York well into the 1970s. Although other US cities followed this line of development, they have had nothing like the influence of Chicago or New York on high-rise construction.

2. The Beginnings in the USA

Chicago – the Block

The high-rise as a specific type of structure originated in the booming city of Chicago towards the end of 19th century. Its development was decisively influenced by the great inventions of the age. The technological preconditions were created with the development of safe elevators and the skeleton steel structure made of rolled iron sections – two of the most important parameters – and with the development of service systems, such as communications systems. Their combined impact led to the development of large office blocks and expensive floor areas stacked on top of one another.

1 Home Insurance Building, Chicago, William LeBaron Jenney, 1884

2 Reliance Building, Chicago, Burnham and Root, 1894

3 Masonic Temple, Chicago, Burnham and Root, 1892

4 Singer Tower, New York, Ernest Flagg, 1908

5 Woolworth Building, New York, Cass Gilbert, 1914

Despite the use of skeleton structures of cast and wrought iron, the first big office blocks in Chicago do not seem to strive for the heavens; the horizontal structure of their brick and natural-stone façades lend them a certain heaviness reminiscent of the Italian Renaissance palazzo (Fig. 1).

However, the development of light and powerful steel skeleton structures soon emancipated architecture from its classical appearance (Fig. 2). Vertical structural elements were accentuated to emphasis their lightweight character and to create the impression of soaring façades. Furthermore, façades were increasingly reduced to lightweight shields mounted on a load-bearing structure separating the load-bearing and boundary functions. Incidentally, the first building to receive the epithet "the world's tallest building" was the Masonic Temple (Fig. 3). It had a public viewing platform almost 100 m above the ground. Thematizing the capital and exploiting the building's view as a popular attraction were quite novel approaches at the time. What are the characteristics of these new soaring office buildings?

Louis H. Sullivan (1856–1924) must be mentioned in this context. Sullivan may be considered the first theoretician of high-rise aesthetics. Between 1880 and 1895, when the first tall office blocks were all the rage in Chicago, Sullivan, and John Wellborn Root (1850–1891) formulated the principles of an architecture in which "form follows function". The new style, which became known around the world as the "Chicago School", helped pave the way for the Modern Movement. The structure became a form-giving element and was clearly identifiable from outside. Louis Sullivan was the first to define the rules for designing high-rises [1]. To render the scale of the tall buildings legible, he subdivided the building into base, shaft and capital. This tripartite division is barely perceptible in the high block structures built in Chicago. Later, however, it was sometimes transferred dogmatically onto the outer form and can be considered typological of high-rise buildings in all epochs of their construction. A law passed in 1893, drastically limiting permissible height to 40 m, temporarily halted any further development of the high-rise in Chicago. As a consequence, Chicago was compelled to surrender its leading role in high-rise construction and development to New York.

New York – the Block and the Tower

In New York, the evolution of the high-rise was determined by two factors: the development of the idea of the tower and the influence of eclecticism. Speculators' demands for maximum exploitation of the land sent buildings constructed on small plots soaring to new heights. We now see the transition from the tall office block to the office tower. An attempt was made to create the high-rise building as a homogeneous whole in historicist style. Gothic, Romanesque and Beaux Arts were employed as metaphors to link the new with the old.

In 1908, Ernest Flagg designed a new tower for the existing 14-story Singer building (Fig. 4). In its form, the top of the Singer Tower imitates the corner towers of the Louvre in Paris. Its tower-like extension made it the most famous building in America and the tallest office tower in the world. Thousands traveled to New York to visit the viewing platform. Its design cites historicist forms in an endeavor to soften the futurist image of the high-rise. The soaring vertical elements of Gothic proved particularly suitable for creating a stylized mask to clad the high-rise. Soon the high-rise buildings of this epoch, such as the Woolworth Building, were to become the cathedrals of commerce (Fig. 5). Attention was given in particular to accentuating the forms of their pinnacles, turning them into symbolic advertisements for the buildings, their clients and architects and, indeed, the entire city. The term "skyscraper" was coined. The public acceptance of the skyscraper's architectural language grew, reaching its zenith in the Golden Twenties.

New York, The 1916 Zoning Laws – the Wedding Cake

It was only when building clients and architects began pushing the exploitation of plots to extreme lengths that the enthusiast response skyscrapers had met with in New York declined. Consequently, there was a shift away from the slender tower form in favor of the more compact, tall block structure. The great bone of contention was the Equitable Building (Fig. 6). Following public protests, limits were imposed on such developments, which threatened to destroy the cityscape and jeopardized neighbor laws. As a result, new legislation was passed: the 1916 Zoning Laws.

6 Equitable Building,
New York,
Ernest Graham, 1915

7 Barclay Vesey Building,
New York, Voorhees,
Gmelin und Walker, 1926

8 Chrysler Building,
New York, 1930

9 Empire State
Building,
New York, 1931

10 PSFS Building,
Philadelphia, 1932

11 RCA Building,
Rockefeller Center,
New York, 1940

These laws prescribed the construction of the so-called "setback building", which meant that the more a building was set back towards the top, the higher it was allowed to rise. This legislation instructed architects which form their buildings were to assume. The Barclay Vesey Building (Fig. 7) is an example of how the Zoning Laws were implemented. Buildings thus constructed may be classified as high-rise structures with three distinct zones and greatly extended pinnacles. This style, created by setting back buildings in distinct levels, is often referred to as the "wedding-cake style".

New York – the American Skyscraper

The race to achieve ever-greater heights continued despite the Zoning Laws. For if the floor area were reduced to a quarter of the ground-floor area by introducing setbacks, a building could be made to rise indefinitely. In the early 1930s, probably the two most famous skyscrapers in the world were constructed: the Chrysler Building designed in theatrical Art Deco style by architect William van Alen (Fig. 8), and the Empire State Building designed by Schreve, Lamb and Harmon (Fig. 9). The Empire State Building, the archetype of the American skyscraper, finally reached the limits of the proven steel-skeleton structure. At 381 m, the Empire State Building remained the world's tallest building for more than forty years: from 1931 to 1972. The economic crisis combined with the radical change in the spirit and style embodied in Modernism brought to an end the era of the Golden Twenties and that of the skyscraper too.

The International Style – Simple Forms

In 1922, radical new goals were formulated in what was probably the most famous international high-rise competition: the competition for the Chicago Tribune Tower in Chicago. A new generation of European architects, such as Gropius and the three Dutchmen Bijvoet, Duiker and Zandvoort (representatives of German Bauhaus architecture and the De Stijl movement in Holland respectively), entered the competition, submitting designs with new radical goals. Even though their designs had little chance of winning, they nevertheless revealed a definite commitment to technology, functionality and clear lines. Modernist architects had entered the arena.
In 1937, Walter Gropius was offered a chair at Harvard; that same year, Laslo Moholy-Nagy founded the new Bauhaus in Chicago; and in 1938, Mies van der Rohe became director of the Illinois Institute of Technology. In the disturbing years between the War and the economic crisis two buildings were erected under the sign of Modernism: the PSFS Building in Philadelphia in 1932, designed by Howe and Lescaze (Fig. 10) and the RCA Building of the Rockefeller Center, designed by Hood & Foulhoux, Hofmeister, Corbett, Harrison & Mac Murrey, which was erected in New York in 1940 (Fig. 11).

The PSFS Building was one of the first unmistakable attempts to apply the principles of the International Style of the Modern Movement to the American skyscraper. However, it was only in 1947 – shortly after the Second World War – that Ludwig Mies van der Rohe initiated an entirely new generation of

high-rise buildings, of which Lake Shore Drive Apartments in Chicago (Fig. 12), with their typical curtain-wall façades, were an early example. Between 1948 and 1969, Mies van der Rohe designed fourteen high-rises in Chicago, which gave him an opportunity to develop and perfect an archetype. His high-rise buildings look very similar to one another, for Mies van der Rohe was fundamentally opposed to the notion that each one had to have a distinct character. His buildings are based on a simple cubic form and display great attention to detail. The Seagram Building of 1958 (Fig. 13), planned in co-operation with Philip Johnson, became the prototype of the modern office tower. Subsequently, office towers were built in Mies van der Rohe style all over the world. However, the replicas did not attain the quality of the originals. The word skyscraper had more or less fallen into disuse; from a certain height upwards the buildings were simply referred to as tall buildings, high-rises or IGH (Immeubles de Grande Hauteur).

New York, The Zoning Laws of 1961 – A High-rise with an Entrance Plaza

The Seagram Building was also innovatory with respect to urban planning. It was set back from the property line to create a large plaza in front. This mode of construction influenced New York's new building legislation, the 2nd Zoning Laws of 1961, which now permitted greater concentration in return for public space on the site. Where the top had once been the most significant element of skyscrapers, this new type of high-rise building

12 Lake Shore Drive
Apartments,
Chicago, 1947

13 Seagram Building,
New York,
Mies van der Rohe, 1958

14 Pennzoil Plaza Building,
Houston/Texas, Philip Johnson
and John Burgee, 1976

15 AT&T Building, New York,
Johnson/Burgee Architects,
1984

16 Humana Building, Louisville,
Michael Graves, 1986

focused attention on the base as the public zone. The greater floor-space index that was now allowed for a building with a plaza triggered a building boom. A problem arose, however, when several of these buildings are placed alongside one another they create a rather unsatisfactory urban setting. The "plazas" pass into one another without interruption, dissolving the property line completely.

Postmodernism

In the 1970s and 1980s, people began search-ing for alternatives to the stereotypical build-ings of the Modern Movement. Clearly defined forms were distorted to create huge sculptural forms; instead of being treated as purely functional components, technical ele-ments were exaggerated to create decorative details or else concealed behind historicist façades. For instance, the Pennzoil Plaza Build-ing in Houston abandons the right angle to make a striking building out of an otherwise anonymous box (Fig. 14). The AT&T Building (Fig. 15) conspicuously draws on historicism. It is designed as a skyscraper in a classical sheath with a crown that New York Times critic Paul Goldberger referred to as a vastly exaggerated version of a Chippendale pedi-ment. The striking tripartite division of the building plays an important role in Post-modernist high-rise architecture. It represents an attempt to use a striking base zone in connection with a tall building and a conven-tional street development. This new aware-ness of the significance of the street space and scale led to another change in New York's

legislation in 1981. The new law stipulated that the base of the building was not to be set back by more than three meters on certain streets in order to preserve the property line. At the same time, appropriate measures had to be taken with new buildings to extend public access routes. This law aimed to ensure that public street space also extended into the building. In the Humana Building, for instance, this is achieved by means of a large front hall lined with tall pylons (Fig. 16).

The tall buildings designed by Michael Graves are characterized by their independent base, which is pushed up against the street edge. The high-rise above is set back from the base, which, in turn, integrates the public zone – a feature typical of this type of building. The high-rise as a structure defined by public uses, communications areas with atriums, conser-vatories for relaxing, shopping zones and other attractions has become the theme of a whole new generation of buildings. The tower and the base receive distinct uses as two sep-arate zones.

In addition to this high-rise family there are other types in which the top of the building is given conspicuous thematic treatment. The skyline and prestigious appearance play a very important role here. Since the 1970s, it has become impossible to consider the typology of high-rises as a chronological evolution as styles have developed parallel to one another. Nor is it possible to focus on the USA alone, because Europe (since the 1950s and 1960s) and Asia (since the 1980s and 1990s) have played an increasingly significant part in the development of the high-rise.

3.   High-rise Construction in Europe

Developments before 1945

At the end of the 19th century, Europe played an important role in developing new building materials such as steel, glass and reinforced concrete and in applying innovatory con-struction techniques. The industrial revolu-tion, which introduced new production methods, created a need for large workshops, factories and warehouses as well as multi-story buildings for the rapidly growing towns and cities. In addition to factories, there was an equally great need for a completely new transport, trade and traffic infrastructure. Industry made a vital technical contribution towards creating this infrastructure as it switched over from producing cast iron to making rolled steel with standardized sec-tions. Powerful lightweight structures permit-ted the erection of structures that spanned great distances and could be used in the new halls and bridges. The use of iron in combina-tion with glass created the aesthetics of a new type of building: the railway, market and exhibition hall. In 1851 Joseph Paxton's Crystal Palace, an all-skeleton building, was erected for the World Exhibition. It was the prototype of the structural mode of construction. Another milestone in the development of iron skeleton structures was the 300 m Tower designed by Gustave Eiffel for the 1889 World Exhibition in Paris. The replacement of unwieldy cast iron by rolled iron and sheet sections and the use of riveted joints made the structure lighter and easier to calculate. Thus were created the technical and struc-tural preconditions for high-rise construction.

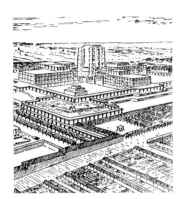

17 Wettbewerb Berlin Friedrichstraße, Mies van der Rohe, 1922

18 Die Stadtkrone, Bruno Taut, 1919

19 Vertikale Stadt, Ludwig Hilbersheimer, 1924

20 Plan Voisin for Paris, Le Corbusier, 1925

In Europe, high-rise buildings were not initially erected due to any real need, but rather as a sign of technological progress and the power of the societies in which they arose. At the time it was built, the Eiffel Tower, with its steel skeleton aesthetics, almost attained the status of a sacred building.

In the USA, on the other hand, the construction of high-rise buildings responded to a very real demand for office buildings in city centers. One need only recall the reconstruction of Chicago after its destruction by fire. American architects initially tended to be hesitant regarding the aesthetics of the new types of buildings. The "Chicago School", with its avowed principle of combining architecture and technology with a functionalism that was visible in the outward appearance of the buildings, was unable to assert itself against historicism.

In the early 20th century high-rise planning was discussed at a purely theoretical level in Europe. Not bound by the constraints of practical implementation, urban-planning and architectural theories on the new type of building were able to develop more freely.

The model of a concentrated ensemble of high-rises in the city center, as implemented in the new American cities that were evolving on grid plans, was out of the question for Europe. The structure of the historically evolved city with a medieval city center and dominant historical structures called for a variety of approaches to high-rise planning. And these were formulated in diverse ways in different European countries.

Germany

In Germany, the positioning of isolated high-rise buildings at major intersections was proposed as a model compatible with the city. High-rises located at a suitable distance from the historical center were supposed to provide points of orientation in an expanding city. Even though this subsequently proved to be a useful model, the capital needed to implement this idea was still lacking in the early days (Fig. 17).

Another striking idea in Germany was that of harmonizing the high-rises and the city, as described by Bruno Taut in his book *Die Stadtkrone*. This model conceived the high-rise as a building in the city center that towered above everything else. The idea was particularly popular among the champions of the various currents of socialism. At the time of the November Revolution *Die Stadtkrone* was seen as an image a socialist society in which the central building served as a superelevated civic center (Fig. 18).

The image of the *Stadtkrone*, which has been taken up by project studies time and again, has remained a purely theoretical construct. The same is true of the rather different approaches adopted by the architect Ludwig Hilbersheimer, who published his designs for a *Großstadtarchitektur* (metropolitan architecture) in 1924. A novel modern cityscape arose that was based on the notion of horizontal traffic layers and high-rise buildings. The commercial zones occupy the lower levels, while

the higher levels are reserved for residential purposes. Rail transport is located below ground, car traffic flows along the level occupied by the commercial zones, while the pedestrian areas, which consist of paths and bridges, are assigned to the residential level (Fig. 19).

France

Approaches developed in France also exploited the new high-rises to create completely new city structures using broken rows of buildings. By greatly concentrating residential and working space, this new type of building – the high-rise – had the potential both to satisfy the city's growing demand for space and to redress its cramped plan which let in too little light and air. Auguste Perret and Le Corbusier were the leading advocates of concept. Their high-rises, which were designed as elements of urban-development projects, reach the considerable height of 200 m and are placed at sufficient distance from one another to create space for large traffic axes and green strips in between the towers (Fig. 20).

The designs of European architects, whose architectural language is radically modern at times, stands in marked contrast to the conceptions espoused by their US colleagues. This was quite evident at the competition for the Chicago Tribune Tower (see p. 13) mentioned above. The design submitted by US architect Raymond Hood of Howells and Hood, which was premiered in Chicago and subsequently built, plainly drew on historicism, whereas

21 Wettbewerb Chicago Tribune Tower, Walter Gropius and Adolf Meyer, 1922

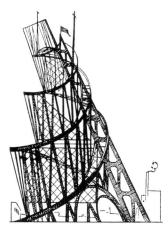

22 Monument to the Third International, Moscow, Vladimir Tatlin, 1920

23 Sky-Hook, design for a high-rise, Moscow, El Lissitzky, 1924

24 Soviet Palace, Moscow, Jofan, Helfrich and Stschuko, 1937

those entered by Walter Gropius, Bruno Taut and the Dutch De Stijl architects were distinctly Modernist. It was only after the Second World War that these currents were able to assert themselves in the United States (Fig. 21).

Russia

The ideas inspiring high-rise building in Eastern Europe, above all in Russia, were quite idiosyncratic. The development of high-rise buildings began with the idea of creating the symbolic representation of a new society. It is in this connection that the Tatlin Tower – a spiraling 300 m iron and glass structure – must be considered. It was conceived in 1919 both as a building and an architectural monument to the Third International, an organization that united all the communist parties of the world. Steel spirals bear a number of large, variously sized glass cubes containing diverse rooms, such as meeting rooms in the base, offices for the executive organs in the middle and press rooms at the top. Although it was never built, the tower become both an internationally famous icon of the ideology of the largest communist organization and a symbol of Constructivism, an architectural current inspired by a strong belief in modern technology (Fig. 22).

Following Lenin's death in 1924, there was a growing desire to construct a Palace of the Soviets as Russia's supreme building: a monument to Lenin, to the memory of the October Revolution and to the founding of the USSR in 1922. Alongside the idea of creating a palace

as a unique building there was also a desire and need for buildings for the central administration. This became the objective of countless competitions and architectural experiments in those cauldrons of ideas, the universities. During the 1920s, studies and designs for office towers up to 225 m high were completed in an astonishingly modern, technological language. Little is known of the theoretical studies then carried out on the proportions and staggered organization of high buildings, such as those designed by Malewitch (a marked contrast to those of Hugh Ferris in the United States). This is mainly due to the difficulties involved in implementing Russian architecture at the time.

Other structures that were never built, but whose fame carried across all borders, are the radical designs for a Sky-Hook by "artist-architect" El Lissitzky in 1924. He wanted to leave street areas free and accommodate the mass of the building in a block floating horizontally 45 m above ground. All together, eight Sky-Hooks were to be erected to mark the important intersections of the Boulevard Ring Road and the radial roads within the city. This great emphasis on public space was seen as a counter model to the dense concentration typical of US cities (Fig. 23).

In the ensuing years, discussions on the design for a Soviet Palace were held in ever wider circles. During the 1930s, comprehensive plans to redesign the city of Moscow were submitted. The masterplan (architect:

Jofan) for Moscow reflected the desire to dramatically present and embody Soviet power in the form of monumental buildings, squares and streets. The supreme building was not to be a mere office tower, but a monument. The building was to be crowned by a gigantic statue of Lenin, which was intended to be the biggest sculpture in the world, even bigger than the Statue of Liberty. In the early 1930s a competition was held. The location was the site of the Cathedral of Christ the Savior in the center of the city. Demolition of the building began immediately. In 1933, the Moscow architect Boris Michailowitch Jofan was appointed chief architect of the palace by the head of the urban planning department. Leningrad architects Helfrich and Stschuko co-operated with Jofan on revising the design for the Soviet Palace, which by 1937 was planned to rise to 419 m. The Lenin statue was projected to be 100 m. Construction of this mammoth project actually began in 1937. After the foundations were completed, work began on the steel skeleton. However, construction came to an abrupt halt as the Soviet Union was drawn into the Second World War (Fig. 24).

Developments after 1945

Lacking the necessary economic power, Europe had yet to demonstrate whether the implementation of ideas that had, in some cases, been radically committed to Modernism were socially compatible. Before the Second World War, high-rise buildings were few and far between and remained well below the 100 m limit. It was only when work began on reconstructing the destroyed towns

25 Zürich Hochhaus, Frankfurt am Main, Udo von Schauroth and Werner Stückeli, 1962

26 Gropiusstadt Berlin, various architects, 1962–72

27 La Défense: Grande Arche, Paris, Johan Otto von Spreckelsen, 1989

28 Tour Sans Fins with Grande Arche, La Défense in Paris, Jean Nouvel, draft, 1989

and cities and capital flowed in from abroad that high-rise planning received a new boost. In Western Europe, projects followed the US model; Eastern Europe, in contrast, consciously pursued a different course expressing its opposed ideological position. In both East and West, high-rise buildings served to symbolize the power –administrative and economic – of the towns and countries where they were erected. The rapid reconstruction carried out during the post-War period to accommodate the expanded demand for office and residential space, as well as the search for new, modern urban models, favored the choice of high-rise buildings as an appropriate for form both the inner-city and the outlying areas. Even then, high-rises tended to be isolated phenomena because planners sought to show consideration towards the historical structures that dominated the old towns and cities (Fig. 25).

High-rises were erected in inner-city areas to distinguish city centers or set landmarks at the intersections of major routes, which were often junctions of radial traffic axes linking city centers with the ring roads around them. Urban models also displayed linear arrangements of high-rises along both the ring roads and the main roads leading out of the city. Dense concentrations of high-rise buildings were also adapted as possible models, although in Europe (in contrast to the USA, where such concentrations were customary) they were generally reserved for specific areas outside the city. Only in Frankfurt am Main did the urban planners bow to the pressure of financially powerful corporations and release land in the inner city for high-rise construction.

Initially, high-rise buildings were welcomed. In the 1970s, however, enthusiasm for these types of buildings gave way to criticism of planning practice. Office tower blocks came to be viewed as negative symbols of the power of capital. Living space disappeared inside cities, leading to a functional separation between home and work and to a dramatic increase in traffic as commuters traveled to work every day. Where concentrated groups of mono-functional high-rise buildings arose, regardless of whether they were residential buildings on the outskirts or office tower blocks inside the inner cities, they ultimately left entire districts empty, creating social powder kegs (Fig. 26).

It was only in the 1980s that people began to identify more closely with high-rises. During this phase, the appearance of high-rises altered. The stereotyped forms of the Modernists gave way to the playful variations of the Postmodernists. The desire to create significant forms and to humanize the world of work led to the design of new types of high-rise structures. Great importance was now attached to integrating them into existing urban contexts. A return to the traditional values of the European city with their dominant historical structures resulted in the demand to keep important visual axes free and locate high-rise buildings outside the city center.

Below, I endeavor to show how the high-rise has evolved as a building form in urban contexts in Paris, London, Frankfurt and Moscow since 1945.

Paris

"La Défense" is a cluster of high-rises built on the outskirts of Paris as a branch of the city directly extending *La voie royale*. The above-mentioned Ville de Tour, built from a design by August Perret in 1922, was located here (see page 15). During the post-War period, the cluster was completed in several stages. An interesting aspect is the consistent application of modern urban planning, which is apparent in the strict separation of traffic flows: the railway lines at the lowest level, the road traffic above them, and the pedestrian level at the top. The first high-rises were built during the 1960s as simple geometric cubatures no higher than 100 m. And although the subsequent Postmodernist high-rises of the 1970s and 1980s are taller, they are still well under the 200 m limit. One of the highlights in the development of the area was the erection of the Grande Arche in 1989 (architect: Johan Otto von Spreckelsen) to mark the 200th anniversary of the French Revolution. This sculptural high-rise constitutes a monumental conclusion of the axis not so much because of its height, since it is only 110 m high, as because of its form. It stands as a monumental gate marking the conclusion of the axis, while providing a view of the countryside. Additional high-rises, also below 200 m, were built in the 1990s in a striking architectural language (Fig. 28).

The design (architect: Jean Nouvel et Associé) for the Tour Sans Fins, which rises to a height of 427 m, was produced during the wave of excitement that swept across the world at the turn of the millennium. The building was

29 Tour Sans Fins, Paris,
Jean Nouvel, draft, 1989

30 Tour Maine-Montparnasse, Paris,
E. Beaudouin, 1973

31 London skyline viewed from Waterloo
Bridge, 2003

32 One Canada Square,
Canary Wharf, London, Cesar Pelli
& Ass. Architects, 1991

scheduled for completion in the year 2000
(Fig. 29). As a result, Paris was also able to
boast a millennium project that reached the
very limits of contemporary technology. Had it
been designed with the aim of erecting the
tallest building in competition with other
nations, the Tours sans fins would have taken
its place among the world's tallest buildings,
making it unique in Europe. In Paris, this
project has currently been shelved – not only
for financial reasons, but also as a conscious
rejection of the fetishization of gargantuan
structures. Paris's heritage comprises a largely
intact historical city structure unequalled
anywhere in the world. Building to extreme
heights is a secondary consideration here; the
enterprise of building the world's highest
buildings has been consciously left to Asia.
In order to accommodate the pressure of
investors and the desire of major corporations
for prestigious buildings, high-rise projects
have been assigned to locations outside the
city center. Among these is La Défense, the
large high-rise cluster mentioned above. There
also exist smaller groupings of high-rises with
a city-gate function at the intersections of the
main access roads to the expressway ring and
at certain points outside this ring at a sufficiently large distance from the old city center.
The Tour Maine-Montparnasse (architect:
E. Beaudouin), which was completed in 1973
and stands alongside the Paris railway station,
is regarded as an urban-planning mistake.
This 209 m structure is the tallest high-rise
building in France. It is the only one that can
be considered a serious rival to the Eiffel
Tower (Fig. 30).

London

While it was possible to keep the historical
center of Paris almost free from high-rise
buildings, these structures have been rising
successively in the center of London right up
to the present. After the War, and indeed well
into the 1950s, London had no high-rise buildings worth mentioning. It was not until the
1960s that high-rise buildings exceeding the
100 m mark were erected. Both single and
concentrated groups of high-rises have been
constructed in the city such as the Bank
Centre to the northeast of St Paul's Cathedral.
Here, too, stands the 183 m Nat West Bank
Tower, which was erected in 1980. These
towers are formidable rivals to the dominant
historical structures (Fig. 31).

This trend has continued even though regulatory instruments were created in the mid-
1970s to control the development of high-
rises by regulating the granting of building
permits for high-rise buildings. Thus, from a
height of 150 feet (46 m) upwards high-rises
must be authorized by the Greater London
Council, which is duty bound to ensure that
they conform with the Greater London Development Plan. This plan was drawn up to
regulate the construction of high-rise buildings and thus preserve historical areas and
visual axes. The regulations have been repeatedly ignored. In 1986, the laws for high-rise
permits were relaxed. Nevertheless, from a
height of 100 m upwards, reports must be
prepared and presented for public discussion.
As a matter of principle, locations selected for
new high-rises buildings must be of both
commercial and visual significance.

In the late 1980s and early 1990s pressure
from investors finally led to the development
of Canary Wharf on the outskirts in the conversion zone of the London Docklands, an area
earmarked for far-reaching redevelopment.
The construction of high-rises there had the
advantage of not adding to the congestion of
the inner-city skyline. At the same time it met
the needs of a modern metropolis by providing locations for high-rise buildings. After
the 1985 Canary Wharf masterplan had been
revised a number of times by the American
architect's and engineer's office of SOM
(Skidmore, Owing & Merill, Chicago) and in
response to initial charges of excessive Americanization, a compromise was forged that
allowed the planned high-rise complex in the
Canary Wharf district to go ahead without
jeopardizing important historical reference
points. In 1984, the central tower of the high-
rise ensemble was erected: One Canada
Square at a height of 254 m (architect: Cesar
Pelli). The other towers have not yet been built
(Fig. 32).

Subsequent development of Canary Wharf
proceeded very slowly, and the high-rise city
also failed to fulfil its promise as an economic
success. In consequence, high-rise locations in
the city center have remained attractive since
they offer better marketing prospects.

In the City of London, towers have sprung
up a moderate height of 100–150 m.
In the mid-1980s, parallel styles asserted
themselves as Postmodernism entered the
scene. Such different buildings as the Post-
modernist bank (designed by architect Terry
Farrel) in Fenchurch Street and the building

33 Fenchurch Street, London, Terry Farrell, 1987

34 Lloyds of London, London, Richard Rogers, 1986

35 Millenium Tower, London, skyline view of building in context – visualisation, Foster and Partners

36 Swiss Re Headquarters, 30 St Mary Axe, London, visualisation, Foster and Partners, 2003

for the Lloyds of London insurance company (designed by Richard Rogers), which seemed to be committed to "true" functionalist architecture [2] have been erected. Whereas Farrel's building abstracts from classical stylistic elements, Lloyd's high-rise is embellished by its technical elements, structure and services (Figs. 33, 34).

At the end of the 1990s, a trend towards extremely tall buildings made itself felt in London, as in other metropolises, too in the form of millennium fever. This is reflected in the designs for the 383 m Millennium Tower by Sir Norman Foster and the City Point Tower by Santiago Calatrava, which was supposed to reach a height of just over 200 m (Fig. 35). Both buildings are characterized by mixed-use: combining office use and public catering areas. High-rises are increasingly becoming investment projects with flexible room structures designed to serve the requirements of future tenants with varied needs and offer additional attractions. Neither of the above projects has been implemented. As in Paris, critical voices have expressed doubts about the need for superscrapers in a European capital like London.

During the past few years, London's high-rise development has evolved a powerful dynamic of its own. After some delay, the building boom forecast for Docklands finally took off: from 1999 to 2005, twenty new high-rises are scheduled for completion. Very few of these will exceed 150 m; the majority will be in fact under 100 m. Their names will mundanely reflect their addresses, e.g. 40 Bank Street Building. Even so, there is still the occasional

spectacular project, such as the tower designed by Renzo Piano – a pointed needle that is supposed to soar to 310 m. It is, however, uncertain whether this project will be realized. One thing is sure, though: the planned Millennium Tower will not be constructed. In its place, the approximately 180 m tower, Swiss Re Headquarters, 30 St Mary Axe, also designed by Foster and Partners, will be erected in the center of London. That this conspicuous structure has already achieved fame prior to its completion is due more to its striking form – which has lent it its name, the Cuban Cigar – than its height (Fig. 36).

Frankfurt am Main

Frankfurt am Main is another center of high-rise construction in Europe, although it is far smaller than the other two European metropolises – Paris and London – described above. The development of high-rise structures in Frankfurt, with its a dense concentration of office towers in the city center, has closely followed the US model. As Frankfurt was the main base for the US occupying forces, its international airport was rapidly extended; this development created the conditions for today's commercial hub. Following the decision of the major banks to move their headquarters to Frankfurt, the constitution of the Bundesbank with its headquarters in Frankfurt in 1957 and the establishment of the international stock exchange in Frankfurt, the city became Germany's financial services center. Corporations have pushed for the best locations and demanded the release of land in the center to develop offices. City planning

has ceded to this pressure in order to ensure Frankfurt a permanent place as a financial and commercial center. An extreme concentration of buildings in the inner-city area has been permitted at the cost of high property prices. Town planners have responded by creating a new office city in a green area (Niederrad).

Considered typologically, the first postwar high-rises were simple geometrical buildings of moderate height. When the original office towers were constructed, the prime aim was not so much to stage a symbolical demonstration of power as to use the land as profitably as possible. Speculation rapidly sent property prices soaring in Frankfurt's inner-city area. In 1970, the city commissioned the so-called Bank Plan, which permitted high-rises that exceeded the cathedral's height of 95 m. Although the first climate reports were made for the Frankfurt inner-city area in the early 1970s they had no effect on planning. A noticeable deterioration in the urban climate coupled with traffic problems caused by the daily flows of commuters provoked criticism of Frankfurt's planning practice. What finally sparked off public protest more than anything else was the destruction of living space and the fact that small businesses were being squeezed out of the inner city. Rents in the center and the surrounding inner-city area were too high. An inner city developed which only came alive during the day when the commuters and financially powerful customers were there and was completely dead at night. Only in the 1980s were there first signs of the public identifying with the city of Frankfurt. At the same time, efforts were made to exploit

37 Deutsche Bank, Frankfurt am Main, ABB Hanig, Scheid, Schmidt, Beckert, 1984

38 Messeturm (Exhibition Tower), Frankfurt am Main, Helmut Jahn, Murphy/Jahn, 1984

39 Kronenhochhaus, Frankfurt am Main, KPF/Nägele Hofmann Tiedemann, 1993

40 Commerzbank, Frankfurt am Main, Foster and Partners, 1997

Frankfurt's high-rises as constituting the city's image; after all, it is these buildings that both symbolize Frankfurt as an important commercial hub and attract additional corporations to this prospering region. During this phase, Frankfurt's high-rises took on a new form, increasingly resembling sculptural forms clad in reflecting façades. High-rise buildings are the symbol of Frankfurt as a banking metropolis; and the aesthetic impact of their combined mass on the city skyline is becoming more impressive as time passes. High-rises are more readily accepted, the more individual their form. High-rise euphoria became evident with the completion of the Messeturm (245 m, architect: Helmut Jahn, Chicago) in 1984. The Messeturm falls back on the typology of American skyscraper styles of the 1920s (Figs. 37, 38).

In the early 1990s, further high-rise buildings reaching 200 m were erected in the inner-city area. Frankfurt applied to be the seat of the European Central Bank. In 1993, the 208 m Kronenhochhaus (architects: KPF/Nägele Hofmann Tiedemann) and the 186 m Trianon, (Architektengemeinschaft BfG: Novotny Mähner Ass./Albert Speer & Partner) were completed. Both buildings are conspicuous for their form and the design of the "capital": the base contains a public passageway, and their striking classical tripartite division recalls the Postmodernism of US high-rise typology (Fig. 39).

The 1990 Bank Plan envisaged additional high-rise locations in the inner city. During the following years further high-rises were constructed. Planning controls affecting the height as well as the ecological and social consequences of towers were introduced, resulting in a new type of high-rise, e.g.: the Japan Center (architects: Ganz + Rolfes, 115 m), the new Commerzbank building (architects: Foster and Partners, London, 259 m), Eurotheum (architects: Novotny and Mähner Ass., Offenbach, 110 m) and the Maintower (Architects: Schweger + Partner, Hamburg, 200 m). A novel feature of these high-rises was their emphasis on mixed use – and not only office use as had formerly been the case. This was reflected in the opening-up of the base and/or top to include catering areas, or turning over the top floors to special uses (e.g. radio stations) and creating apartments above the office floors.

The search for energy-saving concepts and climatic approaches that allowed individual ventilation control via the façade without recourse to air-conditioning created a new room quality and emancipated the high-rise building from its anti-ecological image. "Hanging gardens" and spacious vertical interior rooms created new points of reference to the inside and outside. These approaches resulted in towers that were less slender than they had been in the past, and displayed office areas that could be located on the external and atrium façades (Fig. 40).

With the definitive establishment of the European Central Bank in Frankfurt and the favorable development of the office market, a new

high-rise development plan was adopted in 1999. Increasingly, plans were designed that envisaged renting out space to third parties so that high-rises would no longer be used solely by the owners. This strategy in turn changed high-rise typology. Demand arose for rental units with their own entrances, addresses and tower lobbies. This, in turn, lead to the development of larger core and access areas. The flexibility and interconnectability of the units left its mark on the floor plan and elevation, and allowed for a wide variety of office forms. The workplace of the future calls for an infrastructure that can be shared by all users. A conference room, twenty-four-hour catering services in cafeterias and bistros, as well as recreational and leisure areas close to the offices, create high-rise buildings offering more flexible use. High-rise buildings create worlds of their own. Public access requires greater security.

Access to the top of towers is financially possible only in certain cases, but where the top floors are open to the public, for example in the Maintower, they attract tourists. Enlivening base zones with richly diversified urban activities is hard to imagine because rental areas are too expensive to permit flexible small-scale use. The targeted promotion of cultural establishments and attractive after-work events is a blatant attempt to keep "bankers" in the city after working hours. Frankfurt's inhabitants identify with the metropolitan image their high-rise buildings radiate to the outside world; metropolitan life cannot, however, be created under these conditions.

41 Lomonossow University, Moscow, Lew Rudnjew, 1953

42 Kalin Prospekt, Moscow, Possochin, 1968

43 RGW building, Moscow, Possochin, 1970

44 White House, Moscow, Tschetschulin, 1981

Moscow

Most of Europe's high-rise buildings are in Central and Northwest Europe. The high-rises in Eastern Europe were erected during the Cold War in an endeavor to convey the image of a centrally run society. Moscow assumed the leading role within the Warsaw Pact and served as the model for member countries. It became a city crowned by high-rises. The Palace of the Soviets in the city center had been conceived as an ensemble surrounded by eight high-rise buildings whose overall impact was intensified by a uniform architectural language. Stylistically, these buildings recall both traditional Russian architecture with their pointed, fairytale tower-tops, and the early Gothic-like skyscrapers (those cathedral-like buildings whose outer appearance seems to belie their function as office towers) of New York, with their vertically structured shells. Each of the eight high-rise buildings was assigned a specific use independently of its impressive outward appearance: administration, university, hotel or residence. The form of these high-rises was primarily determined by urban-planning considerations. They all have a dominant function: their highest points are related to those of the Palace and form a silhouette that crowns the city. The decision to build these towers around the planned Palace of the Soviets was taken in 1947 and rapidly implemented over the following six years. In Moscow, the chief architect responsible for this project was Tschetschulin; different architects were chosen for each of the seven high-rises. All but one of the buildings were completed and are popularly referred to as the Seven Sisters. The highest building in the ensemble is the 239 m Lomonossow University building (architect Lew Rudnjew). The other high-rises are shorter – 150 m (Fig. 41).

Following Stalin's death in 1953, the construction of the central project, the Palace, was suddenly questioned: the architectural monument with Lenin's statue was no longer politically acceptable. When Chruschtschow, the new leader, took power a critical attitude to Stalin and the personality cult emerged. This was accompanied by a rejection of Stalinist architecture and finally led to the cancellation of the Palace project, which had been planned for decades and was started before the Second World War.

Even though the high-rise ensemble of the Seven Sisters still lacks a centrepiece, it has nonetheless left an unmistakable mark on the city skyline. Its impact is felt to this day, although new high-rise buildings speaking a different architectural language were also erected in the inner-city area during the 1960s.

Modern high-rise building made its appearance in Moscow with the development of the Kalin Prospekt, a complex comprising nine modern residential and administration buildings erected in a row in 1968 (Fig. 42), and the RGW building (Fig. 43), a government administration building dating from 1970 (architect: Possochin, Moscow's chief architect from 1960). Not the height of the Kalin Prospekt high-rises (a modest 100 m approximately), but the arrangement of the point blocks and slab structures has led to justified doubts about their harmonic integration into the cityscape.

The 1971 masterplan no longer envisaged high-rise buildings in the city center. This does not mean high-rise buildings are being rejected, however, since their construction was still permitted outside the central area. During the 1970s and 1980s a series of high-rise buildings, none higher than 100 m, was erected. One exception among the high-rise buildings at this time was the White House, formerly the House of the Soviets, now the Russian government building, which was designed by Tschetschulin as a prestigious state building in the backward-looking style of Soviet Postmodernist architecture (Fig. 44).

During the mid-1990s, under the changed political conditions of a rapprochement between East and West, the idea was proposed to develop a business center called Moscow City based on the US model and using US architects. The tallest building in the world, with a height of 640 m (designed by SOM architects), was supposed to dominate the ensemble on the outskirts of Moscow. Unlike the current plans in other European metropolises, high-rise buildings are no longer planned for the historical city center, with the possible exception of an "Eighth Sister". Although the Seven Sisters are postwar high-rises dating from the 1950s, their architectural language and original intention makes them a historical testimony to a bygone era. Priority has been given to preserving the buildings and the city skyline.

45 Shenzhen, China, 1998

46 Oriental Pearl TV Tower, Shanghai Pudong, 1998

47 View from the Peak, Hong Kong, 1992

4. Enter Asia

Many cities in Europe and the United States experienced their greatest periods of growth around the turn of the century during the transition to industrial society. Asia's cities, in contrast, have experienced explosive growth rates only during the past few decades with the onset of economic growth. After the Second World War, the victorious powers wielded a powerful influence in Japan and in strategically important locations in East and Southeast Asia. It was considered important to build up military, political and economic strongholds within Asia to counter the influence of communist China. This goal was reaffirmed in 1954 with the founding of SEATO (South-East Asia Treaty Organization), which was dominated by the USA. Dissolved after the Vietnam War, the alliance nonetheless exerted a considerable influence on the region's development.

The Japanese economy began to boom in the 1950s. Somewhat later than Tokyo, the city-states of Hong Kong and Singapore, both British colonies, underwent powerful economic booms as they emerged as economic and financial centers in the 1960s. They were followed by South Korea and Taiwan, the two Asian threshold countries with the most rapid growth rates. Elsewhere in Asia, the cities of Bangkok, Kuala Lumpur, Djakarta and Manila began to grow dramatically during the 1980s. Americanization, technical modernization and higher standards of living fundamentally changed the economic and social structures there. These processes triggered the development of the high-rise building and the related

technical know-how in these prospering Asian countries. For all that, the infrastructures one might expect to find in powerful economies are still lacking. Furthermore, there has been rapid urbanization of formerly rural structures; cities are growing so fast that it has become impossible to create the planning instruments needed to cope with their growth.

On the "opposite side", in China, cities have been growing upwards since the 1980s. The economic reforms introduced by Deng Xiaoping led to the establishment of Special Economic Zones which permit capitalist investment in specified areas. Through these experimental zones, China, its communist system notwithstanding, is opening up to the world economy, giving its stagnating economy a powerful boost. This has created the basis for integrating Hong Kong into the Chinese economy. (Hong Kong, the former British crown colony and international trading center, was returned to China in 1999.) Thanks to its proximity to Hong Kong, growth in Shenzhen, one of the four Special Economic Zones originally carved out in southern China, has exceeded all forecasts. In 1978, in connection with the establishment of the Special Economic Zone, Shenzhen was granted the status of a district with its own legislative authority. Before the Zone was established, the area had had a primarily agrarian economy, growing grain and rice, and had just under 30,000 inhabitants. The explosive development of the economy, which sent job vacancies soaring, raised wage levels and improved supplies of goods and leisure facilities, has increased the number of inhabitants to over three million

within two decades. Achievements in the field of construction are among the most impressive in the world. The Shenzhen skyline occupies eighth place in Wolfgang Leonhard's list of the world's skyscraper cities (Fig. 45).

Shanghai's skyline ranks even higher on the list. Shanghai is the center of economic activity in China. In the late 19th century, during the colonial era, the colonial powers forced Shanghai to open its economy to foreign trade. The growth of trade and industry made Shanghai the fifth largest city in the world by 1911. When the Red Army entered the city after the Second World War, all companies there were taken over by the state and economic ties to the outside world were severed. It was only with the economic reforms of the 1980s and the gradual introduction of market forces that Shanghai again became an attractive investment location for foreign corporations. Centrally located on the Chinese coastline, the city of Shanghai used to be the "gateway to the world" at the Yangtze delta. Shanghai is now continuing where it left off. Of all Chinese cities, it has the most considerable potential for establishing links with the world economy. In 1990, the Special Economic Zone of Shanghai Pudong was created on a hitherto undeveloped site. Shanghai's old city districts are also undergoing a phase of total reconstruction. According to observers, it seems as if a new skyscraper is completed every day.

High-rise buildings are a symbol of economic growth. In Asia, extreme heights are held to be a visible sign that a country has managed the leap into the first world. As a symbol announcing the beginning of urban

48 Petronas Twin Towers,
Kuala Lumpur, Cesar Pelli, 1998

development, television towers of conspicuous dimensions and form have been erected
there. The 333 m Tokyo Tower, dating back to
1958 and clearly inspired by the Eiffel Tower, is
an early instance of this development in Asia.
Later examples include the Kuala Lumpur Television Tower (KLTV Tower), which rises to a
height of 421 m, and the Oriental Pearl TV
Tower, 468 m high, whose construction in
1995 heralded the development of Shanghai
Pudong (Fig. 46).

All of Asia's tallest high-rises dating from the
1980s are below the 300 m mark. However,
this limit was soon to be exceeded: in 1989,
the 368 m Bank of China was built in Hong
Kong, followed shortly afterwards by superscrapers – all above 330 m – in Bangkok (Thai-
land), Shenzhen (China), Guangzhou (China)
and Kaoshiung (Taiwan). The Central Plaza
Building (374 m) built in Hong Kong in 1992
was not far off the 400 m mark (Fig. 47).

The desire to erect the world's highest building
in Asia was finally realized in Kuala Lumpur in
1998, where the Petronas Towers have stood
since 1998 (Fig. 48). With their tops peaking at
452 m (architect Cesar Pelli) they outbid the
Sears Tower in Chicago. The Petronas Towers
are part of Kuala Lumpur's largest building
complex, with a total usable floor space of
1.82 million square meters. In the social
context of a European city, a complex of this
magnitude would not have had a chance;
indeed, it would destroy any sense of proportion and ruin the city. In Asia, however, such
projects are constructed despite the absence
of infrastructure or compensatory space. And
developments such as these not only cause

entire transport systems to collapse at regular
intervals, but also bring about a dramatic
deterioration in climatic conditions.

Kuala Lumpur presents a typical example of
urban development governed by market
forces. Structural plans are designed to be
ignored. Authoritarian governments take decisions and ignore planning instruments. In
spite of this, there are no signs of large-scale
protest, on the contrary: modern urban development pursued on the basis of highly concentrated complexes and extremely tall buildings is welcomed, people seem to accept the
adverse effects. The cultural and sociological
backgrounds of Asian lifestyles are often cited
as explanations for this response. The great
degree of tolerance shown in the face of
drastic changes in living conditions is said to
stem from the old Chinese and Indian doc-
trines of I-Ching and Yin-Yang, which have
been very influential throughout Asia for
thousands of years. The ideas of predestined
fate and continual change are part of a
process in which creation, destruction and
renewal are immanent. Asia's cities grow
unrestrained, adapting continually to new
economic realities until they find a new equilibrium. Only when the optimum size has
been reached can stability be restored.
Then artistic and cultural life can flourish
anew, as is already visible in Japan and, to
some extent, in Singapore too.
A study carried out by the architect Rem Kool-
haas with Harvard University students in 1996
examined the phenomenon of explosive
overdevelopment in the Chinese Pearl River
delta, the region extending from Hong Kong
to Shenzhen to Guangzhou. The individual

studies looked at various aspects such as the
infrastructure, ideology, architecture, politics,
countryside and money in an attempt to
define new forms of urban coexistence. The
study's new vocabulary of patented terms provides a framework for describing contemporary urban reality adequately. To Western
observers, such unbridled growth is as fascinating as it is horrifying. This is as true of the
superscrapers as it is of the structures of the
new megacities.

The Taipeh Financial Center (planned height
508 m) now under construction in Taiwan is
likely to offer fresh nourishment to the obses-
sion with high-rise buildings in Asia. In contrast, plans for high-rise structures in Europe,
with few exceptions, envisage buildings of
a more moderate height. New safety precau-
tions are in demand worldwide following the
catastrophe of 11 September.
Additional investment in both fire protection
and redundant structural systems hike up the
costs of a mode of construction that is expensive at the best of times. In view of the high
costs, questions of durable construction are
becoming increasingly important. How can
we develop sufficiently flexible room structures (for high-rise structures) that are adaptable to new user requirements and new
technologies? Alongside the conquest of
extreme heights, these are topics to which
people involved in high-rise building will
have to devote more attention in the future.
They will also give new impetus to high-rise
building.

01   Project Development

Joachim Tenkhoff

High-rise Projects from the Developer and Investor Perspective

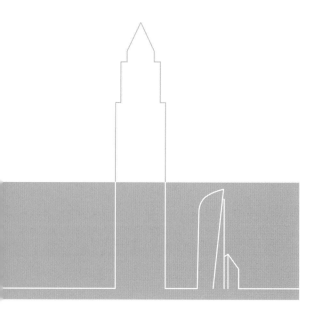

1.1 Introduction

The North American term of project developer was first mentioned in Europe at the beginning of the 1980s and met with rather condescending amusement at the time. After two decades of establishing a professional profile and industrialization in the real estate sector, "project development" has become an established term, albeit one that has yet to enjoy a universally valid definition.

In the United States, "development" encompasses the entire process from land acquisition to building completion and in some cases even project marketing. In Germany, on the other hand, project development is applied specifically to the phase between land or property acquisition and the granting of the building permit, not least thanks to the stringent practice exercised by several market leaders in this sector.

For the purpose of this study, we shall follow the American model and breathe life into the development of high-rises.

The expression "developer" describes companies that develop real estate projects, on the one hand, and individual professional experts, on the other. Once again, neither of these designations is uniformly employed in Germany, and they are used differently from company to company. Thus, a developer can be understood as a straightforward service provider without capital contribution, or as a developer/investor. The following paragraphs address the activities of the developer/investor.

The professional designation of "developer" is nearly always employed for the team leader, who has a high level of competence with regard to the relevant building object.

"High-rise" is understood here as an office high-rise. Whereas individual proprietors base their site selection on specific criteria, the selection criteria of a developer, that is a firm, which is chiefly concerned with renting property, are entirely different in scope. The developer is interested first and foremost in whether he or she can in fact rent out the product. His actions in each phase of the process are user-oriented. This chapter is therefore not focused on the development of high-rises in general, but specifically on the development of a high-rise erected for the sole purpose of future rental and disposal.

1.2 Project Development

Planning

User-oriented developers are increasingly confronted with tenants who insist on the optimum efficiency of the rented areas in response to financial pressures within their own trades or sectors. All major rental agreements today are contingent upon the tenant's consultation with specialists to ensure that the tenant is guaranteed the most efficient use of the space. This influence on the part of the client has considerably elevated the entire planning phase to a higher professional standard in recent years. Today, options for multiple uses, flexibility and efficiency of use enter into the planning considerations at a very early stage.

Functional Concept

This has led to a greater focus on multiple uses and multifunctional planning for developer real estate. Although high-rise planning is always oriented towards small footprints in comparison to a "standard building", there are considerable differences in the efficiency in individual high-rise planning initiatives. It is the task of the developer to guide the building towards an economically acceptable form in collaboration with the architect.

Fire protection is an important factor, which has considerable influence on the planning of the high-rise core as a result of requirements for the number and size of escape stairwells, and smoke extraction. User comfort in terms of rapid response times for elevators also plays an important role in determining the number of elevators and hence the dimension of the core. These issues result in compromises, which impact the profitability of the building.

Architects

While the quintessential high-rise architect was formerly the exception rather than the rule in Europe, the last decade has witnessed a trend among architectural firms to specialize in high-rise construction. It is increasingly evident that high-rise design calls for special experience and expertise, and that many architecture firms are overtaxed by the challenges this poses. The competency of the firm is without doubt an essential criterion in choosing an architect.

Profitability

The experienced developer will draft a pro forma document in the very early stages, which he or she will undertake to continually refine up to the point when a decision to invest is made and a financing contract is signed with the banking syndicate or group of underwriters. The basis for such a pro forma document is both, a comprehensive cost analysis and a cash-flow analysis, which should be based on a monthly scale to avoid inaccuracies.

Areas, Parking

A detailed area analysis is an essential basis for all profitability calculations in the real estate sector. This is where the first decisions are made with regard to realizing the future project. Any developer, who fails to exercise continued vigilance with regard to the area utilization ratio is committing a cardinal error in the project development. Another important consideration, which should not be underestimated, is the issue of required storage areas and parking. In terms of the latter, it is vital to take municipal parking by-laws into consideration, which can greatly diminish profitability in some instances.

Cost Estimate

The quality requirements for the base building are subject to great variations depending on location and the target tenant group. A successful cost estimate must be preceded by the quality definition of the tenant improvement. This can only be achieved through a very direct collaboration with the responsible landlord, who must undertake to evaluate the potential tenant clientele in relation to the anticipated rents. A determination is then made in terms of the standard, which the investor will offer to the tenant and the costs exceeding it, the overbuilding standard, which must be met by the tenant. This standard is contingent upon the landlord's estimation of the market situation at the moment of completion and the degree to which the landlord deems additional costs for the realization of an overbuilding standard feasible if the building is constructed on a speculative basis without advance tenant agreements.

Rent Estimate

The rent estimate is based on an estimate of the relevant net rent exclusive of heating and an additional prognosis with regard to rental periods and anticipated vacancies, factors that affect the cash-flow analysis considerably.

Pro Forma

The developer will seek to realize the capital from the project once profitability has been stabilized, that is, once full occupancy has been achieved. In this respect the free and clear return on costs and the internal rate of return (IRR – internal interest yield based on multipliers determined by the developer according to market criteria – "cap rate") are important indicators of profitability. In the age of investment banking the simple cash surplus analysis of the past is no longer sufficient to achieve financing with an adequate ratio of net worth or share capital to outside capital. Whereas the profitability calculation of the past was still a static system for cost definition, the conditions of today require a dynamic cash-flow analysis, especially with consideration of the time factor and the ability to pinpoint the impact of time defaults on the return on net worth at any given time. The pro forma must also contain various sensitivity analyses to assess potential variable influences, e.g. rents and building costs. It should also present a break-even calculation.

Partners

Owing to the investment volume required to realize a high-rise project, it is generally advisable to secure a partner for such a project with a view to risk-sharing. The number of shares and the structure within which the relevant partners will operate, especially the legal structure of the partnership, must be determined on a case-by-case basis. Changes in tax law, which have considerable impact on the disposal or sale of assets, have made the limited liability company the favourite legal structure in today's market.

It is vital to determine early on, and long before a partnership agreement is signed, whether the partners wish to sell the object or whether one partner may wish to hold onto his share for the long term. This is an important factor in how joint ventures are designed.

1.3 Renting

Optimum project marketing is especially important for successfully renting a high-rise project – whenever possible, this should be done prior to construction in the context of advance rental agreements.

Project Marketing

The marketing activities begin at a very early stage with a development billboard with acquisition characteristics. This is followed by mailings to potential tenants, flyers containing the basic data of the project, and finally the creation of computer simulation and project brochures. The success of a project is greatly dependent on the creativity of project marketing. Once again, the experience of the individual developer with regard to timing and pacing will be an essential factor in the overall success. A marketing campaign that is launched too early can lead to a complete overload in terms of market perception given a completion phase of two to three years. Experience has shown that "renting from the plan", that is, renting without a concrete building that is near completion, is often possible only in especially favorable market situations. The marketing concept must take this parameter into consideration.

Case Study: Sony Center on Potsdamer Platz, Berlin

In a development contract with the property company for the Sony Center, Tishman Speyer Properties assumed responsibility for all marketing initiatives for the object. The marketing strategy based all marketing activities on the excellent location of the object at an early stage. Henceforth, the object was referred to as the "Sony Center on Potsdamer Platz". In addition to the favorable location in downtown Berlin, three further points of emphasis were identified for the marketing strategy:
- The three extraordinary cores in the immediate vicinity of the property: government district, cultural forum and Berlin Tiergarten district.
- The architect Helmut Jahn, the ideas and concepts of his architectural design.
- The Hotel Esplanade and the translocation of historic "Kaisersaal" as a basis for numerous background stories, which were released to the media over the course of the construction phase.

The strategy placed great value on inviting media representatives to the building site regularly, taking advantage of their function as multipliers, and on keeping Berlin's citizens informed in detail with regard to the construction and the progression of the project.

In consideration of the scale of the construction, a communication concept (including setting up an "information panel") was developed to reflect the needs of the city and of neighboring building sites. The next step in the product-specific marketing was focused on positioning the project in a more concrete manner. During this phase, the Sony Center and its silhouette were celebrated as a landmark of the "new Berlin". International appeal, openness, partnership and tolerance, and the mixed-use concept for the new millennium (living and working in the 21st century), together with the fascinating architecture of transparency on different planes (horizontal and vertical), were featured as new horizons of urban design. These aspects provided the platform for the concrete image and marketing campaign. The goal was to distinguish this project from other direct competitors, to create an image and to brand the object, to solicit sympathy and public acceptance and to promote the visibility of the object and its multiple uses. The target groups were users, visitors and investors.

A subsequent step in the campaign introduced the slogan "See you tomorrow", intended to create an appealing, direct and personal line of communication on an international, easily understood and future-oriented level with a focus on encounter, exchange and communication.

The project milestones were the ground-breaking ceremony, the laying of the foundation stone, the topping-out ceremony and the grand opening on 14 June 2000 – reported in all media worldwide.

The goal of the marketing strategy was to solicit as many major users for the rentable areas as early as possible. This marketing concept was almost fully achieved with the signing of rental agreements with Sanofi-Synthelabo and Deutsche Bahn AG.

Upon opening, all rentable areas in the Sony Center were rented.

Rental Management

One essential coordination task of development is the rental management of the participating real estate agency. Even the preliminary step of identifying the principal real estate agency or agencies is only possible with a sound knowledge of the market. Although real estate agencies prefer exclusivity in marketing an individual project, it is in the interest of the developer to preserve a degree of flexibility with budget economies and to entrust at least two realtors with the bid for the object. Another essential element of rental management is the drafting of a practicable rental concept.

Estimates for renting large and small areas play a very important role in this context. Such rental principles must be established even during the prognosis stage of the preliminary pro forma and must be reflected in the rental concept.

Establishing such principles early on and setting the course accordingly has an influence both on the functional planning concept and on the cost factor (completion costs, lower efficiency, etc.). The audacity of an early decision to rent out only large or bulk areas may lead to "punishing" effects later on through higher investment costs, poor profitability and changes in the investment i.e. outside capital, should conversion into smaller units become necessary. Moreover, any restructuring or conversion of this kind will also result in a delay of achieving economic stability for the project as a result of the multitude of individual rental agreements, which have to be negotiated. The consequence of all these factors is an overall decrease in the economic viability of the project.

1.4   Sale/Disposal of Asset

The final stage in high-rise development is the completion of the project, followed by full occupancy at the earliest possible stage. Once the object is fully occupied it can be sold, and here the experience of the developer or asset manager is vitally important in terms of deciding which product should be offered to which group of buyers. Disposal of the asset to institutional investors is generally the preferred strategy in the case of high-rise projects.

The exit strategy should already be taken into consideration when the property or land is purchased for development.

1.5   Summary

This overview has shed light on the many prognoses and decisions that must be undertaken on the path from property acquisition to the sale of a high-rise. The unique risks associated with a high-rise project lie not so much in solving the technical challenges as in the accuracy of the prognosis and consequently the timing when the object is offered on the market.

1.1 Sony Center, Potsdamer Platz, Berlin
Architects: Murphy/Jahn, Chicago

02 Project Management

Frank Spandl   **A Management Tool for Temporary Organizations**

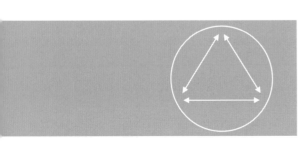

2.1 History of Project Management

Projects are distinctly different than process-oriented, shared labor tasks such as the production of industrial goods. Whereas process-oriented productions progress from design and prototype creation to a production phase, which is constantly optimized and has no defined end, projects are characterized precisely by the quality of being unique with a definite beginning and a definite end. It is common to assemble teams for each individual project – especially construction projects; for the duration of the project, these teams form what one might describe a "virtual company" with the common goal of ensuring the success of the project. For large construction projects today, however, it is hardly feasible to gather all participants in a project on site, as was the case with the building guilds in earlier times. The fact that the individual team members are in turn composed of several sub-teams poses an additional organizational challenge. The management of such temporary organizations encompasses a multitude of tasks. As in classic management theory, the principal tasks are goal definition, organization, control and management. The "Apollo" program in the United States in the 1950s and 1960s was one of the largest project tasks of the 20th century. The variables involved in this project were so complex and intertwined that it would have been impossible to adequately oversee the progress and risks with the prevailing hierarchical management methods. Consequently, new methods were developed for this task, which track the progress of the project according to manageable individual tasks instead of attempting to maintain a constant comprehensive analysis of the entire project. The project management then simply organized the interfaces and interdependencies between these individual tasks, which were coordinated independently by the participating institutions. This approach of tracking the input and output of individual work and service packages and their dependencies led to the method of networked planning in schedule controlling, which is still used today. The statement "The result of team A must be known when team B begins" can be expressed in mathematical terms and processed with the relevant computer software. The next logical step was to ask which resources Team A would require in order to achieve this goal (or how many members must be added to the team to shorten the completion time by 20 percent), with the result that schedule and resource planning became the key functions of project management. Resources, personnel or material, in turn, are closely linked to costs. Hence, the next aspects to enter into the set of responsibilities were cost analysis and dispersal of necessary moneys. Since both aspects are directly dependent on the defined goals of the project, that is, on the qualities and quantities to be achieved, the "magic triangle" of cost, schedule and quality has come to be known as the iconic image for project management tasks (Fig. 2.1).

2.2 What is Project Management?

This magic triangle is a familiar concept in the building trade, as construction projects have revolved around cost, schedule and quality since time immemorial. The responsibility of coordinating the goals and the participants in a building project lies with the clients. The end of the 1970s saw the emergence of the first external service providers for the support of project managers among major building organizations. The task of the "building consultants" of that period was to assume some of the clients' responsibilities, the client tasks, which could be delegated. Experienced building site managers and formerly outsourced building departments, respectively, began to develop these services into a new profession. The methods of integrated scheduling and professional cost management were adapted to the building trade. However, the comprehensive tasks of the client(s), the "project management", go beyond cost and schedule planning. They also include defining the tasks, deciding between alternatives and finally delivering payment for services rendered. When these project management tasks are divided between client and service provider, the domain concerned with the original client tasks is called "project leadership" and the tasks, which are delegated to the project management are referred to as "project management". Hence the term "project management" has generally been adopted to describe the delegated tasks of project leadership. It is

2.1 The "magic triangle" plus organization

important to emphasize that the assumption of project management on the part of an external provider in no way changes the tasks or services of the planners involved in a building project. The project management services must be understood exclusively as supporting and regulating the professional performance of the clients.

2.3 Goal-oriented Management – the Value System

Economic theory teaches that the task of managing an enterprise is comprised of six, independent yet integrated "systems": value, planning, control, information, organization and personnel systems. Given the premise that project organizations should be understood as "temporary companies", all these management tasks should arise for each project. And each of these systems can indeed be translated into the familiar terms of the building trade when describing the services provided by building management. The "heart" of every project is the task itself, the goal formulated by the client. This document describes the desired values of the completed building. These should require no explanation, one would think, yet practice has demonstrated only too frequently that problems occur even at this early stage of a project. This may be due to a client's inability or unwillingness to make decisions with regard to the desired quality or due to a lack of knowledge in terms of methods of defining goals. This problem exists both for fairly simple and rather static tasks and for projects with anticipated dynamic changes. The configuration of the project (and ongoing evaluation by means of so-called "test loops") is the central management instrument with which the project management can assess proposals, costs and schedules and ultimately make decisions on each of these factors.

Integrated Planning of Complex Procedures – the Planning System

In the context of project management, a planning system has little to do with drawing pencils; rather, it refers to the handling of the entire process from project start-up to completion. The practice reveals, that the effort to describe the smallest possible individual processes quickly obscures any clarity one might try to achieve. The dependencies and risks associated with the individual tasks increase exponentially with the number of processes under observation. Hence the only sensible approach to achieve relative planning stability coupled with risk assessment is to describe bundled tasks, accepting the uncertainties within each bundle. The definition of interfaces, the analysis of milestones and intermediate results and the continuous improvement of the planning over the course of the process are complementary tasks within the planning system for project organizations.

Project Controlling – the Control System

As soon as it is evident that no project can be fully described at the initial stage, it is essential to introduce an effective control system. Information on progress and setbacks must be constantly gathered, evaluated and updated for projects. Project controlling has become a collective term for the tasks of recording/retrieving, sorting, collating and evaluating the information prior to making a decision. Most tasks in project controlling are, as the name suggests, controlling tasks. The spectrum surpasses merely collecting and reporting on data. The identification and presentation of dependencies with regard to individual findings and the analysis of possible alternatives are intrinsic components of the performance tasks.

Information Management – the Information System

Information distribution within a project always occurs on three levels. The first level is distribution of information in terms of the goals, contracts and decisions from the client perspective to the planners and executing firms. This level has already been described in the section on "Goal-Oriented Management". The second level, gathering and analyzing of results, is the task of the controlling. However, since a purely hierarchical or "branched" information policy is not suitable for fast-paced projects, special attention must be given to the non-hierarchical, topic-driven communication among participants (lateral communication). It is the blessing and simultaneously the curse of modern information and communications tools that they facilitate rapid distribution of information. To prevent that projects drown in a flood of information and communication, the targeted control of information distribution is an essential management task. It is vital to define who requires and receives which information at any given time, and to ensure that this definition is adhered to and documented.

Team Management – the Organizational and Personnel System

In regarding the different systems for managing projects it is important to remember that they are undertaken and processed by people. This means that one must set up rules as well as provide guidance and motivation. Thus, organizing the decision-making process is an essential element of project management. Specific tools have been developed for these aspects, among them change management and cost management, which are moreover complemented by suitable structures for successful collaboration oriented towards achieving the project goal. A complex project can only be successfully executed if the management establishes a personnel system that creates the appropriate bundles of competencies and engages the individuals in each of these groups to work productively and creatively while avoiding productivity losses through conflicts.

Goal of the Management System: Quality

The success of the project is and must be the only goal of all these management efforts. The measure of this success is the quality of the end result. Project management plays a unique role in this because architectural quality, elegant solutions and the utility of the project are at best secondary considerations. The primary goal of project management is to ensure process quality, that is, to create a framework within which all participants can work without interference, errors or erroneous information. Clearly, this requires a well-founded and deep understanding of the individual steps of planning and building. The project manager should be capable of asking the right questions and of initiating optimizations. Each project organization is faced with a dilemma with regard to quality management. While the individual "products" of a planning and building process must be checked for quality, the standard quality management methods developed for consumer goods are rarely applicable. After all, QM and especially the methods of "Total Quality Management" (TQM) developed in the Japanese industry of consumer goods, are a process of constant optimization defined by the continuous and repetitive production of a consumer product. Such situations are rare in the context of large building projects. To begin with, each building is a unique product. The experience of the project manager has therefore become an important criterion in building projects. Only firms that have already overseen and undertaken numerous projects are able to impose effective quality control. As absurd as it may seem to some planners, definition of the desired quality, which the project controller presents and oversees, is exclusively based on the goal formulations of the client, whose executive arm the project manager is. In some cases this may also translate into a preference for lower product quality given an assessment of the cost-benefit ratio.

2.4 On the Necessity of Project Management for High-rise Projects

What are the special challenges in the project management of high-rises? Are high-rises not simply buildings made extraordinary only through the addition of more stories? Experience has shown that high-rises are far more than simply projects with a greater building mass. The special demands made on the building systems, the logistical challenges, the spatial constraints of the building sites, the number of participants and the frequent economic constraints and tight schedules all contribute to the complexity of the projects. The high cost risk associated with high-rises alone, whose economic viability must frequently be described as difficult due to high downtown property prices and the increased technical demands for construction and operation, compels clients to institute preventative risk management. Moreover, one unique characteristic of high-rise projects is that they are subject to more stringent observation on the part of the public, the press, the neighbors and the authorities than conventional buildings. Given these factors, the best possible prevention of errors is clearly indicated.

Special Organizational Topics

The number of planners and firms participating in high-rises projects translates into a greater effort in terms of coordination than is ordinarily the case for standard building projects. The flow of information is becoming increasingly important, since the high level of integration in planning and execution also increases the risks associated with poor communication. The task division among more specialist services also results in more information, coordination processes and decisions than usual. This calls for a far greater effort in controlling and a structured documentation. The sharpened public interest in high-rise projects, environmental issues, shading, wind effects and security aspects, which are playing an ever greater role especially since the attack on the World Trade Center, have led to excessively stringent legal obligations and building authority regulations. Hence, every high-rise project is subject to far more involvement on the part of regulatory and permit-granting authorities, neighbors and the public.

Special Procedural Topics

While high-rises are subject to the same serial procedures of planning and construction as conventional projects, there is a greater potential for optimization as a result of the high degree of process integration. A planning strategy that accompanies the building is essential for high-rise projects, especially in view of the scheduling pressures generally associated with them. The planning can occur for each individual phase, naturally with attention to the mutual dependencies of the individual planning members. Without doubt, the greatest hurdle for phase-by-phase planning is the need for a coordinated tendering process, especially in cases where a tender is planned for main contractors. It is quite common, therefore, to separate the tenders for the excavation and foundation work and the aboveground work. This makes it possible, for example, to plan the building systems and the execution even as work in the building pit continues. All execution work on high-rise projects is characterized by a high degree of integration. Schedule planning methods developed for line sites such as roads or railroads are often employed. This allows for a finely tuned approach to staggered fixed cycles for the trades following the rough work, with the result that façade and completion work can begin on floors that are only a few levels below the ongoing rough work. Although site logistics and material delivery are important planning areas for every building project, they are especially vital for high-rise projects due to the sheer mass of building components. These topics are addressed in more detail in Chapter 4 (contribution by C. Motzko). However, the project management must also concern itself with logistics, site organization, material and storage. All these areas represent major interfaces with the "outside world" and must therefore be included in the risk assessment.

2.5 The Methods and Tools of Project Management

The methods of effective management tend to adhere to an established scheme. This scheme can be described with the term GTP, or "goal- and task-oriented procedure". This type of procedure is a structured approach to any problem (no matter how small), consisting of five steps:
– situation analysis,
– goal formulation,
– planning,
– execution, and
– control.

To proceed according to GTP is actually quite a trivial challenge; still, it is all too often ignored in reality for many projects and even in the case of large and complex buildings. Individuals who have been trained in planning will too often jump forward to item 3, planning, without completing the first two points. And yet a goal- and task-oriented approach can be applied even when there are small changes, plans and adjustments. Any time and effort invested in the analysis, formulation (and naturally also goal control) translates into higher process quality and lower risk.

Organizational Structure

Project management has developed methods especially for the first two steps of the GTP process, which serve to discipline, structure and coordinate the entire team. The "Organizational Structure", that is, the definition of goals, structures, rules and responsibilities, also contains tools for these domains.

Goal Definition

As described in the introduction to this section, the clear formulation of goals is one of the most important prerequisites for coordination and effective control.
This task can be achieved using methods that provide a context for the various goals.

The most important properties of formulating a goal can be summarized with the mnemonic SMART. Goals that are:
– specific,
– measurable,
– acceptable (and ambitious),
– realistic, and
– timed
are called SMART.

The goal must be formulated for each project in several loops. If only a general direction can be defined at the beginning of the project, it should nevertheless be recorded (and described) with the highest degree of precision. The degree of precision or specificity must increase with each subsequent analysis of the goals to the point where, at the beginning of the actual planning stage, the objectives of cost, schedule, and especially the desired quality of the building, are firmly established. Since it is rare that goals are formulated by a single person, different interest groups will invariably develop competing goals. At this stage, it is the task of project controlling to identify and resolve the resulting conflicts early on. The outcome of this stage is the gathering of all goal ideas and the drafting of a consensus-building "image" which is compatible with all departments of the client.

An architect is often on board at an early stage of the project. Design sketches can thus be included as part of the goal definition.

All information relating to the project goals in agreement with the client(s) is gathered into the project manual. The creation of this "book" is another, clearly set task for the project controlling. At the beginning of the project, such a book will still be a fairly slim volume, containing little more than the location of the object and a few important data. Over time, information is added to the manual as goals are more clearly defined and especially if the client decides to alter them. A carefully recorded project manual can therefore be regarded as a kind of historical record of the project after completion, documenting all decisions over the course of the project – from the first definition to the final selection of door handles.

Convening a Planning Team

As in stationary enterprises, the achievable quality of a building project largely depends on the available personnel. In a stationary enterprise, correct personnel selection and integration is the task of the HR department, which has developed qualified methods for this purpose. In building projects (including high-rise projects) the selection of participants is often determined by factors other than those of qualification and compatibility. Architecture competitions are often the starting point of assembling a team, a highly developed and ambitious design is recommended for realization. This means that the recommendation is often for architects, who have demonstrated with their design that they have mastered 10 percent of the entire sphere of an architect's responsibility. Winning a competition does not make a statement on their qualification to organize a complex process, on delivering error-free detailed planning, or indeed on adhering to cost estimates, schedules and other agreements. When architects are awarded direct or limited contracts, it is therefore recommendable to adhere to a structure and a transparent decision-making process. The method of "benefit analysis", also called "decision matrix" (**Table 2.2**), has proved effective over time. It sets the different qualities of alternative solutions into a benefit context. In cases where adherence to a competition design is mandated, a division of the architects' portfolio of responsibilities among several planning firms or the commissioned working group is one method of minimizing risks.

Client organizations are often faced with problems when several planning partners are engaged for the project, because the elegance and quality of building system designs, fire protection expert reports or elevator plans cannot be judged in the same manner as architectural form. In the end, decisions are often based only on the offered price. This should be avoided at all times from the perspective of the project controller. Even if planning costs account for up to 15 percent of the entire project costs, cutting corners for planner fees is almost always at the root of subsequent cost problems, disputes and debates on the subject of supplementary charges. No other area can save more money

than the adequate involvement of planners and the cooperative management of these teams.

Since the management of the planning team is the key instrument for ensuring that the chosen goal is achieved, particular attention should be given to the collaboration of all participants in the planning process. So-called "project kick-off" events have proved to be effective instruments. At this intensive initial meeting, the goals of the project are explained, interfaces, decision paths and performance expectations are outlined, and rules for the project processing are agreed. Another aspect that should not be underestimated is the human component, that is, the harmonization and coordination of the participants and the opportunity for them to get to know each other during this event, which must be carefully prepared and competently chaired by the project controller.

Execution

In recent years, the selection of general contractors has become entrenched as seemingly the only option for large and complex projects in the German-speaking region. In response, the large rough construction enterprises have also undergone a radical evolution; thus several of these firms have begun to stress that their core competence is that of system management. In fact, with the exception of reducing the interfaces with the client, there is no compelling reason to bundle technical services, completion work and façade work under the umbrella of a general contractor. Since many client organizations have reached the same conclusion, one can notice a slight trend towards modified tenders. The commission of three GC (general contractor) packages (foundation GC, elevation GC and building systems GC) has become common practice for large projects, and the commissioning of a construction manager (project manager/ construction manager responsible for tendering and assigning contracts, settlement of accounts and management of the individual providers), which has been standard in English-speaking countries, is gradually taking hold.

Establishing how contracts are assigned in an early phase, evaluating alternatives and adapting the entire project organization based on these decisions is an important task of project controlling. It is important, in this context, to remember that the responsibility profile and the required effort on the part of the project controllers can vary greatly according to the decision of how contracts are assigned, and that this must be written into the contract.

Contract Management

It is important to clearly identify the performance profile, responsibilities and interfaces for the many individual specialists and trades involved in a high-rise project. The first order is to clearly separate the responsibilities of the project controlling from those of the other planning participants. Lack of clarity in distinguishing between the building management and the building control tasks can often lead to liability risks, which must be avoided contractually. The standard case, on which most building law attorneys insist, is a clear separation of planning and client responsibility. Building management is usually closely linked to the planning (and to the "work performance" of the planners to create a sound building free of errors), while the client responsibilities include the assumption of the client tasks that can be delegated, that is, the control.

The project control responsibility of "contract management" is important for both planning and execution, although the emphasis is clearly on the planning stage.

When contracts are signed with architects and engineers, the expected performance must always be defined and included in the planner contracts. This is especially important when the clients wish not only to demand fulfillment of the contract in terms of the building itself but also to ask for a specific form of project documentation. The use of Internet-supported planning systems or the adherence to rules with regard to handing over the documents to subsequent operators or facility managers must therefore be contractually defined, since standard planner contracts are not suited to enforcing such subsidiary obligations.

General contractor contracts at a fixed price have become the norm for large projects. However, clients and project controllers have often made the painful experience that these contracts only offer security in terms of cost and schedule if little room for interpretation remains due to advanced planning and goal definition. Any changes to the project undertaken after the contract has already been signed are inordinately expensive, and supplementary payments are often a major factor in the profit of large contracting firms. For this reason several attempts have been made in recent years to design contracts in a different manner, for example, the so-called "glass pockets" of the GC or "guaranteed maximum cost contracts" (GMC). These ensure a relatively high degree of cost security, even if the planning has not been finalized, and also motivate the general contractor to initiate cost-saving subcontracts.

The project controller can and must advise and assist the client on these contract management issues. However, the client cannot expect the project controller to provide ongoing legal and contractual consulting services for the entire term of the building project.

Table 2.2 Simplified example of a benefit analysis

Expertise	Valuation	Planner A	Planner B	Planner C
Has already successfully planned high-rises	20%	20 pt	10 pt	0 pt
Has the necessary expertise for organizing complex projects (reference projects)	25%	10 pt	30 pt	40 pt
Has the necessary expertise for detail planning (reference projects)	30%	10 pt	30 pt	40 pt
Designs architecture of aesthetic value	25%	10 pt	40 pt	30 pt
Total	100%	12 pt	28.5 pt	29.5 pt

No = 0 points, little = 12 points, average = 20 points, good = 30 points, excellent = 40 points

Risk Management

Murphy's law – "Anything that can go wrong, will go wrong sooner or later" – is particulary true for building projects. The importance of early risk assessment cannot be emphasized enough, especially if one takes into account the enormous sums that must be raised for high-rise projects. While timely and structured project organization by experienced project controllers is an essential part of risk management, it is not sufficient on its own. The "critical success factors" and the "principal risk factors" can be identified relatively early on based on the goals of the current project and experience drawn from previous, comparable projects. Not all individual steps of the planning or execution are of equal importance; it is the task of the project controller to identify the most important individual steps, to assess and verify them constantly with the help of a milestone plan, to spot any delays early on and to counteract them. However, the risk assessment must also take possible external risks into account, e.g. the insolvency of a firm, damage to neighboring buildings, etc. Once again, it is the task of the project controller to draft reaction plans for the principal risk factors, to prepare checklists and handling guidelines, and to establish a system of rapid reaction by means of ad-hoc conferences.

Organization Manual

The organizational measures described in the preceding paragraph must be documented and continually updated by the project controller. This organization of the project is recorded in an organization manual, which should be made available to all project participants.

It is important to make a clear distinction between the project manual mentioned in the section "Goal definition" and the organization manual.

The project manual is more of a static document, which documents the decisions made with regard to the project. New choices and decisions are added to the document if the project goals have been refined or changed. The organization manual, on the other hand, is updated whenever responsibilities, procedures, rules and agreements change, and does not document the entire history of the project, but only gives the current status of the agreements entered into.

Organizing the Sequential Structure

No project controller is able to describe and pre-plan the entire process of planning and building in all details at the outset of a project. Like all other participants in the planning, his or her work is one of gradually approaching the new task at first on the basis of preliminary observations and experiential values. These observations are constantly refined and more extensively formulated in consultation with the other participants. This means that the project controller's initial role is one of asking questions. This gathering of information on the project in the beginning stage – and especially the identification and definition of organizational procedures – is one reason for the common disillusion that can set in between client and project control during the first three months of a project.

However, experience has demonstrated that any aggressively simulated sense of security and blind activism instead of solid preparation are harmful to projects rather than beneficial.

Planning the Planning

A closer look at the key management processes of a building project reveals that the planning periods are frequently the principal cause for delays, with the result that the organization of the planning itself is an important issue for the project controller. It is essential, therefore, to collaborate closely with all participants in the planning in order to reach a realistic assessment of the anticipated planning periods as early as possible. This assessment should, moreover, be clearly divided into pre-design and design stage, permit planning and execution planning. The question of how long any particular planning process may take is difficult to answer in advance. However, planning firms are also enterprises that must operate efficiently, and this means that a "reverse calculation" of fees in consideration of risk and profit margins, and a calculation of the hourly pay for the planners involved, allows a rough time estimate. Experience from previous projects can then be brought into play to determine the principal planning bundles, to define further processing through other planners and to depict all this information in a network plan.

With the introduction of useful schedule planning programs in the early 1990s, attempts were undertaken in many projects to plot each individual deliverable plan as a separate process in a network plan. The idea was to achieve process control and a qualified record of the "work flow" of the individual plans. Many of these attempts failed, however, because the growing complexity of this type of schedule planning proved too elaborate for both the planners, who were forced to constantly deliver statements on projected plans, and the project controllers, who had to process these continually changing statements. Bundling the planning themes and setting milestones has emerged as a feasible option for planning control, whereby the day-to-day control of the resources employed and the planners' progress is absolutely essential. On the other hand, experience has also shown that the progress report "we have completed 90 percent" has only limited meaning, because the remaining 10 percent tend to require at least another 50 percent of the work time.

Data and Communications Management

The increased use of CAD and other electronic tools have fundamentally changed planning processes in recent years. Planning has become faster, standard postal routes can be bypassed, there are fewer transmission errors, and planning details can be reused.

Yet like all technological advances, the use of electronic tools in the planning process also poses considerable risks in addition to the aforementioned advantages. The possibility of creating and sending files much more quickly can lead to an information overload for the individual participants in the project. This overabundant flow of information can only be countered with clear structuring and rigorous control over information routes. Internet-based project communication systems (e.g. www.conject.com), which permit centralized data and communications management, have been in use for several years. In addition to communicating status reports on the planning, these systems also offer control of information flow and access rights, quality control of planning targets, and finally complete structure project and planning documentation. This enables increased quality of information management and transparency for individual services and performance, which can also protect a project against appeals. Is the project controller called upon to include these new options in basic performance profile? From today's perspective, the answer is more likely to be negative. While the use of an information system provided by the client should have no impact on the project controller's fee, structuring such a system, ongoing control of the planners and, finally, handing the files over to the client can be regarded as preliminary project documentation, which should be remunerated as an additional service. If the project controller assumes additional responsibilities in areas such as CAD coordination or organizing the planning for subsequent operators and facility managers, such services must in each case be treated as additional and remunerable efforts.

Managing Authorities and Neighbors

As mentioned, high-rise projects are also notable for the intensive scrutiny they are subjected to from the public, the authorities and neighbors. The project controller therefore pays particular attention to including these groups to a large extent as early as possible. Planning the site logistics is especially important in terms of authorities management, because all high-rise projects will impose some restrictions on the public. The planning of removing excavation material as well as the delivery and storage of building materials is therefore one of the tasks that the project controller must address early on.

Experience with high-projects, especially in inner city locations, has shown that they also pose considerable risks through changes to the basic load of the building area. Hence timely consultation with the neighborhood, open debate on potential risks and timely documentation of possible cracks, subsidence, etc. are very important. Once again these tasks must be coordinated by the project controller.

Quality Management and Planning Efficiency

The more advanced the planning, the more specialist knowledge is required to assess the planning quality. One of the standard services that a project controller provides is regular checking of the planning with regard to keeping to defined targets. For this reason, the project controller must accompany all stages of the planning process as a knowledgeable and critical inquirer – without interfering in the planning.

The quality of the planning is assessed in several steps. To begin with it is important that all participants adhere to the agreements and rules of the planning process. The use of agreed upon file names, the layer structure of the CAD drawing and adherence to the processes established for change management are only some of the aspects involved. The project controller will also pay close attention to the efficiency of the chosen solutions and regularly assess the progress of the increasingly detailed and advanced planning. Spot checks of individual planning stages and in-depth verification of critical areas must lead to qualified reports, especially subsequent to the submission of intermediate results for design planning, permit planning or tenders.

Planning coordination is still largely the responsibility of the architects, whereas the project controller participates in planning conferences only on an intermittent basis. The "jour-fixe" meeting, a scheduled weekly meeting for large projects, is the project controller's forum. These meetings are not intended for discussions on planning details or quality improvement; rather, they focus on the interfaces, the necessary decisions and the tasks, which have been completed or are set for completion.

Optimizing the Execution

In high-rise projects, which are erected by general contractors, the project controller's involvement in the execution phase is considerably reduced. The coordination responsibilities concerning the sub-contractors of the GC are not his concern. The controller will only assume a role in cases where the overall contract is split among several GCs or when specific individual services are singled out from the GC contract.

Hence the tasks of the project controller (after the contract has been formulated in collaboration with the GC) during the execution phase are cost management, setting and checking milestones and tracking the change management. Supplementary management, on the other hand, is increasingly becoming one of the controller's principal tasks during the execution phase.

Since obstacle reports from the contractors and demands for supplementary charges in particular must always be responded to in due time, meticulous supervision of these instances is of prime importance. The project controller must always be informed, in a broad sense, of all events and contingencies on the building site, and a regular presence on site is therefore necessary.

Since the project controller serves as an expert consultant for the client during the stage of handing over the project and project completion, it would be irresponsible to censure shortcomings previously noted in the execution at this late stage. On the other hand, it is vital to ensure that the tasks of building management/project controlling remain distinct throughout the construction phase, to avoid lack of clarity with regard to liability for the errors. In recent years, a secondary profile has therefore emerged: quality controlling throughout the construction period. As a representative of the client, the project controller acts as an observer on the site, keeping a record of deviations, errors or shortcomings. The controller reports these observations to the client, who, as the line executive of the building management, can influence the executing firms or contractors. In this manner the project controller can document shortcomings without having to assume responsibility for rectifying them.

Cost Management

In Germany, cost management often begins only some time after the start of the planning phase. In English-speaking countries it is common to engage a cost planner (or quantity surveyor) prior to contracting the other planners.

The quantity surveyor determines the framework of costs for a building on the basis of comparable objects and establishes a budget together with the client. This framework and the contractual obligations of the subsequently contracted planners to adhere to it provide far greater cost stability for the client (3–5 percent in the cost estimate stage alone) than is common in Germany. The effort required to achieve such a degree of cost stability is far greater and must be expended much earlier than is standard in the German planning methodology. Thus it is not uncommon in English-speaking countries to separate cost management from the other planner services and to engage a dedicated cost manager. The cost manager continues to follow the entire planning process and to log a current cost-plan. Alternatives, changes or additions initiated by the planners are evaluated as to cost and included in the budget should a decision be made in favor of these alternatives.

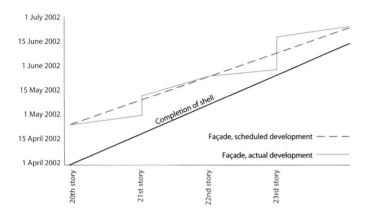

Completion of shell

Façade, scheduled development — — —

Façade, actual development ⸺⸺⸺

2.3 Time-completion
diagram for a façade

As the changes occur, the cost manager maintains an overall perspective, thereby ensuring that additional costs in one area are covered by savings in another. Each of these steps is minutely documented to illustrate, if there are revisions at a later stage, why individual decisions were made in favor of a particular solution.

In the meantime this new division of tasks in cost management has also become more common in Germany. At times, the tasks are embedded in the project controlling, at others, they are separated out as an individual responsibility. International architecture firms have long understood the advantages of professional, independent cost management, and regularly advise their clients to engage a quantity surveyor. The professional expertise of quantity surveyors, their market overview of building methods, materials and costs and their mediating role between planning team and building executive are therefore often regarded as a positive complement by the architects and not as a limitation of their own scope. Although responsibility for cost management traditionally resides with the architect in Germany, it is one of the core tasks of external project controllers to coordinate costs, in keeping with the four phases of cost analysis according to the HOAI (Honorarordnung für Architekten und Ingenieure, or Official Scale of Fees for Services by Architects and Engineers). However, because project controllers do not estimate or determine the costs themselves as quantity surveyors would, they depend on planners' estimates, veryfying their plausibility through spot checks. The project controller also creates and logs a comprehensive overview of all costs, thus establishing a clear default cost structure and

comparing all results of the estimates to the original budget. He or she can then present the client with a timely anticipated statement of accounts for the building. Following this statement, setting up the appropriate project accounting and verifying and administrating all invoices and payments or remittances is simply a matter of using standard professional procedures.

Changes or planning/tender errors invariably result in cost changes. Change management in the context of costs and especially supplementary cost management are therefore essential elements of responsible cost management. Hence, at the beginning of the execution phase the project controller's focus shifts from budgeting and cost estimation to analysis of supplements and changes. Timely definition of supplement submissions and change management in the organization manual are indispensable tools for verifying the justification for and amount of supplementary payments. Maintaining a log of cost development, integrating supplements which have already been submitted or are anticipated, as well as organizing invoicing and payment procedures, allow a day-to-day prognosis of costs and financial requirements and provide the basis for timely controlling options.

Schedule Management

It is often assumed that the most important task of project management is to plan the procedures and schedules on the building site. However, planning the planning, as described above, is far more important. The project controller generally only designs the framework

for scheduling in the execution phase, since coordination of the various individual services is the responsibility of the general contractor, the construction manager or the architect. The participation of the project controller in coordination meetings for the building site is the exception rather than the rule.

On the part of the project controlling, the planning of the processes is therefore usually a scheduling outline planning. These scheduling plans are often incorporated into the execution contracts, thus becoming binding provisions. Ultimately, the general contractor (or the architect in the case of individual contracts) is obligated to deliver a finished job on a fixed day. How this target is reached must be left to the contractor. Unless interim deadlines have been agreed upon as targets, the project controller can therefore only act as an advisor or "early warning system", identifying delays early on and testing measures for catching up.

For complex projects, however, professional project controllers are increasingly favored for this task – similar to the situation described for cost management. General contractors have not only begun to engage external project controllers increasingly often for detailed scheduling for all processes, the suggestions and optimization proposals of the client/project controller are also more often incorporated into project planning. One unique feature in scheduling the execution phase of high-rises is the option for close integration of the processes. It is not unusual to encounter "work cycles" on high-rise building sites, similar to the practice employed for road works. This integration is difficult to visualize with the standard scheduling programs, and project controllers with high-rise experience have been successful in employing methods borrowed from line work planning.

An essential element in scheduling for line construction sites such as roads or high-rises is the learning curve that is invariably involved. Even for the second repetition of a building section (for example, a standard floor in a high-rise) one can assume that execution will be roughly 10 percent faster. This means that high-rise construction displays a trend that is rare in any other area of the building sector: the permanent improvement of the

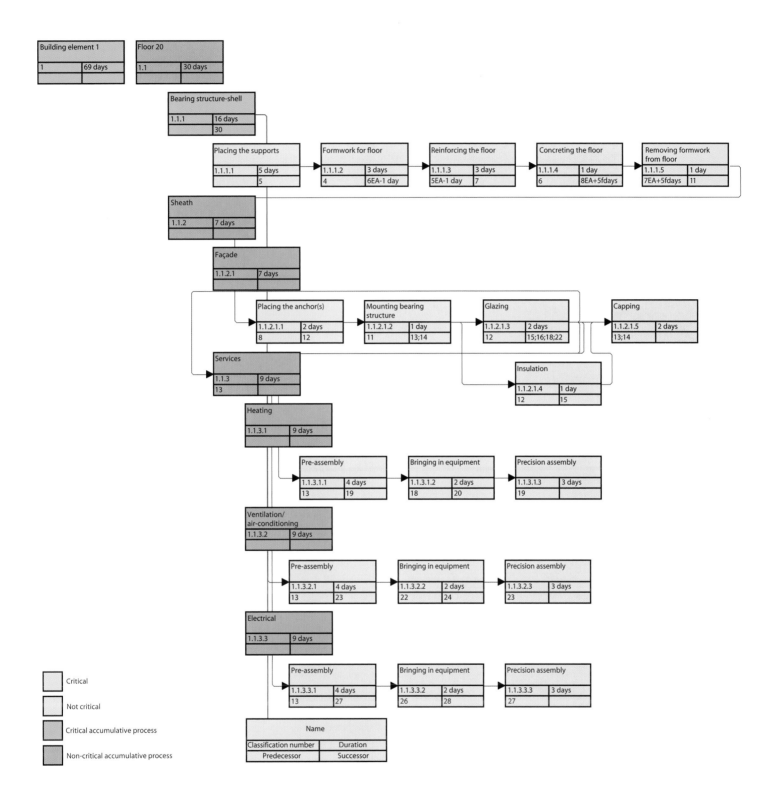

2.4 Network plan (PERT – Program Evaluation and Review Technique), basis for a schedule, developed from project schedules showing the dependencies, i.e. the preliminary and finishing work for specific tasks.

processes. Aside from mass production of residential homes, high-rise buildings are therefore the only real estate products where the "continual improvement" methods of the consumer goods industry can be employed to achieve process optimization and acceleration.

2.6 From Project Organization to Team Organization

The more complex the integration of individual tasks is in a project, the more important the smooth progression of each of these processes is. The role of the social components of collaboration for the success of a project must not be underestimated.

While the entire planning and execution process can be carefully thought out in advance and most risk factors can be identified and monitored, the multiple influence and risk factors in such a complex process make it imperative to apply the "two sets of eyes" principle to checking all individual processes, and to create a project culture where close networking among the various participants and their motivation to successfully complete the project awaken a personal interest in all those involved. Only then will individual participants look "past the end of their noses" and name the opportunities, risks and problems that affect other participants and contribute to finding solutions. The ability of project managers or project controllers to act as a "cultural link" for the project is therefore a qualification that should not be neglected.

Qualifications of a Project Manager

Naturally, the professional and technical qualification of the project manager, project leader or project controller is an indispensable prerequisite for acceptance in the entire planning and execution team. This includes expertise in the methods of project management and an understanding of the planning processes and topics, as well as an understanding of building and planning laws and regulations and comprehension of the processes.

However, the most important qualification for a project manager of a high-rise is practical experience of working with highly complex

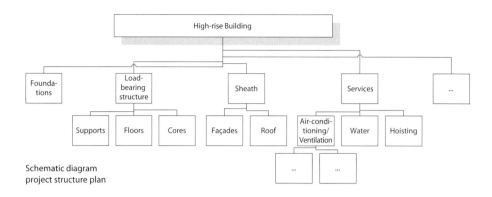

Schematic diagram
project structure plan

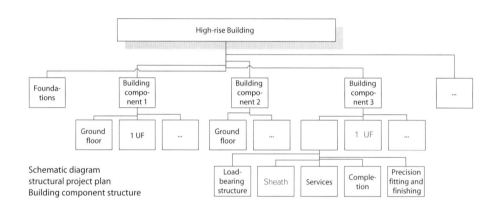

Schematic diagram
structural project plan
Building component structure

2.5 Schematic diagrams of the project structure plan for the overall and detailed structuring of a project

projects. Every high-rise project reaches a critical phase when it is difficult to adhere to schedules, costs and other variables. Only if the project manager is able to demonstrate the necessary standing in this situation, will he or she be able to survive this perhaps deleterious outcome for the project. Is it necessary for a project controller who is asked to control a high-rise project to be experienced in high-rise projects? Surely not, otherwise only few members of the "old guard" would be available as project controllers in the near future. Nevertheless a sound fundamental understanding of all participating trades should be given in addition to the proven ability to cope with complexity. Since the project controller does not engage in planning in any direct manner, he or she must be able to further the process of planning and building in a qualitative manner through constant queries, suggestions and assessment of options. To this end it is helpful to be able to fall back on an organization for professional support. And he or she must speak the language of the

planners and executing firms (and be able to translate it for the client, who is often not as well versed in specialist knowledge).

Social Competence

At different points we have noted that a large project is also a large social construct. Directing this construct is as challenging as maintaining an overview of the various technical issues. A minimum with regard to ability and knowledge of group dynamics and leadership is therefore one of the prerequisites for success as a project controller. Prior to engaging an external project controller, it is therefore sensible to gather some information about leadership and corporate culture in the controller's own enterprise. An employee of a company with an authoritarian management structure will be unlikely to make a substantial contribution to a project approach geared towards finding solutions and establishing consensus. Motivating all participants to give of their best may be possible by exerting pressure. However, experience with countless building projects has shown that this only works if there is a direct relationship of dependency between those who exert pressure and those who are subjected to it. Since this is rarely the case in building projects, a high degree of pressure will soon result in compensatory reactions: through demands for supplementary payment, delays and/or poor quality. A consensus-oriented approach to project organization is therefore always preferable to the authoritarian approach, although it is important to guard against slipping into an anti-authoritarian mode.

Emotional Competence

As soon as one steps into a home, one has a sense whether the person who furnished it had a clear vision of the overall impression or whether individual pieces were simply assembled in a "hotchpotch" manner. The same is true for high-rises. The architect is responsible for the design quality of the project, but every project is composed only in part of "visible" elements. The important goal is to achieve the overall success of the project, whereby the design of the skin, the arrangement of the ground plan and the finishing details are only parts of the whole. If the task is to erect an elegant and intelligently planned high-rise, it applies to all areas of planning and execution, from cost structuring to waste management on the building site. In order to apply the project guidelines to all sectors and to communicate them to all participants on an ongoing basis, the project controller must also possess emotional competence. The ability to sense stumbling-blocks early on and to remain calm in a crisis are abilities that characterize top project controllers.

Quantity Surveying

The origins of the professional profile of a project controller are based on the profile of the British quantity surveyor. After the Great Fire of London in 1666, the building masters of the time were so occupied with reconstructing the city that they needed support in applying for funds from the city. These tasks

were assumed by the so-called quantity surveyors (QS).

Today, quantity surveyors are organized worldwide in the Royal Institution of Chartered Surveyors (RICS), members are listed with the title MRICS (Member of...) or FRICS (Fellow of...).

The quantity surveyor is specialized in determining volume and mass and managing building costs. He may work directly for the client or as the chief calculator for a building firm.

In the UK, cost planners are brought into the project at a very early stage. The quantity surveyor is often the first consultant engaged by the client. His or her task is to create a cost model even before commissions are offered to architects and engineers.

As the project progresses, the quantity surveyor is the contact person for all aspects associated with costs. He or she advises the client on questions of financing and efficiency, on cost-in-use or life-cycle-costing and generates a cost estimate with 5 percent margin of accuracy in the early phase of the project. This accuracy is translated through the "design to cost" or "target costing" model. Once the budget has been defined, the planning as a whole is oriented to achieving this budget target. Planners, who are contractually bound to the budget, must consult the quantity surveyor for each additional detailing or change and clarify how this affects the cost development. If additional costs are incurred, the planners must reduce costs elsewhere in order to meet budget requirements.

This can only function if there is a high degree of cost transparency. As the ultimate cost advocate, the quantity surveyor is therefore responsible for the current and exact cost data of all participants. These are the general "project public", and the principle of "public ownership of the budget" means that each participant is given access to the figures and is responsible for meeting the budget.

In this process the quantity surveyor assumes the cost determination tasks of architects and engineers as well as the tasks of the project controller, e.g. cost tracking and cost reports.

The traditional separation of planning tasks in England means that the quantity surveyor often drafts the specifications and is always responsible for issuing tenders.

It is impossible to undertake cost control without affecting quality. In addition to cost, the quantity surveyor therefore also studies scheduling and quality issues, which bear an influence on cost. And finally, he or she acts as a neutral expert and a fair mediator in case of conflict.

2.7 High-rises Require High Performance: Motivating Interdisciplinary Teams

A successful American entrepreneur once said: "There is no need to motivate employees, but one must avoid 'demotivating' them." This insight is equally applicable to building projects and team members. Aside from satisfying the basic needs, the most important motivation is participation in interesting and ambitious tasks. Simply the act of being part of a large and difficult project is motivating. Hence, it is common to encounter highly motivated participants at the beginning of a project, whose interest it is to achieve success together.

Fairness and transparency are essential if one wishes to maintain this basic motivation. And fairness also means that the client must be willing to offer appropriate remuneration to the participants. However, this is an insight that is only gradually being accepted. The norm, even today, is to expect outstanding performance, creative and innovate solutions in an atmosphere of merciless price competition. Synergies are only possible, however, if the environment is fit for all participants, that is, avoiding that one side of the project teams reaps above-average profits to the detriment of all others. This is also the domain of the project controller, who presides over and guides the team process of building a high-rise. Leadership means enabling the success of one's team members.

Organization
03 of Office Towers

Timo Brehme und Frank Meitzner

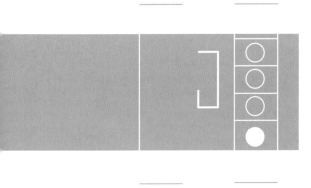

3.1 Market Forces: What Makes an Office Tower Skyrocket

Since the beginning of the last century there seems to have been a nearly inseparable correlation between economic growth rates and the height of office towers – when the economy grows, so do high-rises. The first office towers were erected circa 1870–80 in the conurbations of New York and Chicago. By the beginning of the 20th century, a boom in the economy and on the stock market resulted in a competition for building height, for which there seemed to be no limit. The stock market crash of 1929 and the depression that followed brought an end to the building boom. The tallest building of the world remained as an impressive testimony to the competition: the Empire State Building, built during the crisis and completed in 1931. It quickly became New York's landmark, but economically it proved a failure for many years.

The Empire State Building was only surpassed in the wake of the economic prosperity in the 1960s and 1970s with the erection, in 1972, of the World Trade Center, at 417 m the highest building of the world, and shortly after by the Sears Tower in Chicago, which reached a height of 443 m including its antenna.

Recently, the highest office towers, and most such towers, have been built in Asia: between 1992 and the end of 1997 2,437 high-rises were built in Shanghai alone, of which 966 rise to a height of over 20 floors. The Petronas Towers (452 m), the tallest high-rise in the world, are located in Kuala Lumpur, Malaysia.

Who Builds High-rises?

Real estate funds, which have increased in number and scope since the 1990s, represent a new type of client, building or commissioning buildings increasingly for the speculative sector of renting through third parties. This development gave rise to a multitude of specialized project development companies that erect turnkey real estate objects, a trend that continues today. Another factor is that more and more banks and insurance companies are spinning off their real estate inventory and merging it with their investments in order to repatriate the capital of their owner-occupied properties. This development has resulted in a noticeable trend towards globalization with all the attendant advantages and disadvantages of the real estate market.

One opportunity offered by this new client scene lies no doubt in the mixed use of these objects (in addition to offices, plans often include retail areas, restaurants, observation platforms, fitness centers or cineplexes). This opens the high-rises up to the public, a situation that did not exist with owner-occupancy. The flip side is the cause for concern with regard to the quality of purely profit-driven objects and structures.

3.2 Consequences of Separating the Client and User Roles

Changes in the marketplace and in particular the evolution of the client as owner-occupier to client/landlord for third-party users have resulted in fundamental changes in the project organization of building and the planning process. The classic client was an investor, project developer and user all in one. Once the roles are separated, the number of project participants increases, as does the need for coordination among the parties. Project management and project control take on far greater importance. Another change occurs with regard to the planning process. For the approach of the "classic client" was to determine his qualitative and quantitative requirements and then to set about realizing the task: location, site, planner, design and execution.

When investors are the client(s), the process is far less defined. In fact, it is usually reversed: the project developer readies a property for exploitation by undertaking a feasibility study, initiating the creation of the corresponding design and defining the outline conditions. The next step is to look for an investor, to whom the project is presented in detail and cast in numbers, data and facts. Finally, the user enters into the process as the last actor, and only much later the actual requirement.

Many fruitful projects are proof of the success of such project processes. The decisive factors are the optimal harmonization of the vastly different interests of the individual actors and the decision to make quality competition the binding ultimate goal. In the following, the problems and challenges associated with this process are explained.

The Role of the Investor

The investor has one goal: return on investment. To calculate it, all benchmark data that may influence the financial conditions must be defined and contractually fixed with the project developer at a very early stage. This occurs at a point in time when detailed planning – at least to any considerable degree – is still impossible. Cost and deadline stability is the primary goal. To delegate this responsibility and the risks associate with it as quickly as possible, a general contractor is usually brought on board. Quality is the only variable, since it is the most difficult quantifiable factor in words or numbers.

Investors are on principle interested in long-term rental agreements, because the investments are often for 20 years or even longer terms. In practice, however, the question often arises: Is the investor's thinking truly long-term? To answer this question we must differentiate between the goals of the decision-taker and the corporate goals, which are geared towards the coming decades. Corporations listed on the stock exchange often present the image that current or real-time figures are so explosive and relevant as to render strategies for the medium or long term less important. Moreover, decision-takers are not capital owners but only trustees – and rarely active in one corporation for an entire working life, as is the case in family-owned companies, for example. This is the only explanation for the fact that large buildings have to be demolished even before they reach the 20-year term – even though they have not yet fully depreciated – because renovation would be too expensive and the outcome would therefore no longer be profitable.

The scope for action also depends on the number of interested parties: the greater the number of parties involved in a project, the fewer the options for action. Even a single change results in an enormous number of contract adaptations. There is little room for adjusting the course when the planning is already underway, although the built result is supposed to last for a long time.

The marketing phase is especially challenging when originally calculated rents are changed. The modified return creates an investment loss for the asset holders.

The Project Developer as Client Representative

The project developer is generally the initiator of the project and thus the contact person for all participating parties. The difference between the purchase and sale of the real estate is profit and thus the yardstick for his or her actions. The primary goals are the maximum exploitation of the property and low production costs – sometimes achieved at the cost of quality, although shortcomings are not superficially visible. Project developers are often uninterested in benefits and profits that are realized only after several years. This applies, for example, to energy-conserving concepts, which amortize through savings in energy consumption. Price per square meter still seems to be the key marketing criterion. Investor projects are usually completed to the standards deemed necessary by experience, with the exception of prime locations. The goal is to achieve maximum use of the net floor area. The question of the utility value of these areas is soon delegated to the background. After all, none of the project participants will live or work in these locations and users are never present during the planning stage. It goes without saying that this circumstance effects urban design, architecture and floor plans.

The Interests of the User

The choice of location is based on subjective criteria, which the landlord cannot influence. The price-performance ratio is only of secondary importance. It comprises many aspects and factors, such as:
– options for realizing the tenant's individual space program given the lowest possible rent area;
– low rent exclusive of heating and low utility and incidental costs (which are

becoming increasingly important as a result of rising supply and disposal costs), high finishing comfort, optimum work environment criteria and flexible adaptation of the floor plans to continually changing work processes;
– rental agreements and a building that allows for the expansion and downsizing of organizations;
– services provided by a landlord.

There are no consumer reports for office building users that compare office buildings and publish the findings. The tenant has little insight into the true variables of administration buildings, particularly since the individual seeking a space for rent on behalf of a company is generally a layperson. The downsides of the building are only revealed when it is already in use – at a time when it is far too late to choose alternative solutions.

3.3 The New Criteria for Office Area Efficiency

The seven criteria for the efficiency of office areas listed below are based on the analysis of more than 100 objects. These seven criteria have been established to save more than 30 percent of cost in each category. They were developed for tenants and investors alike. For the tenant they indicate
– aspects that should be considered,
– how to evaluate the individual criteria, and
– what to do in order to secure an advantage.
To the investor they offer an opportunity
– to optimize object planning,
– to be more competitive,
– to devise a marketing strategy geared towards the client's needs, and
– to develop targeted consulting offers for interested tenants.

Criterion 1: Price Transparency

Most prospective tenants search for a specific number of square meters, which they derive from their tenant agreement – including a surcharge or deduction. Few people are aware that the gross rental area indicated in brochures or by agents deviates considerably from the true net rental area (= the area that is effectively usable).

Moreover, the figure indicated in the tenant agreement is not a relevant parameter: the customary differences that result from price distortion reach up to 30 percent. The underlying reasons are a lack of conventions for market transparency, price concealment, charges levied for common areas, and differences in building efficiency.

Criterion 2: Actual Rent

Many tenants – incidentally, much like investors in the planning – base their price comparisons simply on the indicated price per square meter. Yet the actual rent is far more important: it includes the price for rent exclusive of heating, the investment rent for "special requirements" and the incidental costs. Differences in actual rent can be as high as 50 percent in the marketplace, the product of differences in location and outfitting, the differences between minimum standard and medium standard as well as considerable differences in energy consumption and maintenance costs. Given these conditions, there is a need for clients to make detailed demands on the planners and not only demand farsightedness from the tenant. Tenants who wish to avoid unpleasant surprises should request proof of incidental costs or a similar document prior to signing an agreement.

Criterion 3: Occupancy Capacity

Occupancy capacity is calculated based on the number of workstations per square meter of net rental area. The layout module, the smallest possible individual office space with roughly 2.7 x 4.0 m, is a good unit on which to base the calculation. The rental area requirement per layout module can be used as a comparative value, with standard market differences in occupancy capacity at roughly 30 percent. The key factors are the facade grid, building depth and access/circulation paths. A ground plan analysis of designs prior to application planning is therefore highly recommended.

Criterion 4: Area Efficiency

The most important demand placed on the architect is the design of the floor plans. The decisive question is: How much area is lost through access, internal circulation, washrooms and office areas that are difficult to utilize?

Once again, standard differences in the market can be as high as 30 percent. The comparability of objects is ensured through occupancy planning. This should be undertaken with professional support prior to signing the agreement in order to ensure optimum area use from the outset.

Criterion 5: Flexibility

Many office buildings are planned and authorized for only one office concept. Yet the organizational requirements fluctuate for many companies. The potential for savings in space consumption is especially high in the choice of use strategy, depending on the company requirements. Office concepts such as group office, modular office, combination office and business club should all be considered in the planning. Subsequent solutions are generally expensive and not economically viable.

Criterion 6: Use Strategy

Work and business processes, points of contact and synergy potentials must be exploited to the fullest: relocation offers a rare opportunity to do so. Retrospective analysis of past experience is often insufficient as a basis for supplying answers for the future. Careful planning makes it possible to promote employee concentration and communication and simultaneously to reduce vacant areas. Up to 30 percent of space can easily be saved given

the right use strategy. If desk-sharing, alternating workstations, teamwork and teleworking are not yet possible in the company at the time of planning, these options should nevertheless be considered. Combination offices are a good basis for the requirements of tomorrow.

Criterion 7: Productivity

One should not be overly impressed by the cost difference between the minimum and the optimum solution. The decisive factor is the relationship between current work results and potential future gains in productivity or, conversely, loss in productivity. In this area there is no better tool for increasing productivity than improving the efficiency, for the ratio between space and personnel costs is roughly 1:15 in a service undertaking.

3.4   Office Organization and Building Grid

In times when only modular offices or open-plan offices were known, there were two fundamentally different grid typologies:
- Two rows of modular offices with central corridor and a standard clear building depth of roughly 12.0 m, a façade grid of roughly 1.2 to 1.8 m and room widths of 3.6 m for double rooms. Table depths of roughly 80 cm as well as file storage in built-in closets set along the corridor wall were standard features for modular offices prior to the introduction of computers in the workplace.
- Open-plan offices on a single floor level with a variety of structural and façade grids.

The introduction of the combination office in Germany in 1987 by congena (Corporation for Planning, Training and Organization) offered the opportunity for new solutions. Modular office, group office and combination office are competing office concepts that are suitable for different work requirements. The decisive factor is the option to transform the office areas into any of the three concepts. Façade grids and building depths are affected in various ways, depending on the concept requirements (Fig. 3.2).

The Modular Office

The standard layout is to arrange single and double rooms along the façade. Double rooms are often used to accommodate three employees for lack of other space. A typical functional workstation consists of table, room to move and a filing cabinet within reach of the employee, at times with an additional small meeting area.

The modular office requires a total clear depth of roughly 2.2 m per workstation, while a minimum of 4.4 m must be provided for a double room. With the addition of a dividing wall depth of roughly 10 cm, the center-to-center distance is roughly 4.5 m. Based on these standards, the façade grid is roughly 1.5 m. Two grids with an approximate clear room space of 2.9 m represent the smallest room, three grids a comfortable double room. The uniaxial room with roughly 1.40 m clear space is suitable as a utility space (e.g. copier, printer, small kitchens, wardrobes and storage).

As a result, the majority of office buildings conceived for modular office have a façade grid of roughly 1.5 m. Standard room depths range from roughly 5.0 to 5.5 m. Two rooms and a central corridor that is approximately 2.0 m wide combine into the traditional clear building depth of roughly 12.0 to 13.0 m. Greater building depths are also planned in order to increase the rentable area without considering functional requirements or usefulness. This is the case, for example, for solitary high-rises with one-sided access.

The Combination Office

The first combination offices in Sweden (1979) consist of 20 to 25 single rooms grouped around a common central zone. The façade grid is roughly 1.25 m, the depth of the combination offices roughly 4.0 m. The resulting minimum size for the biaxial combination office is 10 m². The building depth in this instance is determined by the central common area. Combination offices are a combination of workstations in single rooms with direct link to a common central core suitable for a variety of uses – the combination zone.

The individual workstations are single offices with room-height divisions set along the façade, each with a small conference or meeting area. Each workstation offers:
– direct visual contact with the outside,
– individual control of the work environment conditions,
– ergonomic workstation design, adaptable to user requirements.

Each office only contains objects that are directly allocated to the individual workstation. All furnishing and features used by several employees are located in the combination zone. It is available as a common area for all additional functions (printer, copier, mail room, group filing, additional or temporary workstations, meeting areas, café and beverage counter). The combination office facilitates close contact between the individual and their team at any time, while at the same time offering each employee a well-screened area to prevent acoustic distractions and provide the prerequisite for focused work. To fulfill this dual function, the offices are glazed on the side facing the combination zone.

Daylight penetrates as far as the central zone, which also provides visual contact with the outside.

To avoid excessive circulation and the distractions this creates for the employees seated in the area, two typical ground plans have been developed:
– the "comb": combination office areas are arranged along an access wing that accommodates the cores, utility areas and in some cases additional offices – usually modular offices,
– the "star": combination office areas radiate out from a central core or atrium.

The combination office concept offers a solution for the dilemma posed by conventional room arrangements by linking rooms that offer a quiet work atmosphere and focus, while facilitating the desired information exchange with the help of communication in defined areas.

The concept of the business club points the way to other future solutions. For this concept to function, it is necessary to modify work habits, management rules and organizational concepts. The office space is transformed into an active management tool. There is no longer a boss with a particular vision and many employees realizing it – everyone has a vision, and everyone executes tasks. Control is focused only on results, not on processes.

The number of workstations is based not on the number of employees, but on the tasks (e.g. accounting, HR, organization). The office concept is a task-oriented version of the combination office. There are fixed service functions such as lockers, wardrobes, espresso bars, document centers, conference rooms and reception/secretary's offices. The employees do not have assigned workstations. Rather, they operate on the basis of work scenarios, among which they can choose depending on daily requirements: combination offices are available for focused individual work, open and closed team work areas are available for group work, there are standing workstations and open individual workstations grouped around libraries and filing areas, as well as a lounge, which exudes a club rather than an office atmosphere.

A Comparison – Advantages and Disadvantages

To what degree is the described typical modular structure suitable or unsuitable for the combination office? A building depth of roughly 12.0 to 12.5 m is insufficient for combination offices that are roughly 4.2 m deep. The remaining central zone of roughly 3.5 to 4.0 m is too narrow, once the necessary access area in front of the individual rooms (2 x 1.1 m) has been deducted, given a common area of roughly 1.3 to 1.8 m.

Conversely, does the combination office structure work for modular office? A building depth of 13.5 m is excessive for straightforward modular offices.

Triaxial rooms with a clear width of 3.95 m can be used as double rooms only by accepting the compromise that there will be no filing cabinets within reach of the desks. Nearly all documents, etc., must be stored in cabinets set along the corridor wall. Obviously, this only too frequent "standard room" does not deliver the desirable workplace quality in terms of function and comfort.

Table 3.1 Criteria for the operational efficiency and comparability of office propert: 1 m² is rarely 1 m²

Criteria/possibilities	€/m² heated	€/m² unheated	€/WP workplace	€/staff member	€/m²	Δ F'w
Price transparency Net/gross area	X	X	X	X	X	30%
Actual rent Net/gross area		X	X	X	X	30%
Occupancy capacity Façade grid/depth of building			X	X	X	30%
Quadrature efficiency Primary and secondary usable areas			X	X	X	30%
Variable use Flexible				X	X	30%
Use strategy Area utilization				X	X	50%
Productivity Operating result: before/after					X	100%

3.2 Example of floor plan
The standard floor of
the Sigma office building
in Frankfurt-Niederrad
Client: iii-Fonds,
Architects NHT, Frankfurt.
High-rise concept: up to
four rental units per floor,
thanks to the flexible floor
plan, the building can be
completed to accommodate
all standard office concepts.

Business club

Cubicle office

Open-plan office

Combined office

A façade grid of 1.5 m and building depth of 12.0 to 12.5 m will result, with some compromises, in combined offices with biaxial room units that are 3.0 m wide and roughly 3.6 m deep. The remaining central zone is usable at a depth of 4.6 to 5.1 m. Even if the central zone is 4.6 m deep, the space remaining after deducting access areas of 2 x 1.1 m is still 2.4 m wide: sufficient, albeit somewhat restricted space for banks of filing cabinets, a conference area, small kitchen, mail distribution, etc. On the other hand, there is a higher proportion of inefficiency in the façade area to usable area ratio (Fig. 3.3).

Functionality and Area Efficiency

The suitability of the derived structure – 1.5 m façade grid and 12.2 m building depth – is not only reflected in the quality of the office workstations. The arrangement of the ancillary spaces and the occupancy capacity also determine functionality and area efficiency. The areas accommodated in the central zone in combination offices are housed in rooms at the façade in the modular structure.

Experience has shown that combination offices – regardless of the grid – are at least as area efficient as typical modular offices with functional workstations set along the façade

in a single row as result of the highly efficient work area in the façade area and the use of the central zone for all additional functions. The area efficiency rises even further when double combination offices are created.

The Right Concept in the Right Place

Wherever routine work is the order of the day with little need for internal and external meetings and few communal facilities, modular offices are a suitable and even desirable option. Hierarchical traditions and conventions are most likely the principal reasons why this concept is chosen, rather than

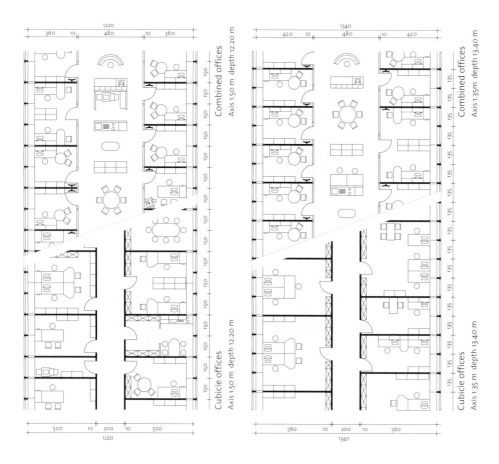

Combined offices
Axis 1.50 m depth 12.20 m

Cubicle offices
Axis 1.50 m depth 12.20 m

Combined offices
Axis 1.35m depth 13.40 m

Cubicle offices
Axis 1.35 m depth 13.40 m

3.3 Combined versus modular office – a comparison

functional requirements. In fact: modular offices are still the predominant choice.

Where constant interaction alternates with focused individual work and the opportunity for communication and conversation as well as the need for many communal facilities are in the foreground – requirements that will be universal and standard in future – the decision should always be in favor of the combination office.

Group rooms (open-plan rooms or "office landscapes") are generally not very popular among employees, and will in future be preferred for special tasks (e.g. distribution groups, call centers, drafting and construction offices).

The Requirement Profile for the Comfortable Office

All concepts for redesigning future spaces and work conditions are based on a fundamental premise: the employee must feel comfortable with his or her work at the workplace – be it at the company location, at home or on the road. If this basic requirement is not fulfilled, all other attempts at creating a contented atmosphere through well-designed space are doomed to fail. The office of the future is the comfort office with a clearly defined set of requirements:

– Flexibility: workplaces must be adaptable to work conditions at any given time, and convertible.
– Functionality: workplaces must allow for different tasks without necessitating any major reconfiguration effort. Air and light must correspond to natural, and to legislated, conditions.
– Social: workplaces must promote identification among the employees with the company and the products. They should

not only facilitate communication, but should act as forerunners of newly evolving forms of communications. The hierarchical status of the employees is irrelevant.
– Sensuousness: workplaces must appeal to, promote and develop all human senses – be it in the home office, on the road or in the company building.
– Space and location: workplaces are any place where the employee is working at any given time. The building envelope must accommodate this. The character, furnishing and outfitting of the workplaces must support the employee at work and provide an appealing environment.

Human beings continue to be the determining factor for the future of workspaces and work locations, even – and especially – in an economic and work environment that is flexible, accelerated and high-tech.

3.5 Ensuring Flexibility through Standardized Office Scenarios

If we were to believe furniture manufacturers, every piece of furniture must be equipped with casters. Everything must be movable, for "flexibility" is the magic word. In the minds of the suppliers, the idealized flexibility scenario seems to be as follows: in the morning, the employee collects a container on wheels at the container station and rolls it to a workstation – there seems to be an unspoken consensus that the latter will change from day to day. Whenever teamwork is required, individual work areas are transformed into teamwork and conference areas. When the moment arrives to return to individual work, everything is pushed back to the previous position. Everything is mobile, everything is flexible, everything is wheeled to wherever it is needed.

The reality, however, is different: the number of casters does not increase flexibility, for:
– Electronic devices will continue to be dependent on cables despite the introduction of wireless systems – power will still be supplied from the socket.
– Every piece of furniture that is moved occupies space elsewhere – this means that each piece of furniture requires at least double the amount of space.

– Foregoing fixed walls invariably leads to
acoustic problems – all compensatory
measures are both expensive and barely
effective.
– The reconfiguration of the work areas not
only requires creativity and mobility, it is
also a waste of time – a table that is to be
moved must first be cleared.
– The mobility of the employees will only
increase if the dependency on paper and
files is reduced, i.e., work processes must
be optimized using of electronic media.
Large containers on casters are inadequate
solutions for unfulfilled organizational
tasks.

The changes in office work are far less dramatic than some would like to suggest. Office
work encompasses relatively few activities:
reading, writing, talking, at times alone, at
other times on the phone, the computer, with
one or more people. Teamwork requires communication; exacting individual work requires
concentration. These are the basic requirements for the office environment. Hence there
is a need for standardized offices with the
greatest degree of flexibility. Flexibility is not
the result of the greatest number of casters,
but of intelligent standardization. One of
these concepts is the combination office mentioned above: Small individual rooms along
the façade and a corridor that is expanded
into a central zone with infrastructure, small
conference islands and glazed corridor walls
are the hallmarks of this concept, where
employees are the "mobile elements" – as
needed – not walls or furniture.

3.4 Central area of the business club of the dvg Hanover

3.5. Floor plan
Detail of one of the six arms of the
main administrative building of
the dvg in Hanover. Each department has been assigned one of
these units. The service functions
(lockers, espresso bars, conference
and project rooms as well as the
secretary's office) are permanently
available to the staff at the business center. The workplaces are
not personalized, but arranged in
accordance with the type of work
performed: the staff can choose
between open workplaces, working while standing, closed single
rooms, group workplaces or the
lounge, depending on the day's
requirements.

The aforementioned concept of the business club is another example of intelligent standardization. It meets the requirements for communication and work scenarios by dividing work spaces into group offices for teamwork, conference rooms, meeting areas, reading areas and lounges for informal communication. The remaining individual workstations are available to all employees as alternate work areas. As a highly flexible work environment, the business club also functions without furniture set on casters (Figs. 3.4 and 3.5).

Ensuring Building Flexibility

As these descriptions have shown, building flexibility is the greatest challenge. It is important to ensure that little effort is required to respond to new usage requirements and aging building systems with differing lifecycles. The more frequent anticipated changes in technology are, the shorter the lifecycle of a subsystem will be. For this reason, subsystems should operate separately and be linked via accessible interfaces or contact points. Complicated façade wall junctions, heating pipes that penetrate dividing walls, heating radiators that bridge window axes, dividing walls, where renovation involves intervention in suspended ceilings, or cables in movable dividing walls are negative examples. As space organizing elements, dividing walls between offices should be free of installations. Circuits, bus bars, the placement of sockets, luminaires and control units must allow for changes in use, without causing work stoppage, dust or noise. Some adaptations are so likely that they should always be included in the planning, and this includes transitions into future office concepts. To this end, higher concentration of workstations must be possible; the same applies to transforming office areas into special use areas and vice versa. This is especially true for objects created for the open market. Office concepts are still undefined at the time of planning and each change of tenant goes hand in hand with renovation or conversion in an occupied building.

3.6 Marketing Strategies: Client Loyalty from the Outset

Ideally, the marketing strategy should begin with the creation of a product profile as the basis for a performance analysis of existing competitors on the market, especially for real estate properties, which are developed by investors for third party users. The product profile must serve as a guideline (including all the data with regard to building, location and service) for continual optimization – for both customer benefit and profitability. Even during the planning stage, a set of simple, user-oriented tools can be developed, which will communicate the benefit to the customer in a more comprehensive and convincing manner than the ubiquitous glossy brochures. They should present competitive advantages as customer benefits and structure the consulting process in consideration of tenant interests. This makes it possible to encourage lasting customer loyalty even during the planning.

Some of the tools that have been successfully employed are:
– determining market demands,
– occupancy planning and area optimization,
– online marketing, and
– service.

Determining Market Demands

The comparability of office locations from the perspective of the tenant interests has little to do with the number of square meters, or rather the price per square meter. It is dependent on the utility of a building and the organization of the office space. Communicating this fact is an important contribution to increasing the competence of the landlord. Office modules should be the calculation unit for a systematic requirement analysis.

An office module corresponds to the optimum workstation for one employee. Based on this unit, derived from the façade grid, it is possible to calculate the real utility value of an area – the occupancy capacity for workstations. The prerequisite is that the required workstation types are known. It is also important to arrive at a realistic estimate of the number of required office modules (Table 3.6).

To begin with the room depth, whether the rooms are completely enclosed, partially glazed or open zones is not important. The result of the analysis is an area requirement per employee, or rather, the total requirement including all necessary ancillary areas.

A rapid test – counting the number of office modules – makes it possible to compare different objects. The lower the ratio of rental area to the number of office modules is, the greater the area efficiency of the project will be.

Occupancy Planning and Area Optimization

Once the requirement has been established, a rough occupancy plan reveals how many square meters of rentable area are needed in a specific object. A simple system allows the prospective tenant to assess an offer for compatibility with his specific needs down to the last meter (Figs. 3.7–3.9).

Each occupancy plan must address the question of options for savings. Some options are universal rules of office planning, others are tied to specific projects and often represent a competitive advantage.

Online Marketing

The utility value of an object can be determined via the Internet. External and internal characteristics of the project can be visualized in three-dimensional images and interested tenants can be informed across great distances at any time. Contacts can be established and cultivated far more quickly and successfully. Any tools, from requirement determination to decision preparation, can be made available interactively. Being equipped with tools that range from requirement clarification to removal planning makes it possible to present an occupancy plan on the day after a conversation – complete with alternative calculations and proof of meeting the requirements, as well as a balance sheet for the achievable area efficiencies.

Table 3.6 Office and special area requirement, establishing the tenant's requirements

Offices	WP/OM	Number of Workplaces per office	WP	Offices	Office space in m²
Manager	(1/2)	1	1	1	41
Manager	(1/1.5)	1	1	1	31
Single office	(1/1)	1	1	1	20
Double room	(2/1.5)	2	2	1	31
Double room	(2/2)	2	2	1	41
Team office	(2/1)	4	2	1	20
Total			9	6	184

Special area requirement	WP	Quantity	Rooms in m²	Special area in m²
Reception	1	1	10	10
Conference	1	1	10	10
EDP	1	1	10	10
Archives	0	1	10	10
Conference room	0	1	10	10
Seminar room	0	1	10	10
Miscellaneous	1	1	10	10
Total	4	7		70

In order to accommodate your space requirement, you will need:

264 m² of rented space or 20.30 m² per workplace

WP = workplace

OM = office module

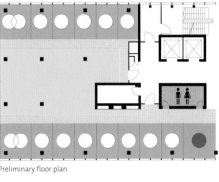

Preliminary floor plan

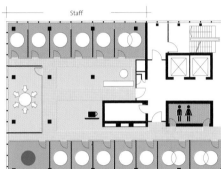

3.7 and 3.8 are examples of a preliminary and a detailed floor plan respectively on a floor of the Vienna Twin Towers, Vienna. Architect: M. Fuksas, Rome

Service

Landlords who wish to become service providers have ample opportunity to do so prior to, during and after tenant occupation. This may include building services, office services and other services for office tasks. The goals are:

– competitiveness through cost and use advantages for the tenant,

– profitability and economic independence of the services,

– financing through synergies between tenants, for example, shared material purchases or joint use of expensive infrastructure.

Different service bundles can be offered to the tenants. Each service can be marketed as a separate module – depending on the needs of the tenant. Nearly all services result in productivity gains for the tenant through savings in personnel costs.

Some examples of service bundles are:

– IT service: LAN system, office equipment purchase incl. maintenance, telerouting, video-conferencing.

– Property management services: area and space management, layout and interior planning, furniture leasing and Rent-a-desk, reconfigurations and conversions, conference sharing, energy (resource) management and cost center accounting.

– Area- and time-saving services: office materials purchasing, printer and copier service, internal and external mail service, in-house catering, travel office, car/truck fleet administration, janitor services for rental areas and errands.

Summary: Reaching for the Sky through Quality and Flexibility

These observations on office organization in high-rises have illustrated that office towers are affected by changes in two areas. For one thing, the client "scene" has become far more varied. The division of roles into client and user mean that the economic and architectural planning process is determined by a multitude of interests. In view of price competition, the various interests must in future be increasingly geared towards quality and

service: aside from the building quality, the greatest competitive advantage lies in being able to offer more flexibility and efficiency and in the area of the quality of services surrounding the office workplace.

This range of services and characteristics provides the basis for a future-oriented response to the second process of transformation in the context of this topic: the change from traditional office concepts to intelligent, standardized office environments that meet the growing demands for flexibility, particulary in the service sector. The office towers of the flexible knowledge- and service-based society must offer the structural, spatial and office organizational prerequisites for more productivity, epitomized, for example, by the combination office and business club concepts.

The only common feature between the office towers of the knowledge industry of the 21st century and their predecessors from the previous century is at best their height – their internal life and office culture are already dedicated to a completely different era of the economic and work environment.

04 Site Operation

Christoph Motzko

Site Operational Issues during High-rise Construction

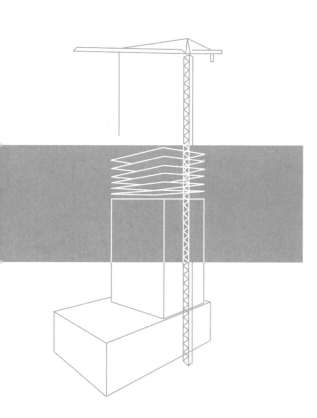

4.1 Introduction

High-rises have a decisive impact on the image of large cities, not only through the completed object but also during the construction, conversion or demolition phases. Many different disciplines must deliver their services in an integrated manner during these periods. Particular attention is drawn to the services provided by the construction firm or contractor relating to process technology, the necessary economic elements of cost planning, and the ecological elements of natural resource protection and environmental waste disposal. The construction phase also plays a role in the building management, making the external observer aware of a project. The rapid construction progress that is usual in high-rise construction is communicated to the public via information billboards, on which the current building height is posted, or visualized by means of webcams on the Internet. Spectacular events in the construction process or equipment components, such as the use of helicopters for assembling building components at a great height, or automated self-climbing machines for formwork systems, enhance the awareness of such a building project. Any high-rise construction site produces a certain amount of noise and will, from time to time, cause traffic congestion near the site. From the perspective of the site operator, the task is to erect a structure on a single footprint with pronounced verticality in the appropriate technical, economical and environmental manner. Clients, architects, expert planners, authorities and executing firms must fulfill a complex and challenging task that is associated with unique risks. In what follows, a selection of issues relating to the execution of high-rises is presented from the perspective of the site operation or management.

4.2 Construction Process

The work on a building site is performed according to the principle of on-site production. The object – the building – is tied to the locality. Workers, working funds and building materials are raised locally at specific times and required volumes. The processes are

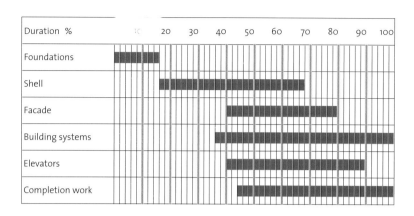

4.1 Typical rough schedule for constructing high-rise buildings

Table 4.2 Comparison of selected high-rise buildings: construction periods and time required to complete the shell of a standard floor

Property	Height	Use	Completion	Construction time	Rough work per standard floor
Business Research Center, Warsaw, Poland	104 m	Office	2000	2 years	5 working days
Taunustor Japan Center, Frankfurt, Germany	114 m	Office	1996	3 years	4 working days
World Port Center, Rotterdam, the Netherlands	125 m	Office	2001	3 years	5 working days
Gallileo, Frankfurt, Germany	136 m	Office	2003	3 years	4 working days
Dresdner Bank, Frankfurt, Germany	166 m	Office	1979	5.5 years	13 working days
Trianon, Frankfurt, Germany	186 m	Office	1993	4 years	5.5 working days
Millennium Tower, Vienna, Austria	202 m	Office	1999	17 months	3 working days
Maintower, Frankfurt, Germany	198 m 247.5 m*	Office	1999	3 years	4 working days
Messeturm, Frankfurt, Germany	256.5 m	Office	1991	37 months	3 working days
Park Tower, Chicago, USA	257 m	Hotel/ residential	2000	3 years	3 working days
Trump World Tower, New York, USA	269 m	Residential	2001	3 years	5 working days
Commerzbank, Frankfurt, Germany	258.7 m 298.5 m*	Office	1997	3 years	3 working days
Petronas Towers, Kuala Lumpur, Malaysia	452 m	Office	1998	5 years	5 working days

*Building height including aerial

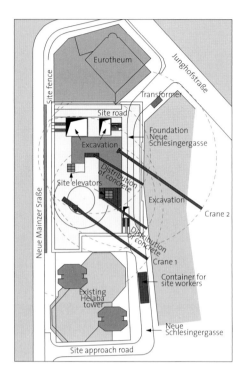

4.3 and 4.4 Site organization for the Maintower, Frankfurt/ Main, above: location plan, below: bird's eye view [5]

coordinated with regard to timing and spatial requirements during the process planning. A typical rough schedule for constructing high-rise buildings has been drafted on the basis of research conducted by the author and a study by Schubert/Racky [1] (Fig. 4.1). It provides a record of data for selected high-rises that have been constructed in Frankfurt am Main in the past 14 years. The schedule illustrates that roughly one third of the entire construction time is taken up by the foundation works and the ensuing rough work, before the other trades can begin to deliver their services.

Clearly, the rough work is a prerequisite for the progress of the construction, even though interest in this aspect is waning. Figure 4.1 plots the percentage of the total construction period taken up by each step and the duration of rough work per standard floor for selected high-rises.

While 13 working days were required to complete the rough work for a standard floor during the construction of the Dresdner Bank high-rise in 1974–1979 (Table 4.2), the same

task is currently achieved in a mere four working days on the Gallileo site [2]. It is important to take into consideration that in the Gallileo project, ceilings as well as defined supports are additionally equipped with building system components (building component temperature equalization).

As a result, the rough work per floor today takes roughly one to two working days longer than the straightforward rough work of earlier years. Rapid construction times were already achieved in the first half of the 20th century with steel-structure high-rises in the United States. The Empire State Building with a height of 381 m was completed in record time in little over one year at a rate of approximately seven million man-hours [3]. In the summer of 1930, the work performance of one floor steel construction per working day was achieved through excellent planning and the site organization of Shreve, Lamb and Harmon [4].

4.3 Site Facilities

Spatial Allocation

The correct spatial allocation of all installations necessary for executing the construction such as transportation routes, storage areas, hoists, containers, etc., is vitally important for efficient and economic completion. It must be planned in the context of the work preparation. There is usually little space available for the building sites of high-rise projects. The necessary containers for site offices, facilities, warehousing and workshops often have to be accommodated in multistory structures in confined spaces, sometimes using temporary steel structures. The number and size of the elevators is also limited by the available space. This results in special requirements in terms of supplying the site with workers, operating equipment and building materials. The vertical focus of the production processes and the small footprint of the ground plans mean that vertical transportation is the most common cause for bottlenecks. The crane capacity and the number of site elevators and of concrete pumps are particulary important in this context.

Cranes

The standard floors of high-rises are generally erected by using two to three self-erecting building tower cranes. More cranes are needed for construction on existing additions (for example, plinth stories) and for the loading and unloading tasks associated with supplying the site. Both derricking jibs and trolley jib cranes are used. The following elements are important in the context of crane planning and selection, especially for high-rise construction in inner-city areas, given the standard technical and geometrical requirements such as covering for the storage and delivery areas, maximum dimensions and weight of the transport goods, overlaps in the revolving range for load transfer:

Neighbor-related Concerns

High-rise construction can cause considerable inconvenience for neighboring properties. In terms of crane use, one important issue is the sweeping movement across an adjacent property. This is a significant imposition that must be clarified with the neighbor(s) in the preparation phase of a building project. There are cases where the neighboring properties are urgently needed as rotation areas and where the indulgence of the neighbor is essential. In practice, the neighbor may demand adequate compensation, which is paid by the client or the contractor. If agreement cannot be reached between neighbors and client/contractor, a court decision will be made on whether defined crane operation is permissible [6]. The structure of the built environment in the immediate vicinity is another important factor for crane selection, for example, if there are other high-rises that could hinder crane operation.

Operating Speed

The operating speed of the crane plays a very important role given the great differences in height. Careful selection of the equipment in consideration of the usual one-to-four-line operation, depending on boom type and the ratio to the load to be transported, is absolutely essential.

Downtimes

The findings of a study [7] have shown that as much as 90 percent must be scheduled in addition to the base time for downtimes and additional service times for equipment. Intensive planning efforts in work preparation reduced this value to roughly 40 percent in the 1990s [8]. According to expert surveys [9], this value can be reduced by an additional 50 percent for the rough work in high-rise construction when appropriate organizational measures are taken. This brings the crane utilization to over 80 percent. These results are contingent on planning and coordinating the use of cranes, and also on the performance of the individual crane operators.

External Anchorage

For high-rise construction, cranes must be anchored at defined distances. The number and design of the crossbars of the external anchorages influence the crane operating costs to a considerable degree. The influence of forces in terms of dimensioning and the construction of the building must also be taken into consideration. Work on the anchorages causes suspension in the disposition of the crane capacity and possibly disruptions for the execution of other trades, for example, work on the façades. Number, location and installation date of the external anchorages must therefore be carefully planned in reference to crane size and crane type.

Site Elevators

In addition to cranes, site elevators are the most important component of the site facilities for vertical transportation of loads and persons. These devices are employed to transport personnel and play an essential role in transporting materials for the finishing trades and for the building systems. The selection criteria are the speed and load-bearing capacity of the site elevator as well as its performance scope and construction speed. In analogy to climbing cranes, the vertical reach of site elevators is expanded as the rough work progresses. Among the high-rises featured in the study, the number of site elevators fluctuated between one and two, each elevator having two elevator cars. The hoisting speed can reach up to 1.5 m/s.

Fresh Concrete Transport

In high-rise construction, fresh or wet concrete is generally transported from the transfer point to the pouring point using stationary concrete pumps for reasons of crane capacity efficiency. Such pumps can transport fresh concrete across installation heights of more than 300 m without intermediate stations. Hopper spreaders are positioned at the top level of the shell to provide fresh concrete for the relevant building components as work progresses. Among the high-rises featured in the study, the number of stationary concrete pumps fluctuated between one and two, the number of hopper spreaders between one and three.

4.4 Formwork

Modern formwork systems guarantee rapid and safe progress in the rough work. The formwork generally determines the rough work in building construction. This requires qualified work preparation with the necessary clock manufacturing planning and the appropriate organization, and work supervision on the building site. In terms of safety, compliance with the installation and application guidelines of the formwork manufacturers as well as standard work safety regulations such as the regulations on accident prevention (in Germany, for example, UVV – Unfallverhütungsvorschriften) are mandatory. For high-rise construction the most efficient formwork systems are those that are largely crane-independent and guarantee the safety imperative for work at great heights. Sliding formwork, self-climbing formwork and self-propelling platforms are used in particular for the production of bracing vertical elements in the structure.

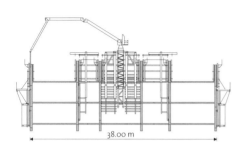

4.5 Section of self-propelled climbing forms, Park Tower, Chicago, USA [11]

4.6 Aerial view of Park Tower

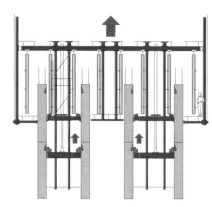

4.7 Example of self-propelled climbing platform, section

4.8 Aerial view [12]

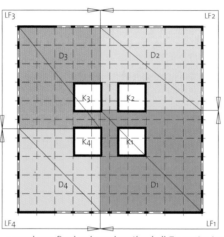

4.9 and 4.10 fixed cycle work on the shell, Taunustor Japan Center, Frankfurt, schematic diagram and aerial view [11]

Sliding Formwork

Sliding formwork is driven by hydraulic power. These systems are employed to manufacture tall vertical reinforced concrete building components and are used chiefly for the construction of building cores. This is not necessarily the standard approach, however, because application is strongly dependent on the ground plan of the building component and on night work permission. The process of sliding formwork requires that work must continue round the clock. Sliding formwork on building cores of high-rises must be interrupted periodically for structural reasons. During the construction of the Messeturm in Frankfurt/Main, for example, the core was constructed in six stages, each comprising sliding formwork across a height of 30 to 40 m. The execution of each sliding formwork stage was completed in 10 to 14 days with an average sliding height of 2.5 m in 24 hours [10]. The sliding formwork stages were staggered four to five weeks apart, to install the standard floors and the perforated façade.

Self-Climbing Formwork

Self-climbing formwork makes it possible to execute single or dual bracket concrete fabrics on any plan. In contrast to sliding formwork, work progresses in defined sections, generally floor-to-floor. The climbing process is crane independent. Hydraulic systems achieve a climbing speed of up to 0.2 m/min. Self-climbing formwork can operate at wind velocities of more than 200 km/h. In building construction, these systems are generally employed for the erection of structural cores and perforated façades. Figures 4.5 and 4.6 depict a section and a bird's eye view, respectively, of the 290 m Park Tower project in Chicago. The special feature in this application is that the hopper spreader operates without a crane on an interior platform and was designed to function with hydraulics together with the climbing unit to save crane capacity [11]. These formwork applications are currently the preferred solution for high-rise construction.

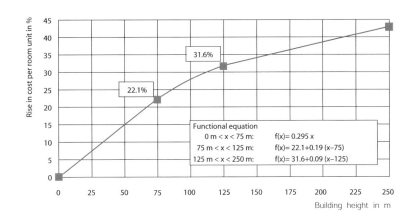

4.11 Plotting the rise in cost per room unit in relation to building height

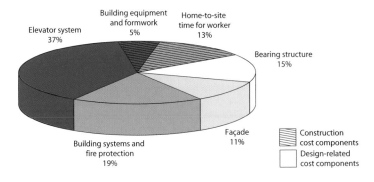

4.12 Allocation of costs (as a percentage) for a 150 m high building

Platform Technology

The latest development in the area of self-climbing technology is platform technology (Figs. 4.7 and 4.8). These are complete "form-work machines" for high-rise cores and tower structures. In these applications, all formwork, scaffolding and stacking grounds for interior and exterior walls are realized in a single self-climbing process. The platform creates better conditions with regard to task ergonomics, intermediate storage of building materials, worker safety and weather protection.

Clock Manufacturing

The goal of clock manufacturing is to create an uninterrupted sequence of repetitive identical processes in different work stages within a structured production process. Decomposition must be carried out in preparation. In the context of construction planning, decomposition refers to a break down of the building processes under consideration of the dependencies in terms of technology and capacity for each process [13]. Figures 4.9 and 4.10 illustrate the manufacture of a single floor on the construction site of the "Taunustor Japan Center" in Frankfurt, a four-day clock manufacture process per rough work for each standard

floor with coordinated construction of all vertical and horizontal components of the structure.

The creation of sealing levels is important for the execution of the tasks that follow the rough work. These can be created vertically by achieving a "sealed façade" state and horizontally by arranging temporary sealing levels on selected floors [15]. This measure is necessary to allow for the parallel execution of other work, which requires weather protection, or of work that requires certain preconditions in the façade area.

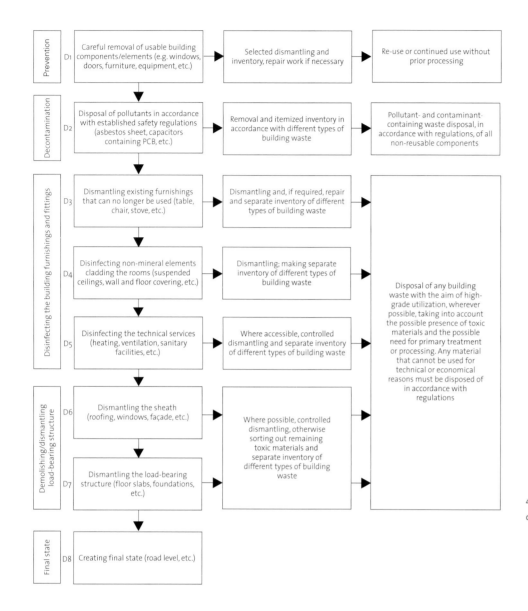

4.13 Procedure for the controlled deconstruction of a building

4.5 Logistics

The unique conditions associated with inner city construction call for special measures in terms of supplying the building site. Ensuring that the delivery of supplies is harmonized with the rate of consumption is a challenging logistical task. Logistics, here, applies to concrete tasks and building materials as well as to meeting planned delivery schedules. A carefully calibrated operating plan for the crane capacity is especially important as is a detailed timetable for other hoisting equipment, such as site elevators or interior elevators used temporarily for specific completion tasks. The operator gives notice of these

timetables in advance, and they must be kept to without fail. Delays or overruns would lead to delays in other areas and create additional costs. Intermediate storage can be set up for highly complex elements of the construction, as was done, for example, during the construction of the Commerzbank high-rise in Frankfurt, where an intermediate warehousing facility was set up for parts of the steel structure outside of the city limits. These elements could then be delivered to the site on schedule late at night [14]. A similar approach had previously been used during the construction of the Empire State Building. A depot was set up outside of New York and the required materials were transported to

the site two days prior to the installation deadline per schedule. The material was then transported on-site to the relevant installation site using cranes integrated into the site construction [4].

4.6 Selected Cost Factors in High-rise Construction

The influence of selected variables on the construction costs of office and administration buildings in relation to building height was studied in a research project at the Institut für Baubetrieb at the Technische Universität in Darmstadt, Germany. The project focused on

reinforced concrete high-rises in Frankfurt. The first step was to chart the governing cost elements that depend on building height. This resulted in two major groups:
– Design elements resulting chiefly from the changing requirements for the load-bearing structure, the façade and the building systems, including fire protection.
– Construction elements resulting from the required construction processes and the site equipment such as cranes, site elevators, concrete pumps and formwork.

The travel time for workers was also revealed as being especially cost intensive.
The results shown in the curve in **Figure 4.11** plot the course of cost increase per room unit according to building height for identical ground plans and completion standards.
The percentages of design and construction-related additional costs for a 150 m building were also researched. A pie chart of these additional costs is shown in **Figure 4.12**, illustrating the dominance of design-related cost factors.

4.7 Construction Waste in the Building and Demolition Phase

The recycling and waste management bill was passed in Germany in 1996 (Krw-/AbfG or Kreislaufwirtschafts- und Abfallgesetz). This created a new legal basis for natural resource protection and environmental waste removal and management. The principal goal is to exploit the technical, economic and ecological options for preventing waste generation, and material- and energy-efficient reuse of waste. The bill has had a major impact on the building sector, since construction waste is a major factor in the waste production in Germany, reaching 71 percent of the total waste produced in 1995 alone [16]. Compliance with the recycling and waste management bill is therefore an important task for all parties in a building project, both during the planning and construction stage and during demolition. The waste management system employed during the construction of the Gallileo high-rise in Frankfurt is a good example of adherence to the Krw-/AbfG for a new building. The general contractor commissioned a specialized service company for expert waste management. This company implemented an on-site waste container system and the relevant logistics, which were contractually agreed in conjunction with the local construction firms. This led to compelling incentives for complying because failure to do so was linked to economic consequences. In addition to adherence to ecological principles, the application of such a system also improved the site operation and made an important contribution to work safety. From an economic perspective, the supply and waste management processes could be charted with great precision and ensure causative cost allocation and cost control in this area. The principles of the recycling and waste management law must also be applied to the demolition of existing buildings. Systems should be implemented for all building demolitions to allow for object specific waste management, pollutant removal and separation of the demolition material.

4.8 Summary

Building a high-rise is a complex and inter-disciplinary undertaking when the technical, economic and ecological parameters are taken into consideration. The areas of work processes, site facilities, formwork, logistics, economy and ecology explored in this chapter are important branches.
Competent construction experts must be consulted during the planning phase to ensure that the available technologies are employed in executing the construction of the high-rise. Planning and execution are closely linked and determine the technical and economic success of the undertaking.

In addition to the erection of a high-rise, consideration must also be given to the fact that growing user requirements with regard to building function and design are catalysts for constant change, which in turn affects the renovation and conversion branch of the building sector.

Demolition is as important as the construction and operation of a high-rise. This, too, must be considered in the planning phase.

05 Geotechnics

Ulvi Arslan and Peter F. Ripper

Geotechnical Aspects of the Planning and Building of High-rises

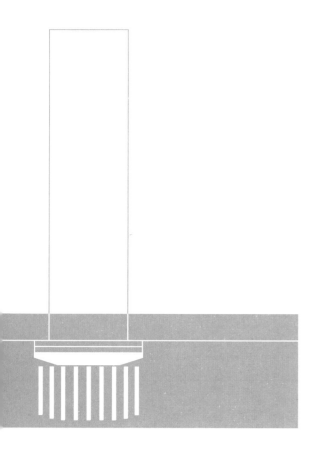

5.1   Introduction

High-rises – A Challenge for Geotechnical Engineers

While architects and structural engineers are able to visually document the success of their planning efforts on each high-rise project, successful geotechnical services remain hidden underground. They are only visible or experienced when errors were made in the ground/subsoil assessment or in case of poor planning, resulting in building damage, construction delays and additional costs.

Although the construction costs for the excavation pits and foundations of high-rises generally account for less than 10 percent of the total construction costs, the ground and the subsoil are major risk factors in high-rise construction. The geotechnical engineer is therefore faced with special challenges and responsibilities in planning and monitoring the construction of high-rises. The added value, which results from professional geotechnical services for the project and the client body, can be considerable and has a decisive effect on the overall success of the project.

A Brief History of the Foundations for Frankfurt's High-rises

In Germany, Frankfurt's emergence as a European financial center has led to the construction of distinct high-rises and the development of a skyline that is unique in Europe. This progressive and dynamic urban development will continue with a high-rise development plan that envisions several additional high-rise projects rising to a height of over 300 m. And yet the building ground in Frankfurt is more vulnerable to deformation than in other German cities, and is therefore not an ideal site for heavy foundations [1].

The foundation conditions for high-rises in Frankfurt are characterized by the presence of Frankfurt Clay, the result of sedimentation in the Tertiary Sea. In the inner city, it is composed of massive clay deposits of over 100 m depth, which include layers of limestone and shell sand. The groundwater sits just above the clay surface and exerts pressure on different layers in the limestone. Superposition of older, already eroded layers place an additional geological burden on the clay. This geological history has characterized the mineral structure with a pre-tension, which continues to exist today and defines the behavior of the ground in terms of deformation and shear strength [4].

Figures 5.1 a to 5.1 c provide a schematic overview of the most important high-rises in Frankfurt's inner city in chronological sequence based on start of construction. We differentiate between the high-rise generation where construction began prior to 1980 (1st generation) and the high-rises erected after 1980 (2nd generation). The high-rises built prior to 1980, in some cases rising to a height of up to 180 m, were all erected on pad foundations of 12–25 m depth and separated from the flat buildings by settlement joints. The predominant range of settlement lies between 20 and 30 cm. All foundations were designed to transfer the load centrally to the

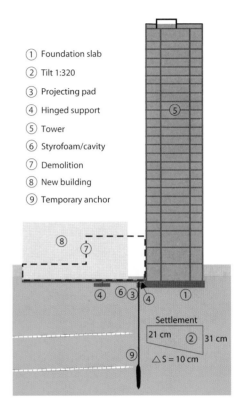

① Foundation slab
② Tilt 1:320
③ Projecting pad
④ Hinged support
⑤ Tower
⑥ Styrofoam/cavity
⑦ Demolition
⑧ New building
⑨ Temporary anchor

5.2 GZ Bank tower, settlement and tilting

5.1 a Chronology of high-rise buildings in Frankfurt. 1st generation, 1960–1980

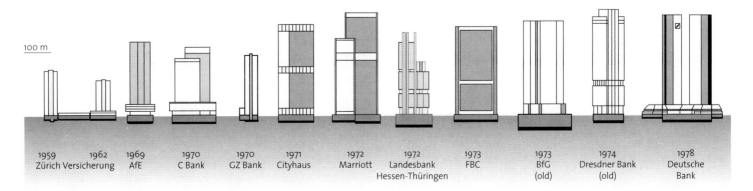

| 1959 Zürich Versicherung | 1962 | 1969 AfE | 1970 C Bank | 1970 GZ Bank | 1971 Cityhaus | 1972 Marriott | 1972 Landesbank Hessen-Thüringen | 1973 FBC | 1973 BfG (old) | 1974 Dresdner Bank (old) | 1978 Deutsche Bank |

60

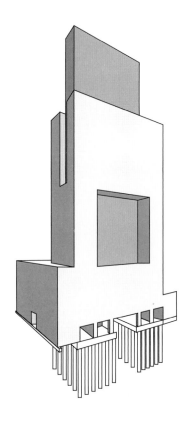

5.3 a

Torhaus Messe Frankfurt, archictect: O. M. Ungers, KPP
foundation: section, plan, load-bearing behavior

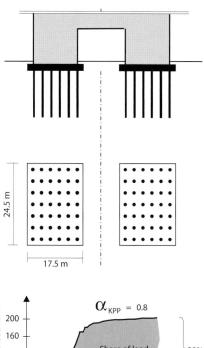

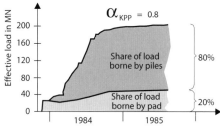

α_{CPP} = pile-pad factor (ratio of bearing capacity of pile / total load of high rise)

foundation pads. In those cases, where this approach was not feasible due to the building or the site geometry, elaborate construction measures were implemented to shift the load center [8].

The roughly 97 m high, extremely slim GZ Bank tower (Fig. 5.2) across from the Alte Oper exemplifies the first generation of high-rises.

This structure attempted to compensate for an anticipated load eccentricity resulting from the off-center core by creating a projecting ballast basement and hollowed-out pad connections to the adjacent underground garages. Even during construction, however, the builders had to contend with a degree of settlement and leaning they had not anticipated. The ballast created by the projecting base-

ment box filled with water and gravel served as a temporary measure to delay the leaning tendency. Undercutting the high-rise pad during construction also failed to produce successful results. The settlement finally subsided roughly 10 years after completion, reaching a maximum of 31 cm and a diagonal settlement differential of 10 cm. The maximum lean today is 1:320. The structure has nevertheless stood without visible damage or operational limitations. The extension was demolished in 2000 and replaced with a new structure. During this process, the foundation pad of the high-rise, already subjected to stresses by the settlement and the leaning, had to be exposed on one side. Additional leaning was prevented with the help of pre-stressed vertical anchors, some of which were put in place in advance while the rest were held in reserve. Deformation measurements during the demolition of the addition formed the basis for a decision whether additional anchors should be installed (see section 5.3, Geotechnical Monitoring).

The Dresdner Bank tower [10], begun in 1974, could not be realized with central load transfer to the foundation slab due to the unfavorable site geometry. Consequently, the foundation pad was undercut around the corner to a total length of 50 m and a width of 5 m. Pressure cushions were then integrated into the resulting cavity. The lean of the high-rise could be continually adjusted by means of the cushion pressure, resulting in virtually no leaning upon building completion.

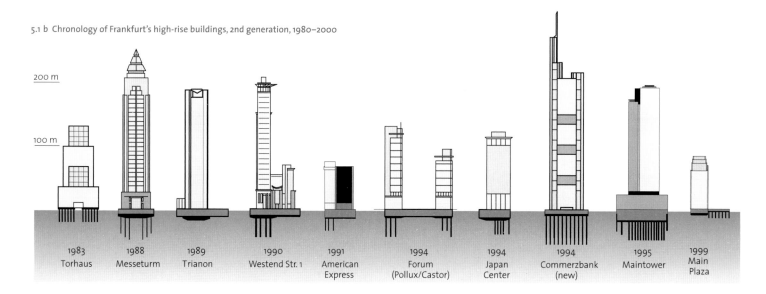

5.1 b Chronology of Frankfurt's high-rise buildings, 2nd generation, 1980–2000

1983 Torhaus · 1988 Messeturm · 1989 Trianon · 1990 Westend Str. 1 · 1991 American Express · 1994 Forum (Pollux/Castor) · 1994 Japan Center · 1994 Commerzbank (new) · 1995 Maintower · 1999 Main Plaza

A new era in foundations for high-rises in Frankfurt began with the "Torhaus" on the city's exhibition grounds (Fig. 5.3 a).

The clients specified that this building should not be designed with a basement, and existing through roads near the gate of the high-rise prevented the excavation of a building pit. It was necessary, therefore, to raise the structure on a foundation of two separate shallow slabs of only 3 m depth below ground surface. Solutions were sought for a low-deformation foundation for the framed load-bearing structure of the high-rise. The answer lay in combining a closely spaced pile with a shallow load-bearing raft. This solution has come to be known as "pile and raft foundation" (PRF) [11], and was employed for most of the high-rises of the 2nd generation from 1980 onwards. When the PRF was designed for the "Torhaus", the engineers were venturing into uncharted territory: at the time, there was no previous experience with this type of foundation in Frankfurt Clay, nor had the relevant design methods been developed.

The structural solution was developed on the basis of experience with load-bearing behavior of a single pile, the raft and the group effect of the foundation pile, and with the help of numerical modeling. The pile foundation carries 80 percent of the building loads, a ratio that would have to be optimized to meet current standards (Fig. 5.3 b).

The geotechnical monitoring of measurements during the construction of the "Torhaus" did, however, provide the basis for further development of PRF. The lessons learned from the "Torhaus" were fully implemented in the design for the foundation for the Messeturm (Fig. 5.4).

The outcome was a comparatively elegant foundation design, which fulfilled the established design goals with astonishing success. Over the ensuing years, all high-rises in Frankfurt were erected on pile and raft foundations, with a few exceptions (Trianon and Main Plaza with pad foundation and Commerzbank with pile foundation). [5]

5.2 Geotechnical Tasks for Project Planning

Legal Background

The building site, i.e. the location, is one of the most important resources in any high-rise project. The client brings the site and the ground to the project, as a platform and material, so to speak, for the erection of the building. Hence, he also carries the risks associated with the conditions of the site and the subsoil.

The following three aspects are important in this context:
- The subsoil, including groundwater as material and medium for integrating (load transfer) the new building (soil mechanics/building structure).

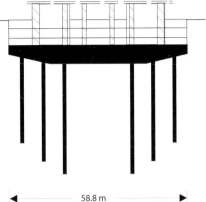
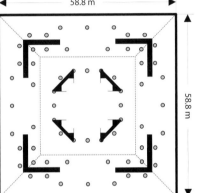
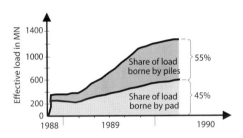

5.4 Messeturm Frankfurt, architects: Murphy/Jahn Assoc., pile and raft foundation: section, plan, load-bearing behavior

5.1 c Chronology of high-rise buildings in Frankfurt, 2000 to the present

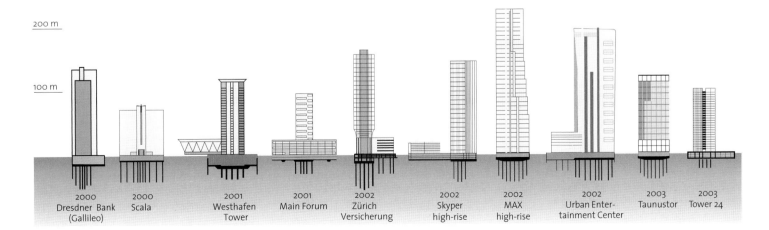

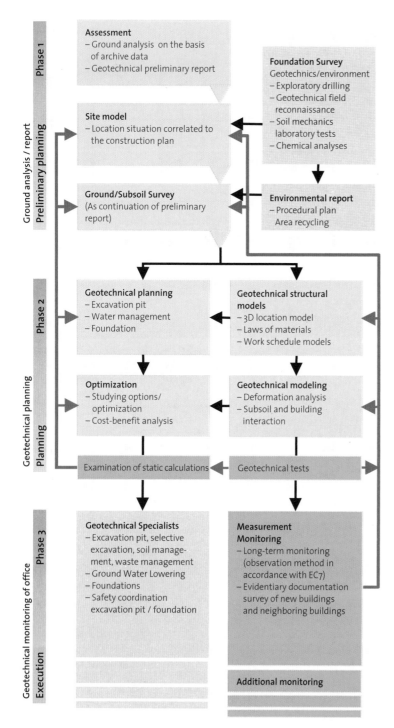

Phase 1

Assessment
- Ground analysis on the basis of archive data
- Geotechnical preliminary report

Foundation Survey
Geotechnics/environment
- Exploratory drilling
- Geotechnical field reconnaissance
- Soil mechanics laboratory tests
- Chemical analyses

Site model
- Location situation correlated to the construction plan

Ground/Subsoil Survey
(As continuation of preliminary report)

Environmental report
- Procedural plan
  Area recycling

Ground analysis / report — Preliminary planning

Phase 2

Geotechnical planning
- Excavation pit
- Water management
- Foundation

Geotechnical structural models
- 3D location model
- Laws of materials
- Work schedule models

Optimization
- Studying options/optimization
- Cost-benefit analysis

Geotechnical modeling
- Deformation analysis
- Subsoil and building interaction

Examination of static calculations

Geotechnical tests

Geotechnical planning — Planning

Phase 3

Geotechnical Specialists
- Excavation pit, selective excavation, soil management, waste management
- Ground Water Lowering
- Foundations
- Safety coordination excavation pit / foundation

Measurement Monitoring
- Long-term monitoring (observation method in accordance with EC7)
- Evidentiary documentation survey of new buildings and neighboring buildings

Additional monitoring

Geotechnical monitoring of office — Execution

5.5 Geotechnical operations during the planning and construction phases

---

- Ground (site including existing development) and groundwater as an environmental medium (environmental factor).
- Ground/subsoil and groundwater as material and thermal resources (resource conservation factor).

The geotechnical engineer fulfills two roles: as an expert and as a planning consultant. These two roles differ in terms of legal obligations and liabilities. While consultants and planners are equally liable under private law for the accuracy, technical quality, safety and efficiency of their solution(s), the expert/consultant also assumes the task of minimizing the building site risk of the building ground for the client.

Geotechnical Safety Concept

The load-bearing system of a high-rise is influenced to a great degree by the deformation behavior of the ground. In this context "to a great degree" means that ground deformations determine not only the stability and serviceability of the building (elevators, transitions, watertightness, etc.), but also the static or internal forces of the load-bearing system (load distribution, stress, bending moment of foundation elements) and hence the reliability and dimensioning of the entire system.

Similar conditions apply to the deep excavation pits required for high-rise construction. With the exception of direct water pressure, the stress placed on the excavation pit sheeting is the result of the pressure exerted by the soil, the scale of which is largely determined by the construction measures and the permissible ground deformations.

Due to this complex interaction between building ground and building and the importance of high-rise safety and deep inner-city excavation pits, all high-rise foundations and the deep pits required for them are classified as especially difficult and high-risk geotechnical tasks according to EC7, geotechnical category GK3. This classification stipulates that geotechnical planning and stability and deformation analyses must be carried out with multistage redundancy in the form of a closed control cycle. The following two additional safety elements are included in the project process to allow for timely modification or adaptation of the systems:

– Independent geotechnical checking of calculation assumptions, models, deformation and stability calculations.
– Geotechnical monitoring throughout the construction allowing for modification or adaptation of the systems (monitoring method).

For high-rise projects, both are compulsory elements in the delivery of stability and serviceability certificates.
The sequence of the geotechnical services to be performed for a high-rise project is illustrated in the process organization diagram (Fig. 5.5) in conjunction with the planning and construction sequence.

Permit Management

The following milestones are important for the overall project sequence:
– Basis data collection/technical and economic viability of the project
– Preliminary planning up to request for development permission/development plan
– Submission of building permit request/permission planning
– Execution planning and issuing tenders for construction services, awarding tenders to executing firms
– Start of construction, completion and move-in date
– End of additional monitoring (geotechnical monitoring).

The geotechnical expert must be included in the process up until the end of the monitoring after completion and the final ground deformations. In areas with sensitive ground conditions (e.g. Frankfurt Clay) this can easily take five years or more after the construction has been completed.

Area Recycling/Environmental Geotechnics

In the dense urban environments of many European cities, new building ground can usually only be provided by redeveloping previous industrial or commercial/residential areas. The preparation of a site for new building uses is referred to as area recycling. In Germany, the preparations for permission for area recycling include a pollution assessment as well as planning for demolition/waste removal and recycling for the existing development on the site. In many cases, an environmental site assessment together with a relevant ground and groundwater rehabilitation plan are also required.

Environmental rehabilitation and the development of a site for construction prior to and during the construction of a new building (excavation of building pit) are often major cost factors for the entire project and hence present a tremendous potential for optimization. A step-by-step approach has proved a viable strategy especially for large and complex area recycling projects. The sequence of these steps is divided into several phases based on the pollution status and risk potential associated with the site.

Aera Recycling Strategy

Phase I: Pre-assessment/reconnaissance/evaluation of archival data
– Long-term utilization record
– Use-specific pollutant potentials
– Risk and problem areas

Phase II: Specific reconnaissance
– Investigation of problem areas
– Assessment of pollution potential and site condition
– Development of rehabilitation options/rehabilitation concept

Phase III: Rehabilitation planning
– Detailed site investigation as basis for rehabilitation planning
– Site model (complete analysis of site condition correlated to construction plan)
– Defining the rehabilitation goals
– Rehabilitation plan including time and cost planning

Phase IV: Rehabilitation execution
– Project management/coordination with construction project
– Supervision/monitoring, reporting
– Health and work

5.6 Area recycling of former freight station, Frankfurt

Depending on the severity of the existing environmental damage, the environmental agency in Germany may declare the entire site or portions thereof a contaminated site. Once this declaration has been issued, rehabilitation is compulsory; it can be implemented prior to or during the site development. Given careful planning, combining rehabilitation with the construction work is the more economical solution.
Detailed rehabilitation plans must be submitted for permission to the environmental agency in charge of contaminated site rehabilitations. If pollution levels in the soil/ground and groundwater are moderate to low, the submission of a procedural concept with regard to the removal or processing of polluted materials is sufficient for the building permit process.

Ground/Subsoil and Foundation Survey

In Germany, the client is obligated to provide the project planners and all executing firms and contractors with full access to all data on the site. To this end, most clients contract a geotechnical expert, to investigate, test and evaluate the ground at the building site to furnish the information for a comprehensive profile of the ground condition at the site. This survey must contain the following data:
– A clear, three-dimensional representation of subsoil strata.
– A classification of the existing ground/subsoil and rock types, and a description of material behavior (shear strength and deformation potential) taking the variations of natural composition into account.

- A detailed description of the groundwater conditions including long-term changes and hydrogeographic interactions (interaction between ground and groundwater).
- A description of possible chemical content in the ground/subsoil and in the groundwater, the type, concentration, distribution, dynamic and effects of this chemical content (pollution potential).

The data for this ground/subsoil survey are collected through subsoil investigation, geotechnical field and laboratory tests and environmental investigations. The comprehensive presentation of the site data in their spatial and interactive context (site model) is the result of Phase I (see Fig. 5.5) of the work carried out by the geotechnical consultant and forms the basis for the rehabilitation and building planning that follows.

Subsoil Investigation

Whereas the materials for all other disciplines of civil engineering (e.g. solid construction and steel construction), are available with standardized material properties and material selection is based on the dimensioning of the load-bearing members, the third discipline of civil engineering, geotechnics, must establish, investigate, test and model the material composition and the material behavior of the subsoil at each new site and for each project. This is one of the recurring core tasks of the geotechnical engineer. Extremely high standards and assurance of design compatibility with the project risks govern the methods and scope of data collection, especially for field and laboratory analyses for difficult geotechnical tasks such as high-rise foundations and deep excavation pits. Not only must the ground risks for the client be covered, but also a solid basis for planning and accurate computational predictions of the load-bearing and deformation behavior of the ground and the building must be created (see contribution by Grohmann/ Kloft, Chapter 6).

Field Investigation

For a high-rise project, reconnaissance of the ground must be facilitated through qualitative exploratory drilling (core drilling) of sufficient density to furnish a complete three-dimensional image of the stratified structure. The investigation depth is based on the assumed depth of the pile foundations. A sufficient number of boreholes must be drilled to collect data on their hydraulic conditions in the form of a groundwater record. Undisturbed soil samples are taken from the trial boreholes to investigate material properties in the laboratory. It is vital to ensure that samples are taken from all existing strata. It may also be useful to carry out geotechnical field test in the borehole (standard penetration tests, vane tests and pressiometer tests).

Laboratory Investigation

In addition to the standard geotechnical tests for soil classification, appropriate geotechnical experiments must be initiated to establish the deformation characteristics and shear strength of the soil materials. In order to achieve realistic results for soils that are prone to deformation, the stress courses of the soil samples in the ground must be simulated for differing load conditions in a triaxial test. The foremost goal of this test is to determine the material parameters for the numeric simulation of the deformation in the soils.

Local data on comparable ground/subsoil conditions are taken into consideration both in the field and laboratory investigations to evaluate the test results and determine the characteristic soil parameters. This task is made more difficult by the natural variety in type and distribution of the materials in the ground and the infinite range of material properties. A comprehensive model of the ground behavior (site model) must be designed for each building project based on the data collected during the investigation – and complemented by the practical experience of the geotechnical engineer and the statistical evaluation of the investigation results.

Site Model

The summary of the background data on the site, the investigation, and the data collected in field and laboratory tests into a single, comprehensive and three-dimensional image of the subsoil condition is called a site model. The site model provides a cogent overview of all important information and data on the site and creates the basis for assessing and calculating the interactions between these data and the following elements:

- Knowledge of previous use of the site (buildings, types of use, previous loads);
- Type and distribution of possible chemical burdens in ground or groundwater (pollution sources/veins/impact potential);
- Existing development and infrastructure in the surroundings;
- Three-dimensional ground model with surface relief and stratification structure;
- Hydrogeological site analysis (groundwater levels, current, sectional pressure level, chemical and physical properties, changes over time);
- Soil and rock mechanics of existing subsoil strata (genesis, composition, deformation behavior, shear strength and rheological behavior).

For complex building sites, the site model may need to be supported by a geographic information system (GIS) with several information levels. The site model must go beyond the boundaries of the building site and should encompass the reach of the possible deformations induced by the building measures. It is the basis for the geotechnical consultation and planning for the entire project, in particular for dimensioning, stability and deformation calculations.

Geotechnical Planning

The geotechnical and environmental tasks during the planning phase are defined as follows:

- Planning for making the site ready for building;
- Planning the excavation pit and water management;
- Planning the building foundations and securing the basement against pressure from groundwater.

The geotechnical planning sequence for the principal tasks mentioned above – excavation pit, water management and high-rise foundation – including the additional elements of geotechnical checking and monitoring is as follows:

A geotechnical plan for the excavation pit, water management and foundation is developed on the basis of the building geometry and the load impact of the projected high-rise.

The foundation plan also includes provisions for securing the structure against pressure from groundwater. The load-bearing structure of the retaining walls with anchoring or bracing and the building foundations must be designed with potential stresses in mind and analytical evidence provided for the structural stability of the all systems. This must include additional loads induced by ground deformation and tolerance of deformation (serviceability).

Geotechnical calculation models: Analysis of the load-bearing capacity and serviceability as well as of the interactions between ground and load-bearing structure is carried out with numerical calculation models. These models take the geometric sequence of loading and the material properties (shear strength, deformation characteristics) into account. The stability of the pit sheeting (retaining walls) and of the buildings neighboring onto the pit is generally established on the basis of ideal plastic material behavior (fracture theory/ earth or soil pressure theory). Simplified settlement calculations are executed on the basis of the elastic half-space theory. These simplified geotechnical models are not suitable for the complex themes that arise from the interactions between the ground and the load-bearing structure of a high-rise. Accurate modeling of the interaction between ground and building during the different phases of construction and the subsequent building use is only possible using three-dimensional elastoplastic modeling (finite element method). Numerical modeling of this kind is an extremely elaborate process and demands years of experience. The results of the numerical modeling of a high-rise foundation, i.e. the identification of deformation areas or coefficient of subsoil response (or bedding value distribution) are applied to the design of

the load-bearing structure. This is the most important interface between geotechnical and structural engineers for high-rise projects.

The structural testing engineer must also test the geotechnical assumptions and models, because the result of the deformation calculations has a defining influence on the stress placed on the load-bearing components (foundation slab and basement). For highrises, this task can only be carried out by a geotechnical engineer with the relevant expertise. This consultant service is generally awarded by the site supervisor, who stipulates that the foundation plan with the corresponding stability and serviceability documents for high-rises – deformation analysis, relevant geotechnical calculation model and material properties – are tested by an independent expert (test engineer) certified for earth and foundation works. Close collaboration with the structural test engineer is essential. The corrections/adjustments recommended by the test engineer must be implemented as compulsory design elements (Fig. 5.5).

Planning optimization: In addition to the geotechnical tasks described above, another essential duty of the geotechnical engineer involves the study of options to identify the optimized economical and technical execution during the design stage. The advantage of numerical modeling has been proved for this process. The intensive effort required to create the model in the first place is compensated by the many possibilities it offers for comparing different design options. Comparative calculation of the building costs for different options is used to establish the optimized economical and technical solution.

Subsoil Deformation in High-rise Construction

The impact of erecting a heavy structure such as a high-rise on the building ground, results in ongoing changes to the natural (initial) stress condition throughout the construction period. This, in turn, results in deformations, the scale, distribution and temporal course of which are dependent on the following factors:
- The properties of the building ground (deformation and shear behavior, rheological characteristics);

- The geometry of the building (areas, volumes);
- The scale and sequence of load impact on the subsoil.

The properties of the subsoil vary according to the natural variety of rocks and soils. The following dominant ground/soil classes can be differentiated; in nature, they generally occur in combinations in sequential vertical strata:

A – subsoil with young limnic or maritime (fine) sediments (peat, silt, clay) has low loadbearing capacity and is highly sensitive to deformation.

B – subsoil with geologically prestressed (fine) sediments (nonyielding plastic clays) and loosely packed sand and gravel has limited load-bearing capacity and is moderately sensitive to deformation.

C – subsoil with densely packed sand, gravel and residual soils (decomposed rock) has good load-bearing capacity and is therefore largely resistant to deformation.

D – stones and rock have high load-bearing capacity and are not susceptible to deformation.

Whereas class A is unsuitable for introducing of heavy loads, appropriate foundation systems and increased effort can make geologically prestressed clay (Frankfurt/London Clay) suitable for high-rise foundations and result in acceptable deformations. Ground classes C and D are suited for pad foundations. The subsoil deformations of high-rises tend to remain below 4 cm in these grounds. In geologically prestressed clays such as Frankfurt Clay, pad foundations have led to settlements of up to 30 cm and leaning of up to 1:300 depending on the building execution.

Experience has shown that the potential tilt as a result of natural eccentricities (lack of homogeneity) in the ground accounts for 10 to 15 percent of the total deformation. This means, that a differential settlement of 3–5 cm can occur as a result of natural geological anomalies alone for an overall settlement of roughly 30 cm. Given the additional eccentricity in the load impact, the tilt of a foundation pad can quickly surpass the tolerance threshold.

For modern high-rise systems, the goal is to limit the deformation of the foundation to the following ratios in order to minimize the risks and guarantee serviceability:
– Settlement max. 10–14 cm
– Tilt max 1:800 (as leaning)
  Tilt max. 1:500 (as bending)
– Differential settlement in joints max. 5 cm.

The critical construction stages with regard to deformation in a typical high-rise project are:
1. Building pit excavation: Destressing the subsoil causes the excavation pit floor or base to heave. In Frankfurt Clay, base heave of 10–15 cm may arise (depending on excavation depth) for long-term de-stressing or, respectively, 8–10 cm heave for re-application of stress as a result of construction soon after excavation.

2. Groundwater lowering or de-stressing: Stress on the subsoil caused by the absence of hydraulic pressure results in settlement in the area affected by lowering the GW level (5–10 cm have been measured in Frankfurt Clay). These settlements are partially compensated by heave when the groundwater level rises again.

3. Construction of the high-rise: Stress on subsoil as a result of construction loads causes settlement, bending and leaning (tilt). These effects are compounded by subsoil deformations in the course of preparing and constructing the excavation pit as a result of the various excavation measures such as injection and pre-stressing of the ground anchors (heave and tear near the prestressing sections) as well as horizontal and vertical sheeting deformation during pit excavation as a result of shifts in the earth or soil pressures (3–8 cm horizontal deformation of the pit sheeting wall in Frankfurt Clay).

These deformation patterns can occur locally or extend across large areas (settlement as a result of GW lowering) and may assume critical dimensions. Geotechnical monitoring is therefore essential for all high-rise projects.

5.3 Geotechnical Monitoring

According to Eurocode EC7, the second compulsory safety element in addition to geotechnical testing is ongoing geotechnical monitoring throughout the construction process (monitoring method). The deformation response of the building ground as a result of pit excavation, water control and new construction measures, as well as the changes in stresses and the flow of forces within the foundation elements must be measured, monitored, evaluated and documented during the construction phase and the subsequent building use, and must continue to be monitored until the ground reactions subside. This creates a real-time quality control record and evidentiary documentation and is also intended to facilitate early recognition of deviation from assumed values and critical conditions in order to initiate modifications/corrections [3].

Some of the requirements for the application of the monitoring method are:
– A forecast of the load-deformation response of the building and the definition of tolerances before construction begins;
– The development of staggered structural engineering countermeasures in case the building measurements reveal critical deviations from the forecast values;
– Geotechnical monitoring and prompt evaluation and interpretation of the measurement results during the construction.

In geotechnical monitoring of high-rise foundations we differentiate between measurements of the excavation pit, measurements of the high-rise and measurements outside of the construction field. Each of these measurements is geodesic and geotechnical. The measurements outside of the building field are also used for the architectural documentation.

Measuring Devices

The geotechnical measuring and monitoring of the load-bearing behavior of high-rise foundations involves the measuring and documentation of the following time variables according to construction sequence and the geotechnical and geometrical parameters:

– Heave of excavation pit floor as a result of excavation;
– Groundwater levels and hydraulic pressures in and near the excavation pit;
– Settlement response of foundation;
– Quantity and distribution of normal stress in/on excavation pit floor and the hydraulic pressures beneath the foundation slab;
– Load-bearing behavior of deep foundation elements, e.g. foundation piles (load-bearing at top of foundation pile/distribution of sheath friction along pile shaft/load-bearing at toe of foundation pile);
– Distribution of vertical displacements in subsoil.

Sensors, characterized by a high degree of rigidity to external influences to withstand the installation work at the building site, are used to record these variables. In view of the long monitoring periods of up to 5 years and more, the sensors must also possess a high resolution and long-term functionality.

Simultaneous to the numerical modeling of the load-bearing behavior of the high-rise foundations, a measuring program compatible with the project-specific requirements should be designed as early as the design and planning stage. This measuring program must be verifiable and contain detailed information on the following parameters:
– Type and scope of measuring program, i.e. number and placement of sensors;
– Requirements and specifications (measurement range, resolution, etc.) of sensors;
– Specifications of measurement sequence harmonized with construction sequence;
– Notation of control and boundary values; complementary measurements or structural countermeasures must be implemented if these values are exceeded.

The following measuring devices are employed for geotechnical measurements: In subsoil or at contact interface of subsoil/foundation slab:
– Extensometer
– Inclinometer
– Contact/base pressure sensor
– Pore-water pressure sensor
– Piezzometer

In foundation piles or at contact interface of pile/subsoil:
- Load cells at the top of the piles
- Load cells at the toe of the piles and strain ganges along the pile shafts.

5.4 Excavation Pit, Water Management and Protection of Adjacent Structures

Tasks

High-rises are nearly always erected in densely built innercity environments. The excavation pits are 10–20 m deep (corresponds to a 6-story building) and often cover a large area because of the extended base structures. They generally reach all the way to the adjacent buildings/urban infrastructure. The geotechnical tasks associated with planning an excavation pit for a high-rise structure consist in:
- Designing the dewatering strategy including water treatment (if chemically treated) and drainage for the specific construction project, local conditions at the site and approval requirements
- Designing a sheeting wall system (sheeting wall/anchorage/bracing)
- Planning the excavation of the pit in conjunction with construction sequence, selective excavation of polluted subsoil and disposal/processing (if required), excavation and transportation logistics
- Calculation of deformations resulting during excavation pit construction and groundwater lowering
- Economic and technical optimization of designs/plans through option comparison. A submission for approval is made for the solution that is most suited to the site; this submission includes the request for approval for groundwater management and for the (sub-)permit for the excavation pit.

Groundwater Management

The task is to keep the excavation pit dry until the new structure has achieved a completion status where sufficient buoyancy safety is assured when the groundwater (GW) returns to its natural level. The technical solution for this task differs enormously from site to site,

depending on the local geotechnical and geohydraulic conditions.

The feasible solutions for deep excavation pits in strongly water-bearing layers, e.g. sand and gravel with permeability coefficients of over 10^{-3} m/s, are outlined in Figures 5.7 a–e. It is often difficult to identify the best technical and economic solution for the conditions at a specific site in advance, in which a comparison of options is required.

Complete GW lowering (Fig. 5.7 a) with external well (1) and water permeable wall (2) is the proven standard solution. Its limitations are:
- Limited GW lowering i.e. extraction for water-resource or environmental reasons, exorbitant disposal costs for pumped-out water (e.g. in case of pollution)
- The risk of settlement damage on adjacent buildings.

Where GW lowering is not an option, the excavation pit must be designed to be waterproof. In addition to the waterproof design of the sheeting wall (3), the pit base must also be constructed to be impermeable to water. The proven solution is to construct excavation pits with underwater concrete floors (4) (Fig. 5.7 c), either with buoyancy anchorage or with deep injection floors (5) (Fig. 5.7 d). Both options are technically elaborate and cost-intensive solutions.

If the site allows for partial GW lowering or de-stressing, option 2 (Fig. 5.7 b) may be a preferable solution: the sheeting of the excavation pit is waterproof (3) and the groundwater pressure is released via de-stressing wells (6). The wells must be sized and arranged to prevent fracturing of the pit base from breaking as a result of de-stressing pressure.

The costs of the sheeting systems (sheeting wall/bracing) increase from options 1 through 4 (Figs. 5.7 a to 5.7 d). In comparing the options, the costs for discharge and, if necessary, treatment of the pumped-out water volumes as well as the potential settlement risks for neighboring structures as a result of GW lowering must be taken into account.

5.7 a–e Different methods of draining excavation pit

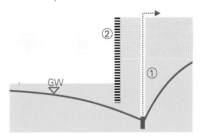

5.7 a Method 1: Complete lowering of GW

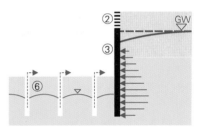

5.7 b Method 2: Waterproof pit wall; groundwater is released via expansion wells

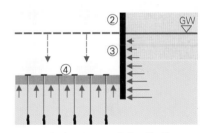

5.7 c Method 3: Waterproof pit wall with underwater concrete floors

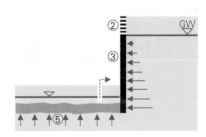

5.7 d Method 4: Waterproof pit wall with deep waterproof pit floor

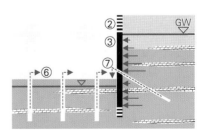

5.7 e Method 5: Partially watertight pit, drainage holes in walls and pit floor

5.8 a Westhafen Tower, Frankfurt,
architects: Schneider und Schumacher

5.8 b, c Westhafen Tower, Frankfurt, partially
dewatered excavation pit next to Main riverbank

In strongly an-isotropic subsoil, e.g. the layers present in Frankfurt Clay where dense clay layers alternate with strongly water-bearing limestone and sandy layers, the geohydraulic effect is determined by the anisotropy of the layers. Interventions into the groundwater result in considerable de-stressing via the water-bearing lime seams, although the water volume that has to be drained to achieve excavation pit dewatering is manageable. Hence, excavation pits in Frankfurt were traditionally designed with permeable sheeting walls (2) and complete GW lowering via external wells (Fig. 5.7 a).

From the 1990s onward, the environmental and water resource authorities in Frankfurt insisted that the intervention into the groundwater household should be minimized. This led to the design of waterproof sheeting wall solutions, e.g. for the Commerzbank and Eurotheum towers, and the undercover design for the Maintower excavation pit. Numerous examples of waterproof excavation pits are found in Berlin (e.g. Potsdamer Platz). When waterproof sheeting walls are used, the full hydraulic pressure must be factored into the calculation, resulting in a highly problematic load distribution onto the sheeting wall with excessive loads transferred onto the anchorage and anchor loads that are almost unmanageable, especially in the lower anchorage levels. An increase of the anchoring depth of the sheeting wall will only relieve the situation at a depth greater than 10 m because the hydraulic pressure continues to increase the lower the anchors are driven. In comparison with a permeable sheeting wall with GW lowering, the costs for waterproof excavation pits in Frankfurt subsoil are increased by a factor of 3 to 5.

This has led to compromise solutions, where the natural groundwater level is largely maintained but the water-bearing limestone strata are dewatered, see Figures 5.7 e (6) and (7). The spatial impact of the dewatering is limited, allowing for compliance with water management and ecological mandates and minimization of the settlement in the vicinity of the excavation pit. The excavation pit of the Westhafen Tower (Figs. 5.8 and 5.9) is a spectacular example for a partially dewatered excavation pit, ending 3 m from the River Main and extending 12 m below the Main's surface.

Sheeting Work and Securing the Integrity of Surrounding Development

Depending on the site conditions and the type of water management, various sheeting works options have been tested for deep inner-city excavation pits. Figure 5.10 gives plans for six common sheeting wall systems [9].

Permeable Sheeting Work:
– Bored soldier piles (steel) with plank or shotcrete infill (1)
– Bored concrete pile wall with shotcrete infill (2)

Watertight Sheeting Work:
– Over-cut bored pile wall (3)
– Reinforced two-phase slurry wall (4)
– Single-phase slurry wall with sheet piling (5)
– Combined bored pile slurry wall (6).

The first two sheeting wall systems can only be used in conjunction with complete groundwater lowering (dewatering). The groundwater penetrating from the water-bearing strata is collected in drain mats and drained off via dewatering pipes.

Over-cut pile walls and slurry wall systems are suitable for high structural stresses. The design must be adapted to the conditions at the site to ensure optimum load-bearing and acceptable deformations. Sheeting wall systems can also be employed to transfer building loads. For the Dresdner Bank tower, for example, sheeting piles were integrated into the foundation to transfer vertical loads. In the Westhafen Tower, sheeting wall piles were utilized as tension piles to absorb the upward pressure on the basements.

The soil and hydraulic pressure forces acting on the sheeting wall must be transferred to the subsoil with the help of appropriate supporting systems. This can be achieved by means of interior bracing the excavation pit wall on the opposite side or through additional anchorage. Beneath the excavation pit base, the passive earth pressure forces are transferred in the area of the sheeting wall base.
The rearrangement of tension in the ground as a result of pit excavation produces unavoidable deformations, which must in turn be

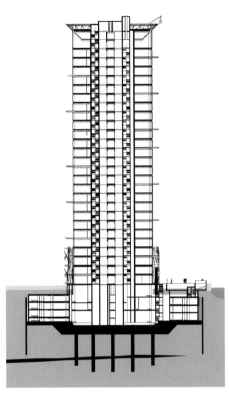

5.9 Westhafen Tower, pile and raft foundation

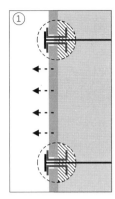

Drilled sheeting with
plank or shotcrete infill

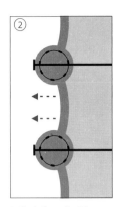

Drilled pile wall with
shotcrete infill

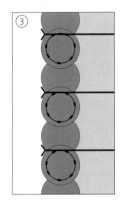

Overreamed drilled
pile wall

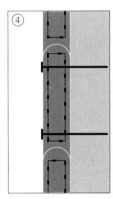

Reinforced two-phase
slurry wall

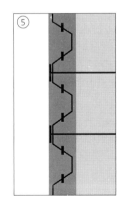

Single-phase slurry wall
with sheet piling

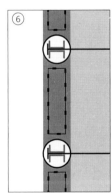

Combined drilled
pile-slurry wall

5.10 Plans of sheeting systems

controlled and absorbed by means of special construction measures and sheeting wall structures. This aspect is characterized by a correlation between the severity of the deformation and the passive earth pressure acting on the sheeting wall. If a certain degree of deformation is allowed behind the sheeting wall, the passive earth pressure can be minimized (active earth pressure). This may lead to displacements in the upper area of the (sheeting) wall, which may account for up to four percent of the excavation pit depth. In cases of very vulnerable neighboring structures, wall displacements on this scale are often not tolerable. The excavation pit sheeting work must therefore be designed to withstand increased earth pressure, resulting in heavy sheeting systems.

In the past, most deep excavations were braced in the deformation-prone Frankfurt subsoil after some spectacular occurrences of damage due to displacements of more than 15 cm in the upper sections of sheeting walls. This was linked to elaborate technical procedures for the bracing systems and interfered with the progress of construction within the excavation pit. The current technical standard is to anchor the sheeting wall from the rear. The following parameters can be adjusted to minimize deformation near the excavation pit: intensity and pre-tensioning of the anchors, anchor placement, anchor length, and, especially in rigid-plastic ground, the length of time during which excavation pit is exposed.

This time of exposure plays an important role because the time-dependent behavior of particular types of clay translates into delayed "relaxation" and hence deformation. It is therefore always advantageous to execute the construction from excavation of the pit to concreting of the foundation slab as quickly as possible for high-rises to minimize relaxation of the subsoil underneath the excavation pit. Optimizing the construction sequence of a deep excavation pit can thus contribute towards minimizing the unavoidable ground deformations.

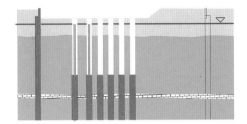

Phase 1: Preliminary excavation, making the drilled piles and installing the primary columns

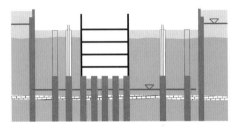

Phase 2: Depression of groundwater and excavation of the central initial pit

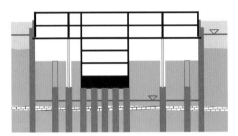

Phase 3: Progressive excavation and simultaneous construction of the first upper floors

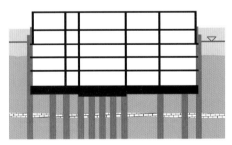

Phase 4: Basement and foundation pad completed

5.11 Constructing the excavation pit in under top cover

Construction under Cover

For excavation pits with a depth exceeding 20 m and no possibility for groundwater lowering/dewatering, construction under cover is often the best solution for managing the earth and hydraulic pressures in conjunction with acceptable deformations. The load transfer of the excavation pit sheeting wall is effected via the basement floors.

Figure 5.11 illustrates the sequence of excavation under cover for the Maintower in Frankfurt. Once a preliminary excavation depth is reached, construction progresses simultaneously upward and downward. Until the walls are built at a later stage, the floors rest on secondary steel columns set into previously bored piles with a diameter of 150 cm. In the case of the Maintower, the heavy load of the high-rise core had to be absorbed separately. To this end, construction progressed in the conventional manner from bottom to top in the core area of the foundation slab. One positive side effect of construction under cover is the shortening of the construction time. The construction above ground on the Maintower had already reached the 15th floor by the time the foundation slab was completed. The disadvantages of this approach lie in the complexity of the construction sequence and the high costs.

5.5   High-rise Foundations

Tasks

The foundation is the interface between the vertical load-bearing structure of the high-rise and the ground. The task is to transfer the high building loads as safely and with as little deformation as possible into the ground. The slenderness ratio H/W = height of foundation bearing area/smallest slab width is one criterion for the stability of a high-rise. Foundation systems must be designed to ensure sufficient external stability of the entire system and maintain the internal load-bearing capacity of the building components through appropriate dimensioning of said components. The serviceability of the building must be guaranteed without limitations for its entire lifecycle.

5.12 a–d Foundation options

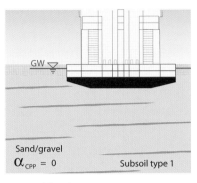

Sand/gravel

$\alpha_{CPP} = 0$ Subsoil type 1

5.12 a Pad foundation

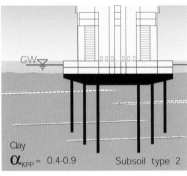

Clay

$\alpha_{KPP} = 0.4-0.9$ Subsoil type 2

5.12 b Pile and raft foundation (PRF)

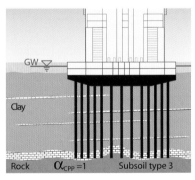

Clay

Rock $\alpha_{CPP} = 1$ Subsoil type 3

5.12 c Pile foundation

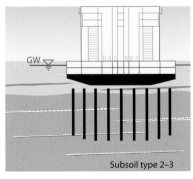

Subsoil type 2–3

5.12 d Uncoupled pile and raft foundation (UPR)

One of the principal tasks is the deformation calculation. The tolerances for tilting are extremely low for high-rises. To prevent unintended leaning of the tall buildings as a result of eccentric load transfer to the ground, the goal throughout the construction should be to center the load resultants in the center of gravity of the foundation slab. In practice, however, eccentric load transfers are virtually unavoidable as result of attached low-rise structures and underground garages. In the past, deformation adjustments for pad foundations of high-rises were therefore fairly common in order to prevent tilting.

Foundation Options

The following principal foundation options exist to transfer the heavy loads from high-rises into the ground:
- Pad foundations, where the loads are transferred to the ground via a foundation slab;
- Deep foundations, where high-rise loads are transferred to a deeper load-bearing horizon via foundation piles or slurry wall elements;
- Pile and raft foundations, where the high-rise load is transferred to a deeper level in the subsoil partly via the foundation raft and partly via piles or slurry wall elements beneath the pad.

These foundation options can also be combined to deal with special subsoil and construction or building design scenarios (e.g. uncoupled pile and raft foundations). In the design stage for a high-rise foundation, a preliminary selection of the suitable foundation option can be made on the basis of the diagrams in Fig. 5.12 a–d. The schematic drawings illustrate four typical foundation options for common subsoil types.

Pad Foundation

In subsoil with good load-bearing capacity, e.g. sandy and gravelly river sediments, pad foundation continues to be the most economic option for high-rises. Exceptions may arise when asymmetric load distribution and high point loads act on the foundation slab. In such cases, supporting the slab with deep foundation elements can help to achieve a

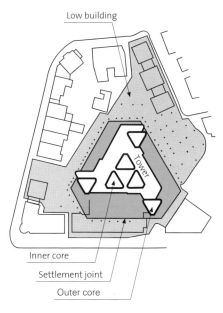

5.13 c Plan of high-rise and low building

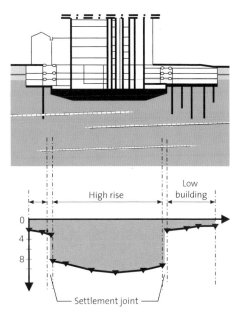

5.13 b Pad foundations and settlement

5.13 a–e Trianon tower, Frankfurt, architects: Albert Speer and Partner, HPP, Novotny Mähner Assoiziierte

5.13 d Steel reinforcement of foundation slab

5.13 e Excavation pit prior to concreting the foundation slab

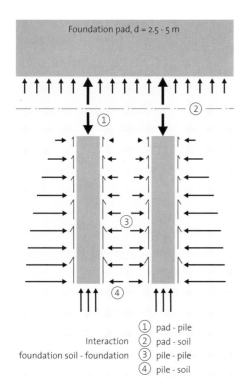

Foundation pad, d = 2.5 - 5 m

Interaction
foundation soil - foundation

① pad - pile
② pad - soil
③ pile - pile
④ pile - soil

5.14 Load-bearing behavior of the pile and raft foundation (PRF)

reduction of the slab thickness or the reinforcement as a result of reduced bending moment, which also translates into an economic advantage. In other words, even for subsoil with good load-bearing capacity, it is important to calculate whether the pile and raft foundation is more economic than a simple pad foundation.

Even in recent years, high-rises have been successfully realized with pad foundations in the deformation-prone Frankfurt Clay. The Trianon (Fig. 5.13 a) and Main Plaza towers can be cited as examples. For both structures, the settlement remained under 10 cm and the tilting less than 1:800. In the case of the Trianon tower [12], the surface pressure was limited by means of a foundation slab projecting far beyond the high-rise. Underground garages were separated by a perimeter settlement joint with coupling fields (Fig. 5.13 b–c). The excavation pit of the Trianon, prior to pouring the concrete for the pad, is shown in Fig. 5.13 e.

Pile and Raft Foundation

For type 2 subsoil structures (Fig. 5.12 b) with deformation-sensitive ground such as Frankfurt Clay, the advantage of the pile and raft foundation is especially pronounced. In this scenario, the arrangement and length of the foundation piles can be used to fully adjust the resultant of the reactionary forces of the subsoil to the load of the high-rise [7].

In practice, the total deformation can be controlled through the configuration of the foundation piles, expressed by the pile-raft factor (ratio of load-bearing capacity of the piles to the total load of the high-rise). The load-bearing behavior of pile and raft foundations is based on the three-dimensional interaction between foundation structure and soil. Figure 5.14 is a schematic diagram of the effects of this interaction between ground and building. The following effects occur:
– Transferring part of the building load to deeper subsoil layers with greater rigidity through the foundation piles via end-bearing piles and skin friction (4)
– Mutual interaction between the foundation piles (group effect) (3)
– Areal load transfer from the raft to the subsoil (2)

– Increase of axial stress on the pile jacket and hence skin friction as a result of surface pressure of the raft (1).

As a result of the group effect, produced by the stress overlap of the closely spaced pile, the numerical load-bearing capacity of the sum of individual piles is greater than the effective load-bearing capacity of the foundation pile group. The foundation piles on the perimeter and especially those at the corners of grouped piles a greater load than the piles at the center. This effect can be diminished through the design of the foundation by creating center foundation piles that are longer than those at the corner or perimeter in order to achieve an even distribution of pile loads (Fig. 5.4, pile and raft foundation, Messeturm Frankfurt). The joint action of raft and piles in the pile and raft foundation means that the stability is primarily ensured by the entire system and not by the load-bearing capacity of the individual pile. Whereas a twofold safety margin in relation to the maximum load-bearing capacity of the individual pile must be given for pile foundations according to the German DIN standard, the piles of a pile and raft foundation can be subjected to loads up to their maximum capacity. The efficiency of the pile and raft foundation by comparison to a simple pile foundation results from this exploitation of the load-bearing capacity of the piles in combination with the simultaneous load-bearing effect of the raft. If, for example, the foundation of the Messeturm had been constructed as a simple pile foundation instead of a pile and raft foundation, the number of piles for the same dimensions would have risen from the 52 executed to over 300.

The dimensioning of a pile and raft foundation is based on a simulation of the ground/building interaction. The deformation behavior of the ground has a considerable influence on the load transfer of the foundation elements and the stress on the building's structure. Due to the complex interactions and the generally asymmetrical and three-dimensional geometry, simple calculation models are accurate enough only for the preliminary design stage. A three-dimensional, numerical simulation of the entire construction process from excavating the pit to completing the building is required to verify the ultimate stability and to size the load-bearing elements of the building.

This can only be achieved with real-time simulation of the non-linear, elastoplastic and time-dependent deformation behavior of the dominant subsoil materials. The material parameters required for this simulation must be derived from laboratory and field investigation and verifiably documented.

Since the results of the model calculations (as bedding values and spring constants for piles and deformations) are included as factors for dimensioning the foundation slab, an independent test of the soil mechanics carried out by a geotechnical expert must be part of the overall structural test.

The concept of pile and raft foundations is a design strategy for high-rise foundations that delivers stability and serviceability (minimized deformation), as well as qualitative technical and economical optimization of the building's socle or base. The advantages and goals of the PRF can be summarized as follows:
– Decrease of subsoil relaxation during pit excavation through the effect of the piles as tension piles (negative skin friction) and hence avoidance of structural "softening" the upper soil layers combined with deformations;
– Limitation of settlement, bending and tilt of foundation raft to a scale that is tolerable for the serviceability of the buildings and technical systems (water tide basement/elevator systems/façades);
– Prevention of settlement gaps between the foundation elements of high-rises and perimeter buildings and thereby avoidance of high-maintenance and expensive settlement joints;
– Centering of resultant soil reaction forces in the axis of the resultant building loads for asymmetrical foundation bodies (avoidance of tilt and settlement joints);
– Centering of piles in load axes and hence avoidance of bending stress on the raft.

The option to safely transfer any eccentric building load with little risk of deformation to the subsoil by means of pile arrangement, staggered pile lengths and pile diameter opens up new possibilities for high-rise construction. Building fabrics, which are subjected to differing loads and asymmetrically arranged, can be realized on a monolithic foundation raft without settlement joint. One example is the Castor and Pollux high-rise complex (**Fig. 5.1 b**). Each project is characterized by individual parameters, which call for an optimized foundation design through option comparison and numerical model calculations [12]. The classic pad foundation should always be included in the option comparison because it does present the most economic solution under certain conditions. The pile and raft foundation offers clear advantages for:
– High slenderness ratios height/width > 4.0;
– Considerable load differential across short distances (high-rises with adjacent underground garages and edge developments);
– Major load eccentricities;
– High base pressures (high building loads on limited foundation area).
– Research and development on pile and raft foundations for unique site conditions and high-rise types are ongoing.

Pile Foundation

Pile foundations are necessary for subsoil with low load-bearing capacity or heterogeneous subsoil. The entire high-rise load is transferred to the load-bearing underground via piles or slurry wall elements. The foundation slab of the high-rise is not, or only marginally, involved in the load transfer. According to the German DIN standard, the piles must be designed to maintain a twofold safety margin in relation to the maximum load-bearing capacity. This requirement results in a far higher number and length of piles by comparison to the pile and raft foundation solution, with the result that the pile foundation is considerably more expensive than the PRF. Conversely, the settlement of simple pile foundations is far less than with the PRF.

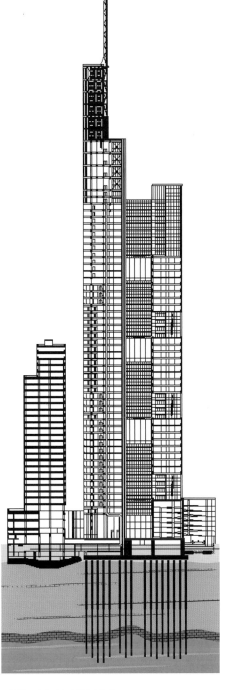

5.15 Commerzbank Frankfurt
architects: Foster and Partners, pile foundation

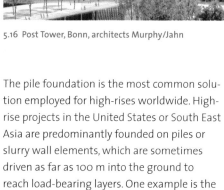

5.16 Post Tower, Bonn, architects Murphy/Jahn

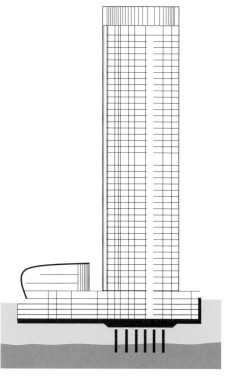

5.17 Post Tower, Bonn, uncoupled pile and raft foundation

The pile foundation is the most common solution employed for high-rises worldwide. High-rise projects in the United States or South East Asia are predominantly founded on piles or slurry wall elements, which are sometimes driven as far as 100 m into the ground to reach load-bearing layers. One example is the BoCom Tower in Shanghai.

The only pile foundation for a high-rise in Frankfurt subsoil thus far is the foundation constructed for the 300 m Commerzbank tower (Fig. 5.15). Because of the close proximity to the 103 m old Commerzbank high-rise, the need arose to find a solution that would minimize deformation. The roughly 1800 MN heavy high-rise was founded on 111 toe- and skin prestressed bored piles, with diameters ranging from 150 to 180 cm (telescopic) and a length of up to 45 m. [6]

Combined Solutions

For smaller high-rises on deformation-prone ground, the combination solution of an uncoupled pile and raft foundation can be an economic option (Fig. 5.12 d). In uncoupled pile and raft foundations, the deformation-prone area of the ground is reinforced by pile elements to the degree required for the raft foundation resting on top to fulfill the deformation criteria of the serviceability specification. One example for an uncoupled pile and raft foundation is the Post Tower in Bonn [13], currently under construction, where the pile heads are separated from the foundation raft of the high-rise by a synthetic slab (Fig. 5.17). The foundation raft absorbs the entire high-rise load until the synthetic slab is fully compressed and full pressure contact with the pile heads is established. This method mobilizes a partial load-bearing effect of the raft, despite integration of the piles in a load-bearing, deeper layer. This fully exploits the construction cost savings of a pile and raft foundation, even though the subsoil is unsuited to it.

Figure 5.16 contains a model photograph of the Post Tower.

5.6   Material and Thermal Use of Ground and Groundwater

In future, the use of the ground and groundwater and their thermal storage will gain in importance due to the increasing scarcity and cost of conventional resources, and in response to growing environmental awareness. The ecological and economic advantages of these technologies, which continue to be the subject of research and development, have yet to be fully exploited. In high-rise projects, the following approaches are of interest for heating and cooling applications:
– Geothermal use of ground as seasonal heat/cold storage in combination with energy piles and/or energy mats;
– Thermal use of groundwater;
– Material use of groundwater as service water.

Implementation of these technologies depends on the geological and hydrogeological site conditions (efficiency and permissibility). The following parameters must be investigated from a geotechnical perspective and integrated into the planning/permission process so as to develop and implement a solution that is ecologically and economically optimized:
– Hydrogeological ground properties (e.g. location and yield of groundwater streams, groundwater flow direction);
– Thermal ground properties (e.g. heat conduction and heat storage capacity);
– (Geo-)chemical and physical groundwater composition (e.g. temperature, anthropogenic and geogenic contents and their impact on the operability of the system).

Efficient solutions for the thermal and/or material use of the ground and the groundwater for heating/cooling high-rises must be developed jointly by HCV engineers (heating/cooling/ventilation) and geotechnical experts. The Maintower and Gallileo high-rise projects in Frankfurt (Figs. 5.1 b and c) are examples of thermal use of the ground and the groundwater. In both projects, the foundation piles are utilized as heat exchanger elements (energy piles) to provide intermediate storage for excess heat/cold energy and to release it when needed. German technology for thermal use of the ground is highly advanced. Dedicated continued development can further this progressive status.

5.7 Summary and Perspectives

The factors that limit high-rise construction are not set by geotechnical knowledge and foundation techniques. On the contrary, much remains to be done to fully exploit the possibilities. It is important, however, to ensure that research and development on modern foundation systems for high-rises are not focused primarily on pushing the safety envelope. The economic advantages can be utilized for improved adaptation of the load-bearing and foundation systems to the site conditions. For high-rise construction, in analogy to aviation, the principle of back-up safety through system redundancies should be applied. The failure of one subsystem must never endanger the entire system. Given this safety

principle, innovation and development trends for high-rise foundations are emerging in the following areas:
– Further development of special civil engineering technology (piles/slurry wall/ anchorage system);
– (Further) development of combination solutions for high-rise foundations (pile and raft foundation/uncoupled raft foundation);
– Integrated solutions through multiple use of load-bearing elements of the foundation and the excavation pit sheeting;
– Perfecting geotechnical calculation models.

The new possibilities, which have emerged through the introduction of the PRF for high-rises, can be expanded with dedicated development. The uncoupling of raft and deep foundation elements (piles/slurry walls), in particular, allows for better adaptation of the ground/building interaction to the building specifications. This represents a considerable economic optimization potential (uncoupled pile and raft foundation).

Further development of special civil engineering technology will lead to more rational and hence economic production processes of piles, slurry wall and anchorage systems. Post-construction prestressing of the deep foundation elements can also optimize the utilization of the load-bearing behavior of the ground (toe and skin prestressing of piles). Integrated solutions allow for multiple uses of building elements. Thus, the bored pile or slurry walls of the excavation pit sheeting can be employed to assist in the vertical load transfer or even assume the function of a watertight external skin for the basement levels. Solutions for drainage/dehumidification ventilation in combination with two-layer walls must be developed to fully implement these techniques.

The foundation elements pad, piles, slurry walls can also be employed as heat exchangers to utilize the ground as seasonal heat/cold storage. One example is Tower 24, currently under development in Frankfurt (Fig. 5.18), where the low-temperature geothermal energy will be used for the air-conditioning in the twin towers.

Finally, another optimization potential resides in the improvement to existing geotechnical calculation models. Standardization of three-dimensional procedures render simulation of the ground/building interaction more realistic and the calculations can be used for the investigating option for technical and economic optimization of the foundation and excavation pit designs.

The prerequisite for the design of high-rise projects that are as safe as they are economic, and for the successful use of geotechnical development potentials, is a comprehensive knowledge of the interactions between ground and load-bearing elements of the structure, experience in working with geotechnical calculation models and sound strategies for foundation design. Herein lie the challenge and the unique responsibility of the geotechnical engineer for high-rise construction.

5.18 High-rise project Kaiserkarree in Frankfurt, architects: Gruber and Kleine-Kraneburg

o6 Load-bearing Structures

Manfred Grohmann and Harald Kloft

6.1 Special Features of High-rise Structures

What are the special features of high-rise structures? How do they differ from the structures of other buildings? The first answer is rather trivial: the structures are higher. This leads to higher vertical loads and, more importantly, higher lateral loads (mainly due to wind stress) in comparison with lower buildings. Both these influences on design are so significant that special demands are placed on the structure of high-rise buildings, which is described below.

The behavior of a high-rise structural system under lateral loading is comparable to a cantilever fixed into the subsoil. Assuming a uniform lateral load, the fixed-end moment on the cantilever increases quadratically with the height. In reality the horizontal loads are not constant over the height (as can be seen in **Fig. 6.1**), but increase. Thus the moment towards the base increases more rapidly.

The absorption of horizontal loads and the ability to transmit the resulting moment into the foundation is a primary task in the structural design of tall buildings. Existing stairwell cores with their continuous vertical elements are highly suited for removing the loading. Another option is to treat the entire high-rise building as a clamped tube. These different systems for reinforcement will later be treated in depth.

With the coupling of forces, the moment can be effectively transferred. However, this causes tensile stresses in the vertical elements, which can only be tolerated in exceptional cases in reinforced concrete constructions. Therefore an attempt is made to distribute the dead loads (mainly the flooring) in such a way that the tensile stresses resulting from horizontal loads are continually compressed or overcompensated. Thus the system of horizontal load removal affects the distribution and transfer of the vertical loads.

In comparison to smaller buildings, the structure of a high-rise building functions more strongly as an integrated whole, and is a fundamental aspect of the design process. What applies to other buildings is even more important for high-rise buildings in view of their

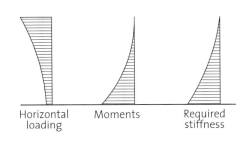

6.1 Behavior of high-rise structure under lateral loading

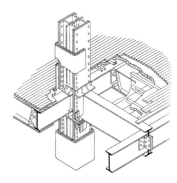

6.2 Connection detail, interior columns of the Fair Building, Chicago, 1892, arcitect.: William Le Baron Jenney

complexity: The design process must be carried out from the very beginning by an integrated team of architects, structural engineers, services engineers, fire safety experts and many other specialist designers.

The height at which lateral loads become dominant for multistory buildings is independent of the definition of a high-rise as set down by the building code. A regulation that buildings are high-rise when the height of the top floor exceeds 22 m reflects the size of fire-service ladders rather than structural considerations. The question at what height in regard to statics one can refer to high-rise buildings cannot be answered. Even for buildings under 22 m the removal of lateral loads can be decisive in the design. Such is the case when the existing core and shear walls are unable to secure lateral stability. The design principles given here could then prove useful.

6.2 Historical Background of the Structure of High-rise Buildings

The evolution of high-rises is closely linked to the urban development of Chicago. Following the devastating fire of 1871, during which a large part of the city was destroyed, new buildings in the reconstruction effort became increasingly higher [1]. This was largely due to a series of technical innovations in building services and elevators, and was motivated by the prestige of tall buildings as an expression of economic growth.

Striving for ever greater height placed new demands on structural engineers. New load-bearing forms had to be developed for these "elevator buildings". The structural system to remove lateral loads in first-generation high-rises consisted of steel frames. Here, steel columns and girders were joined together to form rigid frames. Additional bracing with steel trusses, or infilling with non load-bearing masonry helped in the absorption of wind loads. However, primary rigidity was provided exclusively by a grid of closely spaced steel columns (6–9 m apart) bound together with beams to form a frame.

In 1885 the first high-rise to use this so-called steel skeleton was the Home Insurance Building in Chicago (architect: William Le Baron Jenney), with a height of 55 m. This building became known through a number of innovations, including the use of the first rolled I-beams, a high degree of fire safety with fire walls of masonry, and a safe and rapid occupant transportation system. It was pulled down in 1931. **Figure 6.2** shows a typical connection in the steel skeleton joining a floor beam to an interior column.

In parallel to the development of new structures, more conventional massive building techniques with load-bearing masonry were still popular. In 1891 this traditional approach was used in Chicago's Monadnock Building (Burnham & Root); it is a masonry building with 16 storiesand a perforated façade (**Fig. 6.3a**).

6.3 a Monadnock Building, Chicago

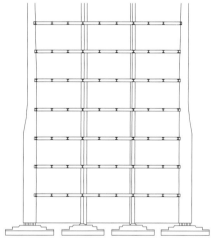

6.3 b Section through base of the Monadnock Building

The load-bearing exterior walls increase to a thickness of almost 2 m at the ground floor (Fig. 6.3 b). The lack of window space gives the façade an air of imperviousness, quite at odds with its use by small retailers. The capabilities of this building technology had reached its limits, and this construction style was not continued thereafter.

Further technical developments seemed to remove all limits to ever taller buildings, and the race to construct the tallest building was underway. The highpoint of the first generation of high-rises was New York's Woolworth Building (Cass Gilbert), finished in 1913.

With its steel skeleton frame, hidden behind a Gothic façade, this building reached a height of 235 m (55 stories). As a highly mechanized building ("The Cathedral of Commerce"), fitted with high-speed elevators, full air-conditioning, electric lighting and telephone systems, the Woolworth Building remained the world's tallest building for 16 years.

After the First World War the resulting economic depression brought an interruption to these developments. However, in the 1920s the construction of high-rise buildings was resumed, culminating at the beginning of the 1930s with New York's Chrysler Building (313 m) and the Empire State Building. The latter, at a height of 383 m, was the tallest building in the world for over 40 years. Then a world economic crisis and the Second World War intervened to prevent any further high-rise construction.

In the 1950s the architecture of Mies van der Rohe invigorated high-rise construction and influenced a whole generation of architects. Buildings such as van der Rohe's residential high-rise on Lake Shore Drive in Chicago, or the Lever House in New York by SOM, are regarded as archetypes of this era. The reduction to essentials as symbolized by the slogan "form follows function" led to a renunciation of elements designed to historicize and conceal the construction, and opened the way for new structural forms.

Engineers such as Fazlur Khan (SOM, Chicago), William Le Messurier (Boston) and Leslie E. Robertson (New York) developed new structures by attempting to increase the efficiency of high-rises and simultaneously designing new load-bearing systems required by the new architecture. To this end so-called tubes were developed; lateral loads could be resisted by rigid tubes located on the exterior. The interior space could thereby remain free of shear walls and reinforcement elements, and was open to diverse usage. Buildings such as the World Trade Center (New York), the John Hancock Center and the Sears Tower (both Chicago) were constructed of steel in this fashion, with the outer tube structures also determining the building's appearance. The tube system was in constant development in the USA and a whole series of combined systems were created: tubes coupled to the rigid core by means of outriggers, tube-in-tube structures, bundled tubes, etc. These will be examined in detail later. Steel, reinforced concrete and composite steel elements were used as building materials.

In 1958 Hubert Beck in Germany published his ground-breaking work on the numerical calculation of regularly spaced walls, which enabled an exact analysis of reinforced-concrete shear walls. Thus the core walls of already existent elevator shafts and stairwells could be used as stiffening shear walls. This method – later developed to tube-in-tube constructions by coupling the core walls with the perforated façade – led to the realization of many high-rise buildings in reinforced concrete, particularly in Germany.

The most recent developments in East Asia, such as the Jin Mao Building in Shanghai or the Petronas Towers in Kuala Lumpur, show that the combination of different building technologies – such as reinforced concrete with composite steel components and elements made from high-strength concrete – produces innovative, hybrid structures, with very high degrees of efficiency.

6.3   Demands on High-rise Structures

General

In addition to stability (ultimate strength), particular attention must be paid to the functionality of the construction when considering high-rise structures. The higher the building the greater the influence of usability will be on the choice of systems, materials and the measurement of cross sections. One important aspect in the functionality of reinforced concrete construction is the differential shortening of vertical load-bearing elements (walls and columns) due to elastic deformation, creep and shrinkage. The maximum size of deflection must be limited in the horizontal direction, as must the lateral acceleration from wind and earthquake loads (see article by Wörner/Nordhues, Chapter 8).

Vertical Loads

The theory of vertical loading for high-rise buildings is identical to that of lower buildings. Dead loads arise from the weight of the individual construction elements and the finishing loads. Live loads are dependent on use. Table 6.4 gives a comparison of live loads from office space using the German DIN 1055, EC 1 and American standards. For normal office use in high-rise buildings live loads should be taken to vary between 2.0 and 5.0 kN/m². Flooring in premium office space is now usually constructed to withstand live loading of 5.0 kN/m², taking into account variable partitioning and higher live loads in the corridor areas. Depending on the number of stories, live loads can be reduced for load transfer and the dimensioning of vertical load-bearing elements. However, the reduction of the total live load on a construction element may not exceed 40 percent.

Horizontal Loads

Owing to the large influence of horizontal stiffening on structure design, the calculation of lateral loads should be carefully scrutinized. The lateral loads generally arise from unexpected deflections, wind and earthquake loads.

Unexpected Deflections

Unexpected deflections arise from imprecision in the manufacture of construction elements and larger components. In addition to this manufacturing problem the uneven settling of the foundation at an inhomogeneous site can also lead to a deflection (see article by Arslan/Ripper, Chapter 5). Any deflection produces additional lateral forces which must be incorporated into the design.

Wind Loads

In general, high-rise buildings are susceptible to oscillation. This means that wind loads should not be viewed as statically equivalent loads, but must be investigated under the aspect of sway behavior. Wind tunnel experiments are usually carried out to determine the influence of the building's shape on the wind load.

The difference between global and local wind loads is more pronounced in high-rises than in lower buildings. Whilst the global loading from wind is an important factor in the design of the main structure, the local distribution of wind pressure over the building exterior affects façade construction design. Here the building's shape and geometry is particularly decisive in determining areas of high drag at the corners. The ability of wind loads to bring a building to sway must also be kept in mind. This oscillation leads both to a perceptible lateral acceleration for occupants, and to a maximum lateral deflection.

The usual value of the eigenfrequency at which a lateral acceleration can be perceived in high-rise buildings (about 0.1 to 0.2 oscillations per second) lies at around 0.5 percent of acceleration due to gravity. At values between 2 and 4 percent of acceleration due to gravity the oscillations are felt as disturbing, and become unbearable at higher values. With a statistical return period of 10 years, it is recommended that lateral acceleration not

exceed 0.2 percent of acceleration due to gravity. In the USA this value is commonly fixed in combination with the building's use. For residential use it should be < 0.15 percent, for hotels < 0.2 percent and for offices < 0.25 percent of acceleration due to gravity, in each case under the assumption of a 10 year return (see article by Wörner/Nordhues, Chapter 8).

In Germany there are no upper limits for the maximum deflection and wind loading of a high-rise building. In the USA a maximum value of h/400 or h/500 is assumed for a 50-year wind. Measurements have shown that for these limits a deflection only about half as big as expected is seen at the top of a building; this is because additional finishing elements bring supplementary stiffening, which helps to reduce lateral deflection.

Earthquake Loads

In areas susceptible to earthquake activity, powerful earthquakes can cause extreme lateral accelerations. However, the probability of a powerful earthquake occurring over the lifetime of a building is relatively small. Therefore it is economically justifiable to design high-rise structures so that they can withstand a major earthquake shock by exhausting all structural strength and load transfer capabilities alone. The main priority is the safety of people, whilst damage to non-bearing finishing elements is allowed and determined relative to the risk. These considerations mean that high-rise structures in earthquake zones should be designed to possess high plastic strength reserves. In concrete terms this means that frame corners should bend without breaking. Structural damage following the Northridge earthquake of 1994 in California has led to the development of detailed construction concepts [2].

Table 6.4 Traffic loads in offices

	USA -1972 ANSI A58.1 [kN/m²]	DIN 1055 [kN/m²]	EC 1 [kN/m²]
Office space	2.40	2.00	3.00
Lobbies	4.80	5.00	5.00

6.4 The Basic Materials Steel and Concrete and their Combinations

General

Steel and concrete are fundamental materials in the construction of high-rise buildings. Allowing for their specific characteristics, they can be combined in a variety of ways to form new construction materials. Floor construction in high-rise buildings is barely conceivable without concrete. Whether it is used as pure reinforced concrete, in a composite steel floor or as a prestressed floor construction depends on different factors. Purely steel vertical components and elements to provide rigidity are of course possible, but reinforced concrete and steel composites are today's common construction materials. The most recent developments in high-rise construction show that previous theories of construction concerning "pure" steel or steel reinforced concrete constructions are outdated. In particular, the rapid on-going development of high-strength concrete in the last few years has made an important contribution. Developments in pump technology, which now enable concrete to be pumped to the top of a high-rise, have also helped to give this material a status equal to steel in the construction of tall buildings. For each project economic considerations are often decisive with regard to the choice of materials and construction methods. It should be noted that in an age of globalization the influence of regional or local construction methods on building costs is continually decreasing. Table 6.5 lists different criteria regarding the choice of construction materials.

Steel Reinforced Concrete

Normal-strength Concrete

Columns and walls in high-rise buildings are subject to compression over their entire height, the compressive stress being generally greater in the columns than in the wall slabs. The design of the structure must take into account the different elastic shortening of the construction elements caused by this compression, as secondary stresses are placed on floors and beams. In addition to these elastic compressive strains, parts made from reinforced concrete undergo shortening by creep and shrinkage, which also increase the secondary strain significantly. In pure reinforced concrete structures, the stressed construction elements absorb a large part of the stress by creep. However in mixed constructions the stresses cannot be removed and must be carefully taken into consideration during planning [3]. In addition to the requirement that the floor should remain horizontal, various axial deformations in vertical structural elements should not result in damage to the finishings. To this end it is necessary to incorporate the different compressions early enough in the design of finishing and façade elements (see article by Gunnarsson, Chapter 10).

High-strength Concrete

Fascinating developments can be observed in high-strength concrete in the past few years. For decades B 55 concrete was regarded as the maximum grade possible for use in Germany, until in 1990 a high-strength concrete of grade B 85 was used for the first time in the construction of the Trianon tower (team of architects: BfG, Novotn, Mähner Assoziierte/ HPP International/Albert Speer und Partner) in Frankfurt. In the meantime experience has been gained in construction with concrete of grade B 115 [5] and it can be expected that this rapid development will continue. The most recent research has shown that high-strength concrete can also be produced to comply with the fire-resistance categories F120 and F180. This is a primary precondition for a wide-ranging implementation of this technology in high-rise construction. The later section "Columns and Walls" gives values to describe the load-bearing characteristics.

Lightweight Concrete

Lightweight concrete specifies concrete with a pure density of 800 to 2000 kg/m². The potential for the use of lightweight concrete in high-rise construction lies in reducing the dead load of the structure while maintaining high material strength. The reduction of density by 25 to 50 percent in comparison to normal concrete is achieved by using lighter aggregates or by aerating the concrete (cellular or foamed concrete). In order to maintain the strength of normal concrete, the precise choice and production of the concrete, aggregate takes on a decisive role. Lightweight concrete is subdivided according to DIN 1045-2/ DIN EN 206-1 in the strength classes LC8/9 to LC80/88, and is regarded from class LC 55/60 upwards as high-strength lightweight concrete. Because of the lower weight of the aggregate there is greater danger of segregation during the pouring and compaction of lightweight concrete than with normal concrete. Previously these difficulties in handling and the more arduous pumping hindered the use of lightweight concrete in tall buildings; but today technology has overcome these problems and opened the way for lightweight concrete to be adopted increasingly in high-rise construction.

Table 6.5 Comparison of various building materials [4]

Criteria	Reinforced concrete, Normal-strenght concrete	Reinforced concrete, High-strenght concrete	Steel construction	Composite construction method
Construction costs	+	++	o	++
Weight of construction	o	+	++	+
Stiffness	++	++	o	+
Flexibility of plan	o	o	++	+
Behavior in fire	++	++	−	+
Construction time	+	+	++	++
Usable area	−	+	++	+

6.6 a and 6.6 b Commerzbank Frankfurt, steel girders in composite floor without and with fire-protective covering

Steel

Steel has the longest tradition in the construction of high-rises. As outlined above, most of the first generation high-rise buildings in America were erected using a pure steel construction. This of course has produced a deep and wide-ranging fund of experience, which gives steel construction an economic head-start, especially in the USA. The main advantage of the material is its high strength, meaning that steel constructions are able to transfer large loads using only minimal cross sections. Moreover, technologies such as welded, screwed or previously used riveted joints enable large forces to be transferred economically [6].

Steel constructions can be prefabricated in factories and, dependent on their size or weight for transportation, can then be delivered pre-assembled on site and incorporated into the construction there. This procedure shortens building time and saves on costs.

The main drawback to steel is its poor fire-resistant qualities. At temperatures as low as 300 °C the strength of steel decreases rapidly. Therefore steel constructions in high-rise buildings must always be protected against fire. This can be achieved with a concrete covering, either as a pure fire-protective covering, or in the form of a composite steel construction to effectively protect the building's statics. Alternatively, the steel construction can be cladded with fire-resistive plates. These outer protective coverings however are very labor intensive and expensive, canceling the cost advantages gained from the short construction period. **Figures 6.6 a and b** show a floor construction of steel girders without and with fire-protection covering. Steel constructions are highly suitable for areas subject to

earthquakes, as steel allows the structure to absorb part of the kinetic energy produced by the earthquake in the form of plastic deformations. In California detailed construction plans are available for steel buildings to ensure they can achieve the necessary security against the effects of earthquakes [2]. Technically a similar ductility can be achieved with steel-reinforced concrete, but the costs increase disproportionately to those of steel buildings.

Composite Steel Constructions

In composite steel constructions steel sections are combined with reinforced concrete to create statically sound structures. The aim is to optimally combine the advantages of both building materials. Using the technology of steel construction joints, these composite steel structures can be assembled at exceptional speed. The reinforced concrete aids the transfer of loads by means of its compressive strength and gives the necessary fire protection to the steel sections [7]. Depending on the type of section there are various combinations of steel and concrete common in composite steel construction.

Concrete-infilled Steel Sections

Standard hollow steel sections or box girders made from steel sheets welded together are filled with concrete, the latter receiving an additional reinforcement. A shear-resistant connection between the outer steel cross

section and the inner concrete cross section is produced using welded studs or other suitable means. In the case of fire (for which the construction can be designed with reduced safety factors), even if the outer hollow steel section fails the inner reinforced concrete cross section will still be capable of carrying the reduced loads.

Steel Sections Partially Encased in Concrete

Open steel sections are infilled with concrete. In this procedure reinforcing cages are placed between the flanges of the section and these areas subsequently filled with concrete. Welded stirrup reinforcement or head bolt studs are used to produce the bondage between reinforced concrete cross section and steel section.

As with infilled sections, the concrete beam alone is able to carry loading – under reduced safety demands – if the steel section flanges fail during a fire.

Steel Sections Fully Encased in Concrete

Composite steel cross sections can also be constructed by encasing steel sections fully in concrete. Here the exterior reinforced concrete functions as a fire-protection covering for the steel section inside the concrete cross section, and also aids the removal of loads by its compressive strength. The type of steel composite to be used depends in the end on a number of different factors. Along with geometric, economic and architectonic requirements, the level of loading and the type of connecting beams play a large role in the selection of the composite element.

Combined Systems

In recent years a combination of systems has become increasingly common. Materials such as reinforced concrete, high-strength concrete, steel, and steel composites are used optimally in structures according to their specific characteristics and with regard to economic aspects. Floors are often constructed as composite steel floors or reinforced concrete floors on trapezoidal metal decks (as permanent formwork). To reduce the dead loads of the floors, the free span is often shortened using steel beams. Vertical supports are concreted in high-strength concrete (columns) or in reinforced concrete (walls). Composite steel constructions are often used for highly stressed shear walls as an alternative to high-strength concrete. Outrigger constructions (coupled structures) to provide necessary reinforcement are usually constructed in steel with a fire-protective covering for reasons of assembly and to avoid cutting into the floor plan. A continuous development of new connections and joints can be observed. Today, for example, composite beams cast into the floor can be connected rigidly to composite steel columns in the façade using steel contact joints. Or new economical specialist bolts and nails are used to transfer vertical loads to steel tube sections [8].

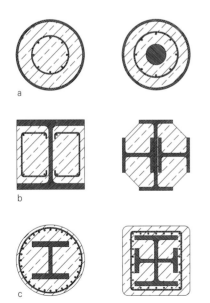

a Concrete infilled steel sections
b Steel sections partially encased in concrete
c Steel sections fully encased in concrete

6.7 Columns as various steel composites [15]

6.5   Systems of Reinforcement

General

Figure 6.8 compares the costs of the individual structural elements for high-rise buildings over different heights: it is clear that the proportion of costs for floor construction hardly changes with increasing height. In contrast, the proportion for vertical load-bearing columns and walls increases linearly with increasing height. Costs for additional measures to ensure lateral stiffness increase even more rapidly.

This shows that with increasing building height the choice of an efficient bracing system takes on increasing importance for the profitability of a high-rise.

In the relevant literature diagrams are given [9,10,11] to show the number of stories that can be achieved with each system. However, the building depth is often left out of consideration. Bracing systems can be sensibly conceptualized by utilizing the maximum building depth as a lever to form a restraining effect by means of coupling forces. Thus in two buildings with the same bracing system, the one with greater depth can be higher.

The slenderness of most high-rises – meaning the ratio of height to width [12,13] – generally has a value up to eight. Higher values usually lead to intolerable lateral accelerations at the top of the building, entailing the employment of active or passive damping elements to allow normal usage.

In Europe, regulations governing office depth mean that for the bracing system the maximum usable building depth is limited to around 30–40 m. With a slenderness ratio of eight the maximum possible height is then 240–320 m. In the USA and Asia larger building depths of 50–60 m allow greater heights to be realized. For example the Petronas Towers in Kuala Lumpur achieves a slenderness ratio of 8.6 (calculated for 88 stories) with a diameter of 46.2 m [14]. This high degree of slenderness is made possible by extremely efficient bracing systems of outriggers. These utilize megacolumns located at the periphery and which have a natural damping effect, allowing a tolerable sway.

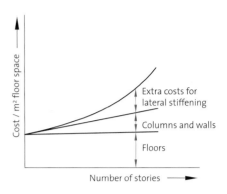

6.8 Breakdown of costs for vertical and horizontal load removal [9]

Fundamental Principles of Reinforcement

Figure 6.9 shows the basic principles in the arrangement of stiffening elements in the plan. At least three elements are necessary in every horizontal plane to reinforce a floor plan. The lines of action of these stiffening elements should not intersect at a point. This arrangement will prevent the deflection of the plan along the x and y axes and will also prevent rotation.

In high-rise construction, existing wall slabs in the access core are usually adopted for stiffening. To enhance lateral stiffening and minimize torsion stresses, it is sensible to locate the core in the middle of the ground plan. **Figure 6.10** shows the increasing effects of non-central cores on lateral loading .

An attempt is made below to give an overview of bracing systems available at the present time and their special characteristics. From simple planar systems to space frame hybrid systems, the principle actions and their boundary conditions are explained.

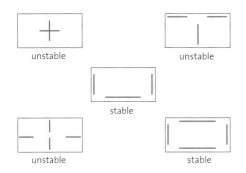

6. 9 Unstable and stable arrangements of structural stiffening elements [9]

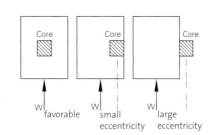

6.10 Influence of core positioning on horizontal loading [9]

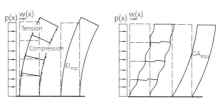

(El$_{equ}$ – Equivalent bending rigidity, GA$_{equ}$ – equivalent shear rigidity) p(x) – function of lateral loading, w(x) – horizontal drift

6.11 Bending and shear drift of walls and frames with equivalent systems (El$_{equ}$ – Equivalent bending rigidity, GA$_{equ}$ – equivalent shear rigidity) [15]

Rigid Frames

When the first high-rises were erected at the end of the 19th century the development of reinforced concrete was in its infancy. The floors of the first tall buildings were constructed with closely spaced steel beams. As described above, the floor supports are rigidly connected to steel columns to form steel frames, and the bracing system thus created is known as a steel skeleton frame. The introduction of diagonal bracing to increase lateral resistance is simple, if the necessary floor plan flexibility is taken into account. In addition, the rigid connections reduced the bending of the floor beams by their clamping effect. Normal, bending and shear forces are produced with the absorption of lateral loads by the frame, and these lead to various deformations. In **Figure 6.11** a breakdown of the lateral deformation into the components bending (flexion) and shear can be clearly observed in the equivalent systems.

The proportion of lateral deformation from "bending drift" comes from the normal force deformation of the frame uprights. A tensile force can be detected in the upright in the side facing the load, with a compressive force on the other side. These normal forces produce a lengthening or shortening in the frame leg, with a resulting deformation of the horizontal member. As the absorption of vertical tensile forces is complex and costly, an attempt is usually made to ensure in the floor plan design that in the frame leg subject to

tensile force from stiffening loads a larger compensating force from dead loading is present. The size of the lateral deformation is directly connected to the axial rigidity of the frame leg. This portion of the total lateral deformation is called in construction jargon the "plate component". The proportion of "shear deformation" of the total lateral deformation is determined by examining the frame deformation while ignoring the normal force deformation. Here, the frame corners remain at the same height. The lateral deformation from shear arises from bending deformations in the frame legs and horizontal members and therefore differs qualitively from the plate component. The deformation of both parts should always be superimposed, and the relationship will change depending on the respective stiffness of the legs and horizontal members. Particular attention in the frame structure should be paid to the moment resistance of the frame corners. Where bending moment is greatest, the moments must be transferred from the horizontal members to the legs. In areas subject to earthquake activity, it is necessary to ensure that during dynamic earthquake loading the rigid connection is not the weakest point and liable to failure, but that the energy can be transferred smoothly by plastic deformation of the horizontal member.

Economic considerations dictate that a high-rise building stiffened only by frames is practical up to a maximum height of 25 stories. Narrow frame systems on a small scale – for example as "tube frames" (on the façade) or frame systems in connection with shear walls and/or outriggers – can still be economical at greater heights.

Braced Frames

With increasing height the bending stresses in the frame legs become so great that pure frame systems are not longer economical. Additional stiffening braces are added to the frame to reduce the cross section of the steel. The braces absorb the lateral loads in these stiffened frames and the frames legs are no longer subject to bending. This statical and constructive advantage must be considered in light of the restrictions in use arising from the diagonal bracing. **Figure 6.12** shows possible arrangements of stiffening braces that allow openings to be integrated.

During the design stage an attempt should be made to arrange the diagonal bracing in the frame in such a way that the connections are always centrally stressed. This means that the lines of action of the individual bars should intersect at a point. For complex beam-to-column joint geometries this is not always possible, and these eccentricities cause secondary stresses, which must be factored into calculations. A further design consideration is the shortening of frame columns under the high vertical loading. This shortening necessarily causes shortening in the diagonal braces, and must be carefully allowed for in the design. Compression diagonal braces are already stressed by axial forces from the permanent loading; however, when tension braces are joined simply by friction connections, they are loosened by the vertical shortening of the columns caused by the permanent load, and can only assume their planned tensile force from the lateral loading when highly deformed. These effects must be incorporated inzo the design of connections, and one recommendation is to perform the joint only after all dead loads have been erected and established.

In view of structural considerations diagonal bracing can be differentiated as follows (see Fig. 6.13):
– Simple diagonal bracing,
– X-bracing (double diagonal bracing),
– K-bracing.

Simple Diagonal Bracing (Alternative a)

Frame stiffening with simple diagonals produces compressive and tensile forces in the diagonal, depending on the direction of the lateral loads. Diagonals should be designed as buckling struts to absorb the compressive forces and must be integrated in the finishing plans.

X-bracing (Alternative b)

This double diagonal bracing is only effective as stiffening when both diagonals are formed as tension members. Under the effect of the lateral loading one of the diagonals of the X-bracing absorbs the tensile force while the other diagonal relaxes under the loading and does not contribute to load removal. As the elastic deformations of the tension diagonals are relatively great the total deformation is correspondingly great in this stiffening option. X-bracing with two tension diagonals consumes the least steel of all three alternatives. During planning it is important to ensure that the tension diagonals still retain strength during elastic shortening of the columns. Thus the tension diagonals are pre-stressed so that even under the maximum lateral loading in both diagonals some tensile force remains. The total stiffness of the system is thereby increased, although extra compressive force is placed on the columns and horizontal members.

X-bracing with tension diagonals is not recommended for conditions of dynamic loading caused by an earthquake, when lateral forces change direction frequently. As a result diagonals which are initially not subject to loading are suddenly stressed at the first change of direction. This places huge stresses on the tension diagonals and individual braces may indeed fail.

K-bracing (Alternative c)

K-bracing is not just used to help absorb horizontal loads but can also contribute to a reduction of span, leading to decreased bending stress in the frame girders. A distinction is made between K-braces that provide support to the girder using either compressive or tensile forces. When the floor beams are hung between the K-braces (Fig. 6.13, right) the diagonals are subject to a kind of pre-stress by the permanent load, and this reduces the compressive forces from wind loading. The elastic shortening of the columns must also be factored into the design. However, because of the relative flexibility of the floor beams, the diagonals in K-bracing do not assume vertical loads to the same extent that columns shorten under the effect of the vertical loading. Another advantage of compressed K-braces in comparison to simple diagonals is their smaller buckling length.

K-braces are particularly suitable in setting up energy-dissipation systems. The building can enjoy considerable reserves of plasticity by introducing specially designed sliding members between the connections of diagonals in the K-bracing. These reserves can be used to compensate for large earthquake loads by means of plastic deformations. Oscillation dampers can also be integrated into the K-bracing junctions to have a positive influence on the dynamic behavior of the building [15,17].

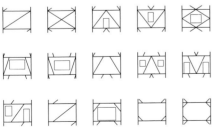
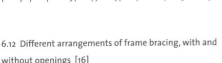

6.12 Different arrangements of frame bracing, with and without openings [16]

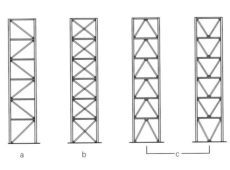

6.13 Different forms of diagonal bracing [15]

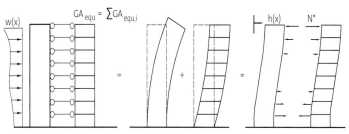

W(x) – wind load function, GA$_{equ}$ – equivalent shear rigidity, $\sum$GA$_{equ,i}$ – sum of equivalent shear rigidity of walls and frames [9]

6.15 Interaction of shear walls and frames, coupled by non-rigid connections

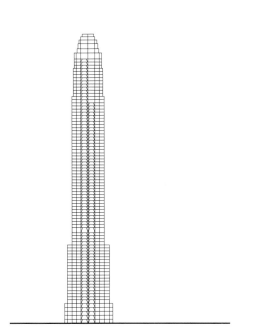

6.14 Braced frame of the Empire State Building [14]

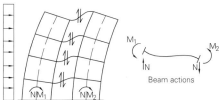

6.16 Rigid beam coupling of two shear walls and stresses in the beams
M$_1$,M$_2$ – reverse bending moments, N – normal forces in columns

Systems using braced frames provided the most effective load-bearing structure for high-rises until the 1950s. The Empire State Building, the classic representative of this style of construction, reached a height of 381 m by using frame braces to provide rigidity, and remained the highest building in the world from 1931 to 1972. **Figure 6.14** shows schematically the reinforcement braces on the frame of the Empire State Building. The riveted steel sections were covered with clinker concrete for reasons of fire safety. However, the subsequent increase in rigidity of this envelope was left out of structural calculations. Later measurements showed a rigidity higher than expected by a factor of about 4.8 [14].

Shear Walls, Coupled Walls and Cores

The elevator shafts, stairwells and respective anterooms necessary for access in a high-rise must be protected by fire walls, as demanded by fire safety regulations. Reinforced concrete

walls are normally used. It makes sense to exploit them in improving the building's rigidity. Reinforced-concrete shear walls, with their high resistance to shear stress, are highly suitable for assuming the shear forces that arise through lateral loads. As with frame systems, attention must be paid that loading from permanent loads is sufficient to prevent tensile stress (particularly at wall ends). To accommodate the increased number of reinforcement bars at the ends of the shear walls, it is often sensible to strengthen the walls in these areas. One way of ensuring this extra strength is to make use of the transverse walls at the wall edges.

Because of functionally necessary openings in the core (elevator and stair doorways, shaft outlets, etc.) the individual walls are not connected to one another directly, but are often coupled by means of girders. These coupled shear walls form highly complicated structural systems. It was only with the research by Fazlur Kahn in the USA and Hubert Beck in Germany at the beginning of the 1960s that it became possible to compute the dynamic structural behavior of these divided walls with

relative ease [9]. These new computation procedures enabled the combination of frames, shear walls and coupled shear walls in the simultaneous removal of lateral loading. **Figure 6.15** shows schematically the interaction of coupled walls and frames. The various behaviors in deformation as illustrated makes clear that the frames drift behind the more rigid shear walls towards the ground. This constraint helps to stiffen the frame, which in turn reduces the horizontal deformation of the shear walls in the upper part of the building.

Coupling with non-rigid elements as shown in **Figure 6.15** merely has the effect that the horizontal deformation in wall and frame is the same on every story. However, if frame and wall or wall and wall are connected to one another with rigid coupling elements (girders or thick floor slabs), a restoring moment is formed in the coupling support and the deformation is reduced further. **Figure 6.16** shows schematically the influence of rigid coupling elements.

As can be clearly seen, the load-bearing behavior of these coupled systems is highly dependent on the degree of rigidity of the coupling agents. Under the theoretical assumption of infinite rigidity the two walls act as one. However, in reality the true values are always lower.

The window openings in many high-rises in Frankfurt – forming so-called perforated façades – cause the reinforced concrete exterior walls to function like shear walls in the removal of interior loads. In removing the outer loads the exterior walls can be said to form a rigid tube, often working in conjunction with the inner core (tube-in-tube) to assume lateral loads. The necessary horizontal coupling of the separate walls to provide

static stability dictates that the maximum window opening is limited, and this restricts the transparency of the façade.

Advances in glass technology and the continued development of transparent glass façades have led to a decline in recent years in the classic perforated façade. Often a reduction of the number of façade elements interfering with transparency is a primary aim. Only columns for vertical load removal are allowed on the façade. This means that all the lateral loads must be assumed in the building interior, i.e. by the core.

An example of this development is the Maintower in Frankfurt, shown in **Figure 6.17**. Horizontal stiffening of the Maintower is effected

by the inner cores, coupled to the outer columns using slender girders. Using this system, together with outriggers on the fifth story, a height of just over 200 m was achieved. The mode of action of coupling by means of outriggers will be handled in detail later.

Figure 6.18 shows that perforated façades are still attractive and can be included in highly innovative concepts in building technology. Here we have a design for the new Zürich Versicherung high-rise in Frankfurt, to be completed by 2005 with a height of 168 m.

Tube Structures

The Maintower is at the upper limit for an efficient stiffening system not integrated into the façade (for high-rises of normal depth). For greater heights it is necessary to remove not only the vertical load but also some of the horizontal load in the façade area. By ensuring rigidity against shear forces of façade corner points over the entire width and depth of the building, the façade is formed into a rigid body, a "tube structure". The whole width of the building becomes structurally more stable. The rigid connection can be achieved using frame structures, jointed walls or even diagonals. In addition to the stiffening elements in the façade, high-rises with tube structures also have an inner core zone, necessary for access, which can be used to contribute to horizontal rigidity. Building height and the coupling of the two systems are determinative here. In statics the term "tube-in-tube" is used. This describes a load-bearing system where the outer tube is coupled to the inner tube using the floor slabs.

The high performance of these tube structures was displayed in impressive fashion as early as the 1970s with the World Trade Center (110 stories, architects: Yamasaki and Roth & Sons) in New York and the John Hancock Center (100 stories, architects: SOM) and Sears Tower (110 stories, architects: SOM), both in Chicago.

These "dissolved tubes" have one significant difference in their load-bearing behavior in comparison with ordinary tubes. This

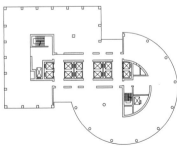

6.17 a, b View and ground plan of the Maintower, Frankfurt, architects: Schweger + Partner, structure: Burggraf, Weichinger + Partner, and Förster + Sennewald

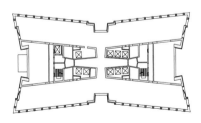

6.18 a, b View and ground plan, a design for the new Zürich Versicherung high-rise, Frankfurt, architects: Christoph Mäckler, structure: Bollinger + Grohmann

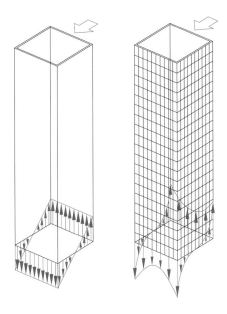
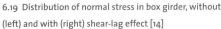
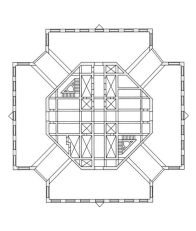
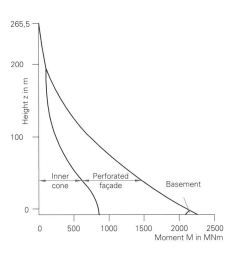

6.19 Distribution of normal stress in box girder, without (left) and with (right) shear-lag effect [14]

6.20 a Messeturm Frankfurt, ground plan

6.20 b Moment distribution in interior core and perforated façade of the Messeturm [12]

difference is made clear in Figure 6.19, left. First, a box girder is considered. This is subject to a lateral load, which, following technical bending theory, causes a linear stress pattern in the two web planes parallel to the direction of the force. For reasons of continuity the normal stresses arising in the corner points will remain constant over the flange planes, lying perpendicular to the direction of the force. This contribution to the removal of loading through the flange plates is secured by the resistance to shearing of the closed box girder.

In an open tube structure consisting of columns and beams, the elastic continuity in the flange planes is only provided by the rigidity of the beams to shear stresses. However, this rigidity is clearly lower than that of a continuous tube. The columns in the middle areas of both web planes can therefore evade the normal force deformation. This effect is called "shear lag" and leads to higher stress in corner columns. Likewise the columns in the middle of the flange planes are not subject to stress, so that in contrast to the closed tube, the distribution of normal stresses is not constant over the width of the flange.

Similarly to the previously described systems for reinforcement, the columns in tube structures are shortened or lengthened by normal forces as a result of the bending component of the horizontal deformation.
The shear force from the horizontal loading of the tube is removed by the bending of columns and beams in the web planes. Additional stresses arise in these web planes, and further deformations of the entire tube are seen. This second component of the horizontal deformation is called the shear deformation. The relative non-rigidity of the frames mean that for tube structures, the proportions of overall deformation resulting from bending and shear forces are almost identical.
The concentration of normal forces at the corner columns in the lower area of a high-rise is greater in comparison to those forces arising from the dead load. Additional bending stresses in these corner columns from the shear effects in the web plane considerably hinders a practical design. For these reasons the stresses should be reduced by activating additional stiffening elements such as shear walls or cores. The high rigidity of these other elements will relieve the large bending stresses in the lower area of the frame tube caused by shear forces.

Exterior Concrete Tubes

All the high-rises constructed in Frankfurt between 1950 and 1970 are reinforced by shear walls, sometimes joined to form cores. As previously mentioned, these stiffening cores function like a bar fixed into the subsoil. The maximum height of these buildings is thereby limited by the maximum permissible and practical dimensioning of the core.

In the new Deutsche Bank in Frankfurt (architects: ABB, Frankfurt; structure: BGS, Frankfurt), exterior walls were used for the first time to provide stiffening. The outer walls were designed as a perforated façade – in other words a reinforced concrete wall with window openings. A frame system is built on sound structural principles using the window pillars and sill supports. This system does not provide the same degree of stiffness as an inner core. However, the larger lever arm, which is at the disposal of the exterior walls, compensates for this. This creates an efficient system, with an inner tube core formed by the elevator and service shafts and an outer rigid frame tube (tube-in-tube).
The Messeturm (Trade Fair Tower) in Frankfurt (architects: Murphy/Jahn, Chicago; structure: Dr.-Ing. Fritz Nötzold, Langen) uses this form

6.21 John Hancock Center, Chicago, architect: SOM/Fazlur Khan

6.22 a and b View and bracing system of the Citicorp Center, New York, architects: The Stubbins Associates and Emery Roth & Sons

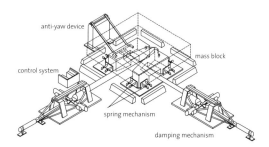

6.22 c Oscillation damper in Citicorp Center

of stiffening and is constructed as a tube-in-tube. **Figures 6.20 a and b** show the load-bearing elements in ground plan as well as the distribution of the stiffening loads between the inner core and exterior perforated façade, the latter functioning as a tube construction. One can see that more than 50 percent of the bending moment from the horizontal loading is removed by the perforated façade.

Steel Rigid Frame Tubes

The use of reinforced concrete in perforated façades to provide stiffening is particularly popular in Germany. In the USA and other countries, by contrast, rigid frame tubes are designed almost exclusively in steel. The same constraints in façade transparency apply here as with exterior tubes constructed from reinforced concrete. The greatest height using this system was achieved in the two towers of the World Trade Center (architect: Minoru Yamasaki; structure: Skilling Helle Christiansen Robertson). Exterior tubes wide approx. 65 m provided most of the necessary rigidity for the towers. The tubes were designed as steel frames with column spacing of approx. 1 m. This approach provided high efficiency, while at the same time demanding an above-average consumption of steel. The fact that the two towers of the World Trade Center did not immediately collapse after the airplane impacts on 11 September can be attributed to the removal of the horizontal loads by the exterior tubes. Although up to 50 percent of the façade columns were destroyed on the impact sides, the upper frames were able to function as vierendeel trusses and remove the vertical loads by redistribution. Moreover, the tube construction was designed for maximum wind load, and the remaining façade columns therefore still had sufficient reserve to remove the higher loads. This gave thousands of people time to leave the burning towers.

Braced Frame Tubes

A rigid frame tube which is additionally stiffened with diagonals is termed a trussed tube.

These trussed tubes assume horizontal loads in the same way as a truss fixed into the subsoil. Analogously to rigid frame tubes, the bending action of horizontal loads is discharged as normal force in the columns. However, the shear stresses are no longer absorbed by girders and columns as secondary bending, but are removed as tensile or compressive forces in the diagonals. This redistribution of shear stresses leads to a considerable saving in building material. The frames in the web planes are no longer subject to additional bending moments and can therefore have a more filigree design. To increase the efficiency of lateral load removal, the diagonals are connected to columns and beams at their points of intersection. The vertical supports are thereby also employed in the removal of horizontal loads and loading is more evenly distributed. Probably the best known example of a tube frame braced with diagonals is the John Hancock Center in Chicago (architects and structure: SOM/Fazlur Khan, Chicago), shown here in **Figure 6.21**. This high-rise with rectangular ground plan has 100 stories. Its tapering walls give the building a particularly elegant appearance. The diagonals are set at an angle of 45° and are clearly visible in the form of mega-X-crosses on the façade. This diagonal bracing assumes the shear force of wind loads and thus stiffens the tube. In addition, the diagonals carry part of the vertical loads, helping to minimize the shear-lag effect and ensuring that the tube construction is homogenously loaded.

Another example for a tube reinforced with diagonals is provided by the Citicorp Center in New York (architects: The Stubbins Associates and Emery Roth & Sons; structure: William James Le Messurier), shown in **Figure 6.22**. In contrast to the John Hancock Center, the diagonals are hidden behind the façade. Another particular feature of the Citicorp Center is seen at the base, where four megasupports carry the entire façade. The reason for this unusual and costly approach was to incorporate a church into the ground plan. As the church could not be demolished it was built over. Shear forces could no longer be absorbed by the building's exterior in the area of the megasupports, and instead shear was discharged by the central inner core.

The body of the building is subdivided into six units, each stiffened with a V-shape brace in tube-like fashion. These units comprise eight stories. As well as assuming horizontal loads the braces remove parts of the vertical load, section by section, and transfer these to the megasupports in the middle of the façade. Because of its susceptibility to oscillation, the Citicorp Center was the first high-rise to be equipped with a resonance damper. A 400-ton concrete block lying in an oil bath was placed on the 59th story, held in both horizontal directions by springs and shock absorbers (Fig. 6.22 c). This oscillation damper reduces the maximum horizontal deflection by 50 percent.

Bundled Tube Structures

Another way of improving the effectiveness of façade-level tube structures is to introduce additional shear-resistant "webs" inside the building. These additional stiffeners ensure that the "flange planes" contribute more to the removal of bending stresses, and in the "web planes" additional frames are available for the removal of shear forces. This compensates for the effect of shear lag (cf. Fig. 6.19).

With these additional "webs" the main tube can be subdivided into smaller tubes, or cells. These can be dropped off at different heights, breaking up the overall form of the building elegantly. Combined systems are also possible, with frame tubes associated with partial diagonals. **Figure 6.23** shows the first and best-known building to use this principle, the Sears Tower in Chicago (architects: SOM/Bruce Graham and Fazlur Khan, Chicago). In the isometric view, additional shear resistant webs can be recognized in the building's interior.

At 109 stories and a total height of 443 m this high-rise was the world's tallest building for many years. At its base the Sears Tower has a width of 3 x approx. 22.9 m = 68.7 m. Two of the cells end at the 50th story, two more at the 66th story and three at the 90th story.

The columns are spaced at 4.6 m, and the floor span in the cells is about 23 m. The direction of span in the individual cells alternates every six stories in order to ensure an even loading of the columns.

6.23 a Sears Tower, Chicago, architects: SOM/Bruce Graham and Fazlur Khan

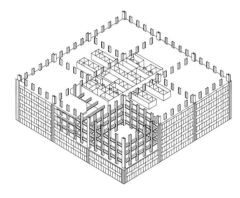

6.23 b Isometric view, structure of Sears Tower, Chicago

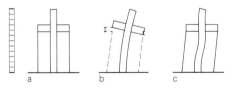

6.24 Action of outrigger structures
a – core-outrigger system without loading
b – deformation without influence of outrigger
c – deformation with reverse rotation caused by outrigger

6.25 Outrigger on the 5th story (machine floor) of the Maintower, Frankfurt

Core-outrigger Structures

When individual cores are too slender to assume the horizontal loads they can be coupled to one another, or to façade columns, using additional boom girders (outriggers). However, in contrast to coupled shear walls, the coupling occurs only on individual stories and is not continuous over the height of the building. This leads to a liberal treatment in the design of the floor plan. Usually the cantilevers are incorporated into machine floors, so that restraints on floor usage do not arise. Figure 6.24 shows the mode of action of outrigger structures. The high rigidity of the load-bearing elements (usually of floor-to-floor height) and their coupling with the façade columns mean that the outriggers are able to return the deformed core to vertical and thereby reduce the horizontal deformation of the building. Sobek/Sundermann [11] compare the effectiveness of different coupling elements. Here the performance of "rigid" beams fixed at end to the core (outriggers) and resting on non-expanding supports can be easily seen (Fig. 6.24, examples b, c).

Outrigger structures are highly stressed load-bearing systems, usually constructed in reinforced concrete to be able to withstand concentrated forces. Figure 6.25 shows the outrigger construction of the Maintower in Frankfurt (architects: Schweger & Partner). Outriggers can also be used to connect two independent cores rigidly, thereby increasing the total stiffness quite considerably. Example of this approach are the currently unfinished Deutsche Post building in Bonn (architects: Murphy/Jahn, Chicago, structure: WSI, Stuttgart) or the BoCom Financial Tower in Shanghai (architects: ABB, Frankfurt; structure: König und Heunisch, Frankfurt).

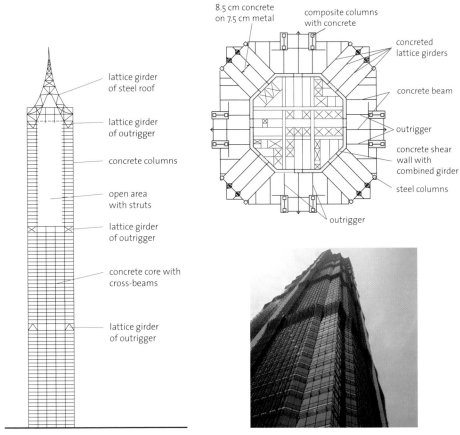

6.27 a–c View, section and ground plan Jin Mao Building, Shanghai, architects: SOM

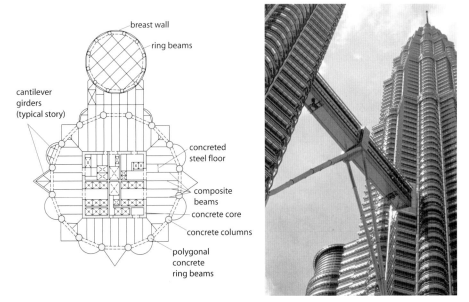

6.26 Ground plan Petronas Towers, interior core and megacolumns, Kuala Lumpur, architects: Cesar Pelli Ass.

The world's current titleholder as tallest building, the Petronas Towers in Kuala Lumpur
(architects: Cesar Pelli Ass.; structure: Thornton-Tomasetti Engineers), also uses outriggers
to connect the rigid inner core with megacolumns hidden behind the façade (Fig. 6.26).
High-strength concrete was used for the inner
core and the megacolumns, while the four
outriggers (each two stories high) are
designed in steel. This intelligent combination
harnesses the best qualities of these two
materials: High-strength concrete in the core
to resist the large surface pressures, and steel
sections in the outriggers to deal with the
highly concentrated forces and provide the
necessary force transfer. This mixed system
also exploits the favorable technical qualities
of concrete in resisting oscillation, such as the
large mass and large inner damping. The
towers of width 46.2 m were thus able to
achieve a height (to antennae tip) of 452 m,
without any additional measures to reduce
oscillation.

The Jin Mao Building in Shanghai (architects
and structure: SOM, Chicago) is also a mixed
construction using both sectional steel and
concrete for the load-bearing structure. A
36-story hotel was placed with an additional
restaurant and observation deck on top of a
50-story office building. The structure for vertical and horizontal loading consists of an
interior reinforced concrete core which –
similar to the Petronas Towers – is coupled
using outriggers to megacolumns hidden
behind the façade (Fig. 6.27). Sectional steel
was used for the outrigger and megacolumns,
the latter covered with concrete and functioning as composite steel cross sections. The
columns also carry part of the dead weight
loads from the floors down the sides of the
building. There are two additional steel
columns in each corner, designed specifically
to remove floor loads.

Each taking up two complete stories, the
outriggers were placed between stories
24 and 26, 51 and 53, and 85 and 87. They are
subject to appreciable secondary stresses,
arising from the various deflections of the
reinforced concrete core and the composite
steel columns. One measure employed to
reduce these stresses to a manageable size
were slot connections in the outriggers during

the construction phase. The individual components were only permanently connected after
completion of the structure.
A further example for the use of outriggers
can be seen in the design for a 400 m high-
rise in Frankfurt, known as the Millennium
Tower (architects: Albert Speer & Partner;
structure: Bollinger + Grohmann). This building is shaped like a lens in its ground plan, and
is stiffened transversely by connecting the
inner core rigidly with half frames (Fig. 6.28).
Additional reinforcement is provided by outriggers, located in the machine floors, which
attach the core to megacolumns hidden
behind the façade.

6.6 Load-bearing Systems for Floors

General

A large part of structural costs – besides
measures necessary to provide horizontal
rigidity – is consumed in the construction of
flooring. This of course means that the selection of a suitable floor system affects the total
costs of the building. As already mentioned,
a floor plan with closed office space – still the
primary design in Germany – restricts workstations to a distance of 7 m from the windows. The maximum floor span in Germany
for high-rises is therefore no more than 7 m,
including corridor width. In America, by comparison, workstations are commonly placed
up to 20 m from windows and consequently
floor spans are much larger. This explains the
differing uptake of the following floor systems
in Europe and the USA.

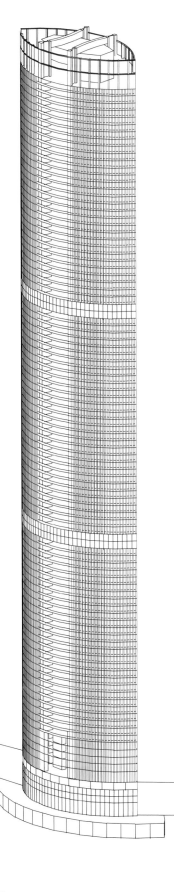
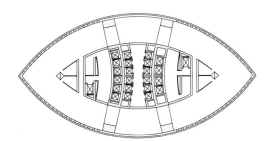

6.28 a and b Ground plan and isometric view Millennium Tower, Frankfurt,
architects: AS & P, structure: Bollinger + Grohmann

6.29 Thermoactive flat-slab flooring in reinforced concrete, Deutsche Post AG, Bonn, architects: Murphy/Jahn, Chicago

6.30 Floor in sitecast concrete with girders

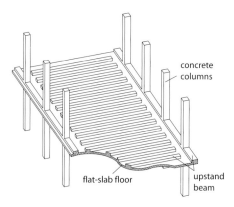

concrete columns

flat-slab floor

upstand beam

6.31 Floor with suspender beams

6.32 Composite floor with steel girders

Flat-slab Floors in Reinforced Concrete

Slab floors in reinforced concrete are economical up to a clear span of max. 8.5–9.5 m. Depending on possible edge stresses in the core or the façade columns, a thickness of 28–32 cm is necessary. The considerable weight of concrete in these flat slabs significantly increases the total weight in comparison with a lighter girder construction, and also affects the vertical load-bearing elements and the foundation. However, the advantages of this type of floor construction can be seen in the smooth girder-free underside. With the freedom provided by the lack of girders, optimization of the arrangement of necessary installations (ventilation, sprinkler system, lighting, etc.) is possible.

The girder-free flat-slab floor also presents the possibility of dispensing with the usual suspended ceiling. In this case installations are fixed directly onto the slab underside. By doing without the suspended ceiling, the mass of the concrete floor can be used to stabilize the building's heat flow. This effect can be strengthened by introducing additional active elements, such as water-filled heating or cooling pipes in the ceiling. Examples can be found in the new Dresdner Bank – Gallileo – in Frankfurt, which incorporates 30 cm thick thermoactive reinforced concrete slabs, and the Deutsche Post AG in Bonn (Fig. 6.29). A precondition for the efficient manufacture of slab floors in sitecast concrete is the efficient formwork system available today. This accommodates the necessary construction cycles in high-rise projects (see article by Motzko, Chapter 4).

Floors with Reinforced Concrete Joists

The employment of joists can considerably reduce the necessary thickness of reinforced concrete floor slabs. This of course decreases total weight and vertical loading. The drawbacks of this system lie in the extra measures necessary for introducing the beams, such as formwork and additional reinforcement cages, as well as the time required for mounting and concrete casting. Modern formwork techniques can be adopted to ensure that construction cycles necessary for high-rises can be maintained, e.g. prefabricated large panel

formwork containing the necessary floor and beam formwork can be introduced floor by floor. Often the beams are laid transversely to the ceiling installations, and the beams cannot penetrate due to their insufficient height. To be able to fit ventilation, sprinklers and other equipment, the ceilings are generally suspended lower in corridor areas, and installations are then mounted underneath the beams. However, in office areas, the services equipment is installed between the beams and the suspended ceiling placed flush with the beams. Figure 6.30 shows the joist floor of the Maintower, with a running ring beam as edge element in the façade area.

Floors with Reinforced Concrete Suspender beams

Suspender beams in reinforced concrete (Fig. 6.31) can be used to combine the advantages of the smooth underside of slab flooring with the substantial weight savings of joists. All installations are laid between the beams on the upper side of the floor. In order to permit lengthwise routing, the suspender beams do not run fully to the end bearers at the core or columns, and the transverse force is transferred to vertical elements by the slab cross section at these points. The false bottom required by this floor construction is laid flush with the beams.

Composite Floors

A variation on the reinforced concrete constructions described above is the composite steel construction. This involves special steel profiled decks which are used as permanent formwork and supported on steel beams (Fig. 6.32). The steel beams are fitted with shear studs or a shear strap so that the floor concrete can be activated as a compression zone for the steel support structure

The steel floor decks have a dovetail profile in cross section and the ribs turn to wedges when stressed by bending forces in the concrete. This means that the decks can be utilized as tensile reinforcement for the floor. For structural and fire safety reasons and to ensure good transverse distribution an additional flat reinforcement is necessary.

The welded shear studs on the beams complete the composite action of concrete and steel to produce an optimal effect (Fig. 6.33). In America trapezoid deck sections with a layer of concrete topping are often used as flooring. For reasons of fire safety and sound-proofing this option is not common in Germany.

The main advantage of composite floors is that the steel decks can be laid by hand and immediately function as working platforms. As no forming and stripping of the concrete floors is necessary, a quicker pace of construction can be achieved. Figure 6.33 shows that composite steel decks can be connected to both steel and reinforced concrete beams. The introduction of trapezoid decks on finished areas in not always possible for technical and logistical reasons. For example, in the Messeturm in Frankfurt, it was decided not to rest the floor decking on the inner core walls; this was to allow the wall formwork in the core to flow without interruption. However, calculations showed that the end reactions could be fully transferred to the core walls through the stirrup reinforcement [7].

Despite the quicker construction pace possible using composite floors, there is still the drawback of higher costs in comparison to other floor formwork systems. In particular, these fixed-shape decks are not practical, or can only be employed with great effort, for ground plans with high curvature or difficult geometries (Fig. 6.34). Therefore, composite floors are generally unsuitable for round plans.

Space Frames for Floor Systems

In some cases it is possible to incorporate the ground plan of a building in support of the floor system. An example of this is the design for the Westhafen Tower in Frankfurt. This building with circular plan (architects: Schneider + Schumacher; structure/preliminary design: Bollinger + Grohmann) was also given a round inner core in the initial planning phase. The dimensioning of the core enabled it to carry all horizontal loads.

In order to maintain flexibility in rental options, the building was designed to accommodate residential, hotel and office use.

A circular plan was used by the structural designers to develop a slab floor haunched towards the inner core. The flooring was supported in the interior by the core and on the exterior it was placed on the peripheral columns (Fig. 6.35). The empty space arising from the haunching could be used for equipment installation. The remaining space was large enough to allow installations such as wastewater pipes in addition to the electrical installations.

Prestressed Concrete Slabs

As already mentioned, slab flooring with spans of more than 9 m are not economically efficient in high-rise construction. In order to achieve larger spans without resorting to beams (and thereby losing a smooth underside), floor slabs can be prestressed. By means of prestressing, plate slenderness of l/40 is possible. So, for example, spans of 12 m can be realized with slab thickness of 30 cm.

As is usual in high-rise construction, the prestressing is achieved without composites. Corrosion protection of the stressed steel is secured by a plastic sheath impregnated with grease. The prestressing elements have an end tie at one side, which is concreted. On the other side the element is led outside using a tie rod. After the concrete has cured this is prestressed against the tension element using external presses. This places the concrete under a compressive stress which counters the tensile stress arising from the bending. Figure 6.36 shows the prestressing elements of a slab deck prior to concrete pouring.

The disadvantages of this process are the additional steps necessary for laying the steel reinforcement and the subsequent prestressing that must be carried out before stripping the formwork. If no outer scaffolding is present then an additional construction is necessary for the prestressing process.

Flat-slab Floors with Displacement Bodies

Another possibility to reduce the own weight of reinforced concrete slabs while maintaining slab thickness is the inclusion of displacement bodies in the slab. The round displacers

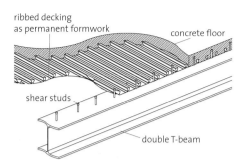
6.33 Composite floor construction with bearing trapezoid decking and concrete topping

6.34 Complex composite floor construction in the Commerzbank high-rise, Frankfurt

6.35 Haunched floor with space for installations. View and section, preliminary design for Westhafen Tower, Frankfurt

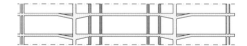

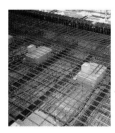 
6.36 Prestressing element without composite in a flat-slab floor
6.37 Flat-slab floor with displacement bodies (Bubbledeck System)

6.38 Diagonal reinforcement cross, new Post Tower, Bonn, architects: Murphy/Jahn, Chicago

6.39 Steel composite walls, Commerzbank Frankfurt, architects: Foster and Partners, London

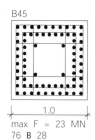

B45

1.0

max F = 23 MN
76 **B** 28

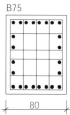

B75

80

max F = 23 MN
52 **B** 28

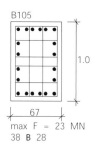

B105

1.0

67

max F = 23 MN
38 **B** 28

6.40 a–c Reduction of column cross section and compressive reinforcement by increasing the grade of concrete [4]

6.41 Steel composite columns with interior steel core, Westhafen Tower, Frankfurt

(Bubbledeck System) are laid together with the reinforcing mesh, thereby being fixed in position (**Fig. 6.37**). Dynamically, this floor construction behaves in the same way as a normal concrete slab floor [18]. Employment of these spherical displacement bodies can reduce the own weight of the slabs by up to 35 percent, which also means savings in vertical load-bearing elements and in the foundation.

6.7 Walls and Columns

The main points regarding walls and columns have already been covered in the section "Systems of Reinforcement", and here only some special features will be mentioned.

Steel, concrete and their various combinations are the materials of choice for the construction of walls and columns in high-rises. The enclosing walls for elevator cores and stairwells must comply with strict fire safety requirements in Germany. Whereas in the USA core walls are commonly steel constructions infilled with insulating material, in Germany load-bearing or stiffening walls are almost always built using reinforced concrete or steel composites. Normal-strength reinforced concrete is adopted when this proves sufficient for structural stability. If stresses are too large, high-strength concrete is used, or steel sections are inserted at weak points to give extra reinforcement. Other factors in the building's construction will dictate which of these methods is chosen.

As previously indicated, creep and shrinkage in concrete must be considered when using steel and concrete elements together for vertical load removal. In particular, the various tolerances of steel construction and concrete construction must be taken into account while planning the building schedule.
If steel sections are used for heavily loaded girders or outrigger constructions, it is often necessary to reinforce the walls in the area of the junctions with elements of sectional steel. **Figure 6.38** shows the diagonal reinforcement cross of the new Deutsche Post AG building in Bonn; the cross connects the facing concrete cores to one another and couples the two circular building halves to form a unified total structure.

The selective strengthening of concrete elements with steel parts improves the pace of construction. Staggered assembly accelerates the building process : either the integrated stiffening elements can be assembled in one run, as in normal steel construction (and the encasement in reinforced concrete can then follow several floors behind), or the concrete core is constructed first and the steel elements are assembled afterwards, as is the case with the Deutsche Post AG building.

In the Commerzbank Tower in Frankfurt, the megacolumns in the outer corners were constructed of composite steel, with high-strength concrete of grade B65 being used in the lower four stories.

Figure 6.39 shows the wall design in steel composite of the Commerzbank Tower (architects: Sir Norman Foster and Partners; structure: design – Ove Arup, London; realization – BGS, Frankfurt). In principle this is a wall structure using reinforced concrete, strengthened in the corners with high-strength concrete and steel elements.

Figure 6.40 clearly shows the possibilities of area reduction in column cross sections and savings in compressive reinforcement when high-strength concrete is employed. Generally, attention must be paid in the design of column cross sections that the elevation width of façade columns should appear constant over height (for formal reasons). The necessary increase in bearing capacity towards the bottom is initially assured by enlarging the depth of the columns. If column sizes become too large, either high-strength concrete can be introduced or the columns are planned as steel composite structures. Apart from the variant of composite columns already shown in Figure 6.7, the load-bearing of columns with purely central loading can also be increased using concrete encased steel (Fig. 6.41).

6.8   Prospects

The ever-increasing building density in the world's metropolises provides a dynamic impetus in the pursuit of height.

The possibilities for building reinforcement offered by the core, tube or core-outrigger systems provide high-performance structures to satisfy all kinds of architectural demands. Megaskyscrapers of up to 200 stories and heights well over 600 m – seen as a utopian vision at the beginning of the 1990s – are taking on concrete features with the furious advance of technology.

The importance of the load-bearing structure is tied to this vertical growth, as with increasing height the ability to meet the large dynamic demands from wind loading becomes a fundamental economic criterion of the whole building. An even closer combination and blending of the presented systems is necessary to optimize the load-bearing performance of megastructures.

Only tube structures (as primary structure) possess the necessary rigidity to assume lateral loads, and these can be skillfully coupled with the core and additional reinforcing elements to produce a hybrid final structure. In addition to these constructive possibilities to enhance performance, optimization of the geometric form is an important step in increasing rigidity and improving aerodynamics.

With increasing height the underlying structure increasingly influences the shape of the building, and lends the design of megaskyscrapers their formal character. For example, the Millennium Tower in Tokyo Bay (Fig. 6.42) developed by Foster and Partners (London) in cooperation with the Obayashi Corporation (Tokyo) has a tower-like appearance, rigorously designed throughout under aerodynamic considerations. The necessary rigidity of the load-bearing construction is provided by a tube-in-tube system, the outer tube of which is at the level of the façade and provides the design with its particular character [20].

The collapse of the World Trade Center will mean a growth in technical demands regarding safety in load-bearing structures. The challenge of designing high-rises so that they are not at risk of collapse when individual components fail presents the designer with new problems, and will greatly influence the future construction of tall buildings.

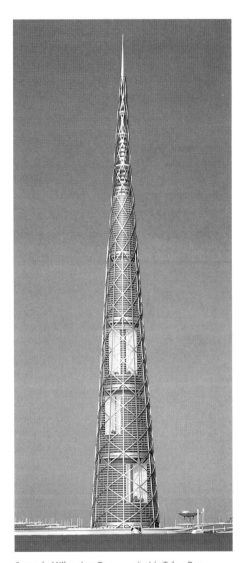

6.42 a, b Millennium Tower, project in Tokyo Bay, architects: Foster and Partners, London, Obayashi Corporation, Tokyo, model: detail and view

07 **Construction and Design**

Johann Eisele

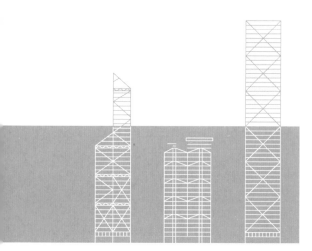

7.1 Design Factors

The design of buildings is influenced by a wide variety of factors. Laws, standards and regulations bring significant influence to bear. The demands of the client can also play an important role, as can function, the envelope, energy and material concerns, building services, the load-bearing structure, and the finishing details. All these aspects generally play a role. Sometimes, however, a single aspect occupies the limelight to such a degree that the others are barely noticed, indeed, they seem not to exist. Ellen Kloft's contribution on "Building Typology" traces how typologies have evolved and changed in high-rise construction. The evolution of form and its impact on the city was a key moment. Legislation had to be brought into play in response to poor planning strategies. Over recent decades, reciprocity has evolved between form and city.

Form and Design

While the evolution of form is merely an aesthetic characteristic, it is by no means insignificant, for, after all the first task is to find the correct form, which must then be filled with meaning. Design therefore presumes the existence of form; however, to define form as design is to put too much emphasis on it. Philip Johnson seems to have mastered this balance and the AT&T Building (Fig. 7.1) in New York (1984) is a paradigmatic example. The building is typologically fairly insignificant in the evolution, leaving the Postmodern revival aside for the moment. Yet the presentation of a high-rise as an Chippendale wardrobe is unmistakable and achieves a powerful symbolic status in the sense of an imprint or company logo. Many of Johnson's colleagues, who subscribed to postmodernism, also tried to achieve symbolism through form alone, although none came close to reaching the power and distinctiveness of the AT&T Building.

Material and Design

In Hans Kollhoff's design for the Main Plaza in Frankfurt (Fig. 7.2), on the other hand, form seems to have played a subordinate role. The structure seems truncated somehow, as if the

7.1 AT&T Building, New York, 1984

7.2 Main Plaza, Frankfurt, 2002

7.3 American Standard Building, New York, 1924

builders had run out of money. And yet a brief glance at the documentation for the competition for the Chicago Tribune Tower reveals a strong formal similarity with the first prize contribution by John Mead Howells & Raymond M. Hood [1]. The design is perhaps reminiscent of the American Standard Building (formerly American Radiator Building) in New York, 1924, by Hood & Fouilhoux (Fig. 7.3), or a blend of it with several other competition entries for the Chicago Tribune Tower.

Whereas architects in New York demonstrated their conservative attitudes in 1922 and hid their load-bearing structures behind eclectic façades, German architects made remarkable contributions, which were firmly dedicated to modernity. The Americans won the prizes (with the exception of the second prize, which was awarded to Eliel Saarinen), the German competition entries toured the United States in an exhibition.

Things have changed since then. The Monadnock Building in Chicago by Burnham & Root, completed in 1892, was the last of its kind to be erected with load-bearing external stone walls: the ratio between ground plan and usable area was simply unacceptable, as was the lighting of the retail spaces behind the 1.8 m thick exterior walls. Clinker-faced façades were unknown. Technology came to the rescue: stainless steel behind the facework could provide structural support for buildings as high as 23 stories and yet allow for 19th-century nostalgia.

7.2 The Meaning of Structure

In her book "Time for Skyscrapers" [2], Ada Louise Huxtable embarks on a different journey. "With all this, or perhaps despite all this, the skyscraper is a form of art and belongs to all other great structures designed according to aesthetic criteria. There are no absolute rules for the design of high-rises, and there never have been, and there is more than one possible façade for each individual high-rise." In the foreword, the author writes: "To describe the phenomenon 'skyscraper' in a conventional way – either from the aesthetic or the structural perspective – is to do an injustice to the architecture, to misunderstand the origin of its power and its weakness, to overlook the difficult translation of vision into reality, to misinterpret the complicated creative process, which transforms necessities into art." This article nevertheless attempts to shed light on the mutual dependencies between construction and design, although or precisely because Huxtable has already identified the aesthetic reciprocity. Although no classification can be entirely complete and correct, there are several reasons to undertake this attempt.

In dealing with everyday tasks, the architect has tremendous leeway in designing the solution. High-rises are more complex and complicated constructs; just as the design freedom decreases the greater the span widths are for bridges, and the load-bearing system plays an ever more dominant role, so does the dominance of the load-bearing system increase for tall buildings – even though cladding obscures the load-bearing structure and prevents it from featuring as a primary design means.

Historically, high-rises are part of modernism, made possible through technical inventions such as elevators, communications systems, supply and disposal systems and the industrial production of iron, steel and glass. Ever since Viollet-le-Duc drew our attention to the significance of the structure in 1864 *["Entretiens sur l'Architecture"]*, it has also become established as playing an aesthetic role. In his seminal essay, Julius Posener writes: "Modern architecture has made us aware of the link between structure and form. It has done so over the course of a long history, longer than the history of overcoming the ornament." [3]

And finally, the beginnings and evolution of high-rise construction in Chicago, as well as architects like W. Le Baron Jenney and L. H. Sullivan and their interpretation of structure and design, also play an important role.

Beginnings in Chicago

Founded in 1804, destroyed by Native Americans in 1812, Chicago was built in 1830 on an American grid pattern and soon developed into a major traffic hub and trading center. The grid and a unique construction method, the "balloon frame", allowed the development and prefabrication of standardized timber battens, which could be quickly and inexpensively nailed together without hierarchical considerations of primary and secondary load-bearing members, if necessary, even by the new owners themselves.

Gradually the timber structures were replaced with iron structures. In 1871, an inferno destroyed a third of the city, the timber structures burnt to the ground and the iron structures melted. After a hesitant start for the reconstruction, the old town was replaced by a center for business. New building techniques and structures were tried and the city began once again to grow rapidly. In 1880 Chicago had half a million inhabitants, ten years later more than one million, and boasting 1.7 million inhabitants by the end of the 19th century. Within a few decades Chicago had developed into the major metropolis of the Midwest.

Because economic pressure was great and the city expanded within such a short time, buildings sprouted out of the ground like

mushrooms. But land was in rare supply and hence expensive, and this led to increasing building heights and dense development. The first architect to master the new technologies was William Le Baron Jenney. He used steel instead of cast iron for his structures, coupled the steel support with the steel girders and thus achieved a rigid, tension- and pressure-proof total structure. The link between the groundbreaking balloon frames and innovative steel structures is evident. What is certain is that the new technologies were first applied in Chicago, the first high-rises were born; although the structures had to be clad for fire protection, the new façades were unprecedented in the history of architecture.

Separating Load-bearing and Envelope

The First Leiter Building by William Le Baron Jenney was constructed in 1879 (Fig. 7.4), at first five stories with iron supports, shortly after increased by two stories, obviously without any structural problems. Since the material was barely capable of absorbing any tensile forces, a framework was still beyond the scope of the possible. The interior was a continuous flexible space that was only divided by 15 cast iron columns (20.3/30.5 cm). To ensure that the façade had to bear only its own weight, Le Baron Jenney arranged rectangular cast iron columns directly behind the supports and laid ceiling girders across them. Although the structure was not exposed or only partly visible – the narrow window mullions were made of cast iron in the First Leiter Building – the large glass areas, the narrow columns and thin window sills could only be achieved by means of a hidden skeleton frame. Moreover, the low own weight of the load-bearing structure could be extended in height. The principle of separating the load-bearing function from the envelope had been discovered for high-rise construction – a forerunner of the curtain wall. The windows can also be regarded as precursors of the so-called Chicago window.

1884 saw the construction of the Home Insurance Building (Fig. 7.5), the first high-rise in steel skeleton construction, followed in 1889–90 by the Second Leiter Building and 1890–91 the Fair Store, for which William Le Baron Jenney developed a new fire-proof structure.

Reliance Building

The Reliance Building (architects: Daniel Hudson Burnham & John Wellborn Root) was erected in Chicago almost concurrently with the realization of the Monadnock Building (1889–91). While the Monadnock Building was the last of its kind with load-bearing external masonry, the Reliance Building (Fig. 7.6) exemplified the Chicago School: steel skeleton as so-called Chicago structure, large glass surfaces, broad horizontal windows, the "Chicago window," with fixed central panel and openable leaves to the left and right. "With its airiness and purity of proportion, the building symbolizes the spirit of the Chicago School, while also being its 'swansong'." [4]

Form Follows Function

"It is the law of all organic and inorganic, all human and superhuman things, all true manifestations of the mind, the heart and the soul, that life is recognizable in its expression, that form always follows function. This is the law." [2b]

Louis H. Sullivan (1856–1924) began his career as a draftsman, worked among others at William Le Baron Jenney's office and left for Paris in 1874 to attend the École des Beaux Arts, where many of his American colleagues were trained. He returned to Chicago the following year, in 1875. Dankmar Adler invited him to join his firm in 1879 to take on the design responsibility for his building tasks. A mere two years later, Sullivan became Adler's partner. Over the next 14 years of collaboration (Adler left the partnership in 1895 because of a lack of building contracts) more than 100 buildings were realized, as well as an impressive theoretical work. Sullivan was the first to recognize that building high called for theoretical aesthetic rules and his motto "form follows function" would become the most-quoted sentence by architects and architectural theorists, often taken out of Sullivan's intended context and misunderstood.

"Is it truly something so wonderful – or is it so hackneyed, so pedestrian and so close to us, that we simply cannot understand that the design, form and exterior of the large office building must adapt to function in the

     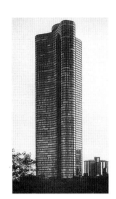

7.4 First Leiter Building, Chicago, 1879   7.5 Home Insurance Building, Chicago, 1884   7.6 Reliance Building, Chicago, 1890   7.7 Guaranty Trust Building, Buffalo, 1894–95
7.8 Lake Shore Drive Apartments, Chicago, 1948–51   7.9 Lake Point Tower, Chicago, 1968–69

manner of all things – that, where function does not change, form must not change?"

Sullivan divided his buildings into three functions: ground floor and first upper floor were classified as one, because they had to fulfill similar functions ("... which call for a large area, much space and much light ..."), and an equipment floor at the top of the building, generally windowless or with very small openings. Between these two functions lie the office floors, which are given the same external treatment (" ... one floor like the other, one office like the other ...") and consist of a grid of intersecting horizontal and vertical lines. To design a building from the inside out, to develop a façade that is virtually self-evident on the basis of the function and not an adaptation of historic stylistic means, was new for the time, even revolutionary, and sparked protest and controversy among architects outside of Chicago.

At the end of the 19th century, the Chicago School had given rise to the most modern architecture in the world, whose influence remained local, however, because wealthy Americans – especially in New York – delighted in eclectic façades, richly ornamented and reminiscent of the splendor of the European Renaissance.

Guaranty Trust Building

The three functions are clearly visible in the Guaranty Trust Building (architects: Adler & Sullivan) in **Figure 7.7** down to the minutest detail: Retail shops and a bank are housed on the ground floor and the first floor, the top

floor (like the basement) are reserved for the necessary technical equipment, and the ten stories in between are occupied by identically arranged offices. The steel structure has a grid of roughly 5 x 7 and 5 x 9 m, respectively, and an additional column, identical in form with the load-bearing columns, although not fulfilling a structural function, is added in the façade from the second floor upward. The diminished distance between columns increases the sense of verticality and attenuates the appearance of the building. Sullivan, it seems, attached so much importance to this effect that he was willing to compromise the clarity of the structure by adding another, non load-bearing column, only to achieve the effect of verticality, which had until then eluded him and the other Chicago architects. The steel structure is clad in terracotta and richly ornamented on the office floors – in contrast to the first two floors. Since the vertical lines intersect the horizontal lines, this building does not feature the windows typical of the Chicago School.

**7.3   Load-bearing Structures/
Load-bearing Systems**

The structural system of a building must be stable when subjected to external loads. Due to their dimensions, high-rises are characterized by high dead and net loads. The greater the number of floors, the greater the influence of the horizontal loads on the structural system: High-rises perform like cantilevered beams fixed into the subsoil (see article by Grohmann/Kloft, Chapter 6). Corner bracing must be part of the reinforcement to prevent torsion. At least three plates are required

across the entire height of the building for bracing, to redirect the wind loads and transfer them to the ground. Ceilings and plates operate in conjunction. The longitudinal axes of the three plates must not intersect at a point, because the building would otherwise be able to rotate around this point (torsion).

Load-transfer systems are classified as direct and indirect systems. Direct load-transfer systems (also called standing structures) gather the various loads from top to bottom and transfer them directly into the subsoil without diversion. This group includes skeleton systems, frameless systems, tubular systems and megastructure systems. Combinations of these systems have also been realized. Indirect load-transfer systems can be divided into three subgroups: support systems, suspended systems and cantilever systems. The loads are transferred into the subsoil from the various floors in different ways, albeit not along the most direct and shortest path; this approach of "taking the loads for a walk" must be justified by good reasons. Examples are used to illustrate the influence of the load-bearing systems on the form of the load-bearing structure and the façade, and hence on the design of the entire building.

Direct Load Transfer

Skeleton Systems

Skeletons are load-bearing systems composed of hinged columns and cross members, which are only capable of transferring vertical loads. The horizontal loads are assumed and transferred via panels.

7.10 Schweizer Nationalversicherung, Frankfurt, 1964   7.11 Seagram Building, New York, 1955–58   7.12 Chase Manhattan Bank, New York, 1957–61

7.13 Atlanta Marriott Marquis, Atlanta, 1985   7.14 Torre Pirelli, Milan, 1956–58

The panels can be designed in different ways: as massive panels or dissolved as (vertical) framework or as a bend-resistant frame. The cores are often utilized for bracing, because they are needed anyway for vertical access and for the supply and disposal shafts, and must be massive in construction as specified by fire protection codes. The panels can be installed on the exterior or interior walls and thus influence the ground plan and/or the façade. In the Lake Shore Drive Apartments (architect: Ludwig Mies van der Rohe, Fig. 7.8) the panels serve simultaneously as dividing walls between apartments, turning a potential disadvantage into an advantage.

Skeleton systems can be employed to realize buildings of varying heights: the Seagram Building (Fig. 7.11) – skeleton with frame struts, architect Philip Johnson – reaches a height of roughly 157 m with 39 stories; the Chase Manhattan Bank (Fig. 7.12) by the architects SOM even soars to an impressive 60 stories and roughly 250 m, with the skeleton executed as a post-and-rail structure and hence structurally very strong through the use of several reinforcements. The end moment, formed by the core or the panels, is the key factor for the height development of skeleton systems. The Haus der Schweizer Nationalversicherung (Swiss National Insurance Building, Fig. 7.10) illustrates a special application of skeleton systems. Meid & Romeick treated the "columns" as building-high frames and stretched the ceilings from upright to upright across the short span length, thereby achieving column-free floor areas.
In theory, skeleton systems permit a very liberal treatment of the ground plan; the Lake Point Tower in Chicago (architects:

Schipporeit/Heinrich Ass., Fig. 7.9) is an impressive example that this need not be restricted to right-angled forms.

The only spatial constraints are imposed on the ground floor as a result of the columns and panels. Large spaces that require column-free design, cannot be realized on this level or require a supporting girder, an elaborate intervention that negates the economic advantage of direct load transfer. Skeleton systems offer tremendous freedom in designing the form and the façade. Interior panels have no impact on the façade. Mies van der Rohe used this freedom to develop the curtain wall (Lake Shore Drive Apartments): in the Seagram Building, he perfected the curtain wall with the typical Mies corner.

Panel and Shear Wall Systems

Panels are massive load-bearing systems, which absorb the external loads parallel to their plane. They differ from the bracing panels of the skeleton systems in that they transfer not only the horizontal loads but all loads. Principally, we can differentiate between transverse panel systems and longitudinal panel systems. The transverse and longitudinal panel system is moreover differentiated from the panel system with a core. Since panel systems are predominantly executed in reinforced concrete, panels can be coupled with the floors to achieve a high degree of rigidity, although the risk of secondary bending must be taken into account.

Transverse panel systems are fundamentally inflexible and are therefore employed in the construction of apartment towers, boarding houses and hotels, where the massive panels are a positive factor for sound insulation. Spatiality is limited on the entrance floor, however, and support girders are required, which undermines the clarity of the entire structure and is uneconomical. In the Atlanta Marriott Marquis (Fig. 7.13) the two room studs are therefore pulled far apart at the bottom to create an open interior without panels.

For this reason, combinations of transverse panels with load-bearing core are employed for office buildings (Torre Pirelli in Milan, architect: Gio Ponti, Fig. 7.14) to increase the flexibility in the plans. Structurally, the Pirelli Tower is nevertheless a splendid building that can be interpreted as an early attempt to transfer loads through megacolumns.

The Thyssen House by the architects HPP (Fig. 7.15) is popularly also known as three-panel house, a reference to the three staggered office slabs. The fronts of the slabs and the panels at the building center act as transverse panels. Load-bearing columns along the principal façades provide flexibility for the ground plans. The Thyssen House can be understood as a transition from the panel system to the skeleton system.

Longitudinal panel systems allow tremendous flexibility in the design of the ground plan, although they impose considerable restrictions on the façade design because they only permit small openings (perforated façade). In the Metropolitan Correctional Center (Fig. 7.16), the city jail of Chicago (architects:

7.15 Thyssen House, Düsseldorf, 1957   7.16 Metropolitan Correctional Center, Chicago, 1975   7.17 Deutsche Bank, Frankfurt, 1984   7.18 United Steelworkers Building, Pittsburgh, 1963
7.19 World Trade Center, New York, 1966–73   7.20 Sears Tower, Chicago, 1972–74

Harry Weese & Associates) an attempt has been made to turn this disadvantage into an advantage: the "windows" widen to the outside to allow more light to penetrate, while measuring only 12.7 cm in width on the inside, in order to obviate the need for bars.

When all exterior walls are constructed as load-bearing panels, the result is a typical perforated façade, whereas structural continuity and composite construction with the floors results in a tubular structure, as is the case with the twin towers of the Deutsche Bank in Frankfurt (architects: ABB; Fig. 7.17), although this is only evident at night when the interior is lit by artificial light.

Tube Systems

This high-performance load-bearing system is based on the box girder principle. The façades are constructed as detached panels and coupled at the corners. The tube thus created is additionally braced through the floor panels. A round plan would be ideal for this application, because the problem of the coupled corner is eliminated. For functional reasons, however, plans that are square or nearly square are more common. Due to torsion, other forms cannot be realized with the simple tube system and with the tube-in-tube system.

In the simple tube system, all horizontal loads are transferred via the façade; since this makes use of the largest available lever arm of the building (entire building depth) and because the two façades running parallel to the wind direction are made to participate in the load transfer, the resulting tensile and pressure forces are correspondingly small. Steel

consumption is minimized, keeping the building's own weight relatively low and permitting enormous building heights.

For buildings with more than 50 to 60 stories it is useful to engage interior load-bearing members in the horizontal load transfer as well, which results in tube-in-tube systems, bundled tubes (e.g. Sears Tower by architects SOM in Fig. 7.20) or a variety of combined systems.

To maintain flexibility in the area between façade and core, large span widths are often tolerated – World Trade Center: approx. 18 m (Fig. 7.19). Theoretically, at least, this offers complete freedom for the ground plan layout. However, the façade is strongly defined by the structural dynamics because a shear effect must be achieved.

There are three fundamental options:

1) Truss Grids
They consist of diagonal stiff-jointed pressure struts or with tie beams along the edge of the floor panels. The many diagonals are difficult to resolve with regard to windows. The two planes are therefore spatially separated and a space-enclosing façade is erected behind the truss grid. However, the necessary penetrations are critical from the perspective of building physics and there is a risk of damage due to secondary bending and settlement. The United Steelworkers Building (Fig. 7.18, architects: Curtis & Davis) features truss grids and façade profiles in one plane.

2) Frames
Façade columns standing close together in

keeping with the distances of the completion grid are stiff-jointed with the girders in the area of the breast wall to form frames. If they are rigorously maintained from the top down to the ground floor, they result in unreasonable openings. The entrances require considerably greater clear openings and supports or props are required unless the façade columns are grouped. The narrowly placed façade columns are dependent on the completion grid and obviate the need for additional window profiles since these can be integrated, also to avoid having to further reduce the clear openings and daylight incidence.

3) Column-Diagonal Frames
The façade consists of hinged columns and girders with economically optimized span widths; the shear effect is achieved by means of large diagonal bracing. Façade grid and construction grid are separated and generally occupy two different planes. Similar problems arise as with the truss grid, although the number of penetrations is considerably reduced, and hence more manageable, as a result of the larger dimension of the construction grid. Tube load-bearing systems are very effective and have a proven record as load-bearing systems for skyscrapers as a glance at the list of the tallest building demonstrates, for example, the John Hancock Center by the architects SOM (Fig. 7.21).

The Millennium Tower (Fig. 7.22), a project by Foster and Partners in the Bay of Tokyo from 1989, is an extreme example of how the increased height of the load-bearing system determines the form (cone) and dominates the design.

7.21 John Hancock Center, Chicago, 1969   7.22 Millennium Tower, Tokyo, 1989 (project, 870 m)   7.23 Olivetti Administration and Training Center, Frankfurt 1967–72

7.24 Citycorp Center, New York, 1979   7.25 Torre Velasca, Milan, 1958

Indirect Load Transfer

Support Systems

Support systems have been employed for several high-rises to create inviting entrance areas. Tube systems are faced with this problem by the very nature of their system design (World Trade Center/John Hancock Tower/Alcoa Building). In this context, however, support systems (Figs. 7.23–7.25) are understood as structures that provide support not to alleviate a problem but because it is an inherent conceptual characteristic.

The core, continuous by necessity, is utilized in the lower floors as the basis for a support structure, which widens with increasing height and thus forms the platform for the upper floors, and which can be developed as a skeleton system (Olivetti) or as tubes with diagonal bracing (Citycorp Center). The horizontal loads are absorbed directly by the core and diverted towards the core on the façade plane. This concentration of loads calls for a central foundation pad, which can be an advantage where difficult subsoil conditions are present, because simple settlements occur. Since the support structure often places static stresses on several floor heights, valuable usable space is lost.

Structural dynamics demand symmetrical forms around a central core, which would otherwise by subjected to eccentric loads and because more material would be consumed as a result of secondary loads.

While this system offers great flexibility for the ground level, because there are no obstructions by columns, the integration of the core and access to the upper floors can be a tremendous challenge.

Egon Eiermann cited several reasons for the shape of the Olivetti Towers (Fig. 7.23): "The narrowness of the lot and the close functional unity between high-rises and hall buildings made it necessary to arrange the buildings as closely together as possible. In this context it was necessary to employ a high-rise structure that avoids any penetration with the hall structure. For this reason, both towers were developed as structures in the shape of inverted chalices with a massive, load-bearing core, where the full stories only begin from the 5th floor upward." [5] It is also possible, however, that Eiermann wanted to reach a certain height before starting the full floors because the views only improved from this level upward.

In the case of the Citycorp Center (Fig. 7.24) the existence of a church was the starting point for the unusual structure: the church administrators sold their air rights and were given a new building on the old site in return. In the end, the architects Stubbins & Associates (with Emery Roth & Sons) solved the difficult entrance situation by creating a sunken square from which access to the high-rise is provided.

Cantilever Systems

The vertical loads are assumed by a central core and transferred to the foundation slab. Cantilevered floors, which assume the horizontal loads project from this core and transfer the loads to the core. Since the core must

assume all loads, the tensile forces resulting from the horizontal load are overcome by the vertical loads in the core: the remaining tensile forces are low (Figs. 7.26 and 7.27).

The floors must be stiff-jointed with the core to transfer cantilever moments, which results in a given construction height. The haunch and the shape of the building and the core may require complicated formwork. Structural dynamics demand symmetrical forms around a central core, which would otherwise by subjected to eccentric loads and introduce secondary loads at the vulnerable point. The boundary of the cantilever usually makes it necessary to work with identical lengths in all directions, which poses considerable limitations on the shape of plans despite the complete absence of columns.

The only fixed point on the ground floor is the core and it can otherwise be developed with complete freedom.

In theory, the façade is also free of all constraints since no load-bearing columns have to be taken into consideration. In practice, however, the completion grid must be considered and the façade must be designed to be light in order to avoid additional stress on the cantilevered floors. The façade joints must be designed in accordance with the anticipated deflection and subsoil settlement must also be taken into consideration.

7.26 Johnson Wax Building, Racine, 1936–39 7.27 Price Tower, Bartlesville, 1956 7.28 Marina City, Chicago, cantilevered balconies, 1962 7.29 BMW Tower, Munich, 1970–72

7.30 Standard Bank Centre, Johannesburg, 1970 7.31 Hong Kong & Shanghai Bank, Hong Kong, 1985

Frank Lloyd Wright's high-rise for Johnson Wax (Fig. 7.26) is a perfect example of how to work with this load-bearing system: the façade is stretched like a skin over the structure, which can also be experienced on the inside, because each second floor is recessed. Yet Wright also demonstrates that the expansion in plan and the development in height are restricted early on in the process.

Suspended Systems

All suspended systems first transfer the horizontal loads upwards via a circuitous route into a (roof) truss, which transfers the load to one or more cores. From these they are, in turn, transferred to the foundations. The horizontal loads are also channeled into the same system via the floors – which are stretched between the tie beams and the cores.
The suspended system is the only load-bearing system to actually "take the loads for a walk". The disadvantages of this must be balanced by advantages, which should be evaluated for each individual case.

A principal differentiation is made between single-core and multicore systems. In terms of the foundation, single-core systems have the same advantages as support systems and cantilever systems: the concentration of loads calls for a central foundation slab, which can be an advantage when difficult subsoil conditions are present because simple settlements occur. Conversely, multicore systems require at least as many foundations as there are cores. All suspended systems can be constructed conventionally from bottom to top, whereby the floors can only be suspended after the completion of the core(s) and the

(roof) trusses. As each story is first completed on the ground and then hoisted, interior work can progress on the upper floors even as the next new rough floor is being produced at ground level.
The process can also be reversed for all suspended systems; in other words, after the aforementioned cores and (roof) trusses have been completed, the individual floors are completed from top to bottom and the interior work follows in the same sequence. There are several possible advantages associated with this reversed process: elaborate protective scaffolding across the entire building height is no longer necessary and only required for one floor at a time, while the individual working levels are protected by the floor above. Less effort is required to set up a winter building site, the ground floor remains open and may be used for site facilities, an advantage on inner-city site in particular. The suspension systems are not at risk of buckling, which permits slender tie bars, an advantage that can be quickly ruined, however, by the necessary fire-protective cladding (e.g. in the case of the Hong Kong & Shanghai Bank, Fig. 7.31, architects: Foster and Partners). The tie bars are subject to changes in length especially as a result of temperature differences between winter and summer, and these changes compound with each additional floor. Partial suspension of different groups of floors can at best minimize these disadvantages and avoid the circuitous diversion across the highest point of the building.

For single-core systems, the plans must be centered on the core. Eccentric loads are difficult to absorb and produce additional moments. The individual floor areas are highly flexible and only dependent on the distance between the individual tie bars. The ground floor is only defined by the cores and can otherwise be developed with complete freedom. Suspended systems permit a very liberal treatments of the façade. The tie bars can be moved to the interior to prevent expansion due to temperature differences or installed on the exterior with corresponding protection. In both cases, the changes in length must be absorbed by expansion joints. Other examples of suspended structures are: BMW Tower Munich (Fig. 7.29, architect: Karl Schwanzer); Standard Bank Centre Johannesburg (Fig. 7.30, architects: HPP).

Mega Structures and Load-bearing System Combinations

Thus far, we have been able to treat the different load-bearing systems as "pure" systems. Yet the limitations of the systems can shift when another system is added. It is difficult, however, to classify these types of load-bearing systems as a separate category, and it is equally difficult to add them to any of the categories described above:

Through additional reinforcement with frame bracing or frame-struts, skeleton systems have reached heights up to 250 m (Chase Manhattan Bank, New York, Fig. 7.12). Tube systems achieve a height of 445 m by adding a truss belt as a framework on the equipment floors (Sears Tower, Chicago, Fig. 7.20).

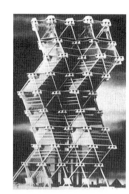

7.32 Jin Mao Building, Shanghai, 1998   7.33 Petronas Towers, Kuala Lumpur, 1997   7.34 Bank of China, Hong Kong, 1990   7.35 Tetraeder Tower, project 1957   7.36 Torres Puerta de Europa, Madrid, 1997   7.37 Vienna Twin Towers, Vienna, 2001

Outriggers

The most recent spectacular high-rises – the Petronas Towers (Fig. 7.33) in Kuala Lumpur (architects: Cesar Pelli & Associates) and the Jin Mao Building (Fig. 7.32) in Shanghai (architects: SOM) – were realized with combinations of different, high-performance materials, but also with using outriggers, i.e. boom girders across one or several floors, which couple the core with the façade columns. This achieves a greater overall rigidity and considerably reducing the tensile forces in the load-bearing structure and the foundations. While the Petronas Towers combine an inner core with a frame tube composed of concreted cylindrical columns via outriggers, the Jin Mao Building is equipped with sets of megacolumns on the four sides of the building, complemented by additional columns at the building corners. However, the design of neither of these buildings reflects the structure, in other words, the megastructures do not seem to have an aesthetic value.

On the Pirelli Tower (Fig. 7.14) in Milan, the mega-transverse panels are visible on the façade and contribute to its division.

Mega Spatial Frameworks

The Bank of China (architect: I.M. Pei & Partners, Fig. 7.34) utilizes a mega spatial framework as a load-bearing system. The plan of the building (approx. 52 x 52 m) is divided into four equal triangles. With increasing height, one less triangle is continued, so that the high-rise grows progressively more slender towards the top. This geometry poses some difficulties in terms of vertical access, and on the 43rd floor one has to transfer across to the remaining triangle.

Structurally, however, this spatial geometry is advantageous: the mega spatial framework creates a rigid load-bearing system that can, in theory, operate without a reinforcing core. A project for a high-rise by Louis I. Kahn (Fig. 7.35), where stacked tetrahedrons demonstrate the same principle, can be understood as a forerunner. But Pei does not reveal the horizontal framework girders on the façade, which can only be explained by the Chinese teachings of Feng-Shui. Consequently, the girders are hidden behind the façade and the visible image of the façade is idealized. The vertical columns at the corners and the building center have a far greater dimension than the even pattern of vertical and diagonal façade cladding suggests. The support structure is especially notable: the mega spatial framework ends at the fourth floor. It rests on a megaframe, which in turn rests on four corner posts and thus creates a generous open space on the ground floor.

7.4 Trends and Perspectives

As early as 1896, Louis H. Sullivan answered his own question on the principal characteristic of a major office building: "It must be tall – every inch of it must be tall. The force and power of height must reside in it – the glamour and pride of enthusiasm." Yet the high-rise is insufficiently characterized by height alone; it must be higher than all others, at least for a time. The Masonic Temple was the first "tallest building of the world," the Empire State Building held the honor for more than 40 years and now the Petronas Towers hold the title – although only by the expedient of designing the antenna as the official building peak and thus outdoing the Sears Tower in height. But the intervals between new records are growing ever shorter. However, this dynamic can serve to inspire work on smaller high-rises as well: They offer opportunities to focus on themes other than load-bearing structure and façade.

Twins – the Wave of the Future

Despite the criticism – ruthless overbuilding of the site – of the Equitable Building in New York, 1915, the structure can be seen as a forerunner of twin towers, which were discovered as an urban event with the advent of the Lake Shore Drive Apartments in Chicago, 1951 (Fig. 7.8). Today, it has become a trend: The Romeo and Juliet towers in Stuttgart-Zuffenhausen (architect: Hans Scharoun) from 1959 referred to their complementary nature already in their name; they were followed by the Marina City twin towers (Fig. 7.28, architect: Goldberg, 1962), the Olivetti Towers (Fig. 7.23), 1972, the twin towers of the Deutsche Bank (Fig. 7.17) in Frankfurt, 1984, the Torres Puerta de Europa (Fig. 7.36) in Madrid (architects: Burgee & Johnson, 1997), the Petronas Towers (Fig. 7.33), 1997 and the Vienna Twin Towers (Fig. 7.37, architect: M. Fuksas, 2001). Several other twins are waiting to be realized on the drawing boards of architects and engineers.

7.38 Haus der Nord L/B, Hanover, 2002, liberation of form   7.39 Tower design at the Technical University of Darmstadt, emancipation of form   7.40 Ford Foundation, New York, 1965-68   7.41 Commerzbank, Frankfurt, 1997   7.42 Menara Mesiniaga, Selangor, 1992   7.43 Tokyo Nara Building, 1999

Liberation of Form

With few exceptions (e.g. Figs. 7.38 and 7.39), most high-rises are rectangular cubes or at least simple geometric shapes; even the Lake Point Tower (Fig. 7.9) can be described geometrically, although it is nevertheless formally distinct. And yet Mies van der Rohe had already demonstrated this liberality in his ideal designs, although he never fulfilled the promise in his buildings.

The Self-sufficient High-rise

The design for the Ford Foundation in New York (Fig. 7.40, architects: Kevin Roche & John Dinkeloo) made no concessions to energy-efficiency; the first energy crisis came later and has affected design in only a few European countries. The Ford Foundation is deliberately restrained on a downtown site, demonstrating size through understatement and offering its employees and the public a high-rise with a park: green space is brought into the interior of the high-rise. The Commerzbank (Fig. 7.41) in Frankfurt has a total of nine gardens, each with a clear height of three stories, distributed on all sides of the tower and winding upwards in a spiral; they bring daylight, air and sun into the interior and are thus far the most current contribution to improving the energy consumption and ecological design of high-rises.

Ken Yeang takes this idea even further. In his book "The Green Skyscraper" [6] he formulates a fully integrated approach towards a solution; in addition to the familiar ecological aspects of building – natural ventilation, movable shading systems, rainwater use and exterior green space – he defines the important urban and regional criteria for his "Bioclimatic skyscraper": Orientation towards the sun and the principal wind direction, shading for neighboring buildings, adaptation to daytime and changing temperatures, as well as the effect of changing local climate conditions on form. Some aspects of this theory have already been realized in a few of his high-rise designs and buildings, for example, in Selangor, Menara Mesiniaga (Fig. 7.42), 1992.

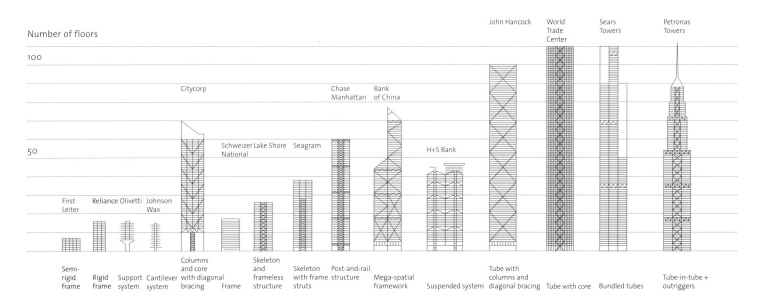

7.44 Matrix: load-bearing structures of towers

o8 Structural Dynamics

Johann-Dietrich Wörner and Hans-Werner Nordhues

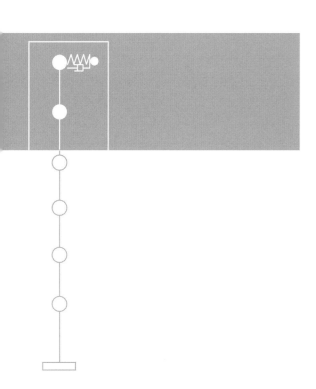

8.1 Introduction

Analyses of structural loads are generally given precedence in calculations/design measurements for high-rises. For reasons of simplicity, a structural equivalent load is often used to analyze the dynamic influences, i.e. influences that change over time, such as traffic loads. And yet dynamics are often especially important both for construction and operation.

This article aims to clarify which aspects much be considered for dynamic influences with reference to both structural stability and to comfort.

8.2 Structural Dynamics in High-rise Construction

General

The dynamic influences relevant for high-rises and similar structures are:
– Earthquakes
– Wind
– Vibrations (traffic, operation)

While extraordinary stresses such as explosions or airplane impact also result in dynamic reactions, events of this kind are not included in these observations.

In broad strokes, the nature of the three influences listed is as follows:

Earthquakes

Origin of Earthquakes

Very simply put, the earth consists of a core with a diameter of roughly 6800 km surrounded by a 2800 km thick mantle. The uppermost layer, approximately 150 km thick, is called the lithosphere. It is formed by seven large, rigid tectonic plates, which shift in relation to each other (Fig. 8.1). Over the course of millennia these tectonic shifts produce high tensions as a result of elastic deformation of the lithosphere. If the stress capacity of the plates is surpassed locally, a sudden movement occurs along a geological fault, which humans perceive as an earthquake. This event generally occurs at a depth of 30–100 km in the earth's crust. The location at which the

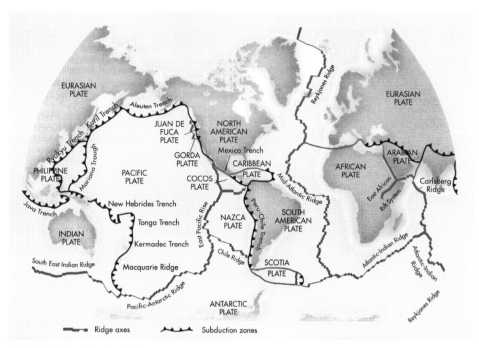

8.1 The Earth's tectonic plates [9]

kinetic energy is released is called the hypocenter, and the location directly above it on the earth's surface, the epicenter.

Characteristics of Earthquakes

Earthquakes are characterized by the type of waves they emit. These are differentiated into space waves and surface waves. When subjected to space waves, the ground experiences either an expansion/compression movement (P-waves) in the direction of the movement of the waves or a shear movement (S-waves) perpendicular to the direction of movement of the waves. Depending on the ground composition, P-waves travel at a speed of roughly 5–6 km/s, while S-waves travel at half that speed.

Surface waves can be divided into Love waves and Rayleigh waves (named after the discoverers A.E.H. Love and Lord Rayleigh). When subjected to Love waves, the ground experiences a shear movement perpendicular to the direction of the movement of the waves, similar to the S-waves. Rayleigh waves are characterized by an upward and downward movement of the ground particles combined with a horizontal distortion and can best be compared to the wave movement of water. These waves exhibit approximately the same velocity as S-waves and reach the observation point at the same time (Fig. 8.2).

The observer of an earthquake is therefore exposed to the following experience: The P-waves of the quake are the first to arrive, causing a tremor predominantly in the vertical direction. In general, this causes little damage to buildings because they are designed for vertical loads including safety coefficients. Next, there is a pause until the S-waves reach the observation point. This stage brings tremors in the horizontal

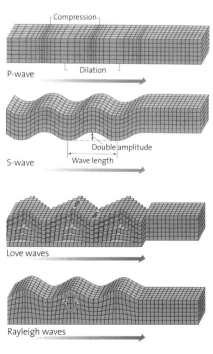

8.2 Earthquake waves [9]

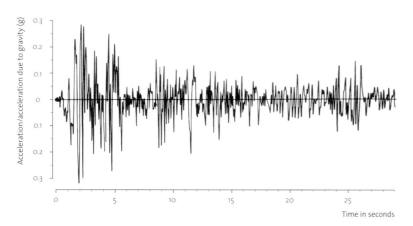

8.3 Course of an earthquake over time (El Centro, 1940)

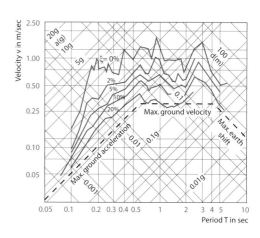

8.5 Elastic response spectrum of the El Centro earthquake

Table 8.4 The intensity of an earthquake on the Medvedev-Sponheuer-Karnik Scale

Intensity (MSK)	Intensity	Perception/effect	Earthquake zone as per DIN 4149, part I
I	Not noticeable	Detected and recorded by seismo-graphs only	
II	Scarcely noticeable	Noticeable by individual people at rest	A
III	Weak	Felt by a few people	
IV	Largely observed	Felt by man people, dishes rattle	
V	Strong	Hanging objects swing; sleeping people awaken	
VI	Slight damage	Slight damage to buildings, fine cracks in plaster	0
VII	Damage to buildings	Damage to buildings, chimneys collapse	1 (a_0 = 0.25 m/s²) 2 (a_0 = 0.40 m/s²)
VIII	Destruction of buildings	Greater damage to buildings, gables collapse	3 (a_0 = 0.65 m/s²) 4 (a_0 = 1.00 m/s²)
IX	General damage	General damage to buildings, landslides	
X	General destruction	General destruction of buildings, cracks of up to 1 m appear in the ground	
XI	Catastrophe	Very few buildings remain standing	
XII	Major catastrophe	Changes to landscape	

direction, responsible for severe damage to buildings. Once the S-waves have passed, the most noticeable impact comes from the Rayleigh waves, comparable to the rolling movement of a ship. Many buildings, already severely damaged by the S-waves, collapse during this phase.

Figure 8.3 illustrates the acceleration of the famous El Centro earthquake in southern California in 1940.

Earthquakes from an Engineering Perspective

The following specifications can be indicated based on intensity and geological conditions:
- Frequency of relevant earthquakes per year: approx. 100–103
- Duration of earthquake: approx. 2–60 s
- Acceleration: up to approx. 0.6 g.

The effect of earthquakes on humans and buildings is best described by giving the intensity of the earthquake on a scale. The most common scale of intensity used in Europe is the Medvedev-Sponheuer-Karnik scale (MSK scale). An abbreviated version is reproduced in Table 8.4.

The response spectrum is especially suited for earthquake analysis from an engineering perspective. It provides information on all characteristic data of an earthquake, e.g. maximum acceleration, as a function of the mode or the natural period of oscillation. A response spectrum indicates the maximum response acceleration experienced by a

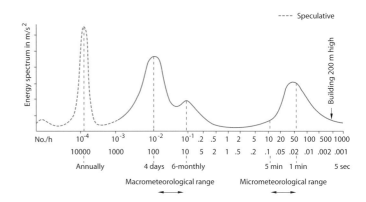

8.6 Spectrum of horizontal wind speed [10]

single-mass oscillator within a given period (or mode) on a given ground acceleration course (e.g. earthquake). The response spectrum is therefore not indicative of the response of a specific building but of the response of many systems with only one mode per system.

This method is ideal for use by (structural) engineers, because one can "compile" the response of the building on the basis of the response spectrums and the calculated modes of any given building. This is the model analysis that is also applied for standards.

Figure 8.5 shows the elastic response spectrum for the famous El Centro earthquake of 1940. The damping of the structure is indicated with x and given in percentages.

Wind

Wind stimuli can be important both in terms of the safety and performance of buildings and in terms of comfort. In the past, the dynamic effect of wind was often the cause for structural failure. A well-known example is the Tacoma Bridge, where relatively moderate wind velocities caused oscillations that were strong enough (galloping) to cause the bridge to fail. Galloping denotes a self-starting oscillation, produced by a pressure field in an oscillating body as a result of its relative movement in reaction to the oncoming flow [2]. The stability of such oscillations is dependent on the scale of the stationary flow. Like

earthquakes, wind fluctuations can be described with the help of spectral analyses. Since the stimulus is influenced in particular by the interaction between wind and building, but also by the geographic conditions (on a large and small scale), general statements on stimulus characteristics are only possible to a limited degree.

Figure 8.6 shows a spectrum of horizontal wind velocity. A macrometereological range (1,000 hours to 1 hour) and a micrometeorological range (1 hour to 1 second) are clearly discernible. The first energy peak of the wind at roughly four days is caused by the changes in the general meteorological conditions with roughly the same frequency. The second peak at roughly 12 hours reflects the wind changes between day and night. These wind frequencies are meaningless for building design. The third peak in the spectrum is the so-called gust spectrum. This gust force of wind is the relevant datum for high-rises. Due to the inherent or eigenfrequencies (also referred to as modes, 0.2–0.4 Hz), they lie on the descending branch of the gust spectrum, and vulnerability to oscillation need only be studied for very slender high-rises.

Vibration

Vibrations can only be described in general for individual scenarios, for example, as a result of subway traffic near a building. Some typical sources of vibrations are:

– Construction (drilling and driving pile foundations, blasting, demolition work)
– Road traffic
– Rail traffic

The degree of vibration transmitted onto buildings is largely dependent on ground or soil composition and on the vibration source, and hence it is impossible to provide general descriptions based on fixed parameters.

The boundary values for structural oscillations vary from country to country in accordance with regulations defining the permissible degree of oscillation dependent on building use. A difference is made between commercial and residential buildings, and settings that call for special protection measures, such as hospitals.

Since oscillations are best perceived by people in a state of rest, the differences in permissible evaluated oscillation forces are considerably greater for day and night than for the various types of use. Generally speaking, the difference between nocturnal and daytime oscillations is at least a factor of 10.

If building use requires more than average requirements, as is the case for strong rooms or computing centers, it may be necessary to set far more stringent limits for building oscillation. These limits or boundary values vary to a great degree. They are not defined by standards or guidelines and must be determined in collaboration with the operator of the relevant establishment.

Table 8.8 General construction principles

Simple load-bearing system	– Regular plan and elevation for building
	– Compact building form
	– No dramatic changes in stiffness as the building rises
Symmetry	– Symmetrical reinforcement system along two orthogonal axes
	– Rectangular ground plan if possible
Connected foundations	– Integrated building sections constructed on common foundations
Spatial load-bearing capacity	– Floors with diaphragm action
Energy dissipation capacity	– Transfer of horizontal loads
	– Sufficient local and general ductility is essential

8.3 Design Principles for High-rise Construction

General

In contrast to standard construction, formal variety is more limited in high-rise construction due to the dominance of the building height. The principal structural principles are nevertheless listed here (Table 8.8).

Plan and Elevation

The design of plan and elevation is a key factor in the building's behavior when it is subjected to dynamic forces. While the floor slabs are designed to transfer horizontal loads to the reinforcing systems, chiefly by rigid body displacement, the reinforcing systems must transfer the horizontal loads to the foundations. Floor slabs should be as compact as possible to allow the transfer of horizontal loads to the reinforcing systems. The disposition of the reinforcing systems in the building ground plan must ensure that the shear center is as close as possible to the mass center of all masses acting in this floor (Fig. 8.9).

The regularity of the buildings in the elevation is especially important for high-rises. The necessity for equipment floors translates into an unavoidable concentration of masses on individual floors. At the same time, the reinforcing system must be less dominant especially in the plinth area of the high-rises for aesthetic reasons.

These two aspects can result in problems for the structural design of the high-rise with regard to dynamic loads. Figure 8.10 illustrates favorable and unfavorable elevations. Another important consideration is that the foundations, especially of high-rises erected on a small footprint, must be capable of preventing the entire structure from tilting.

Material Selection

The load-bearing structure is generally designed as a
– reinforced concrete,
– steel, or
– composite steel construction.

The choice of one system over another is generally a reflection of traditional preferences (e.g. steel construction in the United States and reinforced concrete construction in Germany), and also depends on other construction principles such as fire protection requirements.

Selection of materials is also an important factor in the design and construction of the load-bearing structure. Extensive scientific research has been conducted especially in the area of reinforced concrete construction with the aim of developing safe and economic construction [15,16,17]. This research has resulted in the development of the capacity method, which ensures a load-bearing structure that is capable of calibrated plastic deformation and of dissipating energy in the process without failing.

The capacity method is a tool that allows the engineer to influence the non-linear behavior of the load-bearing structure by defining the zones of energy dissipation and hence the plastic deformation and to design the structure accordingly. When applied to frame systems, for example, an essential goal of the capacity method is to avoid plastic articulations in the columns. This can be achieved by incorporating concrete joints in the beams and stirrups in the columns. Similar principles apply to the design of load-bearing walls, where shear failure must be avoided at all cost. This can be achieved through carefully incorporated plastic articulations in the base area of the wall.

The capacity method has also been incorporated into the new standards for earthquake safety for reinforced concrete, steel and composite steel construction.

Reinforcing Systems

Depending on construction method, three different reinforcing systems are employed for high-rises:
– Load-bearing walls
– Frame systems
– Trusses

Whereas the first two reinforcing systems are preferred for reinforced concrete construction, steel and composite steel constructions are realized with systems two and three.
It is rare – and this is true for all construction, including high-rise construction – for only one

reinforcing system to be employed. Generally, the systems are used in combination both in plan and in elevation. This creates interactions between the reinforcing systems, which must be taken into consideration in the structural and dynamic analysis.

Because of the imperative to avoid plastic hinges in the columns, it is very dangerous to alternate load-bearing walls with column-supported floors in the lower half of a high-rise. These "soft stories" are nevertheless popular on the ground floor of high-rises for aesthetic reasons. The tremendous shear forces, which are transferred from the load-bearing wall to the columns below, would lead to two plastic hinges at the head and foot of the column and thus form a kinetic chain. This story would collapse in an earth-quake, but the rest of the load-bearing struc-ture reinforced with load-bearing walls can remain undamaged.

Floors play an important role in the reinforc-ing system, because all other reinforcing systems are "activated" solely by the shear effect they produce and this alone makes it possible to transfer the horizontal loads to the reinforcing systems.

It is also important to prevent building com-ponents that are designed for infilling and non load-bearing functions alone, such as brickwork infills of frame systems or light-weight partitions, from being inadvertently involved in transferring horizontal loads. This can lead to dangerous load shifts between the reinforcing systems, which, in the worst-case scenario, can lead to a failure of the entire structure. Non load-bearing building compo-nents must therefore always be separated from the actual reinforcing systems by suffi-ciently large joints.

In this context it is worth mentioning façade constructions of high-rises characterized by large glazed surfaces with great rigidity com-bined with a relatively little strength. These façades, generally designed with floor-high components, are also characterized by a negli-gibly small proportion of joints so that defor-mations on a more significant scale can usually not be absorbed.

Table 8.11 Proposals for assigning the measures to specified goals

	G1	G2	G3
M1	+	+	+
M2	+	–	–
M3	+	–	+
M4	+	–	+

+: Measure suitable for achieving goal

–: Measure not very helpful

8.4 Dynamic Design of High-rises

General Design Principles

The following scenarios and critical conditions should be identified using the relevant tests and analyses with regard to the dynamic design of a high-rise. A variety of measures should then be implemented depending on the influencing forces and the situation to achieve specific design goals (G):

G1
Stability in case of earthquake, wind, etc.
G2
Protection of persons/equipment in building from surface effects (traffic, etc.)
G3
Protection of persons/equipment in building from direct effects on building (earthquake, wind, etc.)

Possible measures (M) include:
M1
"Detuning" of building to prevent resonance phenomena
M2
Strengthening the building to increase resistivity
M3
Employing additional passive elements to influence oscillation
M4
Employing active elements to influence oscillation

Table 8.11 gives suggestions on how to match goals and measures.

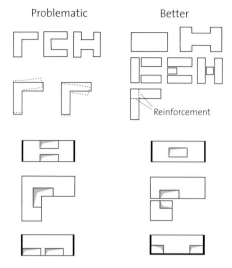

8.9 Plan design taking reinforcement systems into account[16]

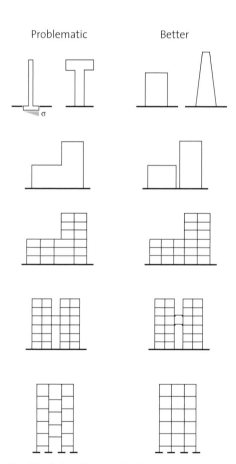

8.10 Plan design of a tower structure taking dynamic loads into account [16]

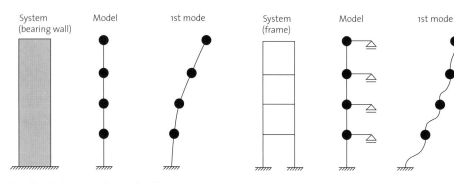

8.13 Models demonstrating earthquakes

Stability

Earthquake Design

The safety of the load-bearing structures must be demonstrated for the different dynamic influences. A lower event probability, e.g. of earthquakes, can be taken into consideration. Relevant regulations have been implement around the world and have proved effective even in strong earthquakes, e.g. Kobe 1995.
Three different types of earthquakes are differentiated for load-bearing structure calculations:

Safety quake: an earthquake with an intensity of IX or X according to MSK
Operating quake: an earthquake with an intensity of VI to VIII according to MSK
Marginal damage quake: an earthquake with an intensity of less than VI according to MSK.

According to this definition, strong earthquakes are those that are statistically described as operating quakes. They recur at intervals of 50 to 150 years, and occur

Earthquake spectrum
↓
Building classification
↓
Regional categorization
↓
Measurement
↓
Structural requirements

8.12 Measurement procedure

statistically roughly once during the lifecycle of a building. By contrast, marginal damage quakes recur at intervals ranging from 10 to 50 years and can occur several times over the course of a building's lifecycle.

The elastic response spectrum of a real-life earthquake is shown in **Fig. 8.5**. If calculations were based on this response spectrum alone, they would only ensure that the load-bearing structure could withstand a comparable earthquake. But each earthquake is different. For this reason, design spectrums were introduced, which represent an envelope of all actual response spectrums. These design spectrums form a plateau at their peak value, which "truncates" the acceleration peaks of the actual response spectrums. This takes the ability of a building to dissipate energy through plastic deformations into account, provided they have been structurally planned in accordance with the standard (see also capacity method).

Most standards wordwide employ the same model for high-rise design calculations (Fig. 8.12).

Dynamic calculations are required for buildings not covered by the classifications in the regulations and which cannot be designed based on a simplified response spectrum method with one or more modes. This applies unequivocally to all high-rises. However, certain factors must be taken into consideration:

The design spectrums of the standard calculations take earthquakes with different variations over time into consideration, whereas the dynamic calculation of a load-bearing framework is executed only for a specific variation over time. It is important, therefore, to ensure that the design spectrum is sufficiently broad, i.e. based on a sufficient number of generated variations over time. Determining a synthetic time-averaged variation curve on the basis of a design spectrum gives unrealistically high energy contents because the envelope of different earthquake events is only transferred in one variation over time during the spectrum determination. Although there is no single solution for this problem, the simplest approach is to investigate several partial response spectrums.

To determine the structural equivalent loads, a model of the building must be created to allow a reliable estimate of the modes. By observing the requirements for the simplicity and symmetry of the load-bearing structure, dynamic analysis can be carried out separately for each direction on the two-dimensional model of the load-bearing structure.
Figure 8.13 depicts simplified models for a load-bearing wall and a frame system visualizing horizontal dynamic loads.
A spatial (or three-dimensional) analysis is required in cases where the simplicity model cannot be applied.

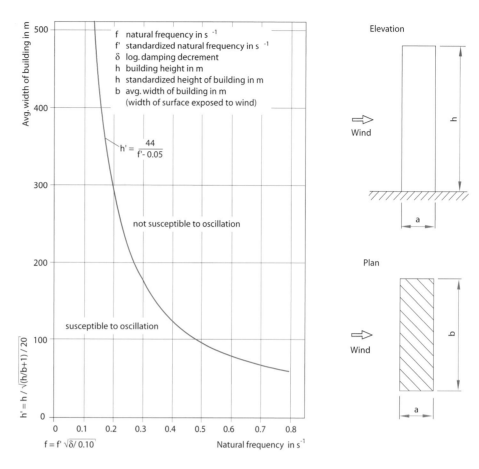

8.15 Mandatory dynamic observations according to DIN 1055 Part 4

Wind Design

Methods based on structural equivalent loads are also commonly employed in designing for wind loads. The first step is a simple determination whether more extensive calculations of dynamic wind effects are required (Fig. 8.15). Involved analyses are necessary for high-rises and an evaluation and calculation taking the dynamic behavior of the structure and its effects into account is therefore required. The calculation models described above can be employed. Specific structural analysis generally requires in-depth knowledge of the influence of wind, which can be studied, for example, in wind tunnel experiments.

Comfort

Comfort of the occupants plays a very important role in tall buildings in particular. Wind and traffic can both be experienced as unpleasant and even unhealthy. Conversely comfort considerations do not play a role for rare events such as earthquakes. Comfort is measured in dynamic quantities, which must take the frequency and type of activity as well as the location of the occupants into consideration.

Oscillation speed is often employed as an indicator because human perception of vibrations is proportional to the oscillation speed in a broad frequency spectrum. The recorded oscillation speeds are usually analyzed and organized into groups based on the "evaluated oscillation strength" according to frequency of occurrence and duration of vibration. These variables are extrapolated for

an evaluation period (in daytime: 16 hours, at night: 8 hours) and compared to limits.

8.5 Structural Design

General

As described in Section 8.4, the load-bearing structure can be detuned to adapt the dynamic properties of a high-rise to the dynamic forces to which it is exposed. "Detuning" is the deliberate modification of the relevant building modes (eigenfrequencies). This detuning (measure M1) is achieved through changes to the reinforcing system or changes in mass. Based on a particular stimulus, characterized

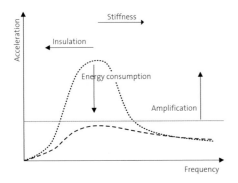

8.16 Detuning a load-bearing structure by deliberately modifying the relevant inherent frequencies of the building

8.17 Insulating the building with spring-damper systems [11] to change its inherent frequency

by a dominant frequency range, the detuning can be achieved through mode amplification (additional rigidity) or damping (Fig. 8.16). It should be noted that mode amplification through installation of additional bracing (rigidity) usually goes hand in hand with a reinforcement of the individual load-bearing members (measure M2). However, this has implications for the load distribution within the load-bearing system and is not necessarily desirable with regard to the capacity for which the load-bearing structure is designed. Building damping is therefore preferable to additional bracing for implementing measure M1.

Building Damping

One extreme example of mode modification is the installation of soft layers, which greatly dampen the oscillations of the building. Damping measures can be employed for the entire building or for selected building components. Spring-damper systems as well as special elastic intermediate layers are used for this purpose (Fig. 8.17).

Reinforcing the Building

Although this measure is aimed directly at resistivity, it also translates into a change in rigidity in practice in most cases. For example, if a steel section with a higher moment of resistance is used, this is generally accompanied by a higher moment of inertia, which increases rigidity and hence the mode of the load-bearing structure.

Using Additional Passive Elements to Influence Oscillation

In this context passive elements are systems that operate without external energy or controls. These primarily include absorbers and damper systems. Damper systems are characterized by the addition of oscillatory systems, which are capable of modulating the oscillation behavior of the building in the relevant frequency range (Fig. 8.18). It should be noted, however, that these systems only operate in relatively small frequency ranges.

The liquid-filled damper [12, 18] is a variation of the standard damper system (see Figs. 8.19 and 8.20). The effect of this damper is achieved by defining a water volume in a manner to ensure that it "sloshes" in the opposite direction to the oscillation of the building in response to an influencing factor (e.g. wind), thereby calming and stabilizing the building. Liquid-filled dampers for high-rises typically hold large volumes of water (several cubic meters) in multiple-layer, stacked tanks that occupy a relatively large

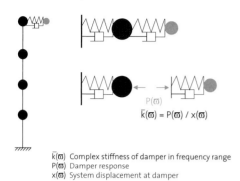

$\overline{k}(\overline{\omega})$ Complex stiffness of damper in frequency range
$P(\overline{\omega})$ Damper response
$x(\overline{\omega})$ System displacement at damper

8.18 Use and mode of functioning of the damper

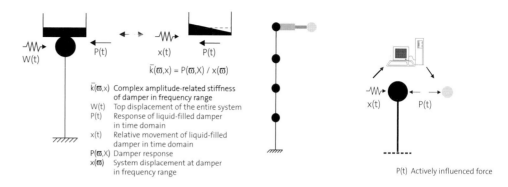

$\overline{k}(\overline{\omega},x)$ Complex amplitude-related stiffness of damper in frequency range
$W(t)$ Top displacement of the entire system
$P(t)$ Response of liquid-filled damper in time domain
$x(t)$ Relative movement of liquid-filled damper in time domain
$P(\overline{\omega},X)$ Damper response
$x(\overline{\omega})$ System displacement at damper in frequency range

8.19 Liquid-filled damper

$P(t)$ Actively influenced force

8.20 Active control of building oscillations

floor area. However, by comparison to standard dampers they offer the considerable advantage of adapting with great precision to the changing building parameters by modifying the water volumes.

Using Active Elements to Influence Oscillation

Contrary to passive elements, the function of active elements is dependent on more or less complicated control cycles. The basic principle is to analyze the behavior on an ongoing basis in order to initiate targeted countermeasures (Fig. 8.20).

In practice, active building control has generally been evaluated as negative with regard to reliability, and the use of such systems has been rejected. However, if one takes the evolution of such systems in other areas into consideration (e.g. car manufacture), these reservations need no longer apply to modern, redundant systems. Rather, these solutions should be realized gradually at first, especially with regard to meeting specific comfort criteria and, once this has been achieved, also with regard to delivering new, efficient solutions for safety requirements.

8.6   Summary

We have described the influences (earthquake, wind, and vibrations) pertaining to the dynamic design of high-rises.
Fundamental design principles such as the symmetry and simplicity of the ground plan must be employed for structures exposed to dynamic stresses, since non-compliance leads to consequences that can no longer be controlled with engineering measures.

In addition to stability, comfort plays a key role in high-rises, because the slenderness of the structures can result in considerable deformation and, when resonance with the stimulus exists, tremendous oscillation speeds. We have presented possible solutions in the form of building shock absorption or the use of dampers. In the future, comfort will play an ever more important role in the design of high-rises, especially if they are once again used for residential purposes, a trend that has already emerged in metropolitan settings.

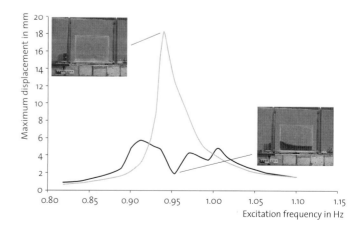

8.21 **Effect of liquid-filled damper exposed to harmonious excitation**
during experimental set-up phase

09 Effects of Wind

Hans Joachim Gerhardt

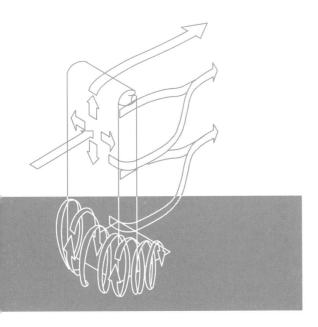

9.1 Introduction

Wind has positive and negative properties, many of which are subjectively evaluated. For the structural engineer of a high-rise, wind effect is a negative factor that inflates construction costs. For the urban planner, wind has positive effects as a result of carrying off contaminants and negative effects by diminishing the comfort of pedestrians. Fire protection experts have only recently fully accepted and understood the impact of wind on guaranteed smoke extraction in case of fire in high-rises. To wind engineers, who study the effect of wind on, inside and near high-rises, wind is a fascinating phenomenon.

Wind technology, the field of wind engineers, is a comparatively young science. It combines meteorology, aerodynamics, structural dynamics and – wind-induced spread of contaminants – chemistry. During the planning and design phase of high-rises and large building complexes, wind-related questions arise in relation to the areas shown in **Figure 9.1**. The answers or solution concepts presented by wind engineers are almost exclusively based on wind tunnel experiments. Even the most advanced CFD (Computational Fluid Dynamics) process cannot calculate the wind-induced flow field near complex building geometries and/or in urban environments with the necessary precision.

The goal of every wind-technological investigation should be to reduce the costs of the planned building. This can generally be combined with lowering the planning risk as well. The conditions for an optimum (i.e. cost-minimized) building with maximum planning reliability can only be achieved if all relevant wind factors are taken into consideration at the earliest possible stage. This chapter explains the influence of wind on high-rises and their surroundings, with a focus on wind loads, smoke extraction, wind-induced noise, wind fields near the ground, and urban ventilation. Knowledge of the wind field near the ground is the prerequisite for establishing an immission prognosis, e.g. with regard to traffic emissions. The changes in the immission field

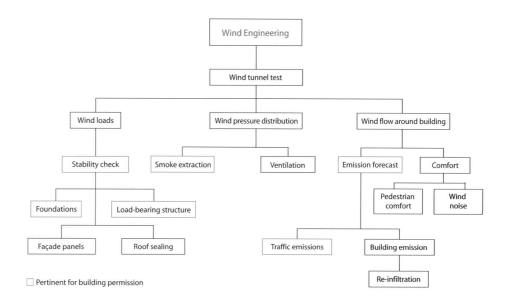

9.1 Schematic presentation of areas covered by wind engineering

and urban ventilation are an important element in environmental compatibility studies, which may be a mandatory requirement of the municipal authorities for permission for high-rise projects.

9.2 Wind Field – Wind Pressure Distribution

The wind-induced flow field, and hence the wind pressure field on a building, is determined by its displacement effect. It is dependent on the size and shape of the building. **Figure 9.2** is a schematic of the flow field for a disk-shaped high-rise, where the approach flow field runs parallel or perpendicular to the principal axis, and for a tower. The overpressure on the leeside facing the wind is the result of dynamic air pressure. The pressure field in this area is barely influenced by the relative building dimensions. The recirculation and the negative pressure caused by it on the leeside subjected to the suction, on the other hand, is considerably influenced by the displacement effect of the high-rise. A strong displacement (disk-shaped high-rise with lateral approach flow field) results in a pronounced and extended recirculation with strong negative pressure, whereas the wake closes off rapidly downstream from disk-shaped high-rises with parallel approach flow fields (low negative pressure).

The wind field near the ground has a considerable effect on both the comfort at the site and the spread of pollutants, e.g. as a result of traffic emissions. While comfort in public areas, e.g. in street cafés and resting zones, requires low air velocities, a high mix of air and pollutants, i.e. a high degree of dilution, is generally the result of high flow velocities. These opposing influences must be taken into consideration when designing open areas near high-rises, and the use of outside zones must be planned in accordance with local wind conditions. Thus, the areas on the ground near the building's corners are critical with regard to comfort, because the displacement effect of the wind can lead to stable eddies with high local velocities (**Fig 9.2 a–c**). Owing to the rather two-dimensional flow around tower-like high-rises, the flow wake in the lee tapers off after a fairly short distance. Downstream from the recirculation, wind effects caused by the high-rise in the flow field are more or less negligible. High-rise development on a fairly loose grid has little impact on the wind field in urban areas that are only several 100 m distant from the high-rises.

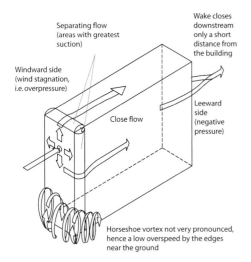

Separating flow (areas with greatest suction)

Windward side (wind stagnation, i.e. overpressure)

Wake closes downstream only a short distance from the building

Close flow

Leeward side (negative pressure)

Horseshoe vortex not very pronounced, hence a low overspeed by the edges near the ground

Great negative pressure on the leeward side due to considerable displacement of wind flow

Three-dimensional wake flow; wake closes only at a great distance from the building

Horseshoe vortex very pronounced, causing a high overspeed by the edges near the ground

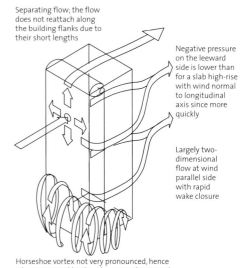

Separating flow; the flow does not reattach along the building flanks due to their short lengths

Negative pressure on the leeward side is lower than for a slab high-rise with wind normal to longitudinal axis since more quickly

Largely two-dimensional flow at wind parallel side with rapid wake closure

Horseshoe vortex not very pronounced, hence a low overspeed by the edges near the ground

9.2 a Slab high-rise, wind flow parallel to longitudinal axis (narrow windward side results in lower air displacement)

9.2 b Slab high-rise, wind flow normal to longitudinal axis (great width of windward side results in large air displacement).

9.2 c Tower

9.3   Determining the Wind Load

Wind Load Concepts

The wind loads of buildings are determined by the characteristics of the wind flow and the shape of the building. The form-dependent displacement effect produces a wind-induced pressure field, which is rendered with shape coefficients. The vortex separation at the building corners results in pressure fluctuations even during stationary flow. The form coefficients are therefore time dependent. The fluctuations in wind velocity as a result of turbulence and the corresponding dynamic wind pressures must also be taken into consideration. The time-dependent wind load (= wind pressure) w(t) is the product of multiplying these two time-dependent variables, that is, the dynamic wind pressure q and the pressure coefficient c_p:

$$w(t) = c_p(t) \times q(t). \qquad (1)$$

In order to determine the design load, i.e. the maximum wind load anticipated over the course of a given time span – usually 50 years – it is necessary to calculate the maximum anticipated product of two time-dependent variables. Several methods have been developed to undertake this calculation and the two most common are described here.

Quasi-static Method

The quasi-static wind load concept is applied, for example, to generate the wind load assumptions for the area of the Federal Republic of Germany, DIN 1055-4. According to this method the maximum anticipated wind load for the reference period is the product multiplying the average shape coefficient $\overline{c}_p$ over time with the maximum anticipated dynamic wind pressure q_b:

$$w = \overline{c}_p \times q_b \qquad (2)$$

The quasi-static method is based on the simplified premise that the pressure fluctuations on the building walls due to vortex separation or building-induced turbulence, respectively are negligible, and that the turbulent eddies of the atmospheric wind flow are fairly large relative to the building dimensions. Given these assumptions, a stationary flow field form around the building during the action of an eddy, and the changes in the pressure field can be correlated directly to the changes in the approach flow. This very simple load concept has proven effective for determining global loads and loads per floor.

Peak Factor Method

The quasi-static method should not be used when the time-averaged aerodynamic coefficients approach zero and/or when small partial areas of the building are analyzed. In the first case, the wind loads would be almost zero even though the turbulence of wind and the separation of vortices may lead to significant load fluctuations and hence considerable wind loads on the building. This is particularly true for urban environments, where the fluctuating load component is often the dominant factor in comparison to the time-averaged component. Secondly, the quasi-static wind load concept should not be employed for measurements on small building components, because the building-induced turbulence, which may lead to short-term, increased wind loads, is not factored into this calculation. Records taken in wind tunnels and in nature have shown that brief suction peaks can be twice as high as the average over time.

The peak factor method proposed by Davenport (1961) [1] takes the principal characteristics of atmospheric wind (e.g. turbulence) into consideration. The changes in the pressure field of the building over time are fully represented by the coefficient, the so-called peak pressure coefficient $\hat{c}_p$ or peak pressure coefficient for suction $\check{c}_p$:

$$w = \check{c}_{\hat{p}} \frac{\rho}{2} u^2_{10min}$$ (3)

$$= (\overline{c}_p \pm k \times c_{pRMS}) \frac{\rho}{2} u^2_{10min}$$

where k = peak factor, c_{pRMS} = coefficient of pressure fluctuations and u_{10min} = 10-minute value of design wind velocity = basic wind velocity. Data on the basic wind velocity are contained in the draft of the European Wind-Load Standard ENV 1991-2-4 and in draft E DIN 1055-4 (March 2001). The standard deviation of the pressure fluctuations as a basis for determining c_{pRMS} can easily be established with standard methods of measuring pressure. The peak factor is established through a statistical analysis of pressure/time curves. This requires pressure measuring technology with high resolution, which is generally available in wind tunnel facilities for building aerodynamics.

The peak factor is primarily dependent on the time of exposure to influence t (= mean time interval) and thus on the characteristic length L of the building component under observation.
According to Lawson (1980) [5], this relationship is expressed as:

$$t = \frac{4.5 \times L}{u_{10min}}$$ (4)

The equation (4) determines the characteristic mean interval dependent on the building component. The pressure/time curves measured in the wind tunnel experiment can be analyzed for different surfaces – façade panels, load-bearing structure components, floors, etc. The result yields minimized design wind loads in accordance with influence area, whereby the surface loads decrease as the influence area increases. By comparison to the wind load definitions according to DIN 1055-5, this approach generally achieves a clear reduction of design wind loads, especially in terms of global wind loads, and hence a reduction of construction costs, a topic that is explained in more detail in section 4.

Dynamic Wind Load Effect, Dynamic Wind Loads

For slender buildings such as high-rise towers, dynamic wind loads resulting from resonance effects may need to be taken into consideration in addition to quasi-static wind loads in order to determine the design wind loads. According to the German DIN standard 1055-4, a building is rated as susceptible to oscillation if the total deformations based on the dynamic wind effect exceed the relevant deformations caused by static or quasi-statically estimated wind loads based on the design wind by more than 10 percent.

Depending on the excitation mechanism, we speak of forced or constrained oscillation versus self-induced oscillation. Oscillation can be forced as the result of the gustiness of wind, the turbulence in the wake of a building upstream (buffeting), and periodic vortex shedding on the building under investigation (Karman vortex street). Galloping oscillations are the most important manifestation of self-induced oscillation.
Tower-like high-rises are generally only tested for gust induced oscillations. Spectral analysis methods are ideally suited for this assessment. The spectrum of fluctuating wind pressure or wind suction on the building walls is given as the input variable. Taking the mechanical transfer function into consideration, the resonance factor is then calculated to provide a basis for estimating the susceptibility of the building to oscillation caused by gusts. The resonance factor R describes the factor by which the quasi-static loads must be multiplied to calculate the static equivalent loads, which contain the dynamic loads induced by oscillations caused by the gust action.

Wind Load Fluctuations – Fatigue Problem

Fatigue problems as a result of dynamic wind loads are not contained in DIN 1055-4. Pressure fluctuations caused by the gustiness of atmospheric wind and caused by vortex separation at the building corners expose, for example, the fastening components of loosely fitted, mechanically fastened roof sealing or the point-fasteners of façade systems, to

alternating loads. The design load for such fastening systems must take these wind load fluctuations into account to prevent damage as a result of fatigue. This is specified in ETAG 006 for mechanically fastened, loosely layed roof sealing. Details were published in 1991 by Gerhardt and Jung [3]. Currently, no analogous test methods exist for façade systems.

9.4 Surface Flow Field – Pollution Spread and Wind Comfort

Wind is a random event (= stochastic variable). Hence, quantitative statements on the effect of wind events can only be made in consideration of the statistic characteristics of wind. Thus comfort in inner city oases or the entrance areas of high-rises is assessed on the basis of how frequently the wind threshhold velocity is exceeded based on statistical probability. Wind comfort is defined not only by the time-averaged wind velocity $\overline{U}$, but also by fluctuations in wind velocity, that is the gustiness of wind. Gustiness is quantified through the standard deviation from the velocity fluctuations. Wind comfort is assessed with the formula for the reference velocity $U_B = \overline{U} + \sigma$. When determining the upper limits of the velocity U_B it is useful to differentiate between the mechanical and the thermal effect of wind on humans. The standard threshhold velocity for quantifying mechanical comfort is generally given as

$$U_{B,mech,bound} = \overline{U} + \sigma = 6 \text{ m/s}$$ (5)

Effects that are perceived as uncomfortable, e.g. stirring up of dust, sensation of pressure on sensitive areas of the body, and eye irritation, begin to set in when this value is exceeded. According to Gandemer and Guyot (1981)[2], this threshhold velocity should not be exceeded, e.g. near building entrances and sidewalks or pedestrian paths, with any frequency greater than 10 percent per year. A 5 percent frequency of higher values is tolerated for urban oases, e.g. parks and planted areas, shopping boulevards. In sidewalk cafés, public (outdoor) pools and other areas, where wind comfort is especially important, the frequency of higher values should not exceed 1 or 2 percent.

When assessing wind safety for pedestrians, wind velocity fluctuations play an important role. This is taken into consideration in the reference velocity through a weighting factor of the deviation from the standard. The following threshhold velocity is based on pedestrian polls in windy areas of Melbourne (1978)[6]:

$$U_{S,bound} = \overline{U} + 3,5 \times \sigma = 23 \text{ m/s} \qquad (6)$$

To determine the frequency with which the threshhold comfort and safety velocities respectively are exceeded, the local wind velocities near the ground must be correlated to the long-term wind statistics of a nearby weather station. Weather stations are generally located in fairly undeveloped sites with little or low-growing vegetation. When relating the wind velocities recorded at the weather station to the urban environment

under investigation, the differences in wind velocity and wind velocity fluctuations must be taken into consideration. The conversion process is illustrated in **Figure 9.3**. The first step is to convert the change of the wind data recorded at the weather station to the wind profile of the urban site and, more specifically, for the height of 2 m above ground, which is relevant for pedestrian comfort. The second step is to assess the influence of the built environment on local wind velocities by means of the velocity factor ψ_∞. Taking this calculation into consideration, assessments can then state the velocity at the weather station, which give the threshhold velocity at the observed location.

Despite increased traffic in inner cities, the immissions loads from traffic emissions have decreased in recent years. This is largely due to improvements in engine technology: imission

loads usually fall below even the more rigorous immission requirements. Immission forecasts for several German cities, for which the wind-induced spread of traffic emissions was tested in wind tunnel experiments, yielded the following result: the relevant test or boundary values are neither reached nor exceeded for the annual averages or the more critical short-term immission values, the 98-percentile values.

9.5 Test Methods

Wind Tunnels

Defining the wind pressure distribution on buildings in boundary layer wind tunnels has become the national and international standard. The atmospheric wind flow is a turbulent boundary layer, which can be expressed through the increase of the velocity with height (velocity profile) and through turbulence (turbulence intensity profile and spectral distribution of velocity energy). **Figure 9.4** depicts a typical boundary layer wind tunnel (measuring width 2.8 m and measuring height 1.6 m). Counihan turbulence generators are placed at the start of the fetch upstream from the test section and the roughness is added to the wind tunnel floor, which can be changed according to the wind boundary layer profile to be simulated. The typical model scales for this wind tunnel range between 1:150 and 1:500.

Wind-induced noise can only be studied in aero-acoustic wind tunnels. They are generally equipped with an open test section and a closed return path (Göttinger wind tunnel). The I.F.I. aero-acoustic wind tunnel has a throat measuring 0.82 m x 0.4 m and a low-reflecting test chamber. The test object is subjected to an extremely silent wind flow and the resulting flow noises are recorded and analyzed. The swiveling nozzle is a unique feature of the I.F.I. aero-acoustic wind tunnel (Fig. 9.5). It makes it possible to simulate fluctuations in wind direction, which may lead to shifting separation lines in the flow around building components. The pressure fluctuations caused by these shifts are one cause for wind-induced noise.

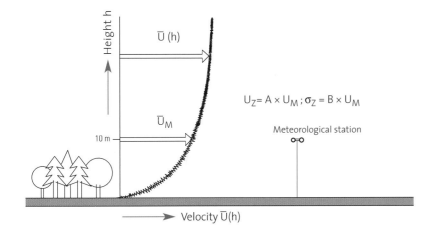

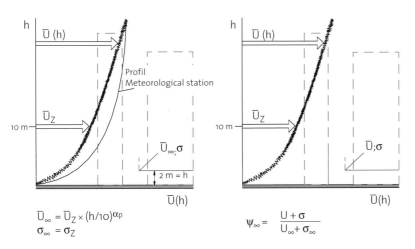

9.3 Comparison of local urban wind field with that at a nearby meteorological station

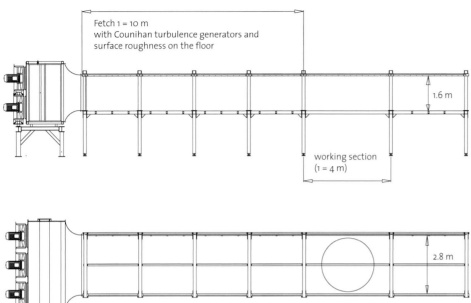

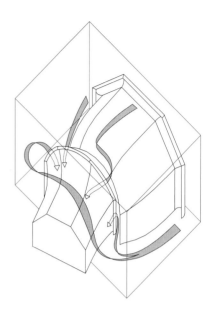

9.4 I.F.I. boundary layer wind tunnel: section (above) and plan (below)

9.5 Swiveling nozzles at the I.F.I. aero-acoustic wind tunnel
(I.F.I.) – Institute for Industrial Aerodynamics, Aachen

Similitude

The results of aerodynamic model experiments for buildings and building complexes can be transferred to the full scale if the flow fields of the model are similar to those in real life. A variety of similitude laws must be observed for the flow near buildings, e.g. calculating the design wind loads, and the flow through buildings, e.g. testing smoke extraction in case of fire. In analyses of the flow near buildings (external aerodynamics) the flow fields of the model and in real life are similar if both the oncoming flow conditions and the flow displacement are similar. The similitude of oncoming flow conditions can be ensured in boundary layer wind tunnels without difficulty. The flow field around sharp-edged buildings is primarily defined by the flow separation along the edges of the building. Aerodynamic similitude must be given even form model-scales of up to 1:800. For bluff round body shapes, e.g. cylindrical or spherical building shapes or buildings with rounded edges, the similitude of the flow field of the model and in real life assumes that the flow separation occurs along equivalent lines. This is given if the Reynolds number is identical for

model and full-scale building. The Reynolds number indicates the ratio of inertial forces to friction forces and is expressed as:

$$Re = \frac{u \times d}{v} \tag{7}$$

where u = characteristic velocity, d = characteristic length, e.g. cylinder or sphere diameter and n = kinematic viscosity = 15×10^{-6} m²/s for air under normal conditions.

Tests on cylindrical high-rises with standard model scales (M = 1:250 to 1:500) typically show that the Reynolds number of the model is smaller by a factor of 400 to 1,000 than the Reynolds number of the full-scale building. This means that aerodynamic similitude is no longer given. It can also not be achieved through manipulation of the boundary layer on the model surface. If the total wind load or the maximum suction load, e.g. on the glass panels, is based on the pressure distribution recorded on the model, the resulting design loads are overestimated by a factor of 2 or 1.4,

respectively. This results in unnecessary construction costs. In these cases, realistic wind load estimates can only be established with the help of section models on a larger scale (Mª 1:50).

The key similitude parameter for model tests of thermal by induced flows inside buildings – thermal-induced ventilation flows and smoke extraction – is the Archimedes number. It indicates the ratio of lifting force to inertia force, which acts on a fluid particle, and can be expressed as follows:

$$Ar = \frac{g \times \beta \times \Delta T \times L}{u^2} \tag{8}$$

where g = gravitational acceleration, β = expansion coefficient, ΔT = temperature difference (e.g. between smoke gases), L = characteristic length and u = velocity, e.g. in the plume above the fire. Typical model scales for smoke extraction range from 1:20 to 1:50. To simulate the temperature conditions of a real fire event (Müllejans, 1973) [7], it is best to simulate the smoke gases with a mix of air and helium (Gerhardt, 2000) [4].

9.6   Case Studies

Methods for

- determining the wind loads,
- carrying out a smoke extraction study,
- assessing wind-induced noise, and
- analyzing wind comfort

are demonstrated in four case studies.

Determining Design Wind Loads for the Sony Center, Berlin

The cross section of the 102 m Sony high-rise on Potsdamer Platz, Berlin, resembles a segment of a circle. The design loads for this high-rise were established in a wind tunnel experiment (model scale 1:500) in dependence on the impact area – from global loads to local loads on the façade panels. **Figure 9.6** shows the city model of Potsdamer Platz, Berlin, in the small I.F.I. boundary layer wind tunnel. The test section measurements are: length l = 2 m, width w = 1.78 m and height h = 0.75 m.

The wind pressures were measured at 228 pressure taps on the model of the Sony high-rise, the coefficients of the time-averaged pressures and the pressure fluctuations were recorded. With the help of the peak factor method, these test data were used to determine the design wind loads in dependence on the influence area. The result is shown in **Figure 11. 7**. While the panel loads are roughly 5.5 kN/m² in the critical façade areas, the loads per floor are w = 2 kN/m² and the foundation loads for wind are roughly 1 kN/m². The pronounced difference between floor and foundation loads is the result, on the one hand, of the difference in area and, on the other, of the negligible correlation between the wind loads on the windward and the lee sides. The area wind loads for the foundation and the glass panels, respectively, differ by a factor of 5.5. Optimized design of the construction, i.e. minimizing costs without compromising structural stability, can only be achieved by taking the size of the influence area into consideration, that is, only by means of employing the peak factor method.

Smoke Extraction Analysis for the Lobby of the Post Tower, Bonn

Deutsche Post AG is currently erecting a 160 m administration building in Bonn **(Fig. 9.10)**. The shape of the cross section is evident in the plan **(Fig. 9.8)**. Smoke extraction tests were carried out for the double-skin façade, for the skygardens (internal atria across nine stories) and for the lobby. The smoke extraction for the lobby is described here.

The fire-induced flow in the lobby is influenced by its shape, the principal load-bearing structure (indicated with hatched lines in **Figs. 9.8 and 9.9**) and the elevator shafts (dark markings).

The southeast section of the lobby rises to a height of roughly 15 m, while the northwest section is only roughly 10 m tall. The fire scenarios shown in **Figure 9.8** were tested for a heat emission of Q = 1 MW for an area of 4 m² and Q = 5 MW for an area of 8 m² with and without wind (wind from SE, SW, W and NW). The annual mean wind velocity of v_M = 3 m/s at an elevation of 10 m was chosen as reference velocity. Replacement air can flow into the lobby through low façade openings with

9.6 Urban model of Potsdamer Platz, Berlin, in the small I.F.I. boundary layer wind tunnel

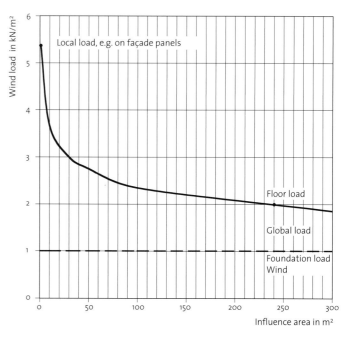

9.7 Design wind loads vs. influence area, Sony Center, Berlin; height 102 m

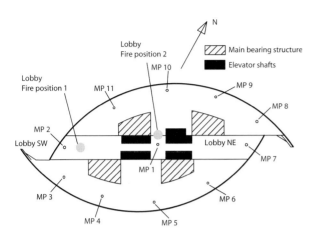

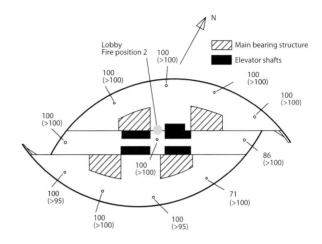

9.8 Post Tower, Bonn, plan, fire and pressure
taps in smoke extraction test

9.9 Post Tower, Bonn, dilution factors for a 1 MW (5 MW) fire

an effective aerodynamic area $A_w = 33.6$ m² and via mechanical ventilation ($V_h = 55,000$ m³/h with injected air velocity of $v_{in} < 0.1$ m/s).

Smoke is extracted via openings set into the upper area of the lobby façade (total effective opening area $A_{w,tot} = 92$ m²), which can be activated in dependence on wind direction.

The smoke gas flow above the fire plume was simulated with an air/helium mix (Gerhardt, 2000) [4]. Archimedes model similitude was maintained. By visualizing the smoke gases, the air movement in the room was optimized to achieve the best results for the replacement air and smoke extraction areas and the wind-dependent regulation of these areas.

A special oil vapor was added to the simulated fumes. Tracer gas was used instead of the oil vapor for quantification. Based on the local tracer gas concentration – taking the tracer gas concentration in the conflagration area into account – makes it possible to quantify the fume dilution and hence the smoke deficiency along the escape and rescue routes. The goal was to keep the escape and rescue routes smoke-free for a minimum period of 30 min. **Figure 9.9** indicates the dilution ratios at 5 m above floor level in the lobby for the critical fire data (fire scenario 2 and $q = 1$ MW) for the critical wind direction. The relatively high dilution ratios demonstrate that the escape and rescue routes remain open for more than 30 minutes given the physiological

effect of the fumes, and that sufficient visibility is ensured.

Assessment of Wind-induced Noise for the ECE Tower on Frankfurter Allee, Berlin

The planned 125 m high-rise has a cross-section in the shape of a ship's hull (**Fig. 9.14**). Horizontal façade sections – four per floor – are planned as a stylistic architectural element.

The sections consist of an aluminum extrusion-press girder, open at the center to avoid snow accumulations, for example. The external element is connected to the element facing the wall at the lateral joints.

The test in the I.F.I. aero-acoustic wind tunnel was carried out on single sections (with and without wall influence) and on sections in series on a scale of 1:1 and on a reduced scale of 1:2. Many different flow directions were simulated by placing the model at various positions in the I.F.I. aero-acoustic wind tunnel. One wind direction for unimpeded flow, i.e. without wall influence, was revealed as particularly critical (**Fig. 9.11**). It produced a noticeable sound, whose intensity (i.e. sound pressure level) increases roughly with the sixth power of the wind velocity, while its frequency remains virtually the same. The level increases up to 20 dB by comparison to the normal flow sound. This effect is influenced by

9.10 Post Tower Bonn, section of model

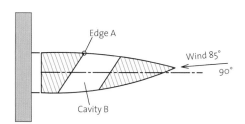

Edge A

Wind 85°

90°

Cavity B

9.11 ECE Tower, Berlin, section of the façade profile "critical flow direction" with unimpeded wind flow, i.e. excluding wall influence

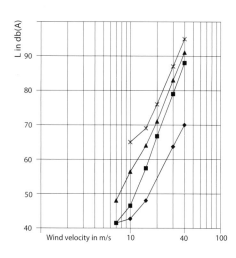

Scale 1:1
85° flow direction

◆ empty tunnel
■ with wall: edges sharp and rounded
▲ without wall, rounded
✕ without wall, sharp edges

9.12 Graph A-valued acoustic pressure level vs. wind velocity: four tested options

the sharp edges of the profile. A slight rounding off already reduced the sound level by roughly 8 dB for a wind velocity of 10 m/s. The A-valued sound pressure level in dependence on wind velocity is shown for several of the tested options in Figure 9.12.

The sound pressure level is greatly influenced by the distance between the wall and the profile. There is no noticeable sound when the gap is closed and all that remains is the broadband flow noise. The sound effect is produced as follows: after passing the windward element, the wind comes into contact with edge A (Fig. 9.11), where an edge tone results. This sound is amplified through the "coupled" cavity B, because the wind does not flow through the cavity itself from this direction and the cavity therefore acts as a resonator. A typical characteristic of this effect is that the frequency of the tone, which is principally defined by the resonator volume, does not change with the wind velocity. Wind from all other flow directions produces in a pressure difference between the upper and bottom sides of the profile; air flows through the cavity and it no longer acts as a resonator. The edge A is no longer exposed to the full brunt of the oncoming flow either.

If the profile is attached directly to the wall

without an interstitial space, the cavity resonator is still present but the stimulus mechanism through the edge is no longer given. Through redirecting the flow and the baffle effect of the wall, the air flow no longer impacts fully on the edge (Fig. 9.13), and no sound is produced.

Wind Field and Wind Comfort

The surface wind field in Frankfurt's banking district may change as a result of an increase in building density due to new high-rises.

By German standards, the banking district in Frankfurt is already marked by a high density of high-rise development. It will be increased by new and planned high-rises in the future. Tests were carried out to analyze the impact on the surface wind field and on the ventilation of nearby districts.

The surface wind velocity field can be visualized across an area using the sand erosion technique. Light-colored sand is strewn onto the black base plate of the wind tunnel model. The sand is blown away by the surface wind flow, if the local wind velocity is sufficiently high. For the tests, the velocity is incrementally increased in the wind tunnel. At each incremental increase, larger areas of the test surface are blown free of sand. The edge of

the cleared area corresponds to a line of constant gust velocity.

A single exposure is taken of the same photograph for each incremental velocity increase. The multiple exposures of the photographs reveal erosion areas in different colored shades. The zones where surface wind velocity is at its highest, that is, areas where the sand has already been blown away when exposed to the lower wind tunnel wind velocity, appear black in the photographs. The greater the erosion areas, the greater the anticipated wind velocities in those areas. Figures 9.15 a and b depict the surface wind field in the banking district in its current condition and after possible increases to the building density for the NE wind direction, which prevails in Frankfurt. The buildings of the existing environment are light, those of the added density are shaded dark. Changes in the surface wind field are only discernible in the immediate vicinity of the added high-rise models. Considerable increases in velocity may occur locally, especially in the pedestrian zone near the new high-rises, as a result of the displacement effect of wind from these buildings or the nozzle effect between the new buildings and the existing built environ-

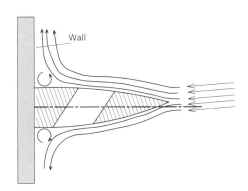

9.13 ECE Tower, Berlin, section of façade profile.
The façade is mounted on the wall without interstitial
space, i.e. with wall influence

9.14 ECE Tower, Berlin, architect: HPP, Dusseldorf with
SOM, Chicago

ment. The impact of altitude wind on the
street level, which is a key factor for great
surface wind velocities, can be diminished
using architectural measures, e.g. plinth
stories or high-rise shape. The necessary detail
optimizations are generally carried out by the
investors in the planning phase, in order to
ensure wind comfort in the entrance areas
and any planned quiet zones.

The effect of wind must be taken into consideration by the various planning departments
for high-rises, e.g. structural planning, fire protection and ventilation. These aspects must be
considered early on to ensure optimized planning and optimal solutions can only be developed through consultation between the
various experts, including the wind engineer.

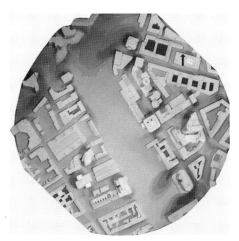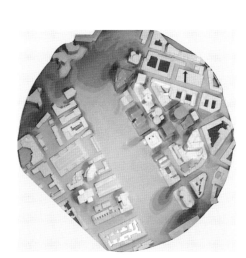

9.15 a, b Wind field close to ground, Bank District, Frankfurt.
Actual state (left) and possible subsequent increases in building density (right)

10 Façade structures

Sigurdur Gunnarsson

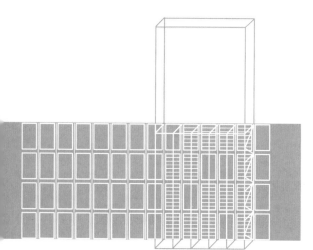

"Modern man, clothed in his modern not [his] historic dress needs [...] housing structures that are appropriate for his time [...] by means of rigorous consideration of modern production methods, structures and materials [...]"
Walther Gropius, Bauhaus Principle 1925 [1]

10.1 The Unique Properties of High-rise Façades

The structural elements of a high-rise façade are per se no different from those of the façade of a "conventional" house: Prefabricated post and beams, cables and tension rods, panes and panels made of glass, metal, stone, wood or plastics – assembled in monomaterial or composite fashion. The palette and variety of structural elements and the material spectrum are not limited by the height of a building. This "normalcy" of the high-rise façade is evident when the observation scale is changed (Fig. 10.1). Still, high-rise façades do possess some unique properties. For one thing, the façade structure must be designed for high wind loads, and for another its concept and design must compensate for the complex deformation response of the corresponding load-bearing structure.

The unique properties of high-rise façades are mainly the result of two factors:
– The height of the principal load-bearing structure, and
– the façade as a surface exposed to wind forces.

Height of Load-bearing Structure

The height of the load-bearing structure is directly linked to the intensity and distribution of the wind loads (see Chapter 9 by Gerhardt) and hence to the absolute deformations of the building. This means that the deformations of individual components, that is, the relative deformations, are greater and above all more complex as the height increases. It is worth noting here that only the height of the load-bearing structure is important, not that of the façade. In keeping with its space-enclosing function, the façade is nearly always divided into floor-high vertical sections. The greater the height of the façade section and hence, the greater the distance between façade attachment points to the load-bearing structure, the greater the joint size.

A force-locked configuration of the façade across the entire building height would result in tremendous vertical shift between load-bearing structure and façade. Due to the limited connection height of the floor system (doors, windows, ventilation elements, etc.) this is hardly conceivable.

Hence, the load-bearing structure of the building is tall, but that of the façade is short. Although separable into individual (short) components, the primary load-bearing structure of a high-rise forms a "long" entity in terms of load-bearing effect. This is not true for the façade of a high-rise. High-rises whose primary structure simultaneously forms the façade structure are the exception, for example, the former World Trade Center in New York with a vertical external support grid of roughly 1 m spacing (Fig. 10.2).

10.2 The load-bearing structure and façade construction merge at the World Trade Center, New York

The Façade as a Wind Surface

Aside from the aesthetic architectural imperative to divide and differentiate a high-rise façade in order to give the building form, the façade must also be divided into zones for the purpose of structural engineering. The principal reason lies in the strong variations in wind loads, depending on building form. Thus up to the middle of the building height, 40 percent of the wind acting on the building flows downwards and this wind energy that is "swept down" overlaps with the wind load still present at the base of the high-rise. Consequently, the local wind loads at the façade may be similar or greater at the entrance level of high-rises than at a height of 100 m. It is important to differentiate between the global wind load of the load-bearing structure – also referred to as structural wind – and the local wind load on the façade – the panel load. The structural load "rocks the boat" and the panel load "tears at the sails". The local turbulence load of a panel may reach 500 kg/m², while the global structural load is only 150 kg/m². The relationship between the dimension of the reference surface and the intensity of the wind load is illustrated in the article by Gerhardt (Chapter 9, Fig. 9.7). Both types of wind load are of importance for the façade structure. The structural load deforms the building and is the basis for designing the principal deformation joints of the façade structure. The peak panel loads and local distortion profiles must be taken into consideration for sizing the façade structure.

10.1 a–c Change in scale and perspective: the Victoria Tower, Mannheim, architects: Albert Speer & Partner

128

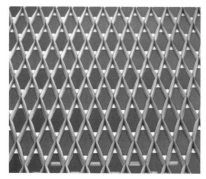

10.3 a, b Cladding – body, façade –
load-bearing structure

10.2 Interaction between Façade Structure and Primary Load-bearing Structure

The Building Skin as a Garment

As mentioned above, the scale of a high-rise has certain consequences for the construction of the façade, which require differentiated analysis. The first prerequisite for designing a high-rise façade is an understanding of the principal load-bearing structure of the high-rise. If one looks upon the load-bearing structure of a high-rise as a body, the components of the façade structure are the garment enclosing it (Fig. 10.3): the façade, generally composed of small components manufactured with machine precision, is draped across the rough fabric of the load-bearing structure, which is constructed with rough work tolerances. The interaction between façade and load-bearing structure is mutual, similar to the friction between body and garment. Thus the façade transfers the wind load to the load-bearing structure and the resulting deformations of the load-bearing structure must, in turn, be accommodated by the façade.

The relative deformations between "body" and "envelope" place varying degrees of stress on the façade structure and create axial, flexial and rotational deformations (Fig. 10.4). As a "precision product", the façade is characterized by a joint grid sized to the millimeter for tolerance compensation, whereas the skeleton structure operates on a scale of centimeters. The outcome is a convergence of two constructs with a large difference in tolerances as a direct result of construction methods. While the difference can be defined

as a design standard, it is difficult to fully determine it with great precision in reality because of the size of the load-bearing structure and the number of influencing factors. The ideal image of the plan can be balanced through measurements during the construction and assembly. In reality, however, those aspects, which can only be predicted to a limited degree, must be taken into consideration.

Relative Deformations between Load-bearing Structure and Envelope

Due to the enormous difference between the measurements of the façade structure and those of the load-bearing structure of a high-rise, the façade is always a structural sub-system. The space between the individual principal load-bearing members is the reference space of the façade. Consequently, the deformations must also be analyzed for different scales. The first step is to study the absolute deformations of the entire structure, which provide the basis for the structural and the dynamic analyses. The second step is to execute a detailed analysis of the relative deformations of the individual members of the load-bearing structure in relation to each other, the boundary condition statement of the façade's reference space. What is a secondary aspect in the load-bearing structure becomes the principal aspect for the façade structure: the relative deformations between load-bearing structure and envelope. The important factors for the façade structure are cause, type, direction and significance of the absolute and relative deformations. The impact of the interfaces between the

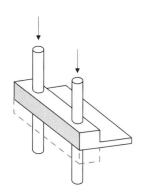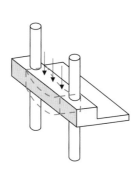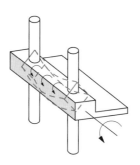

10.4 a–d Images of deformation (compressive strain, deflection, twisting); analogy with the human body

different work processes for load-bearing structure and façade and the conceptual harmonization of planning, manufacture and execution are also very important for the built result, i.e. the deformation of the completed building. The resulting deformations vary depending on these factors. An image of deformation results for each combination: this is the deformation profile. As mentioned above, the load structure has a far greater impact on the deformation behavior and the joint design for the façade structure than the façade structure itself. Whereas as many as six different deformation profiles are differentiated for the façade-related deformation of the load-bearing structure, the façade itself is only characterized by two deformation profiles.

Deformation Profiles of the Façade Structure

Two types of deformation must be analyzed: the deformation of an individual façade component (component deformation) and the deformation of a façade section (section deformation).

Component Deformation

The individual façade component expands horizontally and vertically in relation to the primary structure as a result of temperature changes, or is locally distorted from its plane as a result of wind forces (Fig. 10.5a).

Section Deformation

Section deformations typically occur between two building components, where a long

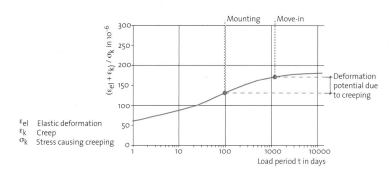

10.6 Creep deformation over time

façade section is suspended and laterally connected to floor-high façade components. The long façade section has only one vertical fixing point, whereas the "short" sections are attached at each floor. The long section must be able to slide along the short section – a vertical offset joint is required (Fig. 10.5 b).

Deformation Profiles of the Load-bearing Structure

The deformation profiles of the load-bearing structure that influence the relative deformations of the load-bearing structure and the envelope, can be categorized as follow, according to direction, duration and cause:

Material-related Overall and Local Deformation

Concrete and composite structures contract during and after construction as a result of material creep and shrinkage.
In addition to the material composition, the degree of this type of deformation is also dependent on the stress condition of the

structure and on local environmental conditions. From the perspective of façade construction, the changes to the form are important in terms of both the entire load-bearing structure and the local deformation of individual load-bearing members. The compression of the entire tower is an especially critical deformation profile for the façade, especially when the construction time is short. To speed up the construction, the façade is assembled on the lower floors even before the principal load-bearing structure is completed across the full height. This puts additional stress onto the lower stories – once the façade has been assembled – through the own weight and construction loads of the upper stories. The shorter the construction time, the more important the measurement and control of the evaluated deformations, which serve as the basis for the façade construction are. This is especially true for concrete construction, because the time-dependent deformation behavior of the entire fabric extends beyond the construction phase and occupation and is only completed after one to three years (Fig. 10.6). The time-dependent deformation of individual load-bearing members at the

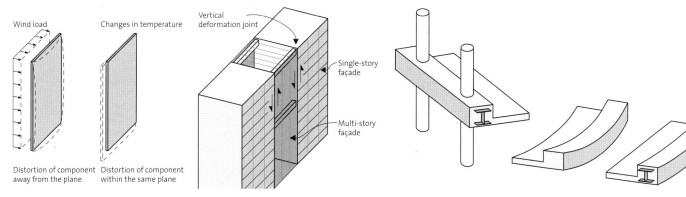

10.5 a, b Deformation of façade components and sections

10.7 a, b Local increase in stiffness – planned reduction in deformation

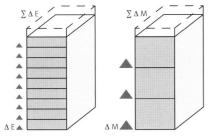

$\Sigma \Delta E$ $\Sigma \Delta M$

ΔE ΔM

Δ E Deformation of single-story façade
Δ M Deformation of multistory façade
$\sum \Delta E = \sum \Delta M$

10.8 Façades with short and long vertical divisions

10.9 a, b Load-bearing skeleton in the façade; the effects of weathering on the load-bearing structure while façade is being mounted, Deutsche Post AG, Bonn, architects: Murphy/Jahn, Chicago

joint with the façade structure is especially pronounced when subjected to deflection. As mentioned, deformations as a result of creep appear in part only after the façade has been attached and after completion. Adjustment is no longer possible once the occupants have moved into the buildings. The deformation joint of the façade structure has to either be (over)sized or the rigidity of the primary structure has to be increased (Fig. 10.6) at the joints to the façade in order to reduce the time-dependent deformations caused by deflection.

Total and Local Deformation as a Result of Live Loads

Deformations caused by the live loads, vertical overall compression and local horizontal deflection appear only after the façade construction and are temporary in nature. Since the proportion of the live loads rarely exceeds one third of the total weight, the potential for deformation is correspondingly low.

The resulting deformation is distributed vertically across the height of the structure (Fig. 10.8). Regardless of the vertical height division of a façade, the sum of the deformations, that is, the joint length remains the same. The deformations are easier to absorb in a façade with small or short-membered divisions, because the expansion of the load-bearing structure can be distributed across many short façade sections. When the façade sections are long, the live load stresses accumulate across several floors and the joint length are grouped together between the vertical fixing points of the façade to the load-bearing structure: many small joints or a few large joints.

Temperature Deformation of the Load-bearing Structure

Form changes in the load-bearing structure as a result of temperature fluctuations occur primarily during the construction phase, when the skeleton is still exposed to the elements (Fig. 10.9). Once the load-bearing structure

has been enveloped and the finishing work has been completed, internal temperatures are established and the fluctuations are less pronounced. The temperature-related deformation profiles of the load-bearing structure are relevant for the façade structure even after construction, if load-bearing structure and façade structure occupy the same plane (Fig. 10.10 a) or if the load-bearing structure is installed in front of the façade (Fig. 10.10 b).

Horizontal Wind Deformation of the Load-bearing Structure

The deformations of the load-bearing structure must be analyzed for wind loads across the entire area and for partial wind loads (Fig. 10.11). The more daring the element displacement is in relation to the primary structure (i.e. the horizontal reinforcement in the façade plane), the more detail and precision is required in plotting the relative deformations caused by partial loads.

Rotational Wind Deformation of the Load-bearing Structure

The rotation of the entire tower shaft or of individual building components towards or away from each other as a result of wind (Fig. 10.12) must be analyzed in this context. As with the horizontal displacement, the maximum total rotation of the tower does not necessarily affect the façade, because the relative movements of individual building components and hence individual façade sections can be greater for a partial load.

10.10 a a Load-bearing skeleton in the façade: John Hancock Building, Chicago

10.10 b Load-bearing skeleton outside the façade: ALCOA Building, San Francisco

Local Deformations at the Façade Junction

The deflection and rotation of individual edge beams/girders at the façade junctions (Fig. 10.4 b, c) as a result of permanent façade loads or temporary traffic loads from the connected floors, or from façade cleaning equipment, must be carefully considered in the planning, execution and assembly (Fig. 10.4 b, c) because the impact of these deformation profiles is difficult to rectify once the building is occupied.

Expansion Joints

As stated at the outset, the façade of a high-rise cannot form a stretchable skin that follows the external contour of the "long fabric". A continually elastic force-locked connection that is "welded" to the load-bearing structure and follows all movements, like a diver's suit, is not possible in high-rise construction. Instead, the different deformations of load-bearing structure and envelope are decoupled through the formation of expansion joints.

Expansion joints do not simply result, they must be planned with great precision. Joints are placed wherever movements are anticipated. The joint length in the façade structure are planned once the deformation behavior has been determined. Once again, it is important to consider that the maximum stress on the load-bearing structure does not necessarily lead to significant deformations in the façade area. In analogy to the human body: "Even if the skeleton is subjected to greater stress in an upright than in a seated position, the folds at the abdomen are larger when seated."

Joints in the façade structure may be vertical or horizontal. The relevant influence for horizontal joint distribution is the relative deformation between load-bearing structure and façade or between vertically separated façade sections (Fig. 10.12 a). It is generally experienced in the areas between the upper edge of the finished floor and the bottom edge of the ceiling. Vertical joints are required at points where there is a sudden increase in the load or rigidity of the primary load-bearing structure, for example the "rigid" girder, or where single-story or multi-story façades

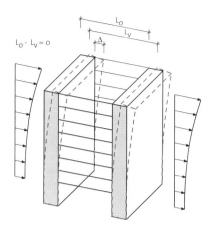

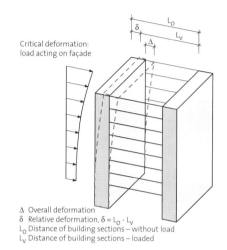

Δ Overall deformation
δ Relative deformation, $\delta = L_O - L_V$
L_O Distance of building sections – without load
L_V Distance of building sections – loaded

10.11 a Wind load on both sides:

high overall deformation – low relative deformation

10.11 b Wind load on one side:

low overall deformation – high relative deformation

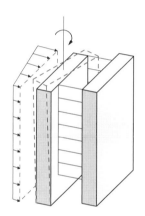

10.12 a Rotation of tower shaft

10.12 a–c Rotation of tower shaft – horizontal façade deformation between two halves of a building, Deutsche Post AG, Bonn

10.13 Measuring up locally prior to installation

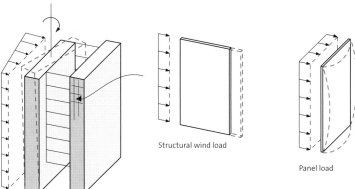

Structural wind load

Panel load

Deformation of structure/panel

10.14 Face: deformation away from a plane (panel load) and deformation within the same plane (structural wind load)

meet and a change in the height division occurs (Fig. 10.5 b).

At the transition areas between load-bearing structure and façade, that is, at the façade junction, special attention must be given to the deformation behavior or the relative deformation of the load-bearing structure. The strategy is either to minimize the deformations, for example, by carefully calculated localized increase of the rigidity of individual building components that are adjacent to the façade (Fig. 10.7), or to define clear deformation and rotation routes by means of a planned joint length that is consistent for both the load-bearing structure and the façade structure.

While the local wind peaks are relevant for the load-bearing capacity and the performance capability (deflection of individual façade element), global wind loads are the reference

parameter for the façade joint design. The performance capacity of the façade is ensured as follows:
– The deformation at the façade plane must be limited. The peak wind load (façade wind) is the determining design load.
– Absorption of the deformation at the façade level must be ensured. The global wind load (structural wind load) is the determining design load for this factor (Fig. 10.14).

The deformations of the primary load-bearing structure (rough work) must be determined with great precision for the design and especially during the execution. Due to the system-related height of a high-rise and efficiency with regard to construction time, the primary load-bearing structure and the façade are not erected in sequence, but to some degree in parallel processes. There is an overlap between the two processes and the half-finished tower

shaft is partially clad, yet only partially subjected to its own weight and compressed. Deviations between the computational absolute values of deformation and the actual deformations during the construction phase are unavoidable as a result of environmental influences, construction speed and deviations between the execution planning of the experts and the on-site planning of the executing firms. Only continual tracking of the deformation history during the execution makes it possible to correct the unavoidable differences between calculation and execution on the spot and for each story. The tolerances established for the rough work are thus prevented from being "dragged along" or even exceeded across all stories. Within the rough work tolerances, which the executing façade firm is given as contractual basis, the trades can operate in parallel without difficulty and coordinate the assembly processes down to the last detail (Fig. 10.15).

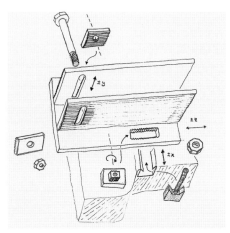

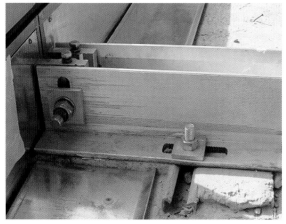

10.15 a–c Equalizing rough work tolerances in the façade – concept and execution

10.3 High-rise Façades as "One-of-a-Kind Products" in Series

The Necessity for Working in Series

The one-dimensionality of a high-rise and the size of the façade areas as a result of the height of the load-bearing structure have an impact on all phases of planning and constructing the façade. The combination of façade construction with the erection of the load-bearing structure cannot be realized without a high degree of prefabrication and in-series production. Vast amounts of façade components must be processed within a short period.

It is the task of the planning departement to identify the different requirements for the façade construction and to establish clearly defined performance profiles, such as
- functional requirements (ventilation, sound and wire tap proofing, etc.)
- influencing factors (increased local wind loads, stability at rest, fall arrest safety) and to seek out synergies for the construction to allow for prefabrication in series.
  This makes it possible to clearly identify and adapt differences and possible synergies between the trades even in the early planning stages. The same construction principle can then be applied to the 38th floor as to the 2nd floor.
  HVAC parameters have a great impact on the design of the façade and the definition of the individual components.

This elaborate effort for each individual planning is soon amortized in high-rise construction owing to the large scale and allows a "separate" series production for the façade. The advantages of series construction are optimized planning, production and assembly. Thus, the intervention of highly qualified planning and production experts decreases over the construction phase, and the error rate declines.

10.16 a Uniform façades – the Lake Shore Drive Apartments, Chicago,
architect: Mies van der Rohe, 1951

10.16 b A differentiated façade –
the GSW Tower, Berlin,
architects: Sauerbruch and Hutton, 1999

10.17 a Sequined dress

10.17 b Tower façade

Table 10.18 Standard values for various manufacturing methods taking stainless steel as an example

Type of processing	Piece No. Manufac- turing capacity	Degree of precision	Necessary finishing	Manufacturing time	Cost of tools
Machining	x	xxx	x	x	x
Extrusion pressing	xx	xx	xx	xx	xx
Casting	xx	x(x)	xx	xx	xxx
Rolling	xxxx	x(x)	xxx	xxxx	xxxxx

 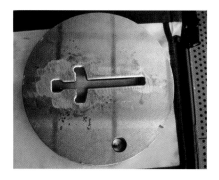  

10.19 a–d Stainless steel extruders: pressing, tool, production line, steel section

This is perhaps a fitting opportunity to respond to the criticism of series production as an undifferentiated tool used to erect monotonous symbols of power.

The greatest potential for façade design lies in the variety of requirements and possible solutions (Fig. 10.16). Series production does not *per se* lead to monotonous results; rather it makes it possible to realize the various functions with efficiency and precision. A sequined dress does not appear monotonous if there is harmony and an interesting tension between the pattern and the body (Fig. 10.17), even though the sequins, which are all identical, are mass-produced. The high-rise façade is a highly industrial product owing to the sheer scale of pieces and yet it remains a one-of-a-kind product, a mixture of Haute Couture and series production.

Collaboration between Client, Engineers/Planners and Contractors

In addition to the technical requirements for a high-rise façade, the collaboration between client, engineers/planners and executing firms remains one of the principal challenges in high-rise construction. The client is determined to create a unique symbol with high recognition value. At the same time, this goal must be achieved with a calculable effort. The executing firms, on the other hand, are able to realize various options in a cost-efficient manner only to a certain degree with their high-performance production lines and equipment and personnel costs.

The production costs are strongly affected by the volume to be produced. The universal rule of thumb is that the price decreases as the volume increases, because the development and tool costs can be amortized for a larger volume.

There are established approximate values for unit number or bandwidths in all industrial sectors, within which the production process is defined. Depending on the number of units, required precision and production period, decisions are made as to machining, casting, extrusion or rolling (Table 10.18).

The same is true for façade construction. There have been fewer and fewer firms in recent years capable of producing and assembling façade structures for high-rises, a fact that is no doubt linked to the continued crisis in the building trade.

The decision for a specific production process and a possible production time is dependent to a great degree on the material selection. Extrusion can be used as an example: A machine that extrudes up to 5 km can be used to produce an aluminum profile. For stainless steel, however, the tool (Fig. 10.19 b) must be overhauled after each extrusion process – that is, after roughly 10 m of production.

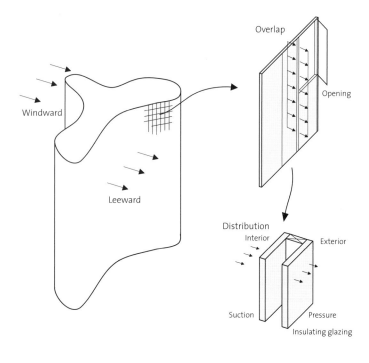

10.20 Wind load – overlap and distribution of the structural and panel wind load. As apertures account for a large share of the façade, the windward and leeward sides must be overlapped.
The hermetic coupling of the single panes in the insulating glazing distributes the overall wind load in accordance with the stiffness of the panes.

Planning Time

The façade is the highly symbolic mask of a high-rise, exuding perfection while being the most expensive part of the building fabric. Nevertheless, the planning schedules are increasingly tighter. Time, rather than money, is frequently the resource that imposes the most restraints. Planning that continues to follow the construction is increasingly criticized for good reason, because this practice is often associated with additional costs. The tender and contract processes held during the planning stage are the principal reason.

The investor tries to keep the investment time – the sum of planning time, tender, production and construction – to a minimum. However, the construction time of a high-rise can only be shortened to a limited degree. While the individual phases overlap, the different trades are always executed by different firms, even when there is a general contractor. There is not a single firm in the German market capable of planning, delivering and constructing both the primary load-bearing structure and the façade of a high-rise with its own personnel. This does not pose a problem in principle, as long as everyone involved understands the need for an overarching plan for the interfaces between the trades. However, the actual constellation of how each trade will be executed can only be determined once the contracts have been awarded and coordination throughout the construction of these interfaces between experts and executing firms is therefore unavoidable. This takes time, a fact that is often swept aside and which must be stated clearly from the outset.

10.4 Planning Criteria for High-rise Façade Structures

Loads

The effect of wind is the key factor for the façade structure of a high-rise. The wind loads, which are used as the basis for designing a high-rise façade, are fundamentally different from the wind loads, which are used to design the primary structure. An incremental analysis is required with regard to wind loads for the façade and for the structure. This

applies to both the intensity and the distribution of the wind load.

The differentiated design of a façade by comparison to the primary load-bearing structure plays an important role in this context. The design wind load is generally based on wind tunnel experiments and, if possible, on data provided by the German Weather Service. The phenomena of overlapping and distributed wind loads (Fig. 10.20) must be harmonized with great precision between the façade planning and the wind analysis. Thus overlaps of the wind loads caused by the structure, such as pressure on the windward side and suction (or negative pressure) as well as the distribution of the total wind load on the internal and the external pane of thermopane glazing, depending on the openings, are key factors for establishing a safe and economical guideline for wind impact.

Dividing the façade into wind load zones in accordance with the wind analysis also allows a differentiated handling of the panel loads.

The size of the façade areas, the effort required for production and the high costs associated with it, create a monetary and ecological incentive for optimizing the material strengths per zone (Fig. 10.21), although this is not necessarily evident in the architectural statement.

Other influences such as temperature changes, pedestrian loads and impact loads are no different for high-rise façades than for "normal" façades. Ice accumulation should be avoided because of the difficult access or elaborate melting systems e.g. by avoiding horizontal projections and small grate areas. The cleaning of high-rise façades and the equipment and loads associated with it must be considered separately. Since there are many different cleaning concepts and because this area is currently undergoing rapid changes, a building-specific coordination with the access engineer is required with regard to operation-related impact load and the pressure and tensile forces exerted by fastening system attached to the façade.

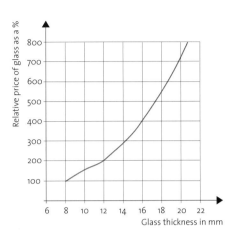

10.21 Price of glass in relation to its thickness

Material Requirements

Although the same materials are used for the construction of a high-rise façade as for a "normal" façade, the materials of the high-rise façade are nevertheless exposed to greater mechanical – weather- and maintenance-related – loads, while having to satisfy ambitious visual requirements. The use of high-performance materials therefore assumes a different economic and ecological relevance in the case of high-rise façades. Titanium, for example, is a possible choice because of its resistance to wear by friction and to weather. High-alloy special steel with high yield point, such as 1.4462 ferrite-austenite steel ($\alpha + \gamma$) is also an option for high-rise façades, despite the high material cost.

Due to the difficulty of access (height) and hence the limited possibility for visual inspection, special measures must be taken to prevent contact corrosion especially at junctions where several different materials converge. Careful planning of the material surfaces is a very important factor in terms of the effort required for maintenance (cleaning) and the visual appearance over time. Self-cleaning coatings – hydrophobic, hydrophilic and photocatalytic – on glass are one viable option. Fairly simple measures, e.g. planning the grinding orientation of metal surfaces, can also neutralize the costs for the self-cleaning process.

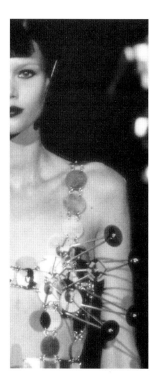

10.22 a, b Slenderness – the principle of suspension: "pinned costume" – façade tie

Structural Criteria

High-rise façade types can be differentiated according to the following structural criteria:
– standing/suspended
– location in relation to primary structure
– non load-bearing/load-bearing (as primary component).

In contrast to human clothing, the façade is observed from the inside and the outside. The scale of observation, however, is entirely different between inside and outside. On the outside the scale is roughly 1:100 (a 1.75 m tall person in front of a 200 m tower). The high-rise is awe-inspiring – one becomes aware of one's own smallness. Conversely, on the inside the scale is nearly 1:1. The familiar proportions no longer apply (Fig. 10.22).

Dimensioning

Façades must be divided into zones according to wind influence in order to achieve economy in the dimensioning and production. Possible failure scenarios must be discussed early on with the relevant authority and defined with the necessary approval. The yield at junctions and the compound effect of individual façade components are dependent to a great degree on the production. Since deformation, e.g. caused by the edging of thermopane glazing, is frequently the principal criterion for dimensioning, a small series of ten test components should be tested prior to production – particularly for façade components that are prone to deformation. This makes it possible to verify planning goals and to ensure that they are achieved.

These criteria (panel load/compound effect) must be established jointly by engineers, test engineers and building authorities prior to tendering and awarding contracts to establish a sound basis for planning and costs.

10.5 Potentials for High-rise Façades

The potentials for high-rise façade development are increasingly linked to material selections, production technology and adaptive construction processes.

Materials

Among the rapidly growing selection of materials, titanium and ceramics deserve special attention.
Titanium (high-tensile such as TiVa4Al for tensile elements, or low-tensile such as ASTM Grade 1 for panels) offers the following advantages:
– extreme weather resistance
– low weight
– very high stability
– a thermal expansion coefficient ($\sim 8 \times 10^{-6}$/K) that is almost identical to that of glass.

Titanium is therefore a viable building material, e.g. for the substructure in long façade sections. The goal must be to minimize the absolute and relative deformations between the glass layer and the substructure and the stresses associated with it.
Ceramics, e.g. in combination with borosilicate glass, will no doubt open up additional possibilities in coming years. The decisive properties of this material are minimal thermal expansion and the extreme temperature stability associated with it, which is especially advantageous for fire protection.

Production Processes

Among production processes, metal foams and nanocomposition should be noted in particular.

Panels of metal foams are produced in three stages. First, a small amount of propellant – approx. 0.5 percent of the weight – is mixed with metal powder. This mixture is then pressed into the desired form, which can also be three-dimensional. In the third step, the pressed form is heated, the propellant is activated and the metal "foams". The volume increase achieved by this method may be as

10.23 Details of the façade construction, Deutsche Post AG, Bonn, architects: Murphy/Jahn, Chicago

10.23 a Intersection – the shed-like form of the façade construction creates a horizontal and thus thermally more effective opening than is the case with vertical arrangement

10.23 b Eye plate – used on weather-protected parts of the façade to support it

10.23 c Tension rod – vertically linking the façade floor by floor. The slenderness of high-strength stainless steel is striking

high as a factor of five. The advantage of metal foams versus compound materials lies in the material purity and the grade-proof reprocessing associated with it. The corrosion risk is not increased by the greater internal surface of the pores, because all air inclusions are hermetically sealed. Metal foams are an extremely viable option for high-rise façades due to the enormous increase in rigidity (against high wind loads) by comparison to other materials.

Nanocomposites are composed of molecular particles, which are characterized by different mechanical, physical and optical properties when combined into functional layers. Glass panels with super-hydrophobic self-cleaning coating, which reduce the cleaning requirements of the façade, are already in use. Further potentials for the high-rise façade will no doubt be linked to the development of the physical properties of nanocomposites as façade coatings and the reduction of operating energy associated with it.

Structural Democracy

The more functions the high-rise façade assumes in its role as an active skin, the more relative and democratic is the load-bearing function of the structure. The structure is but one of many functions in a whole, and forms a scaffold that is increasingly restrained in appearance. Despite this restraint, the high-rise façade cannot help but express sociological aspects of our time as an oversized "garment". Garments and façades have this in common: They must not just be worn but above all borne. However, whereas the impact of garments is generally limited to the personal wardrobe and part of the day, façade design survives generations. The visual and functional character of high-rise façades, often located at the hub of society, play a powerful symbolic and social role as a result of their "eternal" appearance.

Coco Chanel is reported to have said: "I'm opposed to short-lived fashion. I cannot accept that people throw away clothes simply because it is spring." Façade designers are called upon to dissect and re-assemble classic structures and building blocks. "This is not destruction but movement, progress. Dissecting objects and rejoining them with new elements is to act constructively." [Margiela, Die Zeit 2001]. As in fashion, the true potential of façades does not lie in the pursuit of showiness, but in carefully considered development.

11 Façade Technologies

Martin Lutz and Eberhard Oesterle

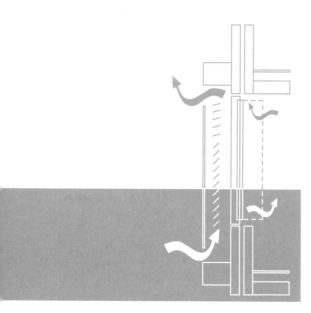

11.1   Façade Types

The architectural design of windows and façades affects construction down to the last detail. This section begins by explaining the different types of façade as a basis for façade design. The sections that follow describe the types of construction (post-and-rail or framed construction) and the building methods (pre-fabricated or conventional) and their effects in more detail. A brief overview of the individual façade types contains built examples of each type.

Perforated Façades

From the perspective of the history of building, the perforated façade can be termed the traditional window and façade construction. Depending on weather conditions, more or less large openings were cut into the carcass in southern countries to provide protection from the sun and long heat waves. Similarly, the practice in northern countries and in the Alpine regions was to create only a few openings in the carcass for protection during the long cold weather period. Windows, usually wood-framed, were set into these openings and sealed with the carcass.

The carcass of the classic constructions in southern countries usually consisted of the natural stone materials available in nature, in the northern countries of timber or natural stone, and in the Alpine regions predominantly of timber. In traditional architecture, the solid, non-transparent surface of the external skin was clad or rendered with the materials available in the region or with weatherproof building materials. In massive carcass structures, for example in natural stone or brick-work, the need for a cladding of the carcass was partly obviated. In modern architecture, and high-rise construction in particular, the perforated façade has no doubt been relegated to second place, although its energy and economic efficiency continue to make it a valuable option. It will be interesting to see whether the introduction of the energy-efficiency law will lead to a noticeable renewed appreciation for these solutions.

The non-transparent area of the façade is insulated and then rendered or clad with modern system superstructures. The ventilated cladding is fastened in front of a weatherproof substructure of stainless steel or aluminum onto the carcass construction.

Traditional Foundations

Neither the box window nor the strip-window façade as a double-skin construction are new inventions. Both building types are based on traditional models in terms of the constructional principle of the second, outer, single-glazed window construction. To provide protection against the bitter cold in winter, box windows and strip windows are built into the thick, well-insulated external solid-wood wall. The internal window, also single-glazed at that time, is installed flush with the internal wall edge, the outer window flush with the external wood cladding.

The example of a traditional family home in the high-altitude Swiss Alpine village of Mürren (**Figs. 11.1 and 11.2**) illustrates how the air cushion (thermal buffer) between the two layers of single glazing was used to increase comfort inside the home.

Box Window Construction

The box window, a doubled window with single glazing on the outside and an intermediate space of roughly 200 to 400 mm, is perhaps the oldest form of a double-skin façade. The intermediate space is vertically and horizontally separated, i.e. sealed. This continuous seal prevents the transfer of air, sound and odor between constructional axes i.e. from room to room. As a result, each box window element requires an individual fresh air and ventilation opening, which must be integrated into the design.

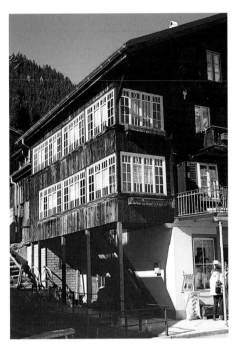

11.1 Traditional residential house in the Swiss Alpine village of Mürren. A glazed veranda serves as a thermal buffer

11.2 Detail of a box window, easily identified by the winter vents

11.3
High-rise at
Potsdamer
Platz 1, Berlin.
Architects:
Kollhoff and
Timmermann,
Berlin

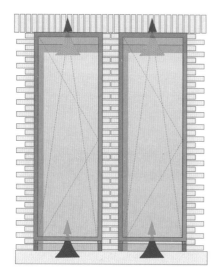

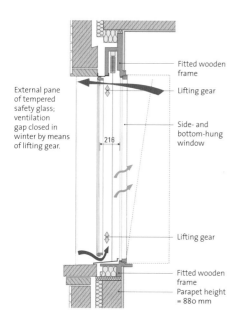

External pane
of tempered
safety glass;
ventilation
gap closed in
winter by means
of lifting gear.

216

Fitted wooden
frame

Lifting gear

Side- and
bottom-hung
window

Lifting gear

Fitted wooden
frame
Parapet height
= 880 mm

11.4 Box window construction, Potsdamer Platz 1,
elevation and section

Built Example:
High-rise Potsdamer Platz 1, Berlin

Architect Hans Kollhoff integrated a modern box-window construction into the traditional clinker façade of the roughly 90 m office building.

The internal window is designed as a side- and bottom-hung casement with low-E glazing in a wood frame with external aluminum cover strips. An optimized shading system with louvered blinds, specially developed for this project, is installed in the roughly 220 mm deep space between the two façade layers. The outer window sits in a side-hung casement to facilitate cleaning. A 60 or 50 mm gap beneath and above the outer pivoting casement allows for ventilation of the intermediate space and the internal offices. The outer pane is equipped with a lifting gear, which enables the user to fully or partially close the gap by raising the window pane. In winter, this design facilitates the utilization of the heat gained in the space between the panes. The simulation carried out at the planning stage showed that the combination of window ventilation with mechanical support resulted in excellent thermal comfort even for extreme weather conditions. The theoretical analysis based on the simulation has been fully vindicated in practice.

Strip-window Façades as Double-skin and Single-skin Structures

This strip-window façade bears a close resemblance to the perforated façade, both in terms of construction principle and in terms of the ventilated cladding materials installed near the window sill or lintel. Instead of the individual openings cut into the carcass – the constructional principles of a perforated façade – the strip-window façade is created by cutting continuous horizontal opening strips into the carcass. This creates floor-high strips around the building consisting of a continuous window strip and a continuous solid apron wall and floor. The vertical loads are usually assumed by slightly recessed columns.

In modern high-rise construction strip-window façades can be designed both as single-skin façades and as double-skin solutions. The type of construction depends on the building location, building height, external noise level, and user requirements. Differences in the performance of single-skin and double-skin façades:

Single-skin Façades

Regardless of the stresses placed on a façade through noise in the surroundings, wind and building height, a single-skin façade can deliver the following performance characteristics only to a limited degree in comparison with a double-skin façade:
- Night cooling in summer regardless of weather conditions.
- Intruder protection when inner windows are open.
- Reduction of wind gusts and pressure fluctuations when inner windows are open.
- Ensuring 100 percent operability of external shading system regardless of wind force.

Double-skin Façades

Generally speaking, double-skin façades make sense whenever buildings are exposed to high noise or wind levels. This applies to high-rises as much as it does to other, lower buildings. If these buildings are to be ventilated via the windows for much of the year, double-skin façades offer clear advantages. Renovation projects, where it is either not possible or not desirable to replace the existing façades, are another application for double-skin façades. Here, the second skin will provide the necessary weather protection and furnish a contemporary design for the façade.

Built Example, Single-skin:
Colorium High-rise, Düsseldorf

For the 62 m building, Alsop architects, London (formerly: Alsop + Störmer architects, London), planned a strip-window façade as a single-skin façade with integrated apron wall panel. The opening casement was designed as a mechanical (manual) top-hinged sash window set into each second façade axis. The stunning color design was achieved with

11.5 Colorium Tower, Dusseldorf,
architects: Alsop architects, London

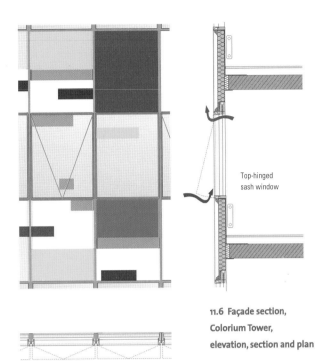

Top-hinged
sash window

11.6 **Façade section,**
Colorium Tower,
elevation, section and plan

11.7 Business Tower, Nuremberg,
architects: Friedrich Biefang,
Nuremberg, Peter Dürschinger, Fürth,
Jörg Spengler, Nuremberg

roughly 30 different multicolored serigraphic patterns on the opaque sill area and on the glazing. The non-transparent sill strip was structurally integrated as a W90-panel (wall component, minimum 90 minutes fire resistance to prevent vertical flash-over) into the fully prefabricated façade construction. The entire façade could thus be mounted with scaffolding (Figs. 11.5 and 11.6).

Built Example, Double-skin:
Business Tower, Nuremberg

The roughly 134 m Business Tower in Nuremberg was realized with a double-skin, permanently ventilated strip-window façade (Figs. 11.7–11.9). The interior façade was fitted with a concrete breast wall for reasons of preventing fire flashover and energy optimization. The breast wall was insulated and clad with glass. The outer façade was designed as a fully glazed façade, the face ends of the floor visible on the outside and the ventilation box area were clad in fritted glass.

The inner façade consists of a prefabricated aluminum frame with side- and bottom-hung casements and top-hinged windows in each second window axis. Aluminum louvered blinds are installed in the roughly 45 cm intermediate space between façade layers for shading. This example represents a blend of strip-window and corridor façade. The authors would also like to cite this double-skin façade as an example of a curtain wall façade (see next chapter), because it was fully assembled prior to the rough work. The double-skin construction was planned as a fully prefabricated façade (i.e. rigorous horizontal and vertical separation throughout) with an extremely high degree of prefabrication.

The façade components were installed in the monorail assembly process with exceptional speed and without scaffolding.
A trolley cab, fitted onto a circumferential rail, the "monorail", transports the elements to the mounting position.

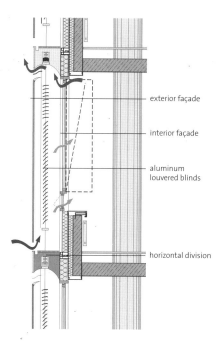

exterior façade

interior façade

aluminum
louvered blinds

horizontal division

11.8 and 11.9
Business Tower, Nuremberg
Double-skin strip-window curtain-wall façade,
plan, elevation section

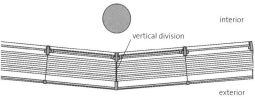

interior

vertical division

exterior

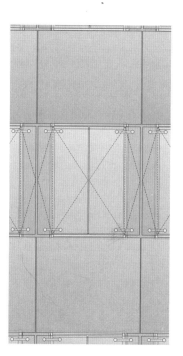

exterior façade

side-hung
plate-glass window

interior façade

existing solid parapet

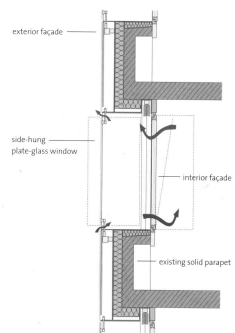

11.10 und 11.11
The Federal Ministry for Consumer
Protection, Food and Agriculture, Bonn,
architects and general planners:
Ingenhoven Overdiek Kahlen und
Partner, Dusseldorf

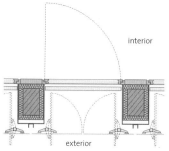

interior

exterior

Plan, elevation, section
Double-skin strip-window curtain-wall
façade with off-center plate-glass windows
Redevelopment: the solid parapet of the
existing shell defined the clearly projecting
reference planes

Curtain-wall Façades

The curtain wall can be defined as a floor-high façade construction suspended in front of the carcass between floors. The continuous external skin that results is point-fixed at the level of the front edge of the floors. It is this building method that makes the rigorous separation of carcass and façade construction possible. The sealed junctions between façade construction and the corresponding carcass section necessary for perforated or strip-window façades are no longer required. Instead the façade sealing is effected within the façade construction at joints between the façade components. The façade components are at times fully prefabricated with great precision, produced in the façade specialist's workshop and delivered to the site as floor-high façade elements. The rough work tolerances are compensated with precise, adjustable, point fixing brackets (see section on fixing and forms of anchoring). The sealing of the façade component joints is achieved with specially developed elastic sealing profiles. The façade expansions are also absorbed by elastic sealing profiles or sliding bolt connections depending on the type of construction – post-and-rail or framed construction.

Evolution

The first instances of "dissolving" the hitherto massive exterior wall designs are recorded from the beginning of the 20th century:
– Department store Hermann Tietz ("Hertie") in Berlin, Sehring and Lachenmann, 1898,
– AEG Turbine Hall in Berlin, Peter Behrens, 1908–1909
– Fagus Factory in Alfeld, Gropius, Feyer, 1911–1916.

However, the literature cites the first building with a curtain wall as being the
– Hallidie Building in San Francisco, W. I. Polk, 1918.

This evolution in dissolving the wall and integrated floor-high glass panes was continued by Le Corbusier, Mies van der Rohe and Walter Gropius in the years that followed. The constructional principle of the curtain wall was also applied to high-rises over the course of this evolution. One example is the
– Lever House in New York, Skidmore Owings and Merrill, 1952.

This high-rise façade was designed in the character of a glazed curtain wall. The formal image is still frequently replicated even today with modern profile constructions and advanced glazing techniques on both single- and double-skin façades.

Modern Double-skin or Single-skin Curtain-wall Façade

Most modern façade constructions, especially filigree constructions, are realized on the principle of the curtain wall. The economic advantages, the opportunities to accelerate the mounting process and the clear separation of the works interfaces are advantages of modern building technology that cannot be denied. This is especially true for large building projects and for façade constructions with predominantly large and identical components.
We have illustrated the double-skin curtain wall façade with the example of the Business Tower in Nuremberg. The built example of a single-skin curtain wall façade is the Vodafone (formerly Mannesmann) high-rise.

Built Example, Single-skin Curtain-wall Façade: Renovation Vodafone High-rise, Dusseldorf

The roughly 89 m Vodafone (formerly Mannesmann) high-rise is a listed building erected in 1954–1956 (Figs. 11.12, 11.13). The architects RKW Dusseldorf were charged with the task of completely renovating the high-profile building near the banks of the Rhine in Dusseldorf. The original single-glazed façade construction had to be reconstructed with great precision, to the latest standards in technology and in accordance with the energy conservation law. Owing to the impact of pollution on the interior building components and the resulting disassembly process from top to bottom, it was necessary to develop a reversed mounting principle for the façade construction. Another joint planning tasks

11.12 and 11.13 Vodafone Tower, Dusseldorf, built in 1956: Prof. Dr.-Ing. E.H. Schneider von Esleben, modernization: RKW Architekten, Dusseldorf

11.14 Maintower, Frankfurt
architects: Schweger und Partner, Hamburg

11.15 Maintower, Frankfurt
parallel-opening sash windows, round tower

consisted in designing the aluminum façade construction to weigh the same or only very slightly more than the original façade, despite the use of antisun glazing and the profile frame material category 1. The static system had to remain unchanged and no additional loads could be added to the floor. Hence, the façade loads had to be transferred to the columns as before. The existing brackets had to be re-used as fixing points for the new façade construction. Since these had been partially damaged over time, repairs were required on individual pieces.

The single-skin fully prefabricated framed construction was mounted by a crane, which the façade contractor had arranged to lift onto the roof of the building with a helicopter. The existing rails of the façade access system were put to excellent use for mounting the façade.

Parallel Ventilator Windows

With the completion of the roughly 170 m Maintower in Frankfurt (Figs. 11.14 and 11.15) a new type of ventilator window – the electronically operated parallel ventilator window – has entered the discussion. This entirely novel ventilator idea makes it possible to extend the openable window parallel to the façade in infinitely variable steps to an opening gap ranging from 2.5 to 200 mm. Notable features of the design are the fittings in conjunction with the installation of the electric motor in the profile frame. The folding fittings have been improved and optimized in terms of technology, maximum ventilator dimensions and weights by comparison to the Maintower dimension. This type of ventilator window is predestined for use in single-skin façades. The comparatively high costs for the fittings due to the technical requirements must be taken into consideration in the cost calculation. Analysis must be precise and critical for high-rise applications of this type of ventilator window.

The wind-pressure dependent ventilator control, which takes the wind gusts at great heights into consideration, results in a comparatively high frequency of ventilator adjustment depending on the building height. This should be analyzed specifically with anticipated motor noise in mind. The ventilation performance in conjunction with the planned conservation solution (internal shading system) must be studied in detail, particularly for room- or floor-high glazing. The quality or the E-value of the glazing and the building physics of the shading system play a decisive role.

When planning the use of parallel ventilator windows, permission granted by building authorities with regard to the risk of crushing is an important consideration. It would be wrong to assume that the Maintower solution – relying on the noise of the motorized mechanism as an acceptable warning signal – will be acceptable elsewhere. The guideline for power-operated windows, doors and gates is the legal basis for implementing these and comparable ventilator solutions. Alternative warning signal options such as light barriers, pneumatic switches, etc. are technologically feasible; they should, however, be factored into the cost calculation because of the additional effort associated with them.

11.2 Types of Construction

Post-and-rail Construction

Post-and-rail construction (Figs. 11.16–11.18) consists of vertical posts and horizontal sections or rails, which are installed in line according to the desired measurements. The predominant materials for the sections/rails are aluminum, steel and, recently, wood.

A post-and-rail construction differs from a classic framed construction principally in the type of glazing. The former is glazed from the outside in a separate work process. The glass and installation elements are attached with a clamping bar or a clamping and cover bar with the specified glass frame depth. Both the clamping and cover bar and the bearing profiles – posts and rails – can be custom designed and manufactured to the architects' preferences, taking the material properties into consideration. The depth and projection width of the bearing profiles are dependent on the static parameters.

The bearing profile joints usually form the profile unions and are designed as expansion and sliding joints. The profile union, for example of aluminum profiles, is often effected with sliding bolt or pin joints. The installation hollows for the union or connecting elements are pressed into the profile wall during the manufacturing process. Steel sections are often connected with screws, for example with welded butt straps or bearing brackets. Cover strip connections are another common solution for U-sections (or channel sections).

Profiles of wood or wood-aluminum post-and-rail structures are primarily screw-jointed with fittings set into the corner joint. All types of fittings are employed for this purpose. Modified furniture mountings are a common option.

Opinions differ as to the technical design of the sealing systems. This is especially true for glass roof structures, but also for vertical post-and-rail glazing applications. Façade specialists often interpret the many different sealing systems offered by the major system suppliers as "default" functional principles.

They are highly competitive and are unfortunately employed more and more frequently without subjecting the necessary parameters to appropriate analyses. Experience has shown that employing these usually two- and three-part sealing systems without matching them to the specific situation results in leaks and possibly damage. The same deleterious results may occur if these sealing systems are installed under adverse weather conditions or without full compliance with the system specifications.

In the authors' opinion, the overlapping joint seals (Figs. 11.19–11.21) developed in recent years as continuous sealing systems are a step in the right direction. These systems can be employed without modification or, when required, as appropriate yet system-neutral engineered solutions. This is particularly true for the second sealing layer, which ensures safety drainage. The overlapping joint sealing offers a high degree of processing and hence quality assurance, because the work on façades is undertaken in all weather conditions today. In the past, the systems sector of the industry was reluctant to fully accept the

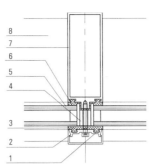

1 Clamping bar
2 Covering bar
3 External seal
4 Insulation
5 Insulating glass
6 Inner seal
7 Section of post
8 Section of rail
9 Insert

Post-and-rail construction in aluminum

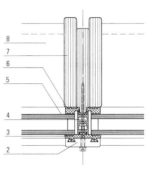

Post-and-rail construction in wood

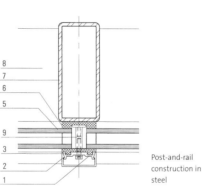

Post-and-rail construction in steel

11.16–11.18 Post-and-rail construction, profile sections

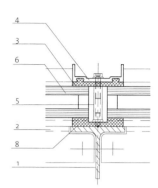

1 Pillar
2 Beam
3 Clamping bar seal
4 Cover bar
5 Screw insert
6 Insulating glass
7 Overlap
8 Post seal
9 Rail seal
10 Safety drainage

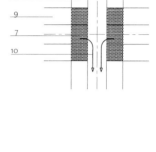

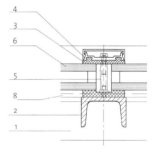

11.19–11.21 Illustration showing the principle behind the overlapping joint sealing, crossing point in horizontal section, elevation and vertical section

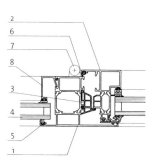

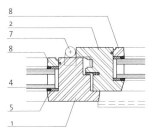

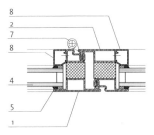

1 Frame profile
2 Sash profile
3 Inner seal
4 Insulating glass
5 External glass seal
6 Interior rebate seal
7 Hinge
8 Glazing bead

Aluminum frame construction

Wooden frame construction

Steel frame construction

11.22–11.24 Frame construction, section of profile

advantages of this profile sealing structure. It is all the more encouraging, therefore, that this type of sealing was in part developed in the "research kitchens" of the leading system manufacturers and is now available on the market.

A continuous insulating web, consisting of glass-fiber reinforced polyamide, for example, should be a component of any high-quality post-and-rail structure irrespective of the selected profile material. The insulating web is mounted separately.

The mounting of a post-and-rail structure is relatively elaborate. The fill elements, i.e. all glass panes, panels and mounting elements, are delivered to the site in separate stages and only installed on site.

This on-site assembly, which must continue regardless of weather conditions, increases the error rate during the mounting process. Scaffolding is required for the mounting, with the exception of prefabricated post-and-rail structures.

The aforementioned fill and mounting elements of the post-and-rail structure must be installed at sufficient distance to the continuous insulating web. The rebate depth must be capable of accommodating the anticipated expansions and tolerances of the fill elements.

Frame Construction

Frame construction (Figures 11.22–11.24) is radically different from post-and-rail construction. The profiles used for frame construction are industrially prefabricated with a pressed-in continuous insulation zone, eliminating this manual mounting process.

For this construction type, the glazing is installed from the inside. The glass and the mounting elements are installed in the frame profiles. Familiar materials, such as aluminum, wood, steel and plastics, are used for the frame profiles. Exotic materials such as bronze or stainless steel are very rarely used in façade construction.

For constructional reasons, the profile joints are executed predominantly with mitered joints at an angle of 45° and invisible, internal angle brackets.

The sealing issue is less complicated for this type of construction than for post-and-rail structures. The most common solution is to use vulcanized corner EPDM strips. EPDM is the acronym for elastic polymer sealant material. Together with silicon, which is generally used for gland seals, EPDM is the most commonly used material for sealing work on buildings.

Structural Glazing Construction

Frameless glazing at its purest, where the glass panes are mounted with adhesive from the outside without visible glass fastening strips or glass point fixings, is called structural glazing (SG).

This type of glazing (Fig. 11.25) is popular in France and especially in the United States. In Germany, on the other hand, structural glazing applications in excess of 8 m height find little favor with the relevant building authorities. A general authorization would be required for SG mounted exclusively with adhesives. Since this authorization has not been issued to date for applications of over 8 m (above ground), applications for permits are necessary in each individual case. However, the responsible higher building authorities are only willing to issue such permits on the basis of proof of long-term exposure or annual safety checks, which are

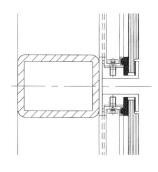

SG construction with ground-in recesses. Mounted with bolted rails

11.25 SG glazing, section of profile

virtually unfeasible from an economic perspective and which are imposed on the client(s). These checks, for example of the entire glazing or of each individual glass panel, are associated with extremely high investments both in terms of money and time as to make SG an impractical construction choice.

Irrespective of the debate on structural glazing adhesives, instances of falling glass in Hamburg, Duisburg and Berlin have demonstrated that these demands on the part of the higher building authorities, i.e. the responsible departments have not been imposed without reason. To date, several causes have been identified for these events, which threatened the lives of passers-by. It would be wrong and entirely inappropriate to condemn individual glass fastening techniques or to dismiss the safety requirements imposed by the building authorities as exaggerated or unjustified. Ensuring public safety is one of the most important tasks of building authorities. As a result of the difficulties we have described with regard to receiving permission to employ structural glazing exclusively with adhesives, a wide variety of combined solutions have been developed. For these combined solutions, the glass edges are worked in various ways, for example

– beveled, with a bevel of roughly 45°
– by grinding recesses into the glass.

These methods achieve flush glass fastenings with additional or entirely mechanical fastening safety. The probability of securing the relevant permission for such combined solutions of glass mounting is far greater than for pure structural glazing, as long as the representatives of the responsible building authorities are informed in a timely fashion and the necessary tests and proofs are delivered.

To avoid unpleasant surprises when planning and scheduling such methods of glass mounting, it is necessary to clarify at the earliest possible point where building component tests are required for the permits. These are time-intensive and can be very expensive. Building component tests are carried out by a relatively small number of specialized, independent institutes.

11.3 Building Methods

Conventional Building Method

Like the prefabricated method, the conventional building method can in principle be applied for both types of construction

– post-and-rail construction or
– framed construction.

The term "conventional building method" is understood to refer to façade assembly of individual components on the building site. Sections or section frames, glazing, panels, fixings and other façade components are delivered separately to the building site and assembled on-site into a façade construction.

In comparison with the prefabricated building method, the conventional method is associated with less material effort and also with less effort in terms of the constructional and technical processing.

For double-skin façades, an experienced façade specialist will only employ the conventional method for small façade areas based on the efficiency in execution. For small volumes, standard façade components are ordered from catalogues. For larger façade volumes, the prefabricated method is preferred because of the high degree of prefabrication it offers and the economic advantages associated with it. The conventional method is moreover justified for projects with extreme differences between the planes of the existing carcass (see for example the BML project in Bonn, **Figs. 11.10, 11.11**).

In cases where different façade profile materials are used, for example wood for an interior façade and aluminum for an exterior façade, a conventional building method may also be more efficient, depending on the project size and the rough work conditions.

Scaffolding/Hoists

In conventional construction, scaffolding, which must be erected in compliance with the relevant codes and guidelines, must be raised on the exterior of the building for the façade mounting work.

11.26 View of façade of the Federal Ministry for Consumer Protection, Food and Agriculture, Bonn

The individual façade elements must be hoisted into the existing skeleton structure or onto the stage floor in consideration of the scaffold load capacity (usually 300 kg/m²) with a rotary tower crane that is already on site, or by hiring a mobile crane.

The available skeleton area and the stage floor of the scaffolding are the intermediate storage area from which the façade is assembled and mounted. Heavy façade elements such as large panes must be fitted into the façade frame with special hoisting equipment, for example a glass suction apparatus.

Since the carcass contractor's rotary tower crane is usually not available for this time-consuming task, the façade contractor is often required to hire a mobile crane for the duration of the glazing or similarly heavy mounting work.

For the site architect, the coordination of the scaffolding with all other trades working in the façade area (for example, stonemasons, facing bricklayers, etc.) is an important task. Key criteria are the load capacity of the scaffolding, especially when heavy types of cladding are used and the distance between the scaffolding and the existing carcass, which must be carefully planned to ensure that the work carried out by trades on the exterior face can proceed unimpeded.

For which trade should the scaffolding be tendered? There is no absolute answer to this question. One thing is certain: When the scaffolding is part of the package of services performed by the façade contractor, he or she will ensure that the work will be completed in as timely a fashion as possible to minimize the time during which the scaffold is required. Practical experience has shown that the façade contractor meets the "façade-sealed deadline", which is generally associated with a contractual penalty in case of non-compliance. The more extensive finishing work often takes months to complete, a source of frustration for the site management. Conversely, the façade contractor is motivated to complete the work and achieve the hand-over target because of the accumulating costs for additional time when scaffolding is used unnecessarily, which put a strain on the budget. If the scaffolding is tendered by the architects as a service separate from the performance delivered by the façade contractor, this motivating factor, resulting from the cost pressures described above, is eliminated.

11.27 Business Tower, Nuremberg, mounting the façade

Little Prefabrication and Time-intensive Assembly

Conventional construction, in the context of double-skin façade construction, should be taken to mean that the entire structure is delivered in individual elements to the site and assembled on-site. Even for this construction method, the level of prefabrication can and must be optimized with a view to construction efficiency.

Thus most elements of the inner façade layer can prefabricated at the façade builder's workshop.

A far-sighted façade builder will try to design the horizontal union in an open fashion and the bottom edge of the union, including the horizontal completion elements of the façade cavity, as a vertically adjustable façade plane that is separated from floor to floor. This approach of designing the horizontal planes in the manner of an adjustable saddle frame construction makes it possible to reduce the on-site work to simply placing the individual façade elements delivered to the site in between the horizontal connecting planes. These horizontal planes are pre-mounted during the first assembly stage and adjusted true to the dimensions. This helps to compensate in part for the lesser degree of prefabrication and the resulting assembly effort.

This saddle frame construction in conjunction with the higher degree of prefabrication for the inner façade structure makes it possible to achieve the "façade-sealed deadline" much more quickly than is otherwise possible. This has a positive effect on the completion of the entire structure, because the sealing of the façade is a prerequisite for beginning with assembly of several interior-finishing works.

The external elements of a double-skin façade can be mounted according to an independent schedule from the outside when this method is used. This does not affect the continuing interior work, because the exterior façade elements are mounted from the external scaffolding.

Prefabrication Method

The prefabricated building method can in principle be applied for
- post-and-rail construction, or
- framed construction.

The term "prefabricated building method" refers to a consistent horizontal and vertical separation or division of a large façade element.

To this end, the façade sections or profiles are axially divided and joined together like a labyrinth.

Most prefabricated double-skin façades are executed as frame structures. Aluminum is commonly employed for divided façade profiles, and is used both for the internal and the external façade. In recent years, prefabricated wood façade profiles are also used for the inner façade layer.

The labyrinthine profile, i.e. joint between elements, is also the mounting joint. This element joint (Figs. 11.28–11.31) is usually individually designed for double-skin façades. Structural expert knowledge is required for the development. Great care and precision must be taken because this element joint has to perfectly fulfill several technical requirements simultaneously.

The profile joint absorbs the expansion movement of the façade element and must also fulfill the function of a waterproof expansion joint as well as all the technical requirements of a horizontal and vertical assembly joint. To ensure perfect watertightness, these profile joints are fitted with custom designed EPDM or silicon sealants.

Prefabricated construction makes it possible to deliver the façade elements including all glass panes, panels and other mounting elements, which have been fully prefabricated in the façade builder's workshop, to the building site.

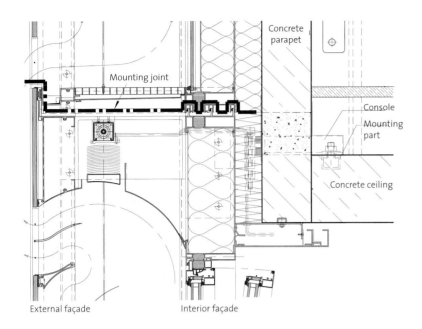

External façade — Interior façade

11.28 Detail of the horizontal course of the joint between the sections at the roof front.
All the examples on this page are taken from the Business Tower, Nuremberg

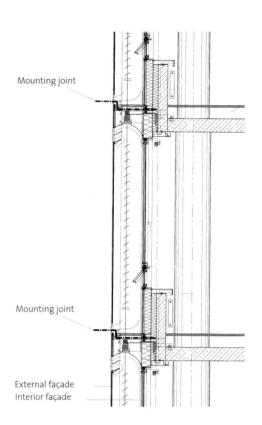

11.30 Vertical section, mounting joint in the façade

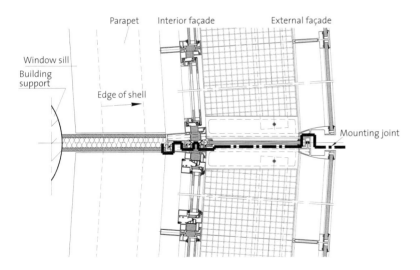

11.29 Detail of the vertical course of the mounting joint at the roof front

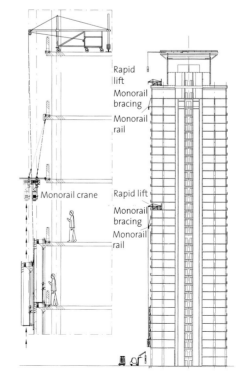

11.31 The principle underlying the lifting gear: the installation of the monorail with which the prefabricated sections were brought into position for mounting

11.32 Vodafone Tower, Dusseldorf,
mounting the single-skin curtain-wall façade

11.33 Colorium Tower, Dusseldorf,
mounting the single-skin curtain-wall façade

Assembly Planning/Hoists

Prefabricated construction offers several great advantages with a view to assembly planning. No doubt, one key advantage lies in the option to execute the entire façade assembly without elaborate external scaffolding. The façade components arrive fully prefabricated on the building site with just-in-time delivery. The floor-high and generally two-construction-axes wide components are lifted with the carcass contractor's rotating cranes, which are already on site, or with mobile cranes hired by the façade builder into the existing carcass.

Experienced façade contracting firms have specialized assembly experts, who plan and adapt the specific approach to each project, because this area offers a tremendous savings potential. The inventiveness with which the assembly experts develop project-specific solution often deserves the unreserved admiration of architects and façade consultants.

It is impossible, therefore, to describe a single, universally applicable method. Nor is it possible to provide an overview of the wide variety of solutions tailor-made for each building. Clearly, high-rise construction calls for different assembly and mounting solutions than large-area, low-story buildings.

One fairly common mounting solution on high-rises is the rail-mounting method. The façade elements lifted by rotary-tower or mobile cranes are hoisted into the building and temporarily stored on the relevant floor with the help of a special stacker truck (Fig. 11.31).

The façade elements are mounted via an external mounting rail, the "monorail", which transports the elements to the installation site in a trolley.

For the delivery and mounting of double-skin façade elements, the mounting specialist strives to eliminate the temporary storage phase on each floor, because double-skin façade elements, in contrast to their single-skin counterparts, occupy large storage areas due to their depth and because handling

them is far more cumbersome. Given the appropriate access routes to the building, the double-skin elements are lifted directly from the truck onto the monorail and transported via a previously planned vertical transportation corridor directly to the installation site, where it is loosely mounted. While the monorail is transporting the next element, the loosely mounted element is carefully adjusted and then fixed in place.

Depending on the size of the double-skin façade elements, a single truck can transport roughly eight to twelve units to the building site.

Using the monorail mounting method without intermediate storage described above, a single floor can be mounted on a circular high-rise in roughly 1.5 to 2 weeks, unless there are delays caused by severe weather conditions.

High Degree of Prefabrication and Efficient Assembly

Like all departments in the building sector, the façade trades have been faced with growing challenges in terms of shortening the time required for mounting and construction. Façade construction is a decisive component in on-time completion of an entire building. Delays in completing the façade have a devastating impact on the subsequent work processes. If the façade has not been sealed at the scheduled deadline or if important individual elements of the façade are still outstanding, the interior work cannot progress according to schedule. This creates a chain of delays, which can no longer be caught up. In some cases, expensive temporary sealing measures must be implemented.

This scheduling dependency alone, especially for large building projects, has resulted in a development towards
– a high degree of prefabrication and
– short mounting times for façade technology and will no doubt continue to do so.

Another important advantage in the high degree of prefabrication employed for this construction type is the "controlled" assembly of the façade element in the workshop of the façade builder. A considerable portion of the

11.34 Mounting the prefabricated double-skin façade, Business Tower, Nuremberg

assembly, which was previously carried out on-site regardless of weather conditions, is effected in a "dry" setting when this method is employed. Workshop assembly results in a considerable improvement of the product quality. The dominant use of ultramodern manufacturing machines in the workshop compensates for the error-prone manual labor on site and achieves far more precision in assembly.

The quality assurance that is possible with workshop production makes an important contribution to minimizing deficiencies in the façade structure.

In the case of double-skin façades, prefabrication is in part advanced to such a degree that the elements manufactured in the workshop are completely pre-assembled, consisting of interior and exterior façade and including horizontal stays and ventilator boxes as well as integrated shading systems.

Individual transport and mounting fittings must be developed to safely transport these relatively large façade elements, which are moreover susceptible to warping due to the double-layer assembly. If the completed double-skin element should become subject to distortion for some reason en route between workshop and building site, the resulting damage is most likely irreparable or at least extremely difficult to repair. Naturally,

the exact degree of prefabrication differs from project to project and is dependent on many factors associated with the façade design. It is influenced by the existing carcass elements and by the available space on the building site.

It is important to note, however, that this construction method, especially when it is associated with a high degree of prefabrication, goes hand in hand with a far greater planning effort, where the intensity of planning and the qualifications of the builders are equally important attributes.

More Cost Efficiency for Mass Production

The planning required for prefabricated construction is far greater both in terms of the façade planning on the part of the architect/ façade consultant and the assembly planning on the part of the façade builder. However, these planning costs and the slightly higher material costs are easily compensated in large building projects and undoubtedly represent a highly cost-efficient solution for the client and the façade builder if the number of individual prefabricated elements is correspondingly great.

On-site assembly and mounting are reduced to a minimum, and downtimes due to adverse weather conditions are diminished. The higher wage costs associated with on-site assembly (travel costs, overnight accommodation expenses, absence premiums) also contribute to reducing the costs for the façade builder. The possibility of scaffold-free mounting also eliminates the costs for enveloping the entire structure in scaffolding and keeping the scaffolding in place over long periods of time. Rational use of automated manufacturing machines in the workshop of the façade builder in combination with a coordinated and qualified workforce plays an important role in optimized economic efficiency, not to mention the improved quality it delivers.

The joint effect of these economic aspects paints a clear picture of how cost-efficient prefabricated construction is for larger and large building projects. At the same time, however, it is evident that the common practice among clients and project controllers to economize in terms of the planning costs (for the architect and the façade consultant) is undoubtedly the wrong approach. Experience has shown that this results in diminished quality and function and a high potential for supplementary work, for which the executing façade builder can no longer be compensated.

12 Insolation and Shading

Helmut F.O. Müller and Hans Jürgen Schmitz

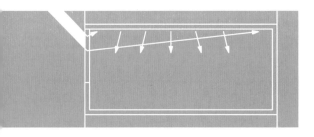

12.1 Introduction

Direct or diffuse sun radiation on a building has an important influence on the thermal behavior of the building, as well as on daylighting and hence energy consumption. With regard to high-rises, this topic is discussed in detail under the heading "Heat" (12.3). For building users, interior daylight conditions are also important beyond energy-consumption considerations (Fig. 12.1).

12.2 Effect on the Surroundings

In an urban environment, buildings block some of the daylight falling on the façades of surrounding buildings. Instead of the sky, all we see is the building on the other side. It is therefore unavoidable that there will be areas where daylighting is virtually impossible in dense development. Urban density increased with the industrial revolution at the end of the 19th century, greater housing density and overall population growth. Berlin's famous "Hinterhöfe" (rear courtyards), measuring 5.3 x 5.3 m to accommodate the turning radius of fire engines, resulted in a building density that caused health problems not only with regard to daylight. The demands for "light, air, [and] sun" promoted by the Neues Bauen movement in architecture was and is not merely a matter of luxury, but a question of function in urban living and working [1]. The urban planning strategies with regard to daylight were no longer defined as a side effect of fire protection, but as minimum health requirements in their own right. In other words, a sufficient supply of daylight is not just a question of creating an appealing interior.

In cities, the preference for tall buildings originates in the need for the maximum use of available space. It is also a question of image and representation. Naturally, daylight conditions are primarily determined by the distance and height of buildings, but also to a considerable degree by façade design. Despite cultural differences, there has been a growing trend towards the International Style in architecture since the middle of the 20th century, a consequence of increasing globalization (see Kloft on Building Typology). Glass as a building material plays a key role in this context, although it seems to be more focused on the

12.1 Residential buildings in Shenzhen, China

image of the building than on supplying daylight. Thus the concept of transparency, a term derived from lighting technology, has come to symbolize an architectural era. However, since each glass surface also reflects a greater or lesser percentage of daylight, reflections across large areas can result on sunny days, which are not necessarily experienced as positive. It is therefore sensible to take the effect of a high-rise on the daylight conditions in the immediate surroundings into account for urban planning concepts.

Shading

Despite the transparency of their façades, the buildings themselves do not allow daylight to penetrate. Standards have been developed with regard to the minimum distance between buildings in developed areas to prevent undue mutual shading effects. However, dispensations are often granted for building projects in urban environments, and this applies not only to high-rises. This can easily lead to poor daylight contact in unfavorable locations.

It is important, therefore, to consider visual contact with the outside in urban planning concepts. Daylight can be utilized right down to ground level, even where very tall buildings are erected, if the position and distance between buildings allows for unobstructed views on the horizontal plane.

Requirements

The expectations and requirements pertaining to daylight in buildings have been defined since time immemorial to a large degree by cultural and climatic parameters. It is easy to understand why a cool and even dark atmosphere is preferred in buildings in warm regions where much of daily life occurs outdoors. In temperate latitudes, however, "light-flooded" rooms are extremely desirable. The minimum requirements for daylight conditions in interiors are therefore not the same across the board.

Daylight under Overcast Sky

In most northern European countries, the sky is more or less overcast on average for nearly two thirds of all daytime periods per year. The brightness ratio of the overcast sky is dependent on the time of day and on the season. However, since light distribution remains constant independent of the solar position, daily and annual internal illuminance can be determined with the help of the daylight factor for overcast skies. The daylight factor can be defined as follows: "The daylight factor D is the ratio of the illuminance at a fixed point on a given plane, produced by direct and/or indirect sky light for an assumed or known luminance distribution to the horizontal exterior illuminance assuming the hemisphere is completely unobstructed (no built environment). The illuminances caused by direct sunlight are not taken into consideration." [2]

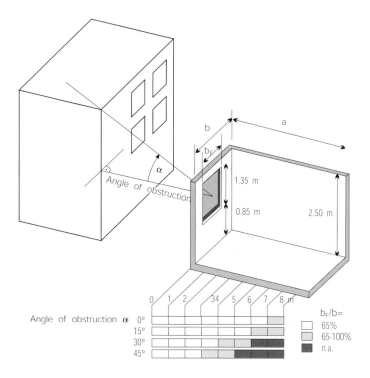

12.2 The minimum width of windows in living rooms should certainly not be less than 65 percent of the room width. In the case of deep rooms with a wide angle of obstruction, even a window width of 100 percent may no longer be sufficient for daylighting

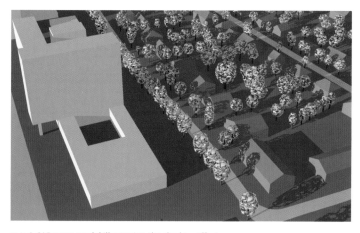

12.3 A CAD mass model illustrating the shadow effect

Since a completely overcast sky is generally the least advantageous sky condition for interior lighting, the minimum requirement for daylighting is based on a reference overcast sky.

According to many European standards, at least 1 percent of the exterior illuminance Ei under overcast sky should be achieved at the working plane for sufficient daylighting of living spaces (and similar rooms). As low as this value may appear at first glance, it is barely achieved in many interiors in densely built environments despite relevant window sizes in accordance with regional building codes. Whenever high-rises obscure the large areas of the façades of existing buildings, daylighting in the rooms behind those façades is virtually impossible (Fig. 12.2). The daylight factor diminishes rapidly, especially in the depth of the room, as obstruction angles increase.

Daylight under Clear Sky

High-rises cast shadows of different lengths depending on the solar position. In addition to the broad area of cast shadow, there are smaller zones in half-shade because sunlight is not entirely parallel (dispersion angle of sunlight roughly 0.5°). Since the luminance distribution of clear sky changes considerably according to solar position, the interior daylight distribution for shade and sun can only be determined for specific solar positions. Hence, it is impossible to formulate a general requirement for lighting under clear sky conditions.

Planning and Evaluation

In most cases a critical analysis of a scale mass model and the built environment will reveal the areas where noticeable changes in daylight conditions must be anticipated. Such a model also makes it possible to investigate the pattern of cast shadows in the surroundings for different seasons with simple means. Whether a workshop or CAD model is used is left to the discretion of the planner, since most programs offer simple calculations for cast shadows for different solar positions. The CAD model offers the slight advantage that the data can be stored and processed for more detailed investigations, which may become necessary at a later stage (Fig. 12.3).

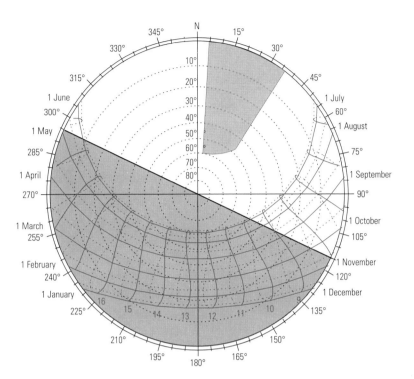

12.4 a, b Mass model illustrating the angle of obstruction and diagram of the sun's position; the new tower stands to the north of the sun; the northeastern façade of the residential building receives daylight. In summer, the northeastern façade of the tower illustrated here receives direct sunshine for up to four hours a day in the morning. The new tower building has no influence on exposure to the sun's rays.

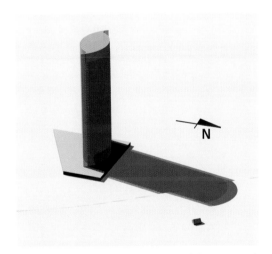

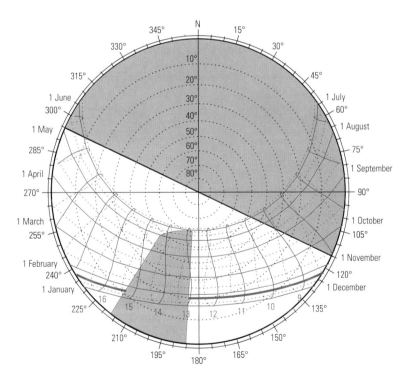

12.5 a, b Mass model illustrating the angle of obstruction and diagram of the sun's position; the new tower stands to the south of the sun, the southwestern façade of the residential building receives daylight. Almost all the year round, the southwestern façade of the tower stands in the shadow for two hours a day.

12.6 Reflection of sunlight on glass façade

This tool should be used at the early stages of any project, however, to explore a variety of options without great effort and precede any firm planning decisions.

If a more detailed analysis of shading is called for, graphic or computer-supported tools are necessary.

While visualizing shading in sun path diagrams requires some practice, it is a good tool to demonstrate all major effects of a development with regard to daylight. This approach is ideal for analyzing and, if necessary, documenting cast shadows and minimum insolation periods at various positions.

Different positions of a new high-rise development – to the north and south, respectively, of existing residential development – are the subject of the study. A fictitious new structure to the north results in changes to the daylight conditions on the NE façade of a residential development at the observation point as a result of obscuring the horizon (Fig. 12.4 a, b).

The shading diagram shows the visible quarter of the hemisphere based on façade orientation and the new percentage of built environment created by the tower. In summer and spring, the NE façade of the building under

observation receives direct sun from sunrise until 10:50 GMT, which can also result in sunlight penetrating into the north-facing rooms depending on the window geometry. On January 17, there is no insolation on this side of the building, and hence no changes for this location. The living areas, which are to receive sun, are located on the other side of the building.

If the high-rise lies to the south of the residential development (Fig. 12.5 a, b) the diagram shows that the sun is blocked for roughly two hours a day on the key day (red line). In this case, the visible width of the building is important rather than the height. Without additional development, the minimum insolation period is not compromised in this example.

Since the daylight penetrating into the interior is analogous to the daylight factor on the façade, the mean daylight factor on the façade with and without the new development is calculated to assess the reduction in daylight. Because of seasonal variations (foliage), vegetation is not taken into consideration.

In this example, the façade overlooking the high-rise experiences a reduction of roughly 20 percent by comparison to the previously unshaded situation, taking roughly 10 percent reflection from a fully glazed façade into account. The degree to which this may pose a problem depends in each instance on the building use and previous daylight quality.

Reflection

A façade does not fully obscure the section of sky it blocks, but reflects part of it depending on the incident light and surface design. Each material results in differing changes to the light in terms of spectral composition, intensity and direction (Fig. 12.6).

The luminance of reflected diffuse daylight is always lower than the luminance of the obscured sky section, which can produce entirely different results for the directed light

of the sun. On the building elevation, specular reflection on glass surfaces displays the mirror image of the sun itself and of the high sky luminance near the sun. Another side effect of sunlight reflected from glazed façades is often observed on the façades of buildings on the opposite side. Shifting light reflections in the immediate environment can be anticipated especially when solar control glass with higher reflectance is used. The glass surfaces, which are never entirely plane, generally cause light patterns that are more or less wave-like. In cases where reflecting films are to be used as sun or glare protection on a high-rise façade, this effect can be considerably more pronounced.

Glare

In most Central and Northern European countries, sunlight is perceived as a welcome enrichment to the spatial environment, provided the heat generated by it does not lead to uncomfortable room temperatures and glare protection is available in case of too much light. Sunlight reflected at glass façades is still sufficiently intense to have both the positive and the negative effects. It is evident therefore, that analysis of the reflection from high-rise façades and their possible effects is important. Knowledge of the most important effects in visual perception is required to assess the effect of reflections.

Glare is a complex phenomenon, which is influenced by an understanding of many different factors. These include the duration of glare in the field of perception, the luminance ratios between the glare source and its environment, and the requirements for the visual task performed in the space. A differentiation is made between absolute glare, resulting from a lack of visible contrasts (snow blindness) or excessive luminance (looking into the sun), which can be temporarily blinding, physiological glare, which results from excessive contrasts and diminishes visual perception (driving out of a tunnel, a dark corridor with a bright window at the far end), as well as psychological glare, which results from reflections and excessively uneven illumination. Psychological glare is the most common type of glare in buildings and leads to fatigue and diminished performance (glare on VDUs). If there are no long-lasting or high-definition

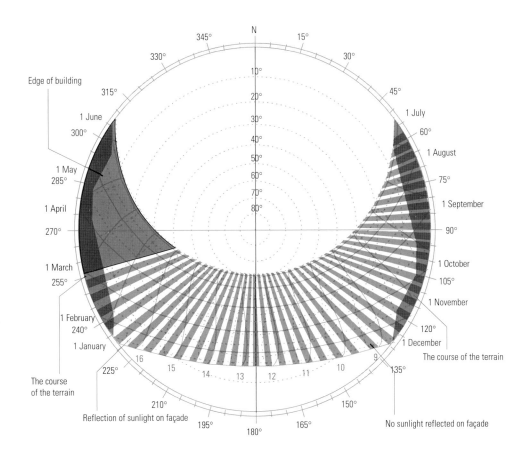

12.7 Illustration of the possible sunlight reflections for convex, polygonal façades; gray areas: no chance of glare, light areas: likelihood of glare.

The sunpath diagram shows the positions from which the sun is likely to be reflected in the façade. On the horizon, the angle of obscuration is presented by the topography of the location. The gray stripes show the positions of the sun when it is not reflected in the polygonal tower façade. The sun path diagram shows that approx. 45 percent of the total hours of sunshine are reflected.

visual tasks, a lighting situation that produces disruptive glare (for office work, for example) may easily be experienced as stimulating in a comfortable manner. Therefore, legislation in Germany only sets limits for absolute luminance and contrast at VDU workstations.

Psychological glare effects depend on the distribution of luminance in the observer's field of perception. Under constant light conditions, contrast of 1:100 can be resolved, with the eye adapting to the brightest larger area (similar to the exposure shutter in a camera). When the angle of perception or the light conditions change, the adaptability of the pupil can regulate the incident light in a split second in a ratio of 1:16. The eye is only unable to fully resolve all contrasts when they exceed 16 x 1:100 in the expanded field.

Looking directly into a reflection of the sun in a glass façade, this contrast ratio is generally exceeded and the eye reacts by squinting. In other words, looking into a reflection of the sun has almost the same glare effect as looking directly into the sun.

Since even a diffuse sky generally has a luminance of up to 10,000 cd/m², most visual tasks in interiors should be performed at a location not facing a window. However, disruptive reflective glare can result if the distribution of luminance from daylight causes excessive contrasts in the field of perception, for example, through sunlight falling directly onto a table surface.

Since glare remains a subjective perception it is impossible to prevent the necessity for additional glare protection against light reflected from façades into interiors that were previously not exposed to direct light.

By contrast to the glare effect, the energy radiating into surrounding buildings as a result of reflection is negligible, because it barely exceeds the amount of simultaneously shaded diffuse radiation over the course of a day – with the exception of high-reflective glass. Hence, problems relating to thermal insulation in summer as a result of reflected sunlight will undoubtedly continue to be extremely rare.

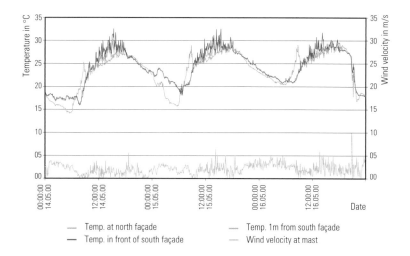

12.8 Air temperature at south and north façades, 16th floor, DLZ Stern Tower in Essen; measurements taken from 14 to 16 May 2000. [4]

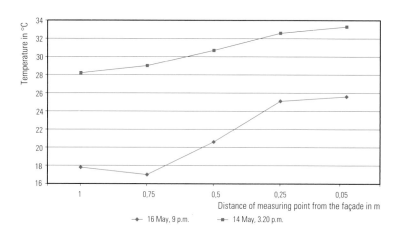

12.9 Temperature layers at the south façade, 16th floor, DLZ Stern Tower in Essen; measurements taken from 14 to 16 May 2000. [4]

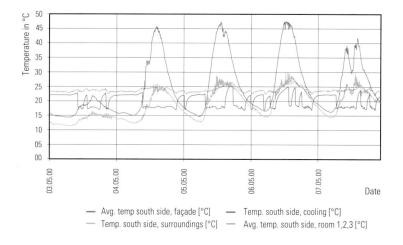

12.10 Façade and room temperatures, on south side, 16th floor, DLZ Stern Tower in Essen, typical summer period; measurements taken from 3 to 7 May 2000. [4]

Planning and Evaluation

The type and spatial distribution of sunlight reflections are a direct result of the façade design of the high-rise. Problematic effects will only be caused by glazed areas. While the spatial distribution depends on orientation and building form, the intensity of the reflections and possible discomfort are determined by the type of glazing. The dark and highly reflective solar control glass popular in the 1980s has contributed to the focus on reflected sunlight as a problem area. With concave façades there is a risk of concentrated reflected sunlight. If a concave curved glass façade is desired, it is important to determine in advance whether potentially concentrated reflections could reach a critical range. Both physical models and computer programs can be used to assess sunlight reflections on façades, although most CAD programs fall short of requirements and closer study is only possible using precise visualization through Ray-Tracing programs. They visualize the sunlight reflected on façades and make photometric evaluation possible. Anyone comfortable with solar altitude diagrams can utilize them to visualize reflection over the course of a year and a day, an effort that requires considerable experience with using this tool especially for more complex façade geometries. A window in a building located on the observation point may receive reflected sunlight from the type of polygonal, convex façade shown in Figure 12.6 (unobstructed view of new building) at the indicated times. Taking the mean sunshine probability into account, an unobstructed north-facing window is exposed to reflected sunlight during roughly 10 percent of daylight time (Fig. 12.7).

With vertical glazing, glare can be avoided only when the sun is very low in the sky. Glass areas that are tilted upwards in the lower area of the high-rise can also reflect sunlight from higher solar altitudes. Hence, sunlight reflection must be analyzed primarily for horizontal radiation. At pedestrian level, this relates predominantly to the plinth story; for facing buildings, however, it refers to the entire insolated glass surface of a building. If reflection occurs in traffic areas, particularly bad conditions may even lead to traffic obstruction. Independent of building height, this problem occurs only with glass areas that are tilted upwards in the plinth story.

Conclusion

The impact on the daylight conditions in the immediate environment must be taken into consideration when planning any high-rise project. First, we must assess the daylight conditions in the existing buildings in the immediate vicinity. Special attention must be given to residential or office buildings that are entirely oriented towards the planned building. It is generally neither necessary nor possible to assess the daylight conditions in all rooms of the adjacent buildings. A simple calculation of the daylight factors on the façades and windows of surrounding buildings can analyze various options for the dimensioning of high-rises.

Elaborate daylight simulation to determine the changes in daylight conditions in individual rooms of surrounding buildings is only necessary in case of doubt.

Reflected sunlight can be a nuisance near high-rises, if façades of office buildings, previously not exposed to sunshine – north-facing façades, for example – require additional glare protection as a result of reflected sunlight. Solar control glass with high reflectance and inclined glass areas in the plinth area can also lead to considerable glare in road traffic. If the horizon remains sufficiently unobstructed for the surrounding built environment as a result of high-rise development, given the aforementioned parameters, the daylight conditions in the urban environment will be no worse, than for more compact buildings.

12.3   Effects on High-rises

Insolation also affects the high-rise itself. It influences the behavior of the building skin and the interior in terms of heat, light and active use of solar energy.

Heat

Insolation raises the temperature in the building, whereby the material properties of the façade components play an important role. Transparent materials such as glass allow a large proportion of the solar radiation to penetrate into the interior of the building.

Opaque elements absorb and reflect solar radiation at the external surface. The greater the reflectance, that is, the brighter the hue, the less solar radiation is transformed into heat and the lower the surface temperature. The surrounding air warms up at the external surface and experiences buoyancy. This is why we observe thermal vertical air currents at high-rise façades, even when there is very little wind. Daniels [3] calculates buoyancy speeds of up to 20 m/s for an assumed maximum temperature difference between surface and outside temperature of 20 K, and draws attention to recorded temperature differences (between surface and outside air) at existing high-rises of up to 50 K on hot and still summer days.

Under clear skies with direct insolation, the heat gain on building fabric surfaces depends on their orientation. Thus at the nearly fully glazed high-rise of the RWE AG, Stern DLZ (service center) in Essen (architects: Ingenhoven, Overdiek and Partners), the outside air temperatures measured directly in front of the south façade are roughly 5 K higher than the air temperature measured at the same time in front of the north façade (Fig. 12.8).

For the south side, these readings reveal a layering of air temperature of 5 K and more (28–33°C on 14 May and 17–25°C on 16 May) at a distance from the façade of roughly 100 cm (Fig. 12.9). This demonstrates the significant impact of insolation on air temperature and airflow in front of high-rise façades, which must be taken into consideration in the building design. Smooth high-rise façades promote buoyancy with corresponding layers of temperatures, while façades with projections and recesses create eddies with less distinct temperature gradients.

Transparent façade components allow for passive heating of the interior through insolation. Far more frequently, however, solar heat gains will contribute to overheating and increased cooling loads. The total window area on the exterior wall and the efficiency of the shading system are key factors. Moveable or changeable shading systems are recommended to allow for an appropriate response to heating and cooling requirements. On high-rises, these

components must withstand relatively high wind velocities if they are installed externally. Consequently, they are frequently integrated into the façade behind a second glass skin (double-skin façade) or inside laminated glass. For the latter, switchable electrochomic glass is an option, for example, as is a shading device in the façade cavity, whereby the surface facing the room must be coated in an insulating material.

In double façades, the closure of the sunshades can lead temporary to high temperature peaks in the cavity if the absorbed incident solar radiation is not sufficiently ventilated to the outside. Natural window ventilation via the gap, on the other hand, allows warm outside air to flow into the room. Measurements in four different office buildings with double-skin façades have shown that room temperatures remained acceptable for most of the time with peaks ranging from 25 to 27 °C, despite short-term gap temperatures of 40 to 50 °C (Fig. 12.10). Analysis of the thermal currents radiating from the solar-heated façade gap revealed that the heat flux was predominantly towards the outside as a result of ventilation and transmittance, while a noticeable smaller flux entered the room as a result of ventilation and transmittance. Limiting window ventilation during peak temperature periods helps to further reduce heat flux towards the interior. The aerodynamically effective opening portion of the exterior skin, ranging from 3 to 6 percent per square meter of façade surface in the studied examples, is the dominant influence. Comparatively moderate increases of the external ventilation openings for cooling can achieve significantly lower temperatures in the cavity of the double-skin façade [5].

Light

In addition to thermal burdens, insolation can also lead to visual discomfort in the form of glare. Glare protection on transparent façades prevents luminance that is unacceptable to the human eye by reducing transmission and/ or direct sunlight deflection. However, any glare protection measures – or, incidentally, thermal sun protection – should not result in diminished daylight or visual contact to the outside.

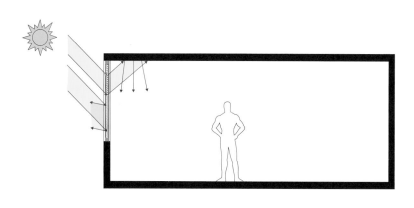

12.11 Venetian blind with light-deflection louvers in the upper window area [6]

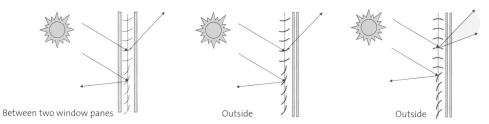

12.11 b Possible placement and setting of louvers

Between two window panes

Outside

Outside

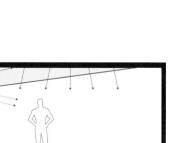

12.12 Lightshelf to deflect light and provide shading [6]

Summer sun

Winter sun

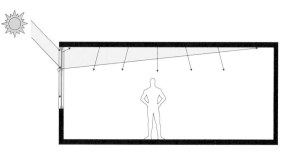

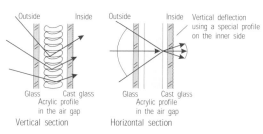

Outside · Inside
Glass · Cast glass
Acrylic profile in the air gap
Vertical section

Outside · Inside
Vertical deflection using a special profile on the inner side
Glass · Cast glass
Acrylic profile in the air gap
Horizontal section

12.13 a, b Light-deflecting glass in upper window area [6]

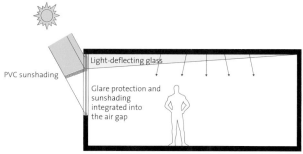

PVC sunshading

Light-deflecting glass

Glare protection and sunshading integrated into the air gap

Façade with PVC sunshading under light-deflecting glass

12.14 Façade with photovoltaic sunshading with sunlight deflection in upper window [6]

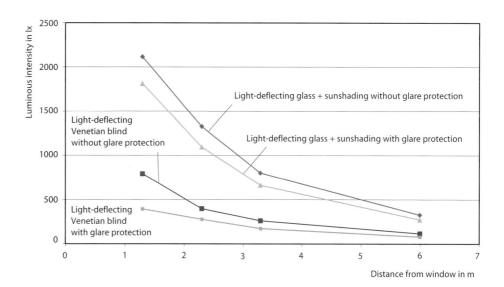

12.15 Comparison of luminous intensity for a façade exposed to sun and façade with integrated sun shading using a venetian blind with light-deflecting louvers (see Fig. 12.11 a, b) and light-deflecting glass in the upper window area (see Fig. 12.13 a, b) at 5 p.m. 3 July, 2001. Measurements of the test façade: Dortmund University

A wide variety of solutions are available, which can all be reduced to the following two principles [6]:
– Selective directional shading from direct sunlight while allowing diffuse light to penetrate
– Partial deflection of direct sunlight for room lighting

The first principle is realized with rigid or movable devices, which are oriented towards the sun to block the high-energy and glaring direct radiation while allowing diffuse light from other areas of the sky to penetrate (e.g. horizontal or vertical louvers).

With applications operating on the second principle, direct sunlight falling onto the upper part of the window is deflected into the interior for lighting, while direct sunlight falling onto the lower part of the window is screened off by a shading device. The simplest solution is a Venetian blind with horizontal louvers, which can be adjusted to deflect light in the upper window area and to shade in the lower area (Fig. 12.11). Concave louvers are more effective for glare-free light deflection than convex louvers. Lightshelves are an alternative: here, a large louver, which both deflects and shades, is placed in the upper window area (Fig. 12.12).

However, low altitude angles require additional glare protection for skylights and when the sky is overcast the louver reduces daylighting if it is a rigid model. A third option is light-deflecting glass in the upper window area, distributing direct light from solar radiation from all altitude angles in the room without glare (Fig. 12.13 a, b). Only the lower part of the window is shaded. Comparison measurement on a test façade at Dortmund University (Fig. 12.15) shows that higher illuminance is achieved in the room with light-deflecting glass than with light-deflecting blinds, based partly on the greater efficiency of the internal total reflectance in the glass in comparison with the reflectance of metal surfaces and the diminished dirt factor of the glass-integrated solution.

The incidence of direct sunlight on the façade can also be harnessed for color and light effects that are perceived inside and outside of the building. Solutions that change with the position of the sun, e.g. in appearance, color or radiant direction, are especially attractive. Figures 12.16 and 17 illustrate examples with transparent holographic films embedded into the laminate glass of the building skin. The holograms deflect transmitted as well as reflected sunlight and separate it into its spectral colors.

Active Use of Solar Energy

In contrast to the options of passive use of solar energy (heating, ventilation, lighting), there are other active uses (thermal, photovoltaic). Collectors that transform solar radiation into heat and modules with solar cells that transform the radiation into electric power are integrated into the building skin. Optimum orientation towards the sun is a key factor. In high-rises the percentage of roof areas with favorable orientation towards the sun is relatively small in comparison with façade areas. Hence, integration across large areas is therefore only feasible on south façades and moreover only in opaque areas such as parapets and sills or in shading systems. Figure 12.14 illustrates a shading system with solar cells, with an optimal angle of 30°, installed underneath light-deflecting glass to avoid any negative impact on interior lighting.

Insolation on high-rises and the shading associated with it must be taken into consideration in the planning and design. The taller the structure, the more serious the many impacts on the surroundings and the building itself will be.

13 Building Systems

Klaus Daniels

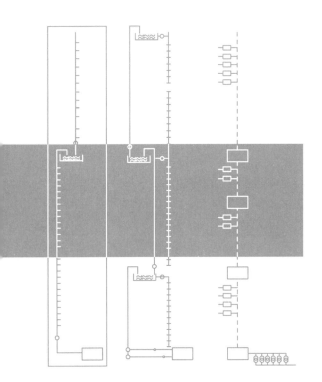

13.1 Comfortable Rooms – Quality Building

Rooms that are suitable for high levels of intellectual productivity and performance place a premium on standards and comfort requirements. The principal factors are:

– Thermal comfort
– Hygienic comfort
– Acoustic comfort
– Visual comfort
– Electromagnetic compatibility
– Influence of colors
– Influence of surfaces and materials
– Avoidance of contaminants and odors

Thermal Comfort

Optimum conditions for performance at the workplace are illustrated in **Figure 13.1**. The image clearly shows that performance levels for demanding intellectual tasks and other work that calls for a high degree of concentration are linked to a very narrow temperature range. Room temperatures are not the only factor, however. Mean radiation temperatures, which indicate the perceived temperature in combination with room temperatures, also play a role (**Fig 13.2**). **Figure 13.3** illustrates the interactions between room air temperature, relative humidity and comfort (comfort zone according to Grandjean).

In addition to temperatures, relative humidity in relation to room air temperature plays an important role, especially in hot-humid climate zones. Occupants need to be able to cool down through convection, radiation and evaporation. Performance is compromised when the relative humidity rises above comfort levels in areas for concentrated work (**Fig. 13.3**). The link between room air temperature and velocity is plotted in **Figure 13.4**.

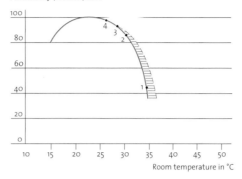

Option 1 all natural ventilation
Option 2 additional mechanical ventilation and night cooling
Option 3 additional mechanical ventilation with chilled ceiling
Option 4 additional mechanical ventilation and cooling of room temperatures to 26 °C in summer

13.1 Human performance

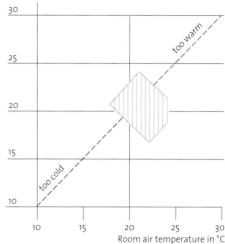

Schematic according to Grandjean
t_r = mean radiation temperature
t_A = room air temperature
Based on air velocity of 0 to 0.2 m/s;
relative humidity 30-70%

13.2 Comfort zone in the t_r/t_A schematic

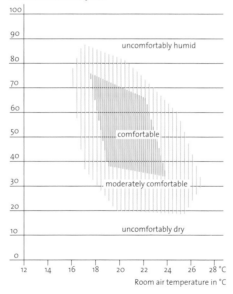

13.3 Comfort zone in relation to room air temperature and relative humidity in room

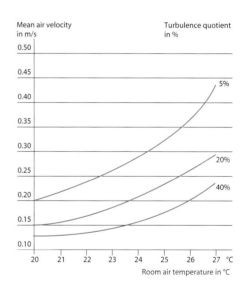

13.4 Relationship between room air temperature and velocity for different turbulence quotients

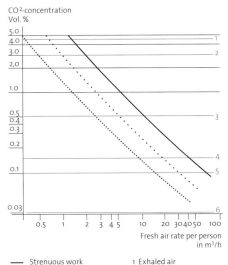

13.5 Fresh air rate per person for different permissible CO2 concentration levels

—— Strenuous work	1 Exhaled air
400 W heat transmission	2 Shelters
· · · Light work	3 Industrial MAK-value
200 W heat transmission	4 Maximum for offices
····· Sedentary work	5 Pettenkofer value
100 W heat transmission	6 Fresh/outside air

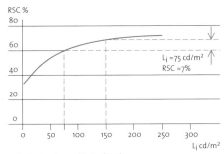

13.6 Contrast sensitivity (RSC)

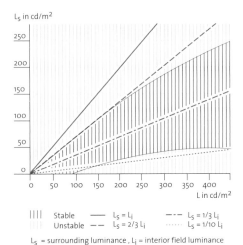

‖‖ Stable	—— $L_S = L_i$	– – – $L_S = 1/3 L_i$	
Unstable	– – $L_S = 2/3 L_i$	······· $L_S = 1/10 L_i$	

L_S = surrounding luminance , L_i = interior field luminance

13.7 Stable/unstable field of perception

Table 13.8 Impact current density and symptoms

Impact current density mA/m²	Symptoms
> 1000	Noticeable damage possible, additional heart contractions, ventricular flutter
100–1000	Possible health hazard, changes in excitability of central nervous system, stimulation thresholds
10–100	well-confirmed effects, not injurous to health, visual sensory impressions, reports of bones healing faster
1–10	No confirmed effects, no confirmed reports on individual discomfort
2	Boundary value established by the radiation protection commission
<1	No confirmed biological effects

Hygienic Comfort

The air quality in a room is determined both by the quality of intake air, and by air-contaminating factors such as room usage. Figure 13.5 contains the familiar Pettenkofer diagram with boundary values for CO2 concentration levels, which can be used as a basis for designing the ventilation system.

Electromagnetic Compatibility

In Europe electromagnetic compatibility is defined by a code for the functional capability of electrical appliances and electrical systems. Electromagnetic compatibility defines, first, the permissible degree of interference radiating from the appliance itself. Second, it defines the levels of interference from other appliances or environmental influences that the appliance must be able to handle. While electromagnetic compatibility refers to appliances, electromagnetic environmental compatibility is used in the context of humans and animals. At issue are possible health hazards as a result of electric, magnetic or electromagnetic fields ("electro-smog").

The impact current densities listed in Table 13.18 (in mA/m²) are related to health issues and to maximum boundary values.

Visual Comfort

Visual comfort exists when the perceptive faculties in the human brain can operate without interference. Incorrect luminance distribution in a room, glare, poor color matching and inappropriate interior design all inhibit perception. Visual comfort also requires a minimum degree of illuminance, which increases with age. Figures 13.6 and 13.7 illustrate visual performance (contrast sensitivity) according to interior field luminance, as well as the fields for stable and unstable perception according to interior field luminance and surrounding luminance (Li, Ls).

Another important factor in façade design is to ensure visual focal points by providing visual contact with the urban environment or the landscape at ground level. Blocking such visual contact would result in considerable disadvantages: window sills at medium or high levels can create a situation where occupants perceive only a grey area as their environment (on overcast or rainy days), sometimes for days on end (Fig. 13.9).

Sick Building Syndrome

Buildings should not cause sickness, but should meet thermal and hygienic requirements to provide an agreeable atmosphere for their users. In the past a number of buildings have been found lacking in this regard. The goal for the future should be not only to use ecologically sound materials, but to avoid basic deficiencies in ventilation and lighting.

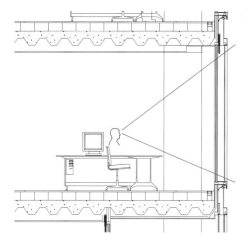

13.9 View of exterior – visual field of perception of a seated person

Table 13.10 SBS complaints after Dr. P. König

SBS complaints	Possible causes
Draft Susceptibility to flues and colds Rheumatic complaints	Excessive flow velocity Excessive turbulence Poor fresh air supply Intake air temperature too low
Mucous membrane irritation of the upper respiratory tract and eyes, sensation of dryness	Microbial allergy (from air-conditioning system) Dust; mites (carpeting etc.)
Fever Respiratory difficulties Aching joints Fatigue	Microbial cell toxins (endotoxins, cytotoxins) from humidifying water, filters and air intake elements
Fatigue Difficulty concentrating Stupor Headaches	Poor temperature control: – Temperatures > 23 °C – Increase in relative humidity – No window ventilation – Low-frequency noise (< 100 Hz) Allergens, endotoxins, cytotoxins Insufficiency of: – Sun protection/shading (none/internal) – Window areas (too large) – Storage mass (too low) – HVAC capacity/maintenance
Poor air quality	Odour from air-conditioning system: – Technical (material, filters) – Microbiological – Insufficient effective air change

The term "Sick Building Syndrome" (SBS) was coined by Dr. P. Kröling. Individual symptoms and related causes are listed in **Table 13.10**. Various sources have been identified as factors in causing the Sick Building Syndrome. These are:

– Excessive air velocity or turbulent airflow in a room.
– Symptoms arising from microbial allergens or cell toxins.
– Malfunction of thermal regulation due to excessively high or low temperatures and poor stimulus climate.
– Problems arising from low-frequency sound (< 100 Hz).
– Odors from poorly maintained humidifiers and filters.

To avoid these problems, air supply to the rooms should be draft-free and the intake air velocity in these areas should be slowed sufficiently (< 0.12 m/s) to ensure comfort. Microbial allergens and cell toxins can be prevented through regular maintenance of humidifiers and filter installations, for instance

by using high-performance filters, which can remove a number of pollutants from the air. Buildings should be designed to function without mechanical ventilation systems, and windows that open are an absolute necessity. By the same token, windowless rooms in constant use to accommodate personnel should be avoided whenever possible, particularly since they are contrary to building codes. Windows should make up at least 50 percent of the façade, and this must go hand in hand with adequate shading measures and large storage volumes to avoid overheating in the rooms. It is vital to ensure that the temperatures fall within the comfort zone (separate temperature controls for individual rooms and options for switching the system off and opening windows for ventilation). Rooms should only be humidified if the relative humidity drops below 35 percent. Indoor plants are a viable option to support humidification. In addition to the principal symptoms Table 13.11 (Dr P. Kröling) also lists secondary symptoms, causes, origins, and means of avoiding SBS.

13.2 Systems for Ventilation, Heating and Cooling

The topic of ventilation, heating and cooling systems as well as water supply is too vast to be included in this volume. Room standards and completion standards are listed in the tables, which indicate options for low, medium and high standards depending on the available investment funds ("low" in this context should not be confused with low energy consumption). Building systems will no doubt continue to evolve, albeit, with the exception of data and communications systems, not at the same pace of progress as has been the case in the past years.
Table 13.12 indicates the use of room and completion standards for different types of office buildings. Table 13.13 lists the different room and completion standards for office buildings. While these tables are not intended to offer a complete overview of all possible scenarios, especially since they are based on the current state of technology, they provide insight into future trends.

Table 13.11 SBS symptoms, secondary (or concomitant) symptoms and prevention according to Dr. P. König

SBS symptoms	Secondary symptoms	Causes	Origin	Prevention
Infectious: Legionella pneumonia	Pontiac fever (similar to influenza)	Legionella bacteria	Aerosol with rich germ burden in air flow (e.g. cooling system)	Hygienic conditions End-stage filters
Allergic: Eye irritation/tears Blocked nose Bronchial disorders Sensation of dryness	Fatigue Headache Impaired concentration Reduced performance	Microbial allergy – Various fungal spores – Various germs – Mites/products – Organic dusts	Humidification – Humidifying water – Moist system components – Filters – Insufficient filtration – Unclean filters	Low-germ humidification (ozone/UV/silver ions) – Regular cleaning – Renewable filters – Electro-filters – End-stage filters
Toxic-allergic: Monday fever Humidifier fever Severe fatigue (fatigue syndrome)	Symptoms similar to influenza Breathing impairment Coughing Allergic alveolitis Long-term risk: Pulmonary fibrosis (wet lung) Reduced performance	Constituents: Various germs – Cell walls: Endotoxins – Cell content: Cytotoxins - Mycotoxins	Germ-infected humidifier water	Low-germ humidification (ozone/UV/silver ions) – Regular cleaning – Renewable filters – Electro-filters – End-stage filters
Toxic: Fatigu Headache Impaired concentration	Allergic symptoms Reduced performance	External sources of contamination: – CO, NOx , SO2 , VOC Internal sources of contamination: – Furniture, carpets	Fresh/outside air Building	– Pollutant-minimizing filters external/end-stage) – Avoidance of sources – Improved ventilation
Olfactory: Unpleasant odors "Lack of oxygen" Need for fresh air Shortness of breath	Discomfort with internal climate Reduced performance Desire to open windows	Malodorous intake air: – Traffic, garages Odor from HVAC systems: – Humidifiers – Filters, system components	Fresh/outside air HVAC system	– Odor-eliminating filters (external/end-stage) Odor prevention: – Odor-eliminating filters (end-stage)

Natural Ventilation

An analysis of the site conditions is vital in the context of natural building ventilation, especially with regard to sufficient air circulation in sheltered areas of the structure (e.g. atria). The wind roses in Figure 13.14 provide an example of conditions in Frankfurt: the principal wind directions are southwest and northeast, and the highest wind velocities come from a westerly to southwesterly direction. The façades exposed to wind from these directions should therefore be designed to ensure that the positive and negative pressures acting on the surface of the building are utilized to promote natural ventilation while at the same time avoiding potential problems in the building's interior (wind pressures on doors, draft, etc.).

The architectural concept in this example features perforated façades (southwest) and generous glazing (northeast), an ideal response to the conditions outlined above. The façade and the individual window

components should be designed so that initial opening of an individual window leaf creates only a narrow gap to minimize wind pressure while ensuring air circulation throughout the room to evacuate contaminants and odors.

Figure 13.15 indicates the frequency of wind velocities in Frankfurt. At this location, wind velocities exceed 10 m/s only during roughly 70 hours per year. Natural ventilation is limited during these periods because high

wind velocities can lead to high pressures. In these conditions it is vital to open windows only briefly and then close them again (instantaneous ventilation), unless the relevant area is mechanically ventilated. This limitation, effective during only 1 percent of the entire year, does not represent a significant downside. Detailed studies should be undertaken of the actual positive and negative pressure quotients, especially with regard to the impact of turbulence on the high-rise. The air currents and pressure quotients are shown in Figure 13.16.

Table 13.12 Applying equipment standards to office buildings

Office building	Low standard	Medium standard	High standard
Mixed residential and retail	x	x	x
Office building/headquarters	x	x	x
Office building/satellite office	x		
Office tower		x	x
Apartment and office building		x	x
Shops and services		x	x

Table 13.13 Room and completion standards for office buildings

Office standard	Low	Medium	High
Room standards			
Room temperature t_m	20–38	20–38 °C	20–26 °C
Room humidity φ	10–80%	40–60%	40–60%
Guaranteed air change	0–10 ACH depending on climate conditions	2–2.5 ACH, mechanical	2.5–3.4 ACH, mechanical
Illuminance e	350–600 Lux (user completion possible)	350–500 Lux	350–500 Lux
Surrounding luminance L_s	150 cd/m^2 (user completion possible)	150 cd/m^2	150 cd/m^2
Completion standards			
Heating	Static heating, conventional energy supply (district heat, boiler)	Static heating, conventional or alternative systems, e.g. heat pump	Static heating, conventional or alternative energy system CHP (e.g. heat pump CHP combined heat and power coupling)
Natural ventilation	Openable windows	Openable windows	Openable windows with window contact (monitoring and switch-off function for heating–ventilation–cooling)
Supplementary ventilation, mechanical	—	Top/top or bottom/top	Up to AC completion standard
Static cooling–building component cooling	—	Supplementary possible, up to 40 kW/m^2	Up to 80 kW/m^2
Sanitary installations	Process water, cold	Includes water-economizing setting, process water cold/warm	Includes water-economizing setting, process water cold/warm
El installations–mains current	Window sill, balustrade duct, possibly exposed installation, visible cabling	Hollow floor, underfloor installation	Hollow floor and double (or false) floor, maximum flexibility
El installations–low-voltage current	Space reserved for exposed installation, visible cabling	Space reserved for duct system or hollow floor	Bus-system technology
Automation (energy management)	Min. (thermostatic valves)	Process control technology for energy management, individual room control	Comprehensive energy management system in combination with bus-system technology
Fire protection	In compliance with legislated standards	In compliance with legislated standards and possibly smoke alarms, etc.	In compliance with legislated standards as well as specific requirements, including automatic fire extinguishing
Retrofit			
Alternative heating systems	None, retrofit possible	None, basic construction for completion in place	Centralized supply, heat pump or CHP, power/heat coupling, possibly earth coils, aquifer storage and photovoltaics
Alternative cooling systems	None, retrofit possible	None, basic construction for completion in place	Centralized supply, heat pump or CHP, power/heat coupling, possibly earth coils, aquifer storage and photovoltaics
Alternative power supply systems	None, retrofit possible	None, basic construction for completion in place, earth coils, aquifer storage and photovoltaics	Centralized supply, heat pump or CHP, possibly power/heat coupling
Rainwater	None, retrofit possible	None, possible preparation through provision of separating system	Graywater system
Expanded passive measures	In compliance with HPR (heat protection regulation), expansion possible, e.g. improved insulating values, windows/AC ratio 1:1 and possibly night cooling	Complemented with automated shading system, night cooling	Highly efficient automated façade (polyvalent wall, TIM), storage concepts (night current, ice storage)
Heating requirement	55–80 kWh/m^{2}a	35–60 kWh/m^{2}a	25–50 kWh/m^{2}a
Daylighting systems	—	Daylight-supplementing lighting, automatic time light switch-off	Daylight-deflecting system, automatic daylight-supplementing lighting, automatic on/off switch when room is occupied/unoccupied

Average distribution of wind direction (%)   Average distribution of wind velocity (m/s)

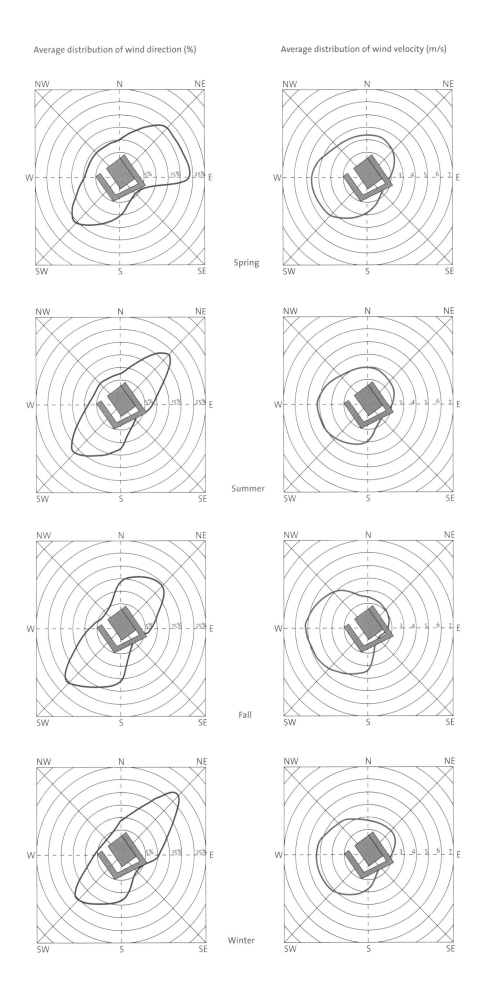

Spring

Summer

Fall

Winter

13.14 Average wind velocity and distribution of wind direction in Frankfurt

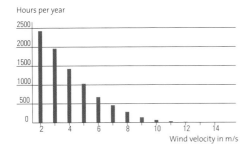

Hours per year

13.15 Frequency of wind velocities in Frankfurt

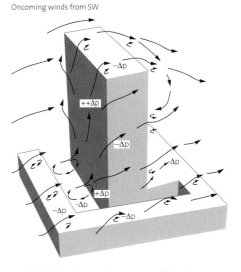

Oncoming winds from NE

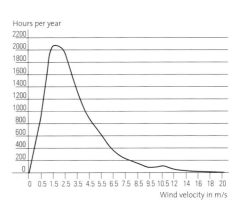

Oncoming winds from SW

13.16 Wind directions and pressure coefficients, example Frankfurt

Seasonal Ventilation Strategies

Natural ventilation of high-rises is particularly viable during the transitional season with average outside temperatures, the only limitation being when the outside air velocity exceeds 8 m/s. In Frankfurt, this occurs only during approx. 200 hours per year (Fig. 13.17).

When outside temperatures exceed 22 °C, supplementary mechanical ventilation is useful or even necessary to avoid uncomfortably high room temperatures on hot summer days. Mechanical ventilation and heat recovery systems are also recommended when outside temperatures fall below 5 °C.

Figure 13.18 demonstrates that natural ventilation is feasible for more than 60 percent of the year, representing circa 1,800 to 3,200 operating hours annually.

The following measures should be taken to achieve optimum operation given a variety of wind and thermal conditions:
– motorized operation of windows and vents,
– automatic settings for opening angles according to wind and thermal conditions and to the temperatures in each individual room,
– optional individual control, i.e. individual override of automatic settings when feasible, and
– use of appropriate bus system with reliable software programs.

Completion Concepts for Offices

The goal for the office building featured in our example was not only cost- and energy-efficient operation but also maximum use of natural resources. To this end a variety of completion concepts were developed with a view to building technology and corresponding façade options. The initial task of drafting a completion concept is to determine whether comfortable room temperatures can be achieved without supplementary technical systems, such as ventilation, cooling with water or air, etc. Figures 13.19 and 13.20 illustrate the different approaches with regard to natural ventilation, natural cooling, supplementary (mechanical) cooling etc., with a focus, in each instance, on which completion standards deliver acceptable and comfortable room temperatures during the height of summer.

Option 1
The premise for option 1 is that all office spaces are exclusively heated with static heating and naturally ventilated through window openings; this option does not include mechanical cooling in summer.

Option 2
The premise for option 2 is that the static heating and window ventilation featured in option 1 are complemented by mechanical night ventilation with outside air (operating approximately 7 p.m. to 5 a.m.), activating the storage capacity of the exposed concrete ceilings.

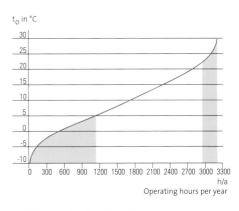

Hours per year

13.17 Frequency of varying outside air velocities per year in Frankfurt

t_o in °C

Operating hours per year

13.18 Frequencies of outside air temperatures during office hours per year

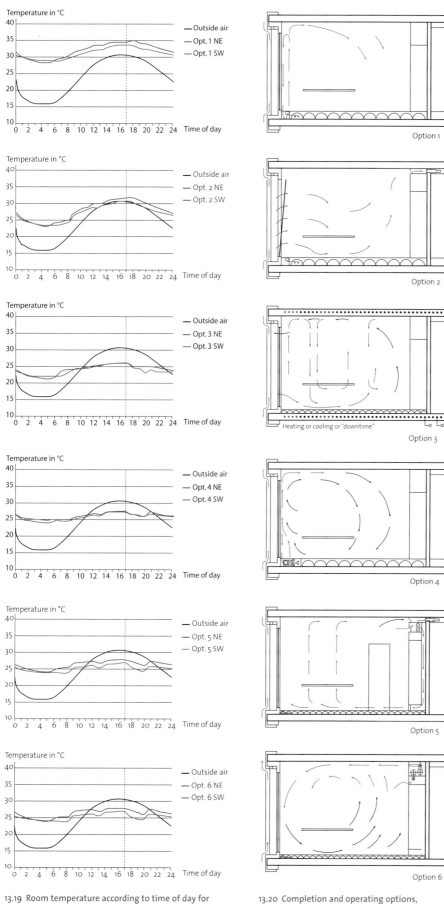

13.19 Room temperature according to time of day for different completion standards

13.20 Completion and operating options, schematic sections

A comparison between options 1 and 2 reveals that the latter reduces temperatures by approx. 3 K. Additional options are explored because the resulting room temperatures are still too high in summer.

Option 3

Cooling of concrete masses using an active cooling water system, integrated into the ceilings. This cooling water system can also be utilized for heating the rooms in winter. The Batiso system (active building component cooling) is operated as follows: For outside temperatures ranging from −12 to +15 °C, warm water (fluctuating flow temperature) is conducted through the pipe system, warming the concrete masses, which in turn radiate thermal energy into the room and raise the room temperature. For heating, the maximum flow temperature is +35 °C, resulting in a maximum ceiling temperature of less than +27 °C in extreme winter conditions. When outside temperatures range from +15 to +18 °C, the rooms are neither heated nor cooled, that is, the pipe system is switched over in readiness for anticipated cooling loads.

When outside temperatures rise above +18 °C, the same pipe system is employed for cooling, drawing the required cooling energy from refrigerating machines (flow temperature approx. +16 °C), earth coils or a free cooling system.

The disadvantage of this system is that, despite the simplicity of its architecture, it does not offer individual regulation per room and has a sluggish response time (similar to floor heating systems).

Option 4

In option 4 the rooms are heated and cooled via fan convectors near the windows coupled with natural ventilation. The fan convector need only operate with or without air to heat or cool rooms along specific axes. The concept is designed to connect the fan convectors to a four-wire installation, allowing for individual heating or cooling operation in rooms depending on cooling loads or heat losses. This system does not have a "downtime" as is the case with option 3. The fans of the subfloor convectors operate only during cooling periods and are regulated continuously.

Option 5

In option 5 (Gravirent System), heating is achieved with convectors (subfloor system as in option 4) and cooling with cooling components that are integrated above the wall units. These components cool the warm air near the ceiling sufficiently for it to sink to the floor, providing ventilation by means of a quasi stack effect. This solution, also described as "static cooling", offers the considerable advantage that cooling and/or heating can be regulated for individual rooms. It also allows for a high degree of load compensation (70 W cooling load per square meter). Another advantage is that the cooling system operates exclusively on a water basis, avoiding undesired noise transmission and increased energy consumption through blowers.

Option 6

This is a well-known ventilation solution (single-duct system, variable volume flow system) in which air is blown into the room at the upper wall-unit level on a tangent and then flows through the entire space. The option illustrated for this example is based on the premise of a maximum 2.5 air change rate, achieving a constant room temperature of approx. 27 °C in the height of summer (intake air temperature +16 °C). Heating in winter is provided by convectors, as in option 1. For the purpose of clarification, options 1, 5 and 6 are subjected to an additional analysis whose principal focus is to determine how they perform during a good weather period (at least seven sunny days in a row). The diagrams in Figures 13.21 and 13.22 show that exclusively natural ventilation and heating results in room temperatures of roughly 35 °C, while options 5 and 6 yielded average temperatures of 27 to 27.5 °C.

A temperature graph indicates the frequency of estimated room temperatures for each individual option in the test office spaces on the northeast and southwest sides, respectively. These graphs show that temperatures above 26 °C are limited to so few hours per

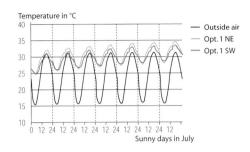

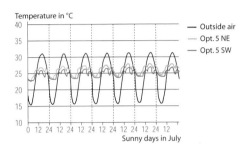

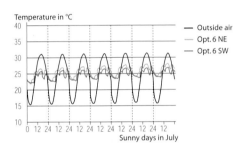

13.21 a–c Transient temperature behavior in rooms with different completion options (summer spell of fine weather)

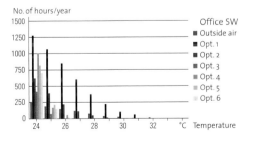

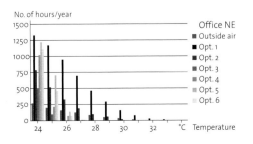

13.22 a, b Annual distribution of internal and external temperature frequencies. The temperatures recorded between 7 a.m. and 6 p.m. are greater or equal to the temperatures marked on the X-axis.

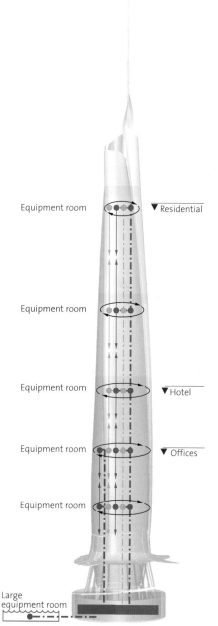

Equipment room   ▼ Residential

Equipment room

Equipment room   ▼ Hotel

Equipment room   ▼ Offices

Equipment room

Large
equipment room

Prewarming/cooling through river or similar feature

13.23 Distribution of equipment rooms in a convertible
high-rise

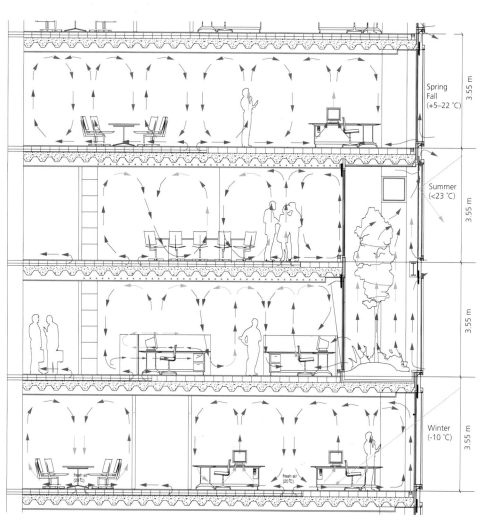

13.24 Seasonal air circulation (offices)

year as to be statistically negligible, while
option 1 results in high room temperatures on
both the northeast and on the southwest
sides for longer periods of time. Natural ventilation alone is therefore not recommended.
The best solution is a combination of supplementary ventilation and cooling as outlined in
the options listed above.

Other Technical Installations

In addition to the technical systems for general office areas, there are a number of heating and ventilation installations for utility
areas, circulation and traffic areas, underground spaces, etc.
In terms of usage requirements and operation
times, these are:
– Ventilation systems for equipment rooms
   Attic floor/ underground levels/ mezzanine
   levels

– Ventilation and cooling systems for confer-
   ence and meeting areas
– Ventilation systems for archives and
   storage/warehouse areas
– Air-conditioning systems for computer
   rooms/central server rooms
– Ventilation and cooling systems for mail
   rooms and shipping and receiving areas
– Ventilation and smoke exhaust systems for
   underground car parks
– Ventilation systems for athletics facilities
– Ventilation systems with cooling for the
   print shop
– Pressure cooling systems for stairwells and
   gates
– Smoke exhaust systems for warehouse
   areas and equipment rooms as well as for
   all rising areas

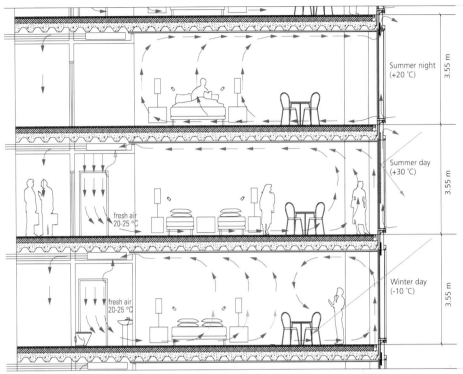

13.25 Air circulation over the course of the year (hotel)

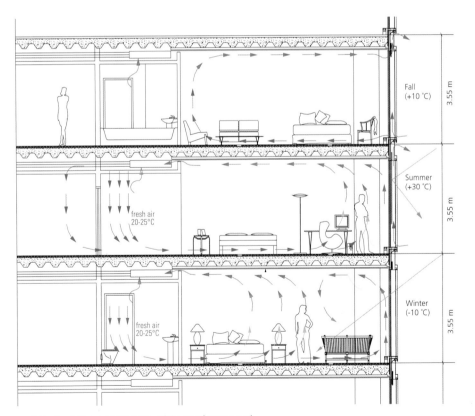

13.26 Air circulation over the course of the year (apartments)

Completion Concepts for High-rise Conversions

Buildings should be conceived with future conversions in mind, for ecological as well as economical reasons. "Flexible real-estate" offers the benefits of a long lifecycle and hence a considerably higher value as a long-term investment.

Conversions of apartment buildings into hotels and vice versa are fairly straightforward thanks to the similarities in installations and structural layout. The same applies to converting hotel areas with double floors into office areas. In this case, adjustments are required to the building systems, especially with regard to fresh air supply.

The double floor design provides space for installation of all air, media and energy-related systems at all positions and areas, where supply to rooms at the core is as easy as supply to rooms at the perimeter. The utility value of the building is thus ensured through infrastructure, provisions for all kinds of user completions and technical options for conversion and different uses. Figure 13.23 illustrates an example of a high-rise structure with different uses in individual sections, which can be shifted as needed.

Offices

Offices on the lower floors of the building are constructed with a basic system comprising floor-integrated convectors, some of which are mounted below the window sills. Fresh air is also injected into the office areas via double or false floors at an air change rate of 1.5 to 2 to achieve guaranteed minimal ventilation for hygienic air conditions. The air volumes supplied in this manner help to compensate for a cooling load up to a maximum of 10 W/m². Based on estimated cooling loads of approximately 50 to 60 W/m² in summer, the room temperature is maintained at roughly 32°C. If users desire a higher degree of thermal comfort or if market demands call for rooms with a more advanced level of technical finishes, retrofit options with capillary tubes (mounted) or suspended cooling ceiling systems (tenant completion) are easily implemented. Both of these retrofit options achieve a total cooling load compensation up to

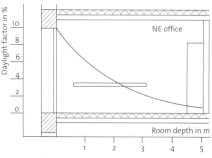

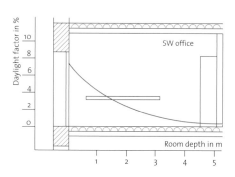

13.27 Daylight factors, diagrammatic sections

approximately 80 W/m². All rooms have flexible access to electrical power via the double floors. All workstations are equipped with connections to information and data communications systems.

Lighting systems may be part of the basic building completion or of the tenant completion, and the initial stage is based on providing general space lighting with an average illuminance of approximately 500 lux (see Chapter 12 by Müller/Schmitz).

The basic interior completion work also includes sprinkler installations in all areas as well as the necessary sanitary blocks. The double floor structure makes it possible to inject air volumes depending on the room division (individual rooms, group rooms or combination solutions, etc.) in areas where they are needed (excluding corridors, for example). Similarly, cooling services (cooling ceiling components) can be installed in those specific areas where cooling loads must be compensated. In addition to fresh air supply, the basic completion also includes ventilation, which results in night-time ventilation in offices constructed with a high-storage capacity (overnight cooling).

Figure 13.24 illustrates air circulation for operation in various seasons.

Hotels

Hotel rooms and hotel bathrooms are equipped with static heating surfaces, taking into account that temperatures in unoccupied hotel rooms are maintained at only +5 °C to +10 °C. The convectors at floor level beneath

windows are therefore used for basic heating. When hotel rooms are occupied, additional heating is provided via fan coil units (systems whose function is similar to fan convectors) coupled with regulated fresh air supply and natural ventilation.

In addition to fresh air, the fan coil unit also draws off room air to supply the necessary cooling energy to cool the rooms. Fresh air is injected in the door and ceiling area in the form of downdraft cooling with stack effect ventilation, the air exhaust is located in the bathrooms (see also Fig. 13.25).

Another basic completion feature in hotel rooms is the lighting in the sanitary blocks, but not the lighting in the hotel room itself. Hotel rooms, like offices, are always equipped with sprinklers (basic completion standard).

Apartments

The basic completion standard in apartments (Fig. 13.26) includes static heating near the windows and fresh air supply at an air change rate of 1.5 to 2, integrated into a suspended ceiling near the entrance. Depending on tenant requirements, fan coil appliances can also be furnished for greater heating and especially cooling performance.

Apartments are constructed with additional floor layers (footfall insulation/total screed approx. 8 cm) in which the cabling ducts are installed to provide floor outlets in all living and lounging areas for all appliances and data/media equipment. Basic completion in the living areas, sanitary blocks and kitchens also includes sprinklers. Stale air from the

living areas is vented via WCs, bathrooms and kitchens grouped around the core to avoid odors within the living areas.

Lighting systems are only provided in the areas with fixtures and appliances (bathrooms, toilets, kitchen) – not in the bedrooms and living rooms.

13.3 Natural and Artificial Lighting for Work Areas

Daylight should be used for work areas in living and office environments (single and open-plan areas) whenever possible. Various concepts are illustrated using a model building.

All offices in the high-rise are daylight-oriented with room depths that lend themselves to daylighting. Problems occur only as a result of high sky luminance or direct sun incidence, and these can be largely solved by providing the appropriate shading and glare protection systems.

Figure 13.27 plots the daylight factors in northeast and southwest offices, respectively. Larger window areas in the northeast offices (lower radiation loads) result in considerably higher daylight factors by comparison to the rooms with a smaller windows (e.g. perforated façades), with the result that the brightness ratio is usually sufficient in northeast offices even in the depth of the rooms, whereas daylight in offices that face southwest more often need to be supplemented with artificial lighting.

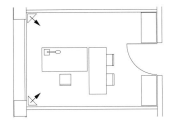
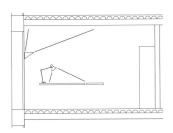

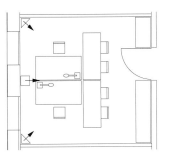
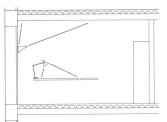
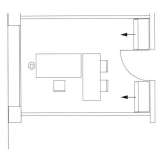
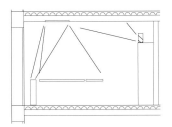
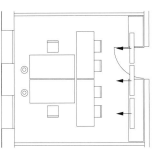
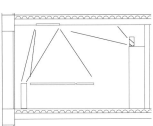

Option 1, NE

Luminaire	Corner lamp HIT 70 W
	Desk lamp TC-T 18 W
Connect load	2 x 82 W
Total connect load	184 W
Specific output	10 W/m²

Option 1, SW

Luminaire	Corner lamp HIT 70 W
	Desk lamp TC-T 18 W
Connect load	2 x 82 W + 1 x 20 W
Total connect load	286 W
Specific output	12 W/m²

Option 3, NE

Luminaire	Downlight (ceiling fixture) HIT 70 W
	Cabinet lamp T 38 W
Connect load	1 x 82 W + 2 x 37 W
Total connect load	156 W
Specific output	8.7 W/m²

Option 3, SW

Luminaire	Downlight (ceiling fixture) HIT 70 W
	Cabinet lamp T 38 W
Connect load	2 x 82 W + 3 x 37 W
Total connect load	275 W
Specific output	11.5 W/m²

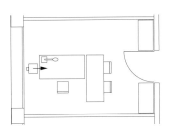
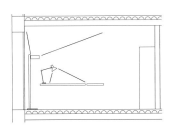
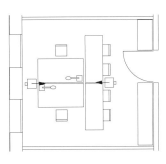
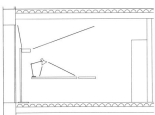
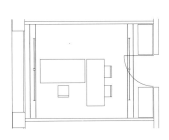
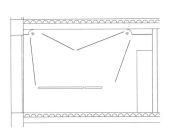
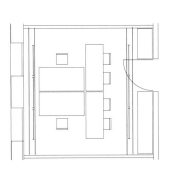
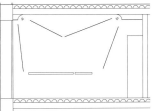

Option 2, NE

Luminaire	Floor lamp 3 x TC-L36 W
	Desk lamp TC-T 18 W
Connect load	102 W + 20 W
Total connect load	122 W
Specific output	7 W/m²

Option 2, SW

Luminaire	2 x floor lamp
	2 x TC-L36 W
	2 x desk lamp TC-T 18 W
Connect load	134 W + 40 W
Total connect load	174 W
Specific output	7.5 W/m²

Option 4, NE

Luminaire	Reflector lamp T 58
Connect load	4 x 55 W
Total connect load	210 W
Specific output	12.2 W/m²

Option 4, SW

Luminaire	Reflector lamp T38
Connect load	6 x 37 W
Total connect load	222 W
Specific output	9.4 W/m²

13.28 Options for lighting systems in an office tower; plans and sections of typical office rooms

Absorption chiller, DH, utility

Supply — Generation/distribution — Requirements
DH
Winter → Heating
ARM → Cooling
Summer
Utility → Power

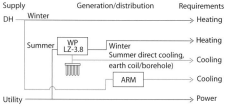

Probes (earth coils), HP, utility, DH, absorption chiller

Supply — Generation/distribution — Requirements
DH
Winter → Heating
WP LZ-3.8
Summer — Winter → Heating
Summer direct cooling, earth coil/borehole) → Cooling
ARM → Cooling
Utility → Power

ARM	Absorption refrigerating machine
RM	Refrigerating machine (also chiller)
CHP	Combined heat and power
DH	District heat
HP	Heat pump

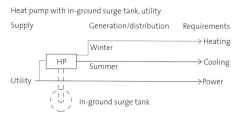

Heat pump with in-ground surge tank, utility

Supply — Generation/distribution — Requirements
Winter → Heating
HP
Summer → Cooling
Utility → Power
In-ground surge tank

Gas powered absorption chiller and CHP, utility

Supply — Generation/distribution — Requirements
Gas → Heating
Winter Summer
ARM → Cooling
CHP ARM
Utility → Power

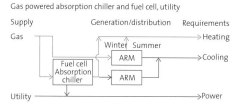

Gas powered absorption chiller and fuel cell, utility

Supply — Generation/distribution — Requirements
Gas → Heating
Winter Summer
ARM → Cooling
Fuel cell Absorption chiller ARM
Utility → Power

Electrically powered chiller with ice storage, DH, utility

Supply — Generation/distribution — Requirements
DH → Heating
Ice storage
RM → Cooling
Utility → Power

Electrically powered chiller, solar collector, DH, utility

Supply — Generation/distribution — Requirements
DH → Heating
RM → Cooling
Utility → Power

13.29 Refrigerating plants

13.30 Heat, power and cooling supply

As explained, visual comfort must be ensured by preventing excessive luminance in the visual field of office users (glare protection). Installation of blinds between the glass panes (external glazing/internal glazing) is also recommended. These should be covered in a metallic coating on the outward-facing surface, and gray on the inside. These blinds can be adjusted by each user to prevent glare as a result of sky light or direct sun incidence. The coating of the louvers is optimized so that artificial light is rarely needed, even when the glare protection and shading device is in full use. Visual contact with the outside is also maintained (diffuse daylighting/angle adjustment). Louvered blinds with optimized design offer a solution for the challenge of harmonizing the surrounding luminance and the

interior field luminance and may even obviate the need for additional glare protection.

In addition to visual comfort, lighting systems (options, see **Fig. 13.28**) also have considerable influence on energy consumption, on the sizing of cooling systems and on power consumption.

Option 1
Option 1 features a lighting system with wall-mounted lighting luminaires in the corners and on walls, respectively, which illuminate

the room by means of asymmetrical radiation. This systems achieves a basic illuminance of approximately 250 to 300 lux, similar to supplementary daylight systems. Workstation luminaires are required to provide additional illumination of the interior field.

Option 2
Option 2 envisions the use of a floor lamp next to the workstation, which casts its light towards the ceiling (metallic surface) for indirect lighting. This indirect lighting can be complemented by an additional light source (wall cabinet area) to increase the basic lighting level.

Option 3
Option 3 illustrates a formally restrained solution with a simple floor lamp (compact fluorescent lamp) and an additional desk lamp (to increase interior field luminance).

Option 4
This is a proven lighting method with asymmetric light-distribution from cove lighting. Luminaires with reflector illuminate reflecting surfaces (distortion following an E-function) and thus the work area. Cove lighting also has the advantage that they can also be designed to act simultaneously as sound absorbers. They can also be combined with cooling elements and contribute to room cooling in summer.

The specific connect loads of the various lighting systems are listed for each option. The aim is to reduce the energy requirements of the lighting system itself as a secondary measure for diminishing the cooling loads.

13.4 Central Energy Supply

Cooling Energy Supply

Cooling energy is currently still supplied through electrically powered chillers, because they are cost-effective despite their high rates of energy consumption. Absorption chillers, which utilize waste heat to generate cooling energy (district heat in summer, waste heat from machine installations), offer a viable alternative.

Where soil temperatures range from +12 °C to +14 °C, direct cooling through probes in combination with a pile foundation is a feasible option. Generally speaking, the heat exchange produced from probes or horizontal earth coils is insufficient for a tall building, resulting in the need for bivalent cold energy production. In-ground surge tanks can be a useful complement, although these may require drilling deep boreholes. In some cases it is possible to tap into natural aquifers to create a seasonal surge tank. Total energy systems, that is, gas-operated combined heat and power plants (CHP) in combination with absorption chillers, may be recommendable, as long as they are backed up by standby systems with a sufficient capacity to furnish the required emergency power. Such installations can be very sensible from both an ecological and an economic perspective due to the high rate of primary energy use (approximately 80 to 85 percent).

One approach to reducing initial investment costs for chillers and re-cooling plants as well as the connect load and operating costs of electrical systems is the use of ice storage or vacuum ice generators, which store a portion of the cold energy produced overnight and release it over the course of the following day. Figure 13.29 illustrates the various technical solutions for the production of cooling energy.

Heating Energy Supply

The most efficient approach to supplying heating energy is the use of district heat, with particular emphasis on heating energy from thermal power stations.

An equally cost-efficient alternative is the use of gas-powered boiler systems based on combustion technology. A combination of heat and power plants and absorption chillers as heat pumps delivers cost-efficient operation that can offset higher (initial) investment costs.

In-ground surge tanks in combination with heat pumps and earth coils can be integrated into a bivalent structure on a case-by-case basis – an ecological choice where applicable. Fuel cells – the latest system solution for optimum primary energy use – are still in

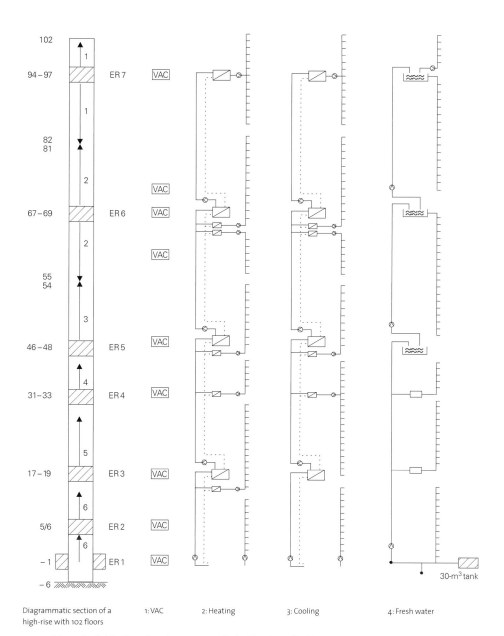

Diagrammatic section of a high-rise with 102 floors

1: VAC   2: Heating   3: Cooling   4: Fresh water

13.31 a Schematic distribution of equipment rooms (ER) with principal building system components, ventilation and air-conditioning (VAC), heating, cooling, fresh water

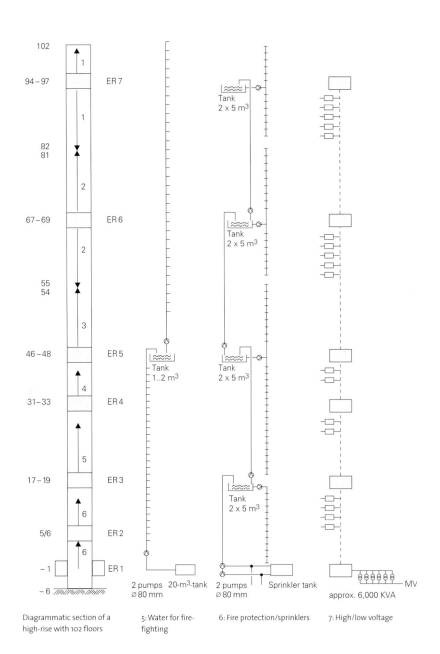

102

94–97   ER 7

82
81

67–69   ER 6

55
54

46–48   ER 5

31–33   ER 4

17–19   ER 3

5/6   ER 2

−1   ER 1

−6

Tank
2 x 5 m³

Tank
2 x 5 m³

Tank
1..2 m³

Tank
2 x 5 m³

Tank
2 x 5 m³

2 pumps   20-m³-tank
∅ 80 mm

2 pumps   Sprinkler tank
∅ 80 mm

approx. 6,000 KVA   MV

Diagrammatic section of a
high-rise with 102 floors

5: Water for fire-
fighting

6: Fire protection/sprinklers

7: High/low voltage

13.31 b Schematic distribution of equipment rooms (ER) with principal building system components, water for firefighting, fire protection/sprinklers, high/low voltage

their infancy in terms of standard use because the investments costs can be prohibitive. However, they should be considered for individual cases.

The active use of solar power through evacuated tube collectors or focal point systems is a feasible solution when combined with architecture designed for this purpose. The inclined surfaces of the building must offer angles that are suited for collector installation. **Figure 13.30** provides a schematic overview of these system solutions.

Electrical Power Supply

Conventional power supply of buildings from the public utility is still the most efficient option with regard to initial investment costs. Decreasing electricity rates (deregulation) result in lower operating costs.

Since high-rises must be equipped with larger stand-by or back-up power supply systems for emergency supply, a combination of power from the CHP and mains input may be the best solution in individual cases. If the

waste heat of the CHP can be utilized at the same time, these solutions can be quite cost-efficient. For optimum use of primary fuels (especially gas), one might consider fuel cells for the production of electrical power (and simultaneous production of heating energy). Solar power can be converted through photovoltaic components, although the profitability of this solution rarely matches the positive image associated with it. Due to the fairly low efficiency quotients, photovoltaic components are at this time still best employed as a complement to electrical power supply.

13.5   Power and Media Distribution

Vertical and Horizontal Distribution

The high-rise illustrated as an example in **Figures 13.31 a and b** contains seven central equipment rooms; the schematic section identifies their location and illustrates sample floors.

As the illustration demonstrates, the equipment room 1 (basement) and the equipment room 6 occupy the most space. For the purpose of illustration, these two spaces were fully furnished and are depicted with the full complement of appliances and machines.

The schematic illustrates the location of principal machines and essential characteristics for the following building services:
− Heating
− Cooling
− Water supply/sewage
− Fire-extinguishing systems
− High-voltage and low-voltage supply
− Central power supply for the entire complex is provided via central installations located on level -1.

Heating is supplied exclusively from the municipal district heat network, with bilateral feed for safety reasons. This supply is transformed in the equipment rooms 3, 5, 6 and 7 and transported from these stations to the individual floors.

Cooling energy is supplied by large-scale electric heat pumps. To reduce investment and consumption costs, the plan envisions

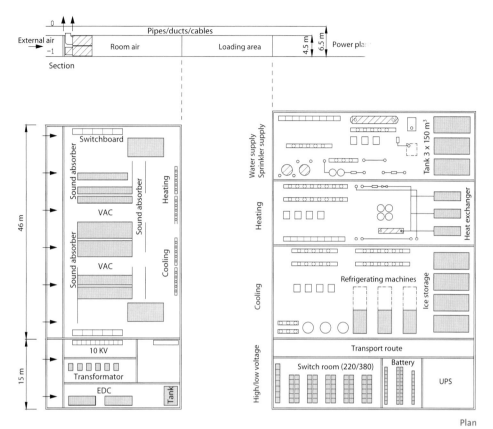

13.32 a Equipment room 1 in basement, including central energy supply

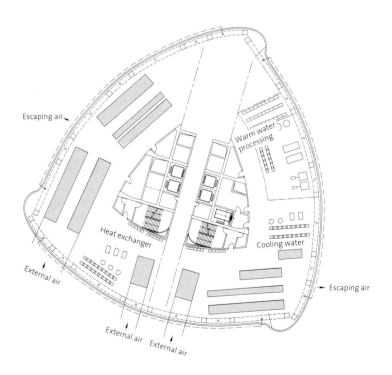

13.32 b Plan of equipment room 6, floors 67–69

ice-storage systems, which store part of the required cooling energy overnight. Cooling energy on the basis of 6/12 °C or 6/20 °C (cooling ceilings/fan coils) is supplied from a decentralized source at graduated pressure levels, similar to the heating systems. The central water supply is designed to operate on four pressure levels to avoid excessive network pressures. The relevant transition stations are housed in the equipment rooms 5, 6 and 7. Water supplies for firefighting and sprinkler systems are similarly decentralized, scaled to ensure an inexhaustible source of roughly 150 m³ of water.

The central electrical power is supplied from the municipal medium high voltage grid. At level -1, the entire electrical supply is stepped down from medium high voltage to low voltage. From this point onwards, distribution occurs via low voltage main distribution cables installed at levels 1, 3, 4, 5, 6 and 7. Power is then distributed from the various low voltage main distribution cables, which are connected by busbars, on each individual floor, where distribution cabinets are installed for change-overs and modifications.

A broadband network for data and communication technology is designed in an analogous manner.

An emergency power supply system is provided in case of power failure (despite the dual feed). It supplies power to the primary emergency power points (elevators, fire-extinguishing systems, emergency lighting, emergency aggregates, computer processing systems). UPS – uninterruptible power supply – can also be installed (tenant completion). The UPS is an element of the building's "intelligent network".

The building systems are complemented by a central process control system, which supports the building operation and regulates the various operating processes. This central process control system registers all system malfunction messages, prioritizing them in order to satisfy all necessary safety requirements.

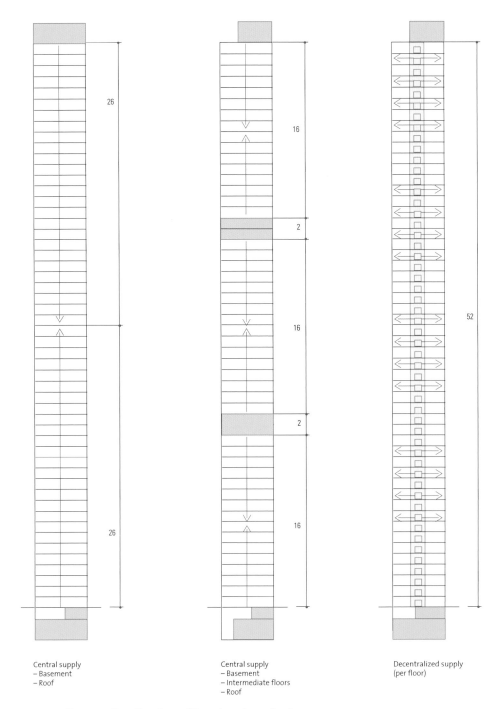

Central supply
– Basement
– Roof

Central supply
– Basement
– Intermediate floors
– Roof

Decentralized supply
(per floor)

13.33 a–c Diagrammatic sections for possible equipment room locations

13.6 Equipment Areas – Centralized versus Decentralized

A common topic in all high-rises is not only the location of the equipment areas but their integration into the overall design. The most difficult challenge seems to arise with regard to designing an appropriate "head", which should, of course, also house or serve a function. Another important issue is the decision whether heating and air-conditioning systems should be integrated in a centralized or decentralized fashion, in order to provide separate service for rental areas on individual floors. The schematic sketch in **Figure 13.33** provides a comparison of the various options, considering that centralized installations are practical only up to a height of approximately 25 floors in very tall buildings, because any greater height would result in elevated pressure levels especially in the water systems, which would require installation of heavy-duty industrial fittings.

The space requirement for the necessary equipment areas and corresponding shaft areas is roughly as follows:

Centralized Supply

(up to max. 25 upper floors)
– 20–25 m² per 1000 m² usable space for centralized energy supply
– 50 m² per 1000 m² usable space for central heating and air-conditioning systems
– 4 m² per 1000 m² usable space for central shaft installations

It is important to remember that centralized systems generally do not occupy valuable rentable areas; instead they are housed in central equipment rooms in underground levels. However, many underground levels are too small to accommodate equipment rooms and still provide space for other uses, leading to the construction of additional underground levels.

Decentralized Equipment Areas

Decentralized heating and air-conditioning systems (per floor) result in the following space requirements:
– 20–25 m² per 1000 m² usable space for centralized energy supply
– 20 m² per 1000 m² usable space for central fresh air processing
– approximately 40 m² per 1000 m² usable space for the installation of decentralized heating and air-conditioning units (processing units installed separately on each floor)
– approximately 1.5 m² of shaft area per 1000 m² usable space

Case-by-case studies are required for comparative analysis to determine what areas must be constructed at what cost and what the specific value of the rentable areas is. A "core and shell" solution (Fig. 13.33 c) can be used to add the required installation space for heating and air-conditioning systems to the rentable areas on each floor to avoid losses. High-rises of fifty floors or more should include two-story

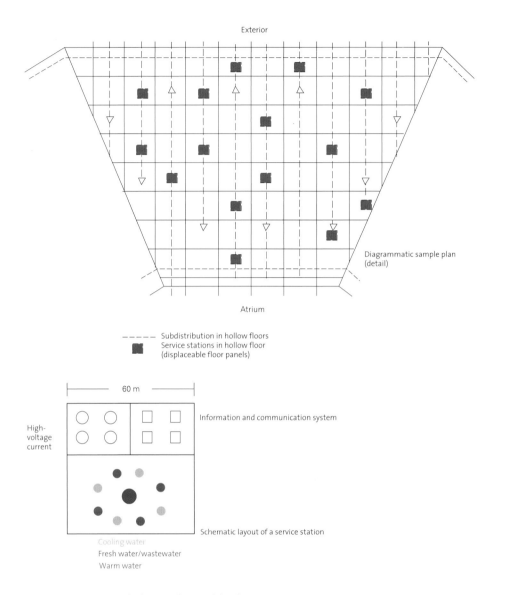

Exterior

Atrium

- - - - Subdistribution in hollow floors
▮ Service stations in hollow floor
(displaceable floor panels)

Diagrammatic sample plan
(detail)

60 m

High-voltage current

Information and communication system

Schematic layout of a service station

Cooling water
Fresh water/wastewater
Warm water

13.34 Service stations in a high-rise with vertical distribution

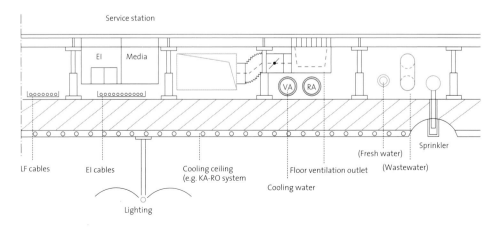

Service station

EI   Media

VA   RA

Sprinkler

(Fresh water)

(Wastewater)

LF cables   EI cables   Cooling ceiling
(e.g. KA-RO system)   Floor ventilation outlet

Cooling water

Lighting

13.35 Section, flexible hollow-floor installation

transition levels from which the areas lying above or below can be supplied.

13.7 Horizontal Distribution

While steel structures generally feature strong girders because of the sheer depth of each girder, many tall buildings today are constructed with flat (or girderless) slab floors on top of which the entire complement of building services can be installed. This achieves a high degree of flexibility. The complete set of installations (except air exhaust) located beneath a hollow floor is readily accessible at all times and hence suitable for conversion or retrofitting. Figure 13.34 illustrates relevant service stations in a section of the building area as well as a schematic section of a service station, while Figure 13.35 contains a cross section of a hollow floor with flexible installation.

As a rule of thumb, horizontal distribution of air, media and data communications requires at least 50–60 cm hollow installation space per floor in order to satisfy all requirements. This hollow installation space is distributed as follows:

- Installation above ceiling only, approx. 60 cm (shaft connection, max. length 20–25 m)
- Installation above floor and above ceiling, approx. 20 cm in ceiling area and approx. 30 cm in floor area (shaft connection as above)

In standard areas, the installation height can be reduced by roughly 20 cm, for example through increased cove height, by employing a comprehensive integrated approach (construction and building systems).
The installation heights listed above for various building systems apply only to rooms with low heat loads (up to approx. 60 W/ m²). In rooms with considerably higher heat loads and higher occupation rates, the space required for a hollow floor in which to install the required heating and air-conditioning channels can be proportionately greater (e.g. retail spaces). The wastewater system also has considerable influence on the installation heights when it is required to accommodate flexible sanitary blocks and when shafts (fixed points) are located at some distance.

14 Integrated Concepts

Matthias Schuler   Ideas, Realizations, Perspectives, Ideas for the Future

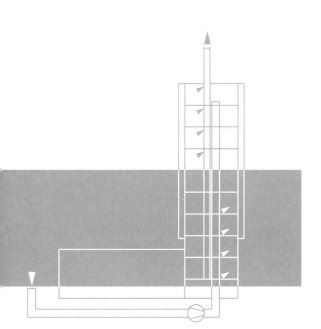

14.1   Integrated High-rises – Why?

The demands for high efficiency and thus maximum use of rentable areas on a minimized footprint make a compelling case for integrating the load-bearing structure, building systems and façade concepts in the architectonic design of high-rises. Multiple uses, e.g. of load-bearing and air-conducting components or complementing building systems through façade concepts, must be taken into consideration. The sheer height of these structures intensifies the effects of the climate parameters, which, in turn, has an impact on concepts for façades and building systems, and also on the demands placed on the load-bearing systems.

In addition to heat gain from internal heat sources, the energy balance sheet of modern administration buildings is very much influenced by the energy that flows through the building skin – including ventilation. This plays a dominant role in the internal climate and the requirements in the building systems and technical equipment. Vast improvements to the thermal insulation properties of glass, and the viability of fully glazed façades that has gone hand in hand with these advances make this role even more important. In Central Europe, understandable user requests for openable façades and individual control over room comfort in terms of temperature and lighting, have translated into additional demands.

An adaptable building skin can minimize the external loads and at the same time optimize individual comfort in each room. Building systems can be reduced, in turn, and this leads to favorable results both in investment and in operating costs. This concept is explained with examples of projects, which have been realized, planned or are currently under construction. Naturally, integration cannot be achieved without an interdisciplinary approach to planning, since the building skin alone no longer fulfills architectonic requirements.

14.2   Integration Ideas

Load-bearing Structure and Ventilation

In high-rises, vertical ventilation shafts waste valuable usable space. In the past, the strategy was to minimize ventilation shafts by reducing the supply distances and hence the dimensions of the ventilation shafts by means of creating several equipment floors. The disadvantage of this approach is that valuable areas are "consumed" by the equipment floors. Minimizing the air volumes to the minimum volumes required for hygienic conditions by employed water as a cooling medium has already allowed noticeable savings.

Another step is to integrate air-conducting shafts and ducts into the load-bearing structure. Thus, pipes can be integrated into the load-neutral zones of floors/ceilings to effect air distribution or extraction without the need for additional construction height, as is the case with false floors or suspended ceilings (Fig. 14.1).

Cavity ceilings, which provide installation space for media distribution, and minimize the dead weight while maintaining the same span widths, are another viable example. The premise for using vertical structural elements for load transfer and air control is based on the comparable load-bearing behavior of a pipe/tube and a solid element. As we shall see in the example of the DLZ Tower (Fig. 14.3), the principal load-bearing structure of a high-rise can be realized as a central stack, which assumes the functions of air supply and air extraction in addition to the load transfer. This basic structure also lends itself to construction with sliding shuttering, which helps to minimize the construction time. In contrast to buildings with standard heights, the cylindrical columns in high-rises cannot be used for air movement because of the number of floors and the required shaft dimensions.

The Building as Air Shaft

This concept is based on the idea of utilizing building areas as air-conducting shafts and horizontal distributions. Double-skin façades are ideal, but circulation corridors and vertical links such as atria or skygardens are also viable

options (see the project on the headquarters for the Deutsche Post AG, Section 14.4). This dual use amortizes the additional investment costs for the elaborate and complex façade through a reduction in shafts and horizontal distributions. However, the calculation does not apply if the dual use is limited over the course of a year – e.g. 70 percent – and a complete alternative concept must be furnished at the same time. Fireprotection and the stringent requirements in this area for high-rises are important considerations in this context. When corridors are used for air supply and spent air venting and the façade is designed with openable ventilators, measures must be taken to reduce the door opening forces and to prevent draft. High air spaces act like chimneys towards the exterior, especially in winter as a result of the increased temperature differences, and should therefore be planned in conjunction with increased impermeability requirements at the façade openings.

Fresh Air Ventilation on the 66th Floor

In addition to the classic solution of a complete double-skin façade, localized solutions for wind pressure control at the opening ventilators can also be implemented. Like selected arrangement of box windows or defined fresh air elements with control components, these alternative solutions can contribute to reducing the incoming airflow. In the MAX tower (architects: Murphy/Jahn, Chicago), currently under development in Frankfurt, the functions of the visual and air-regulating contacts to the outside were treated separately in order to further develop and simplify the double-skin façade concept.

14.1 Air-conducting pipes in the load-neutral floor/ceiling zone

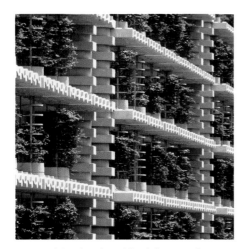

14.2 Façade jungle – planted façade "East Gate", Harare, architect: Mike Pearce, Zimbabwe

14.3 Air extraction via a Venturi wing, Hermannsberg II, Gross-Gerau, architects: m+Architekten, Moos und Matern, Darmstadt

The façade is composed of transparent areas and opaque opening ventilators. In addition, each room is equipped with a decentralized fresh air device, which allow individual basic ventilation without the need for large distribution shafts or a double-skin façade. This arrangement results in very high demands on the wind-pressure dependent control of the fresh air device, and on the wind-pressure resistance of the opening ventilator on the 66th floor. The space savings with regard to shafts and building systems make it possible to increase the efficiency of a high-rise beyond the 75 percent limit (HNF/BGF) without compromising individual comfort control.

The Façade Jungle – Helping Buildings Breathe

The popular solution of temporary or seasonal façade shading by planting trees cannot be applied to the high-rise structure. The distance between users and planted areas on the ground is extreme. The logical solution is to create green spaces closer to the users in the form of "skygardens". The gardens in the Commerzbank tower in Frankfurt exemplify this concept. The offices overlooking these gardens are equipped with openable windows to allow a fresh breeze from these green spaces to enter into the rooms. Façade plantings create microclimates, which are far less prone to heat gain from solar radiation than metal- or mineral-clad surfaces. Evaporation effects result in temperatures that tend to be lower than those in the surroundings. Wind-resistant plants can also be employed as wind breaks, although additional protection must be provided for gusty storm conditions. This idea has been pursued by the Malayan architect Ken Yeang with his "green" façades, for example on the Menara Boustead tower in Kuala Lumpur. Mike Pearce from Zimbabwe experienced one side effect of planted façades with his "East Gate" project in Harare (Fig. 14.2): the green surfaces attracted birds back to the city.

The Building Skin as Power Plant

Given the exposed position of high-rise façades and especially of high-rise roofs and of the wind forces acting upon these surfaces, it seems self-evident that these energies might be harnessed. Wind-supported spent air extraction in the form of a chimney addition or Venturi wing (Fig. 14.3). A rise in velocity in a jet diminishes the pressure, which is then used to transport spent air. Integrating wind power stations into building skins remains are a design vision to this day. Too many obstacles, for example the safety distance required for wind power stations, still stand in the way. Wind power stations are differentiated with regard to their location. In principle, implementations at building peak or between two building components are conceptually interesting, aside from the façade integration mentioned above. Despite the problems we have identified, this topic is addressed in many futuristic high-rise concepts, e.g. in the concept for a high-rise in Shanghai by the architects Theilig & Partner (Fig. 14.6.).

Pile Foundation as Energy Source

Depending on the quality of the subsoil or building ground, high-rises are founded in some locations on many individual piles with depths of up to 100 m. These "pins" thrust into the soil are ideal geothermal heat exchangers, reaching depths where the seasonal temperature fluctuations are irrelevant (see article by Arslan/Ripper, Chapter 5). The soil masses can be utilized as seasonal heat and cold storage, which preserve waste heat produced in summer for use as supplementary building heating source in winter, to provide one example. Heat pumps are generally employed to widen the range of useable temperatures. This is a classic example of dual use. Little additional effort is required to design the piles of the foundation for use as an energy source. It is important to take the limited storage capacity and performance of these systems into consideration for the dimensioning and system architecture.

14.3   Concept – DLZ Tower, Neckarsulm

Parameters

At the entrance to the town of Neckarsulm, a service center is being erected as the gateway to a new industrial park, where some 550 employees of different companies will be provided with a variety of work environments and conditions. The principal motifs of the design are the complex lying parallel to the area boundary and the nearly 100 m office tower, visible from afar (Fig. 14.4). It functions both as a symbol for the client and as a landmark for the entire commercial district. Thanks to a clever energy concept, the tower will be the first glass high-rise to function without a refrigeration plant.

The location of the complex on the highway, a federal highway and the planned by-pass calls for appropriate measures for protection from noise and immissions, which must be reflected in the design.

Goals

The building systems will be designed towards achieving the following goals:
–   Minimizing energy consumption in the form of heating, cooling, and lighting.
–   Optimizing the fabric to avoid unnecessary heating and cooling loads.
–   Minimizing the investment costs through multiple use of building components.
–   Minimizing the building costs through "intelligent" concepts.

Measures

The formulated goals translated into a series of measures aimed at minimizing the heating and cooling requirements:
–   High insulation standard for the external building skin;
–   Utilization of natural temperature decreases in summer (night air/soil);
–   Optimized climatic zoning of the building (atria/circulation areas as buffer zones);
–   Gaining solar energy in the form of light and heat;
–   Using the building fabric as heat and cold storage.

Complete daylighting for work and circulation areas will also contribute towards reducing energy consumption.

The Basic Concept

The 20-story administration tower designed by the architects Ziltz + Partner is conceived with a double-skin façade with single glazing on the outer skin and floor-to-floor separation in response to the wind and sound conditions at the site – location near an expressway interchange.

As a result of its height, the tower is exposed to strong wind forces, which translates into special requirements for façade protection (double-skin façade).

The double-skin façade is continuous on each floor and equipped with ventilators at varying positions. The wind-induced pressure differentials are thus compensated by means of controlled cross-currents allowing for indirect, individual window ventilation. The seasonal changeover of the façade cross-ventilation is achieved almost exclusively with the support of thermal and wind-induced effects. To this end, the tower is equipped with an internal double stack, which serves for fresh air intake and spent air ventilation and simultaneously transfers the principal loads of the structure. In winter, the upper section draws spent air from the office areas via the stack effect, while fresh air flows into the spaces through the double façade (manual control) or prewarmed via a heat-recovery plant through the lower section of the stack. In summer, solar heat in the double façade is ventilated in daytime as a result of the thermal lift of the shading system in conjunction with the wind-pressure controlled ventilators. Cross-ventilation in the offices is effected through the wind and thermally induced exhaust air in the upper stack and fresh air, which is precooled in foundation ducts, is introduced via the lower stack, complemented by mechanical ventilation if necessary (Fig. 14.5).

14.4–14.6 DLZ Tower, Neckarsulm, architects:
Ziltz + Partner, Esslingen
Climate concept: Transsolar, Stuttgart
Heating, ventilation, sanitary systems:
Schreiber, Ulm

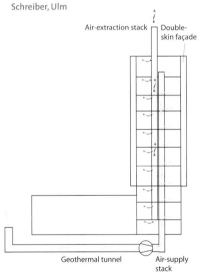

14.5 Climate concept, diagrammatic view

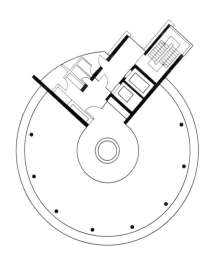

14.6 Diagrammatic plan of tower

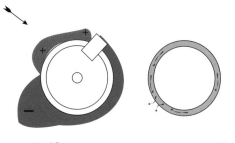

Wind flow   Pressure equalization

14.7 Wind flow and pressure equalization in
the façade, plan

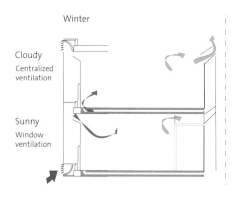

Winter

Cloudy
Centralized
ventilation

Sunny
Window
ventilation

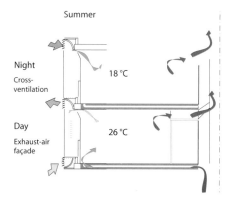

Summer

Night
Cross-
ventilation   18 °C

Day
Exhaust-air
façade   26 °C

14.8 and 14.9 Section showing cooling, heating and
ventilation

14.7–14.10 DLZ Tower, Neckarsulm

The Tower

The 20-story tower accommodates roughly
3,400 m² office area and a cafeteria on the
ground floor. The office tower is surrounded
by three- to four-story annex buildings and is
spatially linked to the "rear", where access to
this section of the complex is provided
(Fig. 14.6).

The office tower is fully clad in a roughly
70 cm deep double-skin façade, which fulfils
the following functions:
– Noise insulation;
– Weather protection for integrated shading
  system;
– Heat insulation (especially in winter and on
  sunny days in spring and autumn);
– Optional individual window ventilation and
  natural ventilation for external temperatures above 5 °C (even for higher wind
  velocities);
– Effective use of geothermal tunnel in
  winter and summer.

The offices located behind the double-skin
façade profit from generous glazed areas,
which allows maximum natural lighting.

Daylight Use and Shading

Sufficient daylight and glare-free lighting of
the workstations are important factors for a
healthy working climate. At the same time,
the rooms must be protected against overheating through direct penetration of solar
radiation.

While antisun glass blocks some of the solar
gains, it also increases the requirement for
artificial lighting and cannot eliminate the
need for air-conditioning. Heat protection
glass, on the other hand, allows a lot of light
to penetrate into the interior. In combination
with an external, movable shading system, it
also provides more effective protection
against overheating than antisun glass. To
ensure daylight in the rooms even when the
shading system is in use, the façade must be
designed accordingly: The windows should
reach all the way to the ceiling. The shading
system is conceived in a manner that leaves
the area at the top unshaded. With combined
light-deflecting and shading systems, light is

cast towards the ceiling and diffusely distributed across the room from that surface (even
room lighting). Sufficient daylighting is thus
ensured even on days with overcast sky.

Ventilation Concept

The cooling and heating concept of the tower
is founded on two basic principles: night ventilation and a system of earth tunnels.
Mechanical fresh air supply is ensured
through the connection to the earth tunnel.
A combined fresh air/spent air stack transports prewarmed (or cooled) fresh air into the
rooms via floor vents. At the same time, part
of the spent air is evacuated via the spent
air duct integrated into the fresh air duct
(Figs. 14.8 and 14.9).

Night Cooling

Massive air change rates at night play an
essential role in reducing the cooling load in
summer. Open storage masses are activated
through night ventilation in the buildings.
Cool night air flows through the offices and
cools building components that were heated
up during the day (ceilings, walls, floors).
During the day, these solid building masses
can once again store part of the thermal load.
Temperature differences between the surroundings and the building and the lift of the
air masses generate a pressure difference
between inside and outside. Cool outside air
flows into the building through the earth
tunnel as a result of this pressure difference.
The lower the external temperature, the
greater the flow velocity of the air. In winter,
the flow rate of escaping air must therefore
be modulated to limit air change rates to the
minimum hygienic and thermal requirements.
Manual ventilation is possible via tilting fan-
lights and can be employed regardless of
weather conditions because of the external
glass skin.

14.4   Concept – Deutsche Post AG
Headquarters, Bonn

A high-rise is erected on the Rhine meadows
in Bonn to house the new headquarters of the
Deutsche Post. The high-rise is in the shape of

two elliptical segments slightly offset from each other. The offices are arranged along the perimeter, and conference rooms, circulation paths and skygardens are located at the center. The elevation of the building is divided into four nine-story units, with the skygardens forming a continuous open space across nine stories. The two floors at the top are reserved for the board of directors.

The ground floor is designed as a four-story-high lobby in one segment and contains meeting rooms and offices in the other. Five basement levels accommodate underground parking, storage areas, utility areas and equipment rooms. A three-story socle or base structure with restaurant, conference facilities and presentation rooms lies in front of the tower. The two main façades of the high-rise face to the north and south, respectively, while the façades of the skygardens, which are inserted between the office slabs, have a west and east orientation.

Comprehensive Concept

The energy and climate concept of the new Deutsche Post headquarters includes the following system components, which combine into a logical comprehensive concept because the each individual component supports the function of the others:

– Double-skin façade with high-reflective shading;
– Concrete core temperature regulation (building component cooling and building component heating) in the massive floors;
– Non-suspended concrete ceilings, which can be activated for thermal use; they absorb large volumes of heat in daytime and are cooled overnight;
– Mechanically supported window or gap ventilation with heat recovery through temperature regulation of the skygarden with evacuated air from the offices;
– Fresh air supply from double-skin façade to offices via window elements and sound insulated gap openings with underfloor convectors, which can be individually controlled as heating and cooling sources;
– Individual window ventilation.

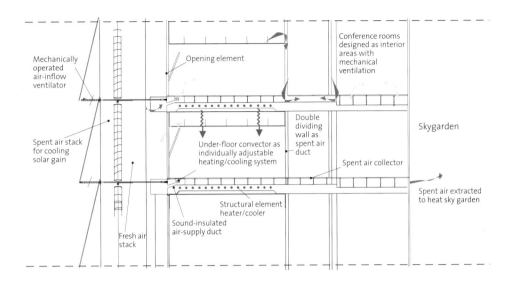

14.11 Section of building showing the system components for the climate and ventilation concept

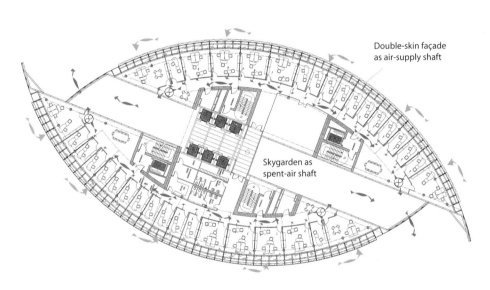

14.12 Diagrammatic plan showing circulation of ventilation air

14.11–14.13 Headquarters of the Deutsche Post AG, Bonn, architects: Murphy/Jahn, Chicago, Climate concept: Transsolar, Stuttgart Structure/façade: Werner Sobek Ingenieure, Stuttgart

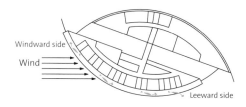

14.14 Double-skin façade to reduce wind pressure, diagrammatic plan

14.15 Simulation (computized fluid dynamics) of the air flows past the building, top view

The individual system components of the climate and ventilation concept are illustrated in a section shown in **Figure 14.11**, while **Figure 14.12** is a diagram of the ventilation air movement (plan).

Double-skin Façade

For architectural reasons, the façade is designed as a fully glazed façade. With conventional thermopane glazing (U-value = 1.1 W/m² K and frame class 1), this design stipulation is associated with the potential for low surface temperatures when outside temperatures are extremely low, because the frame component raises the U-value of the façade to 1.4 W/m²K. The thermal transmittance coefficients of glass elements are moreover generally referenced to a temperature difference of DT = 10 K. When outside temperatures are low, increased convection in the façade cavity tends to reduce the insulating properties of the façade. This leads to diminished comfort, at least near the façade, caused by radiation asymmetries (warm internal wall surfaces for cold façade temperatures) and by the cold air.

The building form and the height of the highrise result in high wind velocities and pressure differences on the external façade, which are problematic for the function of an external shading system and for window ventilation for long periods.

Under the circumstances, a double-skin façade is the logical response for several reasons:

– To decrease the U-value of the façade to well below 1.0 W/m²K;
– To enable permanent activation of the shading system to prevent increased cooling loads in the office on sunny days and high wind loads;
– To ensure window ventilation through controlled openings in the external skin.

Glass Qualities

The external skin of the double-skin façade consists of single glazing with uncoated white glass and the lowest possible iron oxide content. Together with the highly reflective shading, this configuration ensures that a maximum percentage of the solar radiation is reflected back to the outside and does not contribute to heating the intermediate space between the façade layers.

The internal façade constructed with gas-filled thermopane glazing (U-value = 1.1 W/m²K, g-value = 60%) is the true thermal boundary of the skin.

The double-skin façade is a pure supply-air façade characterized by ascending air currents as a result of the solar heat gain and the transmission losses. Ideally, a horizontal thermal gradient should develop in the air cavity in hot weather conditions, with relatively high temperatures between the single glazing and the shading system and lower temperatures between the shading system and the thermopane glazing.

In addition to the improved U-value, the supply-air façade also offers the advantage that the transmission losses through the thermopane glazing are regained with the supply air. The solar gains are moreover used to pre-treat the supply air. With regard to utilizing the natural cooling potential, the aim is to increase night ventilation. The external glass skin offers additional protection during night ventilation in rainy weather.

When the double-skin façade is used to supply fresh air it serves as a quasi-fresh air stack, eliminating the need for supply air stacks in the building interior and creating additional space for other uses. This is a considerable advantage in high-rises. The fact that air temperatures in the space between the façade layers may be considerably higher than outside temperatures in hot weather can present a disadvantage, however. This is especially true if warm air from the solar stack between shading system and external façade is allowed to penetrate into the offices due to incorrect shading system position and design.

Given these advantages and disadvantages of the double-skin façade, it is especially important to integrate it as a central component of the ventilation concept. This approach alone can ensure that unnecessary additional investment is prevented, for example by leaving out provisions for a mechanical supply and exhaust air system with subsidiary air-conditioning, and optimum comfort is provided.

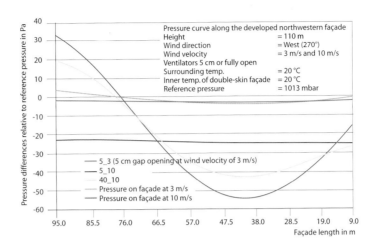

14.16 Pressure curve along and in the north façade for the regulated and open façade ventilators at different wind velocities. The western end of the façade is shown on the left of the diagram with the high dynamic pressure values.

The Double-skin Façade as Regulator

Each obstacle in the path of airflow produces a characteristic pressure field. If we look at a building as a flow obstacle for air, the side facing into the wind is characterized by dynamic pressure, while the side facing away from the wind is characterized by suction (Figs. 14.14 and 14.15). These pressure differences greatly influence the air-change action inside the building. Thus, extreme pressure differences result in draft and strong door opening forces, which can cause doors and windows to slam shut.

A double-skin façade can help to reduce the pressure differences at a building in the façade cavity. For example, the dynamic wind pressure, which is the result of gust, can be reduced by closing the openings in the external façade.

The static pressure produces pressure differences between the windward and the leeward sides. On the Post Tower, this pressure difference can dissipate because the façade cavity has no vertical partitions. The air can flow freely within one floor from the windward to the leeward side, thereby reducing the pressure difference for the static wind pressures.

Effects of a Reduced Façade Ventilator Gap

Figure 14.16 plots the pressure curve for an opening gap on the external ventilators reduced to 5 cm for oncoming westerly flow velocities of 3 and 10 m/s, respectively, and for the façade ventilators opened to a 40 cm gap for oncoming wind velocities of 3 and 10 m/s. In analogy to the calculation results, the gap reduction to 5 cm and an oncoming flow velocity of 3 m/s yields a nearly constant negative pressure of -2 Pascal (Pa) in the space between the façade layers, whereas the outside pressure fluctuates between +3 and -5 Pa. When the wind velocity rises to 10 m/s, the pressure on the façade shifts towards increased negative pressures, fluctuating between -22 Pa on the west side to -25 Pa on the east side. The difference of 60 Pa in the space between the façade layers when the gaps are open (40 cm, wind velocity 10 m/s) can thus be reduced to a mere 3 Pa by reducing the gap (5 cm, wind velocity 10 m/s). All calculations were carried out for temperature equilibrium between inside and outside to focus on comparing the wind effects. All gaps are opened in the same direction. Calculations for localized opened and closed gaps on the façade demonstrate that the dynamic pressure progresses virtually unimpeded from the outside to the inside at the individual open gap. The curve in the space between the façade layers represents the connecting line of localized pressure levels, but does not allow compensation.

14.5 Perspectives – What Next?

Is the comprehensive concept for the headquarters of the Deutsche Post AG the cutting edge of integrated high-rise design? In 2002, this was undoubtedly true. Yet building materials and hence new options will no doubt continue to be developed. The following paragraphs introduce perspectives that are already being implemented at the laboratory level and in experiments on buildings, and which have a profound impact on building comfort and energy requirements.

Decentralized Ventilation without Double-skin Façade

Is the decentralized supply air concept of the Post Tower discussed above imaginable without the elaborate double-skin façade? The concept was further developed by the same planning team led by the architects Murphy/ Jahn for the planned MAX high-rise in Frankfurt. Decentralized supply air devices were to replace the function of the adjustable double-skin façade to achieve wind-dependent pressure control. The goal is to maintain a defined supply air volume for wind pressures as high as 400 Pa and more and equally strong wind suction effects. When the system is not in operation, the building must be fully sealed. In case of increased dynamic pressure on the façade, the supply air volume must be limited because excessive air volumes would otherwise penetrate into the building and the pressure differences would progress towards the interior. The consequences are increased door opening forces and slamming doors. While the supply ventilator can overcome certain pressure differences for the far more frequent scenario of increased negative pressure, the volume flow collapses for a defined rated voltage once a given pressure difference is exceeded. The task is to develop simple regulating concepts, which increase the rated voltage feed and thus ensure the minimum volume flow. Since pressures may differ at each air supply device depending on building form, this cannot be effected with a central regulating console.

The integration of these elements into the façade will no doubt be further developed and improved. Whereas the today's façade modules are delivered to the site almost completely prefabricated – sometimes including shading systems and drives – and all that remains to be done on site is to clip them onto the carcass, the installation and connection of decentralized heating and ventilation elements continues to be carried out via individual pipe fittings and even butt-welded connections – a far cry from industrial prefabrication. In this area, integration into the façade modules and prefabricated connections to heating systems will drastically reduce installation times and increase quality.

Façade Developments

Aside from the integration of additional functions described above, research and development in façade technology will focus on the double-skin façade. The price point will demand simplified solutions for double-skin concepts, without compromising their performance in terms of sun protection and insulation. Concepts that combine the three layers of the double-skin façade into a single glazing unit are currently in development. Shading will either have to be integrated or provided through a combination of coatings and glass qualities. The latter solution allows the use of internal shading systems without significantly increasing the solar heat gains. It is

important to pay particular attention to the reflection of solar radiation in the short-wave range.

In addition to the protection it offers for the shading system, noise and wind protection of openable façade elements are the principal arguments for a double-layer façade. These protective functions must therefore also be met by more advanced single-layer solution. Wind protection can be provided by means of a openable façade elements (gaps), which can be adjusted very precisely, a solution that was realized with the parallel ventilator windows on the Maintower in Frankfurt (architects: Schweger and Partner, Hamburg).

An external baffle pane, which forms a localized box window in combination with the opening wing, is a more far-reaching solution that improves sound as well as wind protection. Pane-integrated shading systems, in the form of miniature shading louvers or a more advanced technology such as electrochrome glazing, must be developed with particular attention to the heat gain response of the combination pane because of the adverse effects such gains have on comfort. Even 15–20 percent of absorbed solar radiation produces a notable increase in the pane temperature and hence the internal surface temperature of the glazing. These temperatures can easily rise to 10 K above the room temperature, which results in a considerable increase of the perceive temperature near the façade and greatly diminished comfort.

These interactions document that innovative shading systems should possess high reflection properties, while avoiding reflected glare directly behind the pane and in neighboring buildings. Holographic layers, the basic principles of which were developed by Professor Stojanow at the RWTH in Aachen, offer an interesting alternative. These coating layers make it possible to reflect direct solar radiation from a specific incident angle, which can

be selected according to the hologram, while transmitting diffuse incident radiation. An additional advantage lies in the virtually full transparency for angular fields outside of the reflection range. While the holographic shading and light-deflecting elements, which have been installed on a few buildings, were applied onto films, Professor Stojanow is currently working on the industrial application of coating glass directly with holograms.

Storage Capacity without Mass

Many innovative high-rise concepts operate with the activated storage masses of the floors, be it in the form of night ventilation or direct activation through building component cooling, with cooling energy drawn overnight from a recooling plant. The premise of the concept is to buffer the external and internal loads in daytime using the storage mass, which has been cooled overnight, without allowing room temperatures to exceed comfort levels. One adverse effect is the dead weight of these reinforced concrete floors/ ceilings. At component heights of 22 to 30 cm per floor, this concept increases the load stresses on building structures and foundations, especially in high-rises. At the same, this correlation explains why this concept can only be applied for high-rises with reinforced concrete structures. Pure steel structures do not possess sufficient storage masses and require additional system adaptation. One logical solution for utilizing the cooling concept via convection is to employ metallic chilled ceilings or capillary tube matting with gypsum plaster board, although storage capacity is clearly diminished in comparison with building component cooling. Consequently, the required cooling energy must be supplied when needed without an option of storing it cost-efficiently overnight for the next day. The option for free cooling is thus null and void, and mechanical or thermal-operated chillers are required instead.

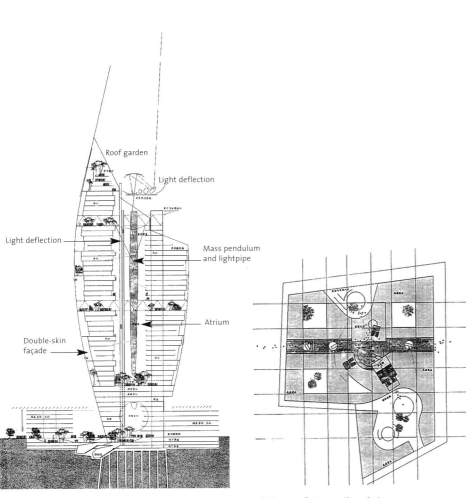

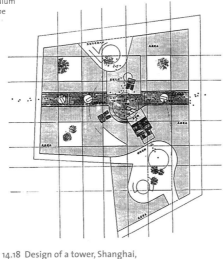

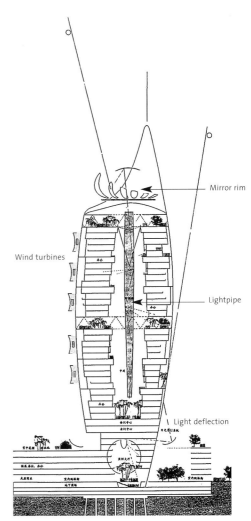

14.17–14.19 Design of a tower, Shanghai,
architects: Kauffmann, Theilig & Partner, Stuttgart,
Structure: Pfefferkorn & Partner, Stuttgart,
Climate concept: Transolar, Stuttgart

14.18 Design of a tower, Shanghai,
Plan of passage

14.19 Section

One solution for this problem may lie in the use of special gypsum plaster board, for which the gypsum is mixed with micro-encapsulated phase commutator material. This material – phase change material (PCM) – is composed of waxy materials or special salts, which melt or solidify at a specific temperature. The material absorbs great amounts of energy upon dissolution or bonding of the phase state "solid", or releases energy upon solidifying. These processes are reversible and prevent a temperature increase in the material upon melting despite the energy gain.

When this principle is applied to the ceiling, phase change materials with melting points of around 24 °C are needed. This means that the gypsum plaster board ceiling can be recharged overnight as the entire material solidifies, because thermal energy is withdrawn. In daytime, conversely, the storage is available to absorb large heat volumes without an increase in temperature. Several joint research projects in the chemical and plaster industries are currently working towards an implementation. It is important to ensure that the inclusion of high percentages of PCMs in the gypsum does not result in a loss of stability or thermal conductivity. The aim is to achieve the storage capacity of a 15 cm thick reinforced steel ceiling with a 2 cm thick gypsum plaster board, which is doped with PCM.

14.6 Ideas for the Future – High-rise Concept for Shanghai

The competition brief for a progressive high-rise in Shanghai called for vision for the future. Brainstorming sessions by the planning team composed of architects, structural engineers and climate engineers led to a visionary high-rise concept, which is both specific to the site and seeks to solve typical high-rise problems with new ideas.

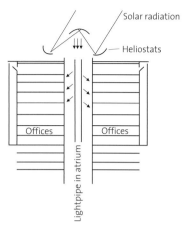

14.20 Tower for Shanghai, diagram of lighting principle

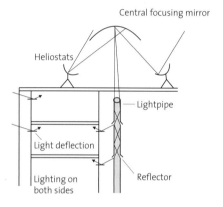

14.21 Section showing light deflection

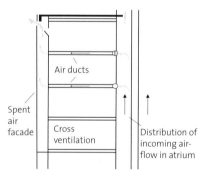

14.22 Section showing air distribution

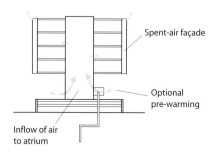

14.23 Section showing ventilation principle

Urban Design

The project consists of two fabrics, a six-story socle or base building and a 40-story tower rising to 160 to 220 m. The shape of the socle building follows the established block edge development of the district. Lightwell insertions ensure natural lighting and offer options for window ventilation during the cooler seasons. The height of the tower is compatible with the existing high-rise development in the area, although an effort was made to transform it into a significant marker through distinctive design (Figs.14.17–14.19).

The Climate-oriented High-rise Form

The streamlined cross-section and ellipsoid plan of the high-rise is the result of aerodynamic optimization of the wind-exposed surfaces. Two principal annual wind directions characterize the situation in Shanghai. In winter, a cool dry wind blows predominantly from a northwesterly direction, resulting in outside temperatures near the freezing point. In summer, on the other hand, the main wind direction is from the southeast, carrying warm, humid air across the China Sea to Shanghai and resulting in outside temperatures of 38 °C and very high humidities. The logical answer was to choose a building form that offers the smallest possible attack area in these two directions in order to minimize the dynamic stresses resulting from changing wind directions. These stresses play a very important role for the high-rise and for user comfort in terms of sway.
The curved areas on the south side direct the wind around the building and capture it with projecting windcatchers. Wind turbines are suspended between these windcatchers and the façade. They harness the energy of the accelerated flow around the building (Fig. 14.19). The five windcatchers distributed across the building height each span across four stories. The rudder-like extension on the north side forms a defined soft wind deflection edge and minimizes the formation of eddies, which would lead to high suction peaks. The wind loads increase with the building height as a result of increased wind velocity – the plan varies accordingly and has been optimized for the height development (Fig. 14.17).

The great building depth dictated that the ground plan had to be designed with a central atrium to ensure at least partial natural light for the areas at the core of the building. This atrium extends to nearly the full height of the high-rise as a light and air shaft (see Fig. 14.17). To transport light into the depths of the space, the light must be focused and redirected. This is achieved with heliostats, i.e. mirror-coated surfaces in the form of a mirror rim that follows the sunpath. A central focusing mirror is also required to dispatch the collected light force downward in the atrium. A central lightpipe was inserted from the top in the form of a metal pipe mirror-coated on the inside to allow for individual light direction on each floor. Allocated mirror elements make it possible to reflect the daylight on each floor and in each section (Figs. 14.20 and 14.21). Discussion in the planning team revealed that these elements could also assume an additional function as oscillation dampers – see Load-bearing Structures.

Figures 14.24 a–c show a built lightpipe in the Mercedes Benz AG pavilion at the IAA, Frankfurt, 1995.

Load-bearing Structure – Oscillation Damping and Oscillation Control

As a result of its dimensions, the high-rise has low natural bending and torsion frequencies and a strong tendency towards wind-induced natural oscillations. Two closely spaced resonance frequencies are achieved by coupling the structure to a second mass as counteroscillator (see article by Wörner/Nordhues, Chapter 8). Damping elements are installed between the two masses. These elements destroy the oscillation energy in a opposite oscillation phase, reducing the oscillation amplitudes to roughly 10 percent of the values anticipated without damping. This principles of passive oscillation control can only function if the frequency of the damper is carefully calibrated to the frequency of the building. For this high-rise, an oscillation damper in the shape of an ideal simple pendulum is envisioned. Since the natural frequency of the pendulum depends on the length of its suspension alone, the damping frequency can easily be adapted to the natural frequency of the building at a later stage.

A purely passive damper requires little maintenance and no additional energy; however, it is active only in an oscillating condition and hence effective only in response to wind excitation. In earthquakes, this condition may only be achieved after the earthquake has passed. Up to that point, a purely passive damper can even amplify the oscillation. Semi-active oscillation damping is therefore introduced. In this system, the passive damper (pendulum) is blocked at the fully extended position. In a catastrophic earthquake, the blockage is unlocked as soon as a previously defined acceleration is exceeded and the damper begins to swing immediately to its maximum extension. This unlocking process is programmed to cause the damper to swing immediately into the phase opposition to the main system, thus preventing undesired amplitude increase in an earthquake.

Bracing

The aerodynamic design of the high-rise plan reduces the formation of eddies and hence air resistance. The wind load is therefore smaller than for an angular building. Eight cores, which are continuous down to the foundation, provide the necessary bracing. The cores are rigidly connected through three cross members. This frame construction reduces the vertical deflection of the building by roughly 70 percent.

Energy Concept

The goal was to create a self-sufficient high-rise, which creates as much energy as it consumes through the building skin and by tapping into the energy source of the soil. The first conceptual prerequisite was to minimize the consumption of transmission and ventilation losses. However, since the cooling potential via natural resources is very limited, it was equally important to minimize the cooling load. Conversely, there was to be no compromise in terms of user comfort; the aim was to optimize thermal, visual and acoustic comfort. The concept was to be realized with a compact construction, equipped with a climatic

skin to minimize the surface exposed to wind forces. In combination with individual window ventilation in the areas facing the central atrium, this concept also allows for heat recovery from exhaust air. Open storage masses create a buffer for the internal loads and a wind-protected shading system integrated into the climatic skin provides the necessary sun protection. When needed, additional cooling is provided from the connection to the soil via an energy pile – that is, heat exchanger tubes in the pile foundation – and surplus heat in fall can be stored for the winter. The high groundwater level in Shanghai supports this concept. Heat pumps make it possible to ensure the necessary spread in temperatures. They are powered by wind power plants integrated into the façade. The ventilation concept is based on the stack effect principle via the climatic skin and by integrating the suction effect at the top of the high-rise.

Conclusion

This concept, which has unfortunately not been realized, exemplifies how closely form and function are linked if mutual interaction between the relevant disciplines is encouraged. This makes it possible to develop integrated visions, which can only benefit construction projects – especially high-rises. Openness and tolerance among the different participants and joint planning from the very beginning is an essential prerequisite for these concepts, whose strength lies in the integration of different functions.

14.24 a–c Mercedes Benz exhibition stand, IAA 1995, Frankfurt, architects: Kauffmann Theilig & Partner, Stuttgart, climate concept: Transsolar, Stuttgart

14.24 a Lightpipe prior to installation

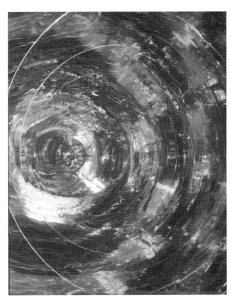

14.24 b Highly reflective lining of lightpipe

14.24 c View into a lightpipe

15 Fire Protection

Wolfram Klingsch

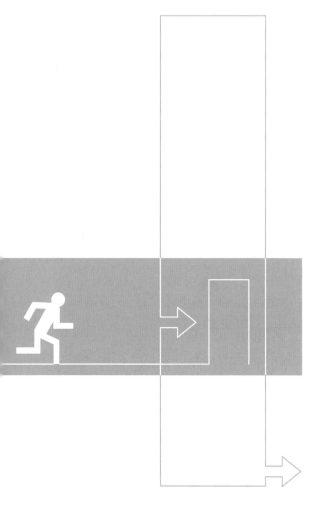

15.1 Systematics of Fire Protection Classification

All buildings where at least one occupied floor lies above the reach of the standard fire-engine ladder are designated as high-rises. This maximum height H is defined differently in the various national codes. The maximum height also applies when special ladders with a higher reach are available in individual cases. The reference height is measured from the set-up surface of the fire engine working level. In other words, a building with lowered access areas (e.g. sunken courtyards) may be categorized as a high-rise, although the actual building height falls below the maximum height limit. Conversely, if a raised or elevated access area is provided and if ladder access to the entire building is given from this point, the high-rise designation may be adjusted accordingly. The maximum height H is based on the building sections above a specific line where ladder access is no longer guaranteed.

All firefighting and rescue operations must be carried out inside high-rises, resulting in more stringent requirements for structural safety and stability. The relevant requirements are defined in the national building codes in each individual country and state. There are notable differences not only between, but also within states, and some local authorities adopt special regulations. Timely consultation with the responsible authority, site supervisor and fire department, and sometimes the insurance company, during the pre-planning stage is highly recommended. High-rises belong to the group of "special buildings". Special requirements from the authorities that exceed the standard one should to be expected and must be taken into consideration from the very beginning when planning high-rises in order to avoid costly design errors.

High-rises are often characterized by a wide range of mixed uses. Additional consideration of the relevant special building regulations is therefore required. Dedicated and exclusively residential or office uses are the exception rather than the rule, and most high-rises include underground parking levels. Conference zones, entertainment areas, restaurants and the like are often included as well. The corresponding special regulations for each of these uses must be met in addition to the high-rise specific requirements. It is important to verify whether the high-rise requirements are applicable to the basement levels and annex structures. The high-rise boundary must be defined early on and approved by with the authorities to establish optimum and efficient design parameters. Dispensation of compliance with regulations applicable to high-rises is only possible, for example, for annexes to the high-rise that are designed as separate fire compartments from the actual tower – the general minimum requirement is an R-90 rated fire wall, if necessary with connecting lobbies and fireproof doors. The annex buildings can then be assessed separately, as low-rise structures, in accordance with the relevant national building code.

The fire protection requirements for high-rises may differ greatly depending on the total building height. The relevant height limits and the allocated fire protection requirements are very different on a national basis. These categories are explained here, taking the requirements in Germany as an example.
According to German regulations, high-rises are divided into four groups:
Buildings with a relevant height of 22 to 30 m fall into high-rise group I. The principal distinction between this group and non-high-rises lies in the more stringent requirements for escape routes: 20 m are permissible instead of the standard 35 m. The building component fire resistance rating remains at R 90.
High-rise group II includes buildings of 30 to 60 m height, which must be equipped with at least one dedicated firefighter's elevator. Buildings over 60 m tall are categorized as high-rise group III. More than one firefighters elevator may be required for these buildings. The structural components must be rated for fire resistance class R 120.
High-rise group IV is reserved for buildings of more than 200 m height. The relevant authorities may stipulate additional requirements for such buildings on a case-by-case basis.

Despite the quantitative differences in fire protection requirements for each nation, a superordinate uniformity of assessment applies.

15.2 Building Requirements

Building Materials and Components

The principle of minimizing the fire loads applies to all building materials used in high-rise construction. Load-bearing building components, separating components and internal partitions, as well as insulating materials must be manufactured from incombustible materials (e.g. class A building materials according to Eurocode). Exceptions are only granted on a very limited basis.

Incombustible building materials are especially important in the area of the building skin or envelope, that is, the façade and the roof, because most firefighting must be undertaken from the inside since the tremendous building height makes it virtually impossible from the outside. Planar wood elements on the external façade are therefore not allowed due to the high risk of fire spreading to an extent that would be difficult to control. In prefabricated metal façades, flammable materials used to seal component joints of façade joints can lead to the entire façade being engulfed in fire, even though the materials are only employed in specific local areas with considerable distances between them.

It is important to ensure that all insulating materials are incombustible. Meeting this requirement can be problematic for some building system applications, e.g. diffusion-proof insulation for cold water pipes. Careful expert planning is needed in these cases. Combustible insulating materials can generally be employed and still meet fire protection requirements if additional safety measures are implemented, although all highly combustible building materials are strictly prohibited. Thus, building materials with low combustible potential (class B/C building materials according to Eurocode) may be acceptable in areas with sprinkler systems; similarly, building materials with medium combustible potential (class D/E building materials according to Eurocode) may be allowed if they are permanently encased on all sides with fireproof class A materials of a thickness equivalent to R 90. One typical application of the last example is thermal insulation in floor/ceiling panels, which is covered on all sides by a sufficiently thick screed; special care must be taken at face or end planes, expansion joints, penetrations for installations and so on, to ensure that these areas are equally and permanently encased. Electrical and data communications cabling are a fire hazard that must not be underestimated. Such cabling must never be laid along essential escape routes, except cabling necessary to supply components required to keep these routes operational. These are generally restricted to electrical wiring for lighting, smoke detectors, and the PA system. All other cables must be laid away from the escape routes, and, in some exceptional cases, encapsulated. The installations required for stairwells, connecting lobbies and elevators must be fed in separately on each floor and not installed as a continuous line.

The fire resistance of the load-bearing components is determined according to risk, taking building height, the structural function of the components and their significance in terms of the protection they offer to the building's occupants into consideration. Compliance with the various national requirements for this aspect is mandatory. The minimum fire resistance rating for all load-bearing components in high-rises is generally R 90/REI 90. The structural components of taller structures (skyscrapers) must be designed for R 120/REI 120. This applies at the very least for load-bearing columns and walls, including their stabilizing elements if applicable. The requirements for floors vary: In some case the REI 90 requirement is applied regardless of which high-rise group a building belongs to; in other cases the horizontal components (floors) must match the quality required for the vertical components. In this area, requirements may vary within individual states. The building regulations in some nations classify the R-ratings for load-bearing components within a building according to elevation: A higher R-rating is required for the lower floors than for the upper ones. However, this relaxation of standards would not seem to be in the best interests of overall safety.

The walls of stairwells and connecting lobbies, anterooms or escape tunnels must be sufficiently resistant to mechanical impact; they must therefore meet the same requirements as fire walls.

The R-classification and dimensioning of building components is generally based on established standards, e.g. Eurocode. Computer-aided engineering procedures, Level-3 procedures according to Eurocodes, are recommended for non-rated building components; the same is true in special cases for the purpose of improving economic efficiency. All deviations from the standards and the application of special verifications should be cleared with the permit-granting authorities at the earliest opportunity.

Smoke Compartments, Fire Compartments

Fire compartments are created to limit the spread of fire. Large areas are generally partitioned off with walls constructed to a high fire resistance. These fire walls must usually be rated for a minimum REI 90 class and be additionally resistant to increased mechanical impact loads. National standards for the dimensions of these fire compartments vary. In Germany, for example, a 40 m distance between fire compartments is the standard, resulting in maximum fire compartment areas of 1,600 m². Larger fire compartments are acceptable and the requirements for the non load-bearing building components within these areas can be stepped down if appropriate, for example in buildings with good fire safety concepts, such as area sprinkler and alarm systems and smoke detectors for all floor areas.

Shafts without horizontal divisions must be regarded as independent, vertical fire compartments subject to the relevant requirements for wall composition and inspection/maintenance hatches. Appropriate fire partitions must be created between the shafts and the corresponding equipment rooms. In the event of fire, shafts are susceptible to chimney effects, which are difficult to control; it is therefore essential to employ only incombustible installations in shafts without divisions and to avoid mixed installations of the individual building systems. Cabling shafts must be designed with qualified barriers. Maintenance openings and similar access points to the shafts should not open directly onto corridors, but always onto lobbies. Naturally, the same requirements also apply to elevator shafts. Since elevator doors have limited fire endurance, access to all elevators should be via anterooms or lobbies. This requirement does not apply to observation or scenic elevators. Stairwells and landings must be designed as independent vertical fire compartments with the requisite qualities in terms of the enclosures (walls) and access points (doors).

Floors provide the horizontal division of individual stories into fire compartments. Connecting elements between floors, which are not classified in terms of fire protection, represent multistory fire compartments: Special fire protection measures must therefore be implemented for atria, open internal stairs and similar features to compensate for this construction-related deficit.

Smoke compartments are designed to prevent the spread of smoke within a fire compartment. Corridors are divided into short smoke compartments to ensure smoke-free escape routes. The division into smoke compartments is effected using smokeproof doors at distances prescribed by national codes and sometimes subject to special requirements from local authorities. Each smoke compartment is connected to a stairway section, setting a limit for the maximum stairway distance.

Escape Routes

The requirements for escape routes are more stringent in high-rises than in other buildings. Since the building's height does not allow evacuation through the windows, it must be designed to provide rapid access to safe escape routes inside the building. Escape routes are comprised of all necessary corridors and stairways, and the allocated links and connecting lobbies. Firefighters elevators and their assigned safety lobbies are also considered as part of the escape route because they provide safe access to the building for the rescue workers and because these elevators are used for evacuating occupants with disabilities or injuries. Standard passenger or freight elevators and, where applicable, escalators cannot be used as escape routes. Whereas standard corridors provide means of escape in both directions and towards the stairwells, dead-end corridors offer a means of escape in one direction only. To compensate for the risks associated with this option, the use of such corridors is limited to short distances if there are no other exits or paths, for example, via balconies, other rooms or similar options.

As essential escape routes, corridors must offer sufficient evacuation security in the event of fire. Minimum fire protection standards are therefore required for the walls between corridors and adjacent rooms. However, it makes little sense to apply higher R-classes to these walls alone, if the doors set into the same walls do no meet minimum fire safety requirements. In combination with an appropriately designed fire safety concept, e.g. smoke detectors, individual alarms and sprinkler systems, the joint use of R 30 or EI 30 walls and self-closing fire doors (EI2 30-C) is a logical and effective means of securing corridors as essential escape routes. This approach also offers attractive design options, e.g. using REI 30 glass walls, without compromising the safety level of the fire safety concept.

Stairways are the most important escape routes in a high-rise. They allow egress from the building and, in combination with firefighters elevators, are safe access routes for firefighters and rescue teams. Stairways, and especially the entrances to stairways and stairwells, must be designed to prevent the ingress of fire and smoke and to promptly evacuate smoke that has penetrated into the space as a result of floor-to-floor evacuation. This translates into special measures for internal stairways. A stairway is defined as internal unless an openable window is available on each floor to effectively ventilate the space in the stairwell. Internal stairways must therefore be "flushed out" with air, with the airflow in the stairwell always flowing in the opposite direction to the evacuation. While air can usually escape easily at the top of the stairwell, special building measures must be implemented for the same process at the foot of the stairs for the basement levels. According to national regulations, compliance with the rule that two structural escape routes, i.e. stairwells, are required is not always necessary for high-rises of medium height if a safety stairwell is provided. For tall high-rises, however, at least two safety stairwells are essential. External safety stairs must be accessed from the outside via an external corridorwithout any openings onto the building interior. This minimizes the risk of smoke spreading directly from one floor into these stairs. The quality of external safety stairs must nevertheless be viewed with some skepticism, as fires resulting in widespread smoke damage to the façade have shown.

Interior safety stairwells are preceded by a connecting lobby on each floor; they also require ventilation with pressurized air. This ventilation system must be designed so that the pressurized air flowing out of the stairwell when the doors are opened from an interior space onto the connecting lobby and from the lobby onto the stairwell can hold back any smoke that may have accumulated on that floor level in the building.

The pressure difference between the safety stairwell and the connecting lobby, and the lobby and the adjacent floor area, respectively, must be sufficient to ensure this airflow from stairwell into the interior. This translates into a need for suitable pressure compensation openings best realized with fireproof connections to shafts; openable windows can also be employed for evacuating the airflow, provided they are equipped with automatic controls. Smoke that is unavoidably allowed to penetrate into the stairwell in the course of floor-to-floor evacuation is strongly diluted by the airflow within the safety stairwell and quickly flushed out. All construction and system-related measures for air-pressurized safety stairwells must be planned and executed by qualified experts.

All necessary stairwells must be equipped with exits leading directly to the outside. The same is true for access to the firefighters elevators. Access that crosses through other occupied areas, including lobbies, entrance atria, etc., is generally not permissible, because people exiting from the stairwell in the course of an evacuation would be forced to enter into a fire zone should these areas be affected by fire. Any necessary exits or entrances, respectively, must be linked to the exterior if necessary via independently enclosed tunnels built to REI 90 rating. Any deviation from this standard must be approved by the authorities. There are rare exceptions, where it is acceptable to locate these entrances and exits on the first basement level and provide secure passage to the outside from there. One example is when the basement level opens directly onto the exterior, for example a secure interior courtyard with an open staircase leading up to street level.

15.3 Fire Protection Systems

Fire Detection and Alarms

All fires begin with an initial phase that develops into a localized fire and can expand into a full-blown fire. The localized initial fire is often not critical in terms of its thermal impact on the room and can be effectively extinguished with simply means. The initial phase of a fire may, however, release smoke volumes large enough to pose a risk for safe evacuation. Hence, early detection of fire combined with an alarm system is one of the most important measures to protect the occupants of a building. It is important not to overestimate the building users' natural sensory perception: the visual and olfactory senses of occupants are not sufficiently safe detection "devices". The automatic detection systems available today offer a far superior quality and safety of automatic early fire detection than the perceptive abilities of the occupants. It is equally important to understand that the visual link between people and their environment, which is often regarded as especially safe and effective, and expressed, for example, through large transparent partitions between individual offices and common areas, is only relative. The technical components are undeniably preferable in terms of safety and reliability. Fire detection systems should be selected in relation to the specific risks and the protection target in each case; factors such as efficiency, maintenance and control should also be taken into consideration. These systems are available for the detection of smoke, heat and flames, as well as combination detectors (multicriteria detectors). The new technology of gas sensors completes the range of available options.

Smoke detectors can be employed as individual or spot detectors, line or linear array detectors. Spot detectors are usually employed in rooms with standard heights, shafts and similar areas. Line detectors, in the form of smoke suction extraction systems, are the preferred choice for false floors, intermediate or suspended ceilings and similar areas, which are difficult to access and poorly ventilated because these systems actively induct (suction) and detect smoke. Linear array detectors operate on the principle of infrared radiation and are capable of detecting smoke across great distances. They are preferably used in atria, entrance halls and similar areas. As their name suggests, combination detectors combine different types of detection in one unit, e.g. smoke-heat combination detectors. The new generation of intelligent or neuronal smoke detectors can also be employed in critical areas, where the high false-alarm risk previously limited the utility of smoke detectors, e.g. kitchens, delivery zones with truck traffic and similar areas. These detection systems must be designed to sound an alarm in the danger zone and simultaneously relay it to a central alarm console, which is manned 24 hours a day, and if necessary, directly to the fire department.

As soon as fire detection has been confirmed, the alarm is automatically triggered in the danger zone. A variety of sirens or similar acoustic devices as well as automatic PA announcements are available as alarms. Verbal announcements have been demonstrated to meet with far greater acceptance than sound signals. Language chips can also be employed to automatically broadcast the appropriate message with evacuation summons in several languages. Alarms with evacuation summons can generally be issued for the localized danger zone at first. This zone is demarcated, for example, by the corresponding fire compartment or firefighting section. In these cases, alarms are sounded, e.g. through smoke detectors, at an early enough stage to ensure safe evacuation. Should the smoke spread into adjacent areas, alarms are automatically triggered in these areas in the necessary sequence. Critical situations, e.g. bottlenecks in front of stairwell entrances, streaming lines of people into the stairwell etc., can be avoided by staggering the evacuation processes in this manner. Early evacuation of the relevant risk areas also prevents collisions with the incoming firefighting and rescue teams.

Firefighting

National regulations relating to the necessity of sprinkler systems are different. Irrespective of this situation, suitable systems for automatic firefighting should be part of the basic safety features in all modern high-rises today; this also applies to apartment and condominium towers. The standard solution is to install sprinkler systems. Since sprinklers are

selectively triggered only in areas where high levels of heat are released, any concerns about water damage are entirely unfounded. Additional options, which have been tested and proved in practice, are available to guard against erroneous sprinkler activation in especially sensitive technical environments. In high-rises with standard uses, such as residential or offices, it is reasonable to assume that only one sprinkler will be triggered and have sufficient impact to effectively control the fire. The new technologies of micro-water dispersion, often described as water-mist or water-fog systems, open up new possibilities for structural protection, e.g. for horizontal glass-steel divisions on multistory, staggered atria, or in areas where the effectiveness of sprinkler systems is limited, e.g. in ducts, shafts, equipment rooms, etc. Micro-water dispersion with standard pressure can be linked to the sprinkler system at low cost, providing a high level of safety for different risk scenarios. This solution makes it possible to effectively compensate for risks related to the construction or the building uses, and obviates the need for structural R-rated barriers.

For high-rise applications, gas extinguishing systems are suitable for server rooms or other sensitive areas. New extinguishing gases expand the options in terms of minimizing structural measures and investment costs while optimizing the protection goal and utilization. This is especially true for the new nitrogen fire-extinguishing technology and the permanent state of intertia it delivers. At an early stage, the initial fire is prevented from developing, while allowing the maintenance staff to access and work in the affected areas without risk.

Wall hydrants as self-help equipment are generally required as part of the basic equipment standard for high-rises. With the exception of garage levels, the usefulness of such hydrants is diminished, however, when large-area automatic firefighting systems are installed at the same time. A more sensible choice is to ensure that a sufficient number of hand-held fire extinguishers in appropriate sizes are available. Initial fires that do not generate enough heat to trigger the sprinkler system can be easily and effectively controlled by targeted action on the part of the building users. To support the effectiveness of firefighting

operations, risers for the fire-extinguishing water supply and sufficient hook-ups are required on each floor as well as pressure boosting pumps at different height levels. Details should be discussed with the local fire department.

Smoke Extraction

Defined requirements for smoke extraction apply to all necessary escape routes, including corridors on each floor and stairwells all the way to the exit to the outside. Smoke extraction must also be provided for underground areas. Special requirements are generally not imposed for the floor areas such as offices, apartments and similar areas; they do apply, however, to spaces designated for special uses such as meeting rooms, restaurants with commercial kitchen facilities, etc.

Smoke extraction measures are designed to safeguard a relatively smoke-free environment along the escape routes for the duration of evacuating a building's occupants. The expectation is not to maintain a completely smoke-free atmosphere in the escape routes during evacuation from one fire zone. However, ensuring sufficient vision all the way to the exits, as well as limiting smoke penetration into the escape areas to prevent interference with safe evacuation procedures, are essential and minimum requirements. The spread of smoke is limited by means of dividing the escape routes into smoke compartments by smoke-proof doors. This structural measure is complemented by dedicated smoke extraction, either through natural ventilation or with mechanical systems.

Natural smoke extraction of user units is effected via openable windows or – at the top of the building – smoke vents set into the roof. Along the escape routes, these smoke extraction openings must be automatically activated as soon as the presence of smoke is detected; heat activation of smoke extraction openings would be too delayed to be truly effective. High-rise façades with openable windows offer effective smoke ventilation in each room regardless of weather conditions. If the opening action is automatically coupled with the smoke detector in the room, the quality of smoke extraction is very high and smoke is not allowed to accumulate to levels

that would have a critical impact on adjacent areas.
Mechanical smoke extraction is effected with extraction fans. The volume output and temperature resistance of these fans must be based on room size, type of use and extinguishing system.

Standard ventilation systems may sometimes be utilized for smoke extraction; the increased volume capacity required for smoke extraction in comparison with ventilation can be provided by separating the unaffected areas in the event of fire using louvers, thereby focusing the ventilation capacity on the area where smoke extraction is required. Mechanical air supply systems, especially air-recycling systems, must at all times be monitored by duct detectors, which immediately shut down the corresponding air supply systems as soon as smoke is detected.

Pressurized airflow is required for internal safety stairwells, normally located in the core; the connecting lobbies must be equipped with pressurized air control to keep these areas as smoke-free as possible and hence safe for use.
The volume flow and the maintenance of pressure in both the stairwell and the connecting lobby must be carefully calibrated to ensure these qualities. The pressure level must be limited to keep door opening resistances at acceptable levels in the case of evacuation. The volume flow is sized in relation to the door dimensions, the type of connection between escape route and floor area and the required flow velocity of the air into the corridor. To ensure this airflow into the corridor, each floor level must be equipped with relevant pressure compensation features, e.g. duct connections to evacuate air, or automatically openable windows. Given a system designed with the object- and risk-specific parameters in mind and careful consideration of the evacuation procedures, pressurized safety stairwells offer a high degree of safety. Critical interactions with the thermally induced external pressure, e.g. extremely low outside temperatures, are avoided when these factors are considered. Extensive tests and measurements in tall high-rises confirm the safety of these escape routes.

Firefighting Installations

Since fires can only be fought from the inside in high-rises, there are a number of necessary special safety and supplementary measures. In addition to secured stairwells, tall buildings that rise above a certain height also require one or more firefighters elevators. Compliance with applicable national regulations is essential, and coordination with the district fire department is recommended. The firefighters elevators must be installed in a dedicated shaft with no direct links to other elevators or user areas. Access is provided through an allocated elevator lobby, which must be designed to provide ample space for rescue teams to transfer injured people from a floor into the elevator. The requirements for the technical equipment of firefighters elevators must be fulfilled, and the same applies to the additional space requirements for transporting stretchers. Firefighters elevators must be located to provide maximum radius action in each area of a floor level; cross-over through foreign rental areas not associated with the fire compartment should be avoided.
The elevator lobbies must be ventilated to prevent smoke accumulation. The process of indirect air pressurization in safety stairwells has also proved especially advantageous for firefighters elevators. Air is blown into the base of the shaft of the elevator and flows into the elevator lobbies through openings. Pressurization thus ensures that the elevator shaft and all lobbies for the firefighters elevator are charged with pressurized air in the event of fire. When an access door is opened, the pressurized air flows into the floor and keeps smoke out.
Risers for the supply for fire-extinguishing water must be installed all the way to the top of the building. Supply points for the firefighters must be placed within easy access of each user area. For reasons of functional safety, only wet standpipes or dry-wet systems are recommended for application in high-rises.
The necessary installations for radio communication between the rescue teams inside the building and the command post outside of the building must be planned and implemented. Current high-rise design and their building systems generally translate into an urgent demand for such internal wireless system because communication might otherwise be dangerously limited not only in the basement levels.

15.4 Project Organization

Planning and Implementation Tasks

Modern high-rise concepts usually call for a multitude of deviations from the standard regulatory demands for reasons dictated by the architecture and the dedicated uses. Even challenging high-rise concepts can be safely designed and realized when planning and design for fire protection is integrated into each phase of the design and building process. As long as proof of the required fire safety is established for custom or non-standard solutions, permission is usually granted, a fact that is demonstrated in many built examples of extraordinary high-rise projects. To ensure the necessary quality of fire safety, a fire safety consultant must be part of the design team at the very least from the pre-planning stage onward, and should continue to accompany the entire planning and construction phase of the project up to the time of handing the completed project over for occupation. For quality assurance purposes, a conformity certificate prepared by an expert should be presented upon handover, confirming at least the correct implementation of the approved fire safety concept. A more comprehensive quality assurance requires the relevant proof through constructional realization in accordance with the approved standards and the technical regulations. This can only be achieved when fire safety monitoring is organized from the outset as part of the overall quality assurance accompanying the entire project. Since the implementation of the fire safety concept is part of the execution planning, in-depth fire protection consultation for the architect and the technical expert planners and engineers is of great importance. Design or planning errors at this stage can lead to severe problems if they are only discovered during the construction monitoring or even at the point of completion.

Modern high-rises are characterized by complex interactions between structural and mechanical system components, including in the area of fire protection. From design to object supervision and monitoring when the building is in use, qualified management is absolutely essential to ensure the required level of fire protection quality.

Close coordination between fire protection planner and all involved technical experts is required in the design stage to avoid conflicts during the execution phase. Timely coordination with the responsible authorities must be initiated and documented for all deviations, compensation measures and specialized solutions. In the construction phase, especially during the installation of the mechanical building systems, expert fire safety construction supervision is sensible for quality assurance for all high-rises with ambitious technical systems. Spot checks of the fundamentally correct implementation of the fire safety concept are rarely sufficient. Experience has shown that design and execution deficits are only discovered at a late stage when controls are anything less than rigorous. This may compromise the issuance of the acceptance certificate by the authorities and hence the moving-in date. Because these fire safety controls touch upon all trades involved in the building's realization, the requirements for staffing and expert qualifications are very high, especially since this stage often calls for the ability to quickly develop special solutions in response to specific situations on site.

Control Matrix and Functional Testing

For reasons of system security and efficiency, the fire safety concepts for modern high-rises are based on a multitude of interactions between the individual components. Thus, the individual functional tests carried out by the technical expert are not sufficient for higher acceptance. What is required instead is a final complex system test to check that all interactions operate in accordance with the regulations. This is effected by smoke tests to simulate fire scenarios in the building, which produce the interactive system reactions defined in a control matrix. This alone

can deliver final proof of the functional performance of the fire protection systems in accordance with regulations and the fire safety concept.

The control matrix describes the interactions between the individual fire safety system components according to different alarm scenarios. The links between the systems for automatic early fire detection, extinguishing systems, alarms, mechanical and natural smoke extraction, elevators, pressurized air ventilation, closing or releasing or opening of doors, etc. are described in the matrix. This complex task must be performed in collaboration with all participating disciplines and at least checked by the fire safety expert. The control matrix then serves as the basis for the execution planning for the individual trades and provides instructions for the installation work. The internal functional controls as well as the acceptance by the authorities can be planned on the basis of this control matrix, which also serves to assess the performance of the system. The control matrix is an important tool in ensuring the quality of the fire safety measures once the building is in use, because the permissibility for and/or necessity of subsequent modifications can be verified, planned, and safely executed in accordance with the data it contains.

Visualizing the Fire Safety Concept

The visualization of the fire safety concept has evolved into an effective planning and assessment tool in recent years. Ground and section plans are employed to render a detailed, color-coded visual image of the fire safety concept. Visualization makes it possible to identify the location and course of fire-safety classified building components, which demarcate zones with sprinkler protection or special fire extinguishing systems, zones with natural or mechanical smoke extraction, or smoke and fire compartments. These plans facilitate assessment by the authorities of the chosen fire safety concept and are also a valuable working tool for all participating expert planners/consultants and executing firms. The plans are also helpful with regard to quality assurance during building operation because they make it easy to discern whether desired modifications are permissible and how they should be executed.

Facility Management and Fire Safety

The successful final functional tests of a high-rise is only a snapshot of the quality of the fire safety concept. Realistically, interventions into the fire safety concept are unavoidable as soon as the first tenants move in to the building. Over time, this can lead to a critical reduction in the safety level of the fire protection system for the entire building. Although building users generally notice and draw attention to any deficits in building systems related to comfort, which are then quickly remedied by the technical support staff, critical changes to the quality of the fire safety concept are frequently only evident at a far later stage. Since modern high-rises no longer derive their quality purely from construction and design, but often from a wide variety of mechanical components, facility management specifically for fire safety is a vital responsibility for which few strategies have been developed to date. The tasks required to fulfill this responsibility include rigorous testing, monitoring and acceptance of all structural and system-related interventions in the building. Updating and managing the control matrix and the fire safety concept visualization also fall into this domain.

15.5 New Technologies

Today's requirements for modern architecture, contemporary concepts for building uses and user comfort requirements generally lead to conflicts with the standard regulations established by the building authorities. This is hardly surprising since building codes and regulations, despite all efforts to create differentiated and up-to-date guidelines, can only ever describe standard situations. This is compounded by rapid development in the area of planning and concepts for building use, construction technology and mechanical building systems. However, a number of new developments make it possible to overcome these conflicts without compromising safety.

Limited Area Concept (LAC)

An LAC is a helpful tool for realizing transparent internal design concepts. The codes requiring R-rated walls for the corridors in necessary escape routes within user areas generally create conflicts if these walls are designed to be transparent (glass walls). A similar conflict arises in the design of reception areas, lobbies and similar zones and the floor areas intended as extensions of these corridor or circulation zones. The fire load resulting from the use of these areas is in direct conflict with the requirement for preserving escape routes as areas that are not exposed to fire loads. This conflict can be overcome by applying the LAC. User units up to a defined maximum size do not require internal corridors in the sense of necessary escape routes. Requirements for wall quality ratings, limitations in terms of permissible materials and inventory etc., thus no longer apply even if internal corridors are created within these user units. Instead, they can be regarded as separate fire compartments in their own right, and must simply be appropriately divided from adjacent areas or compartments. Within this "unit" itself, no further requirements are imposed with regard to necessary external escape routes or staircases, and this, in turn, allows for the creation of transparent internal corridor walls without fire-rated quality, to name just one example. If national regulations do not contain provisions for LAC, the relevant approval should be requested for individual cases. When combined with the sprinkling, smoke detection and evacuation plans necessary for such scenarios within the LAC unit, the risk assessment remains unchanged (i.e. no higher risk), and the effective fire safety of the users may even be higher as a result of this fire protection infrastructure than in the standard scenario without all these additional safety measures.
The standard value for defining an LAC area can be set at 600 m².

Fully Glazed Façades, Double-skin Façades

In high-rise constructions, fully glazed façades are problematic from a safety perspective and hence not allowed in many countries. Since firefighting from the outside is not possible because of the tremendous height of these structures, there is a fundamental risk of fire spread from story to story via the external façade, a risk that has been demonstrated in large-scale fires. Constructional measures are required to prevent this from occurring. Vertical, R-rated balustrade walls of 1 m height, for example, are a standard solution, while the option of R-rated cantilever slabs of 1.5 m depth are not desirable for aesthetic reasons and because of the restrictions they impose on room lighting. The need for balustrade wall components thus prohibits the realization of fully glazed façades. However, a new fire safety concept does make it possible to implement unrated fully glazed façades for high-rises. Indeed, this concept achieves a higher degree of protection against fire spread than in buildings with conventional façade structures.
The basis for this special safety concept for fully glazed façades in high-rise construction is the normal floor sprinkler system, which has been developed for higher quality and reliability on the interior along the perimeter near the façade. The main design parameters are limited distances between individual sprinklers and between sprinklers and the façade, modifying the RTI of the sprinklers (RTI = Response Time Index), and redundant water supply to the floor sprinklers. The additional investment efforts are minimal.

Double-skin façades can increase the risk of vertical or horizontal spread of fire on the façade depending to a great degree on the specific façade design. A special developed risk analysis procedure designed especially for this topic is used to determine the necessary compensatory measures. Double-skin façades can therefore be realized in high-rise construction without incurring additional risks.

The combination of the safety systems for fully glazed façades and double-skin façades also allows for the implementation of fully glazed double-skin façades in high-rise constructions.

Dynamic Elevator Control in the Event of Fire

In the event of fire, all elevators are generally returned to a default position, e.g. its ground floor. However, if this is the fire zone, the resulting risks are enormous, especially for local elevator groups that operate for a limited number of floors. Dynamic control in the event of fire can serve to improve the safety of passenger elevators by ensuring that they always travel to a safe area, regardless of which floor the user has selected on the control panel. This prevents inadvertent travel to a floor engulfed in fire. This new control method, which makes interactive use of the building's automatically fire detection system, uses a set of variables in a control matrix to direct the elevator car to a safe area, which provides direct access to a stairwell or another safe area or directly to the outside.

Special Verification Procedures

The common specifications for fire protection measures are based on codes, standards, regulations and legislation, etc. However, these normative specifications are only applicable to standard situations. They are not designed to take the current status of technology and new technological developments into consideration either. The general protection goals stipulated in the respective national regulations do make allowances, in principle, for the development of a general risk-oriented concept as an alternative to the normative guidelines. This type of concept is referred to as performance-based fire safety concept. One prerequisite for such concepts is to include modern engineering processes in the verification process. Moreover, the individual components are no longer implemented in a purely additive manner, but considered with respect to all their interactions. These interactive concepts and the multiple redundancies they entail result in solutions that offer much greater safety coupled with greater operational reliability while at the same time decreasing costs. The engineering processes employed for such concepts operate with mathematical tools, computer simulation and experimental studies.

Suitable fire experiments are designed to assess the reliability of new material combinations, for example, for interior finishing, or to test the permissibility of upholstered furniture in waiting and reception areas located in escape routes. Full-scale on-site tests or scaled lab experiments provide the basis for goal-oriented development and the safety assessment of new technical systems or building methods as well as assessment of the actual quality of existing buildings.

Full-scale experiments in the building itself undertaken as part of the final acceptance tests allow for realistic assessment of the achieved safety, e.g. by means of simulations with suitable synthetic smoke gases.

Computer supported fire simulations can depict the spread of a fire, with and without automatic fire extinguishing technology, as well as accumulation and spread of smoke or the effectiveness of smoke extraction measures. Model experiments on a precise physical bases are an effective tool in generating a safe and reliable design for smoke extraction measures.

Computer models for calculating the load-bearing capacity of building components can be used for the design of nonstandard structural elements or to assist in evaluating the quality of existing buildings.

Computational programs for dynamic simulation of evacuation scenarios make it possible to calculate evacuation times. This approach represents considerable progress in comparison with the more simple statical evaluation of the evacuation quality according to the normative specifications solely on the basis of geometry, or with other known approximation methods, e.g. NFPA. In combination with the simulations for the spread of fire and smoke, the time required to evacuate occupants through smoke-free areas can be calculated. These simulation programs make it possible to take into account the total building geometry of the floors and the staircases as vertical links between individual floor levels all the way to the outside. Internal obstacles, individual corridor routes, the influence of disabled persons on the evacuation, or the blockage of individual exits as a result of fire can all be taken into consideration. The results help to evaluate the fire safety of deviations from normative specifications or to optimize escape routes and times.

The application of advanced engineering tools for fire safety design demands a high degree of responsibility and qualification on the part of the expert. His or her tasks include a realistic definition of the scenarios to be investigated and the parameters for these scenarios as well as critical evaluation of the results. It is also important to check whether the intended computational model is suitable for the relevant task. Strict compliance with physical modeling laws is essential for all experimental model verification procedures.

The evaluation criteria must be conjointly defined in advance with the authorities and fire department or insurer and documented to ensure the acceptance of the trial results. This applies in particular to acceptance tests (smoke tests) in the building.

15.6   Super Skyscrapers

Building codes and regulations stipulate fire safety requirements for high-rises according to height. From a certain height – although this height limit does differ from country to country – additional measures may be required, which go beyond the standard definitions of the relevant high-rise codes. Current discussions focus on high-rise projects that rise far above 500 m. The user concepts of these buildings are no longer restricted primarily to office use; instead, distinctive mixed uses have entered into the debate, envisioning projects where people who work in the building also live there. Buildings rising to such heights demand new considerations and additional measures to safeguard the necessary fire safety standard. Another consideration is that the number of occupants in such buildings can reach levels that also necessitate new safety provisions. Analyses of such planned super skyscrapers indicate that the anticipated number of people in such buildings will be well above 100,000. The specific timeframes when users are present in the building for working hours alone – the common occupancy profile today – will no longer be possible in such projects. Instead, these buildings will represent "user units" in which people live and work, and which they will only leave for special occasions, e.g. a vacation. New requirements for fire safety concepts in such buildings are necessary even in the case of less futuristic user concepts for protecting occupants and the measures to provide technical support for the firefighting and rescue teams.

Anytime defined fire resistance classes are defined for load-bearing building components, there is an implied acceptance of building component failure when the anticipated intensity of the fire impact is surpassed. This intensity depends on fire temperature and fire duration. A building component rated for R 120 is designed to resist the impact of 120 minutes of a standard fire; depending on the actual fire, the true resistance period may be shorter or longer. The logical answer is to no longer simply establish a defined resistance time for the load-bearing building components of super skyscrapers, but to add the requirement that the load-bearing capacity of the building components does not fall below a minimum safety level even in the most critical fire scenario. This model expands the normative building component evaluation in a manner that takes natural fires into consideration, which factor in the real risks dependent on building design (ventilation) and use (fire load). The damping effect of sprinklering should not be included in the model. This requirement need not result in raising the building component qualities by comparison to hitherto applicable regulations; however, it does considerably improve the overall evaluation of the safety concept. Economic advantages can also be achieved, for example, by minimizing the necessity for extensive building component repairs following a fire. The scientific engineering tools are available and consists of a fire load analysis, a simulation of the course and spread of fire, and a realistic calculation of the load-bearing and deformation behavior of the entire structure and the individual components for the natural worst-case fire scenario. It is important to take into consideration that reinforced concrete, which has cooled again after a fire, has less load-bearing capacity than during the actual fire.

The building height and occupancy numbers of super skyscrapers no longer allow for rapid building evacuation as we understand it today. In combination with the heightened structural quality we have just described, which does not even allow for the partial failure of building components, it seems only logical to create safe rescue areas in the sense of protective zones within the building as a destination to which occupants are evacuated. These zones must be distributed throughout the building according to building height and number of occupants and must be equipped with autonomous safety systems. Acceptance of such an evacuation strategy can only be achieved with relevant training for the building users and regular internal evacuation exercises. These safety zones can be equipped with fireproof elevator systems. These elevators can then be used, in particular, for the internal evacuation of disabled occupants, while others make their way towards these internal safety zones via safety stairwells. The stairwells themselves must be designed to withstand heavy mechanical stresses and loads; lightweight construction methods are not suitable. The stairwells must be arranged at sufficient distance from one another in the building. Qualified personnel, i.e. an internal team of firefighters, should be present at all times to organize these evacuation strategies and to provide a targeted first line of firefighting in the event of fire.

The quality of reliability of the sprinkler system is especially important in these highrises. At least two separate risers in different fire compartments, i.e. in separate shafts, must be allocated to each floor level. Supply on each floor should be in a ring arrangement and connected to both risers. The sprinkler layout per floor must be designed to ensure that only partial sections of the entire sprinkler network need to be shut off for renovation or conversion work, even when this work is undertaken across larger areas (comb system of floor network). All power and water supply systems must be designed for complete redundancy. The minimum operating time, effective area and minimum water supply must be higher than currently stipulated for high-rises. Additional fire-extinguishing water tanks, distributed at regular intervals across the entire height of the building, are an efficient means of increasing the reliability of the fire-extinguishing measures. Micro-mist or minifog systems can be employed to drastically improve the fire-extinguishing efficiency while at the same time decreasing water consumption. This would allow effective protection along escape routes without impeding the evacuation process.

The standby power supply to such high-rises must comply with the increased requirements. The energy supply for the standby power feed (power grid backup, emergency power) must fully autonomous.
To facilitate the firefighting and rescue efforts, risers must be planned to achieve sufficient redundancy on each floor; the same principle applies to water supply, feed, pressure increase, etc.
Given a certain overall building height and number of occupants, the firefighting elevators should be equipped as autonomous mobile firefighting units. The internal firefighting team can assume the responsibility of regular maintenance and upkeep of this facility.

All of the aforementioned special measures for super high-rises can be staggered, depending in each case on building height, number of occupants and building use. However, it seems inevitable that the fire safety techniques employed to date will be adapted to these new challenges in order to apply and maintain the high safety standards currently in place for modern high-rises to super high-rises.

16 Elevator Installations

Hans M. Jappsen

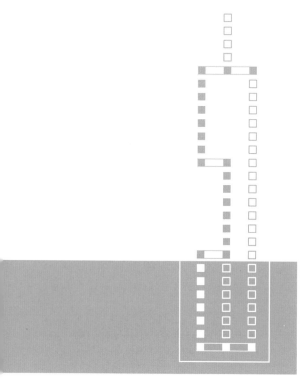

16.1   Introduction

It was the invention of rope and pulley, first used thousands of years ago to help raise a basket in some forgotten place, that really gave birth to the elevator. Of course baskets can also be used to transport people, although this is neither comfortable nor particularly safe.
In 1854 in Crystal Palace, New York, Elisha Graves Otis presented his elevator safety device in a free-fall experiment to an enthusiastic audience. This mechanism made the use of elevator cars safer and opened up new possibilities in architecture: high-rise buildings.

Regulations on the Construction of Elevator Installations

For European countries these regulations are to be found both in EU law and in the respective national laws; for non-European countries the respective national laws apply.

EU Law

– Regulation 95/16/EC of the European Parliament,
– Regulation 89/392/EC of the European Parliament,
– CE Identification regulations 93/68/EWG,
– EN 81, Safety rules for the construction and installation of elevator,
– EN 81-1 Electric elevator,
– EN 81-72 Firefighters elevator,
– Conventional control systems.

National Laws

– Building codes and tall building regulations,
– Regulations from the responsible fire safety authorities.

16.2   Passenger Elevators

One must differentiate between elevators in residential high-rises, elevators in normal office buildings, elevators in "small" office buildings and elevators in "tall" office buildings. Different usage places various demands on architects, elevator designers and elevator constructors. Elevators in high-rises must ensure a building-specific handling capacity. The elevator planner's job is to determine required capacity and calculate the number of elevators necessary to realize this while taking waiting times into account. Depending on expected usage, demands to be placed on elevators should be clearly defined beforehand. After this step, detail planning of elevator installations and necessary traffic calculations can go ahead.

Building Parameters

Usable Floor Space

The basic parameters for elevator traffic calculations are as follows: for office buildings the (planned) office space, for hotels the number of hotel rooms, and in residential buildings the number and size of the apartments. Office space or the number of hotel rooms or apartments must be determined for each story. The number and height of the individual floors must also be known.

Number of Passengers

The population of each story is determined by the usable floor space. In the relevant literature (Barney + Santos 1977 [1]) the following values are given:
– office building with one user
  8–10 m² net area/person,
– office building with multiple users
  10–12 m² net area/person,
– residential buildings and hotels
  1.5–1.9 people/room.

Slightly deviating from the above, the following values are recommended:
– residential building
  13 m²/person,
– hotel
  1.5–1.7 people per double room,
  1 person per single room,

– residential building
  depending on apartment size, 1, 2 or 3 people per apartment.

These values apply to high-value buildings in Western Europe, the USA and Canada. While the aforementioned values determine the likely average population of floors and buildings, the actual occupancy of individual floors can vary considerably.

Required Handling Capacity

The total of probable mean occupancy for each floor is used to determine the necessary conveyance capacity of each elevator group during in-rush periods. The traffic model calculations are based on this period because demands at these times can be standardized and compared. However, the in-rush period is not always the critical period during the day for many buildings. A weighting of critical traffic outside the in-rush period can be achieved by selection of a particular percentage in the five-minute handling capacity (HC5).

Elevator Parameters

Five-minute Handling Capacity

An elevator installation is regarded as sufficient for all normal types of traffic if the five-minute handling capacity during building filling corresponds (at a minimum) to the following staff percentages, taken from the relevant literature.
– Strakosch, 1967 [2]   11–20%,
– Barney + Santos, 1977 [1]
  office building with several users   11–15%,
– and with high prestige   17%,
  office building with one user   15%,
– and with high prestige   17–25%.

Elevators in high-rise buildings in Frankfurt are designed with a five-minute handling capacity of 15 to 16.5%.

Average Waiting Time or Average Interval Time

In Germany the average waiting time is commonly taken to determine elevator efficiency, while the average (or suitable) interval time is used in the USA. The average waiting time is defined as half of the average interval time. This latter time is defined as the average period between two elevator runs at the main lobby during morning in-rush.

The average waiting time (interval time) is a value used to determine the quality of an elevator system. In specialist literature the following interval times are given:

Barney + Santos, 1977 [1]
– office building with prestige   20–25 s,
– other buildings   25–30 s,
– residential and hotels   40–100 s.

The average interval times in office buildings are evaluated as follows:

Table 16.1 Average Interval Times

Average time in seconds	Rating
20–25 s	very good
25–30 s	good
30–35 s	fair
35–40 s	adequate
over 40 s	unsatisfactory

Waiting times are subjectively felt, and longer times are tolerated when waiting areas are improved in their arrangement and design. Transparency of waiting times is also a positive factor here.

Cab Capacity

The necessary floor area of cabs is calculated using the number of passengers to be transported each run to achieve the designated handling capacity with good average waiting times. A net floor space of at least 0.22 m² per person is desirable. Cabs with greater height are a positive contributory factor, as passengers in high cars are more prepared to squeeze together than in cabs with lower ceilings.

Table 16.2 Travel times and speed

Speed (m/s)	2	3	4	5	6	7	8	9	10
Shortest distance (m)	4	9	16	25	36	49	64	91	100
Travel time for 100 m (s)	52.0	36.3	29.0	25	22.7	21.3	20.5	20.1	20
Time saving against 4 m/s (s)			0	4	6.3	7.7	8.5	8.9	9
Time saving against 7 m/s (s)						0	0.8	1.2	1.3

Time Lost at Stop

The "time lost at stop" is the time difference between a trip from floor A to floor B without intervening stops and a trip from B to A with one intervening stop, plus a defined door-opening time. The term "time lost at stop" [3] was coined by the author to create a suitable mark of quality, easily testable, and useful for traffic calculations, tendering and quality approval. It can be quickly determined for every elevator installation using a stopwatch. During traffic calculations for high-rises, advanced elevator technology is a prime requisite in minimizing both elevator numbers and the uptake of building volume. With efficient drives and drive controls, as well as top-grade center-opening sliding doors of 1.1 m width, lost times of between 8.5 and 10 s can be achieved, depending on elevator speed. The door opening time ("using time") of 2 s is already included in these values.

Speed

Elevator speed in high-rises is dependent on hoisting height and chosen on the basis of traffic calculations. Table 16.2 shows in simplified form the effect of speed on travel times for an average acceleration of 1 m/s². It can be seen that high speeds only make sense when distances between stops are large, meaning that the maximum speed is indeed reached. Savings in time even with maximum speeds However, are small.

In Germany the fastest elevator in an office building can be found in Berlin's Potsdamer Platz. The elevator leads to a viewing platform, and a maximum speed of 8.5 m/s is reached (for one second only) going up.

Coming down the maximum speed is 7 m/s. In Japan there are elevators that travel at 12.5 m/s, again only for very short periods. Elevators are planned in the Taipei Financial Center (architects: C.Y. Lee & Partners), currently under construction that will have a speed of 16.7 m/s going up and approx. 10 m/s coming down; distance between stops is 370 m. The limits for acceleration and speed are not in fact set by technology, but by passengers. High accelerations and decelerations are disagreeable to many people. Speeds above 7 m/s, particularly when traveling down, lead for some to an unpleasant pressure in the ears, such as experienced when driving uphill fast. This is caused by the rapid change in air pressure.

Fast elevators require complex equipment for the drive mechanism, cars and counterweight design, buffer and tension sheave in the shaft pit; they need costly measures to ensure structure and air-borne noise insulation and they have a very high electricity consumption.

16.3 Firefighters Elevators

In accordance with national laws firefighters elevators must be incorporated in new high-rises above a certain height. This regulation height in Europe is between 18 m and 30 m, depending on the country. In Russia the figure is 28 m, in Japan 31 m, in Australia 25 m, and in Canada 18 m for residential buildings and 36 m for all others. All elevators in the USA are firefighters elevators.

The primary objective of firefighters elevators is to help fire-service personnel get to a fire. These elevators can also be used for rescue, if the fire chief deems it necessary.

Firefighters elevators are otherwise normal in function, and are used to transport passengers and freight.

Building Requirements

The distance from workstation or gathering place to firefighters elevator is set by national law. In Germany, for example, this distance must not exceed 50 m.

The elevators must be located in a separate, fireproof shaft.

The elevator landing must be large enough that a gurney can be brought out of the elevator into the landing, with the elevator doors being able to close behind. The minimum size of an elevator landing is 5 m², under EN 81-72.

Technical Requirements

Requirements for firefighters elevators are set out in EN 81-72. This is additional to EN 81-1, or EN 82-2.

Cabs in firefighters elevators must be at least 1.10 m wide and 1.40 m deep, with the entry doors at least 800 mm wide. The minimum load capacity is 630 kg.

If the specified use of a firefighters elevator is for evacuation and the accommodation of gurneys/beds, or if both sides of the car are intended for entry, the car must be at least 1.10 m wide and 2.10 m deep, and the doors must be at least 900 mm wide. The minimum load capacity is 1000 kg.

Firefighters elevators require a separate electricity supply that must remain active at least 90 minutes (or 120 minutes) during a fire. Firefighters elevators must also have a redundant electricity supply.

The car of a firefighters elevator, including paneling and flooring, must be made of non-combustible materials.

Firefighters elevators require an escape hatch in the roof, as well as a ladder (or steps) to reach it. Fire services are able to leave the cab by means of this hatch, with or without outside assistance. A ladder must be kept on the elevator roof to enable fire services to unbolt and open the next upper exit, and thus leave the elevator shaft.

The speed of firefighters elevators must be sufficient to ensure that all floors can be reached from the entry level within 60 s.

Certain parts of the firefighters elevator must be protected against water.

16.4   Freight and Cargo Elevators

Freight elevators in office high-rises are required for all types of transport related to daily operation. This includes deliveries to the offices, the transport of waste to collection points, the transport of technical equipment and parts to the machine floors, transportation of furniture and fittings during office relocation, or even the transport of partition walls. The freight elevators are usually already in use during construction, for transporting people and material. Cab sizes must be designed appropriately. If necessary, freight elevators can be used to transport sick or injured people.

Freight elevators in particularly tall high-rises make suitable firefighters elevators, as integration of firefighters elevators with passenger elevator groups is not possible.

The job of freight elevators in hotels is similar to that in offices. In addition they serve as service elevators for laundry transport and are used to bring meals to hotel rooms.
Freight elevators are usually not included in residential high-rises. Instead, loads are transported in normal passenger elevators.

16.5   Elevator Technology

Drive Mechanism

Passenger elevators in high-rises are fast traction (rope) elevators with gearless drives, reaching speeds of 2.5 m/s and above. Gearless drives have slow-speed drive motors, with the drive wheel sitting directly on the drive shaft. Freight elevators in tall high-rises are equipped with such gearless drives; only in exceptional cases is a drive with gearbox installed.

Of importance for traction elevators is the ratio rope diameter to sheave diameter. Regulations dictate that this must be at least 1:40. Large sheaves increase rope life and smoothness, while requiring more space for the shaft head and drive mechanism. The elevator drive must accelerate the car quickly to the specified speed, and decelerate so that the car arrives flush at the correct stop without additional maneuvering. Acceleration and deceleration, as well as changes in these, must be high without compromising passenger comfort. For trips over short distances when it is not possible to reach the optimal speed, the aim should be to run at the highest possible speed.

Ward-Leonard Drive

The Ward-Leonard system employs a DC motor and a dynamic transformer that produces the DC current. The dynamic transformer consists of a DC generator, mechanically connected to an asynchronous three-phase generator which gives it power.

Control of the Ward-Leonard drive is good. Demands placed on the power mains for the harmonic component are very good. Current spikes formed during acceleration of the elevators only reach the mains in attenuated form as the transformer functions as a damper. Electricity consumption is relatively high as the transformer practically runs continuously and is only switched off during longer periods of elevator inactivity. Current is not fed back into the mains. Braking energy is transformed into heat by resistors, and must be removed from the machine room.

Direct Current Motor with Static Transformer

Around the middle of the 1980s the development of power electronics allowed DC current, used to drive DC motors, to be directly transformed from three-phase current using transistors. Control of these drives is good. Demands placed on the power mains for the harmonic component are very high. During start and braking a very high reactive current is produced. Current spikes during acceleration of the elevator go directly into the mains. Electricity consumption is somewhat lower than with the Ward-Leonard drive. Current is not fed back into the mains.

Asynchronous Three-phase Motor with Frequency Transformer

Around the middle of the 1990s further developments in power electronics led to frequency transformers which could also be sufficiently controlled around speed range "zero". Asynchronous three-phase motors with identical performance to DC motors are smaller and save space, and require much less maintenance.

Control of this drive is good. Demands on the mains supply for harmonic component is considerably lower than with the static transformer. The reactive current is very small for all loads. Current spikes during elevator acceleration go directly into the mains. Electricity consumption is lower than for a DC motor with static transformer. Current can be returned to the mains with some additional steps.

Synchronous Three-phase Motor with Frequency Transformer

The latest development in elevator drive systems are synchronous three-phase motors. With the development of more efficient magnets and advances in power electronics these drive systems, out of fashion for around a century, are once again the focus of interest. Synchronous three-phase motors are even smaller and make greater savings in space than asynchronous motors.

Control of these drives is very good. Demands on the mains supply are low for harmonic component. Reactive current is low for all loads. Current spikes during elevator acceleration go directly into the mains. Electricity consumption is the lowest of all the discussed drive systems. Current can be fed back into the mains with some additional steps.

Doors and Door Monitoring

In efficient high-rise elevators, the doors must open quickly and already have opened when the car stops. They must stay open while passengers enter or exit, and close quickly afterwards. No person or object should be caught between the doors during closing. To ensure this, the edges of the doors must be fitted with surveillance units that detect any obstruction early enough to brake and reverse the doors without hitting the obstruction.

High-grade doors must be able to operate for many years without noise and with low maintenance. Unfortunately only a few door types that fulfill these requirements are available worldwide. It must be pointed out that doors are those parts of elevator systems which can affect, for better or worse, the handling capacity dramatically.

Door Operator

Drive mechanisms for efficient high-rise elevators must be designed so that the mass of the door leaves can be quickly accelerated with low oscillation and, more importantly, speedily decelerated with low oscillation, accommodating a change of direction. Door motor and drive control must be able to direct the movements of leaves along predetermined speed curves even if dirt is present in the grooves of the door threshold, or if problems are created by differences in air pressure between shaft and landing.

Door Leaves

In efficient high-rise elevators the door leaves must be resistant to torsion effects – first, to ensure that narrow tolerances between door jamb and door leaf are not overstepped even with variations in air pressure in the shaft, and second, to avoid abrasion marks through contact with the door jambs. The importance of maintaining rigidity increases with the height of the door.
Door rollers must be so arranged and of sufficient size to enable the leaves to run smoothly and without tilting.

Door Edge Monitoring

Monitoring of door edges during closing should prevent people or objects from being caught between the doors. Around 30 years ago, high-grade elevator doors were fitted with electro-mechanical edge monitoring systems: A freely-moving strip placed in front of the door edge moved relative to the leaf when hitting an obstruction and caused the door to stop or reverse by means of a microswitch. In Hong Kong, for example, this electro-mechanical edge monitoring is mandatory.

For a period there were systems that produced an electric field in front of the door edge – if the field was disturbed the doors were stopped or reversed. The electric fields were unstable and dependent on regulation by maintenance staff, and this system has been abandoned.

Nowadays, photoelectric grids are used to monitor door edges. They cover the entire door gap and can halt opening if a beam is interrupted. Two-dimensional grids cannot monitor the whole width of combined car and shaft doors. However, newly developed three-dimensional grids are able to cover and monitor almost the entire door space.

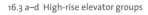

16.3 a–d High-rise elevator groups

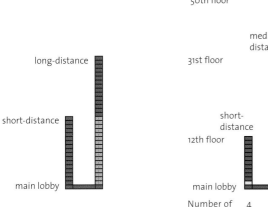

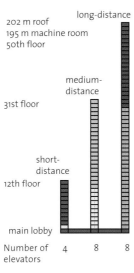

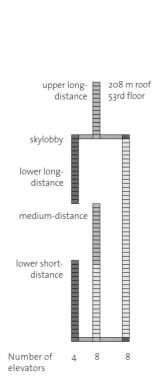

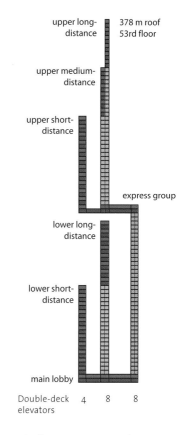

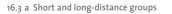

16.3 a Short and long-distance groups

16.3 b UEC high-rise, Frankfurt

16.3 c Westend Straße 1, Frankfurt

16.3 d Petronas Towers, Kuala Lumpur

Elevator Controls

The controls of high-rise elevator groups should ensure that every passenger can enter a cab after a short wait and will be brought to the correct floor with a minimum of intervening stops. Arriving cabs should have enough room for at least one or more passengers. Today we differentiate between conventional and group elevator control ("goal oriented" or "Port System").

Conventional Controls

Outside on the start landing the passenger chooses the desired direction and takes the next car traveling in this direction. The correct floor is only selected once inside the elevator. Modern conventional controls for high-rise elevators are advanced adaptive systems with short-term and long-term memories; they continually update passenger numbers in combination with floor and building populations. With every call the system initiates an ongoing calculation and extrapolation of how much time has elapsed between initial call and arrival of the car, in order to prioritize calls with longer waiting periods. The aim is to keep waits as short as possible and to avoid large discrepancies from the average waiting time.

Group Dispatching

In this system the passenger selects the desired stop while outside on the start landing and takes the indicated car to the correct floor without further prompts being necessary. Using information on the desired end stops of individual passengers, the control system is able to reduce stops by transporting people with the same goal together. Handling capacity can be raised considerably by such an elimination of stops. This is at the expense of waiting times, as passengers cannot simply take the next car after selecting the desired floor, but must wait for the indicated car to arrive. It may be the following one, or the one after that. The technology of group dispatching is still immature and striking improvements can be expected. The choice of control system has an influence on the number and arrangement of elevators in a high-rise.

16.6 Elevator Configurations

One Group for All Floors

Buildings with up to approx. 25 stories are usually served on all floors by just one elevator group. All floors can be reached with a single trip with no change of elevator necessary.

This solution is exhausted when more than six elevators are necessary. Then the possibility must be explored of dividing the elevators into two groups.

Elevator Groups from the Main Lobby

The division into short and long-distance groups (Fig. 16.3 a) reduces the number of stops for each elevator, increases handling capacity and shortens waiting times. The number of passengers in the cars declines, and these can therefore be smaller. The upper floors are served faster and with fewer intervening stops.

Short and long-distance groups are appropriate for buildings of between 20 and approx. 35 stories. For taller buildings up to about 45 stories it makes sense to include an extra group (short, medium and long-distance), and for high-rises up to about 60 stories four groups make sense. It is then possible to reach all floors from the main lobby without changing cars. Traveling from a random floor to a floor served by another elevator group requires just one transfer. From the perspective of transport technology these solutions are perfectly suited for the comfortable access of high-rises. One drawback is the large shaft voume required for more than three elevator groups and the high floor space necessary in the entry level. With increasing building height these space requirements grow excessively.

Stacked Elevator Groups and Skylobby

For heights above 200 m it is possible to reduce total shaft volume and required floor space in the main lobby by stacking elevators on top of each other. Examples of this approach can be found in Frankfurt in the 208 m Westend Strasse 1 (DG Bank, completed 1993) and the 200 m Maintower (completed 1999). Both buildings have a skylobby, directly connected to the main lobby below by an express elevator. From the entry lobby one short-distance and one middle-distance group serve the lower building half, and from the skylobby, one upper and lower long-distance group serve the upper building half, as can be seen in Westend Strasse 1 (Fig. 16.3 c).

In a project study from 1999 conceived by the architects Albert Speer & Partner, two sky-lobbies were planned for the approx. 370 m Millennium Tower in Frankfurt (Figs. 16.4 and 16.5), with separate express elevator groups connecting them to the main lobby. The sky-lobbies divide the building roughly into three equal zones, each zone being served by a short-distance and a long-distance group. The shafts housing the stacked elevators run the entire height of the building and help to provide reinforcement.

Express groups are the only economically viable and structurally acceptable solution for buildings of this height. The current world-wide trend in many tall high-rises for stacked elevators in combination with one or two skylobbies will continue for the foreseeable future.

Double-deck Elevator Groups

Double-deck elevators have one car frame containing two vertically stacked decks. These elevators require a two-story main lobby. During building in-rush the lower deck stops, for example, at all unevenly numbered floors and the upper deck serves the even numbers. Double-deck elevators offer a much greater handling capacity during filling and emptying of a building in comparison with normal elevators. Handling between floors, however, is not improved. A drawback for passengers are those stops which serve only one car deck and landing, when no stop is required by occupants of the other deck or people on the landing. Double-deck elevators are suitable both as express elevators for trips between the main lobby and the skylobby, and as normal elevator groups for buildings with large floor areas. The express elevators in the Millennium Tower are planned to have double-decks. And in the world's tallest building, the Petronas Twin Towers in Kuala Lumpur, all passenger elevators are double-decked. There are around 120 to 200 workstations on every floor (the number decreases with height). In European high-rises, however, more than 50 or 60 workstations can seldom be realized, and thus double-decks are employed only in express elevators.

As long as transport by "beaming", seen in science-fiction films, remains a fantasy, we will need elevators in tall buildings. Technology will be further developed in the future, elevators will become more effective and will require less shaft area and volume, and all this will contribute to ever higher and more economically efficient buildings.

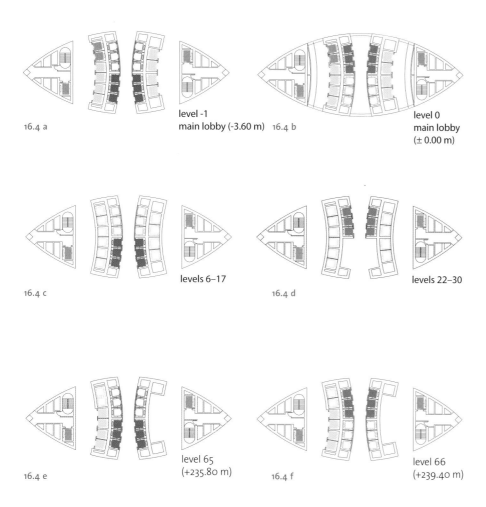

16.4 a

level -1
main lobby (-3.60 m)

16.4 b

level 0
main lobby
(± 0.00 m)

16.4 c

levels 6–17

16.4 d

levels 22–30

16.4 e

level 65
(+235.80 m)

16.4 f

level 66
(+239.40 m)

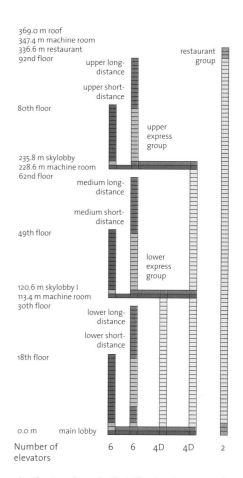

369.0 m roof
347.4 m machine room
336.6 m restaurant
92nd floor

upper long-distance

upper short-distance

80th floor

restaurant group

upper express group

235.8 m skylobby
228.6 m machine room
62nd floor

medium long-distance

medium short-distance

49th floor

lower express group

120.6 m skylobby I
113.4 m machine room
30th floor

lower long-distance

lower short-distance

18th floor

0.0 m   main lobby

Number of elevators   6   6   4D   4D   2

16.5 Elevator scheme for the Millennium Tower, Frankfurt

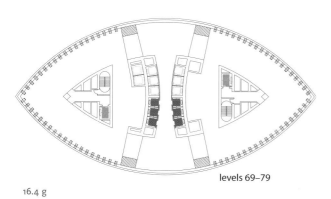

levels 69–79

16.4 g

16.4 a–h Floor plans of the Millennium Tower,
Frankfurt, elevator configurations,
project study 1999, architects: Albert Speer & Partner

16.4 h

levels 84–92

17 Facility Management

Siegfried Schilling

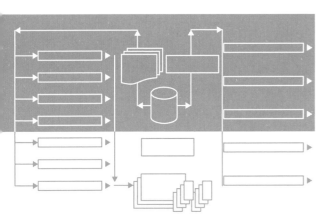

17.1 Introduction

In metropolitan centers, both economy and politics are driven by real estate and especially high-rises. Their architecture and function inspire respect in the observer and give users a sense of aesthetics, comfort, cleanliness, and functionality.

Due to the prestige value of such properties, efficient operation over their lifespan is a challenge for the management. Efficiency is not achieved through reactive economies once the cost situation has been identified, but through a process that begins in the early development phase of building projects and continues to the end of a building's life. Acceptable ancillary costs and attractive service contracts should not be a contradiction, and should offer effective support for the marketing of the development. In the 1980s a new market emerged with the erection and management of large, connected usable areas in high-rises.

17.2 Supporting Architecture Competitions through Cost Benchmarking

Until recently, the standard claim was to bring the manager on board only after the completion of the object. He or she was to participate in the acceptance of the installations in order to be introduced to all the various functions. The object handover was the implementation indicator for the facility management (FM). Today, these processes are seen in a far more complex light and are set in motion during project development. The aim is to tap into facility management know-how in a timely fashion in order to avoid errors, and to create favorable conditions for operation in the future. The following examples illustrate the effectiveness of FM consultation even during architecture competitions:

There are a multitude of design options in high-rise architecture. The differences between perforated and fully glazed façades alone result in considerable cost differences for the management. These are caused by the additional installation of façade maintenance systems and the labor-intensive requirements for cleaning the external surfaces of the property.

Complicated joints and cantilevered elements often lead to increased additional expenditures, which greatly impact the operating costs. The ratio of total area to rentable area also influences the ancillary costs. The smaller the ratio of rentable area is to the total, the greater the ancillary costs. Optimum area use is therefore one of the essential prerequisites for the subsequent success in marketing the properties.

Naturally, operation costs are not the only decisive factor for the competition selection. The ratio of gross area to principal usable area is a key factor in the efficient use of the property. The rule of thumb in this respect is: The greater the ratio, the greater the challenge to achieve a profitable balance between construction cost and rental revenue. In other words, a property where this factor reaches the highest ratio must charge higher rents for equal revenue in order to finance the project.

Other factors are the technical prerequisites within which the comfort conditions must be fulfilled.

Studies have been carried out on the efficiency of building systems in the context of façade structures. The studies explored centralized and decentralized heating and cooling systems, as well as the expenditures for maintenance and energy consumption.

All these examples demonstrate why a profitability study should be executed prior to competition.

Naturally, an exhaustive cost calculation is not required at this stage. The influencing factors can be determined with a benchmark system and are relatively easy to obtain.

Estimating the Operating Costs

After roughly ten years of optimized operation in the marketplace, there are sufficient data to estimate the operating costs with a fairly high degree of accuracy. This can only succeed if the chosen building option and the performance targets are reflected in the completed property.

Benchmark software is a valuable tool for estimating the operating costs of real estate if the databases are updated regularly and the building structure and user profile are compatible.

Table 17.1 shows the results of a complex calculation. Three properties are compared, each on the basis of operating costs in terms of gross area, net area and principal useable area.

The numbers are interpreted exclusively with a view to operation. The other evaluation factors that are standard in competition are not taken into consideration in this chapter. In addition to evaluating the benchmark results, the aforementioned practical examples provide sufficient reason to consult experienced facility managers during this phase.

Table 17.1 Architecture Competition: Comparison of Ratios and Costs

Operating costs	Applicant 1	Applicant 2	Applicant 3	
Total / gross area	2.85	2.47	2.37	€/m² and month
Total / net area	3.03	2.62	2.54	€/m² and month
Total / principle usable area	4.44	3.59	3.93	€/m² and month
Building ratios	**Applicant 1**	**Applicant 2**	**Applicant 3**	
Floor space index	14.52	15.66	13.06	ratio
Site occupancy index	0.50	0.76	0.36	ratio
Cubic index	67.01	102.39	46.20	ratio
Gross area / net area	1.06	1.06	1.07	ratio
Gross area / principle usable area	1.56	1.45	1.66	ratio
Principle usable area / workstation	31.25	36.17	26.43	ratio
Property value / gross area	2.89	2.37	2.68	ratio

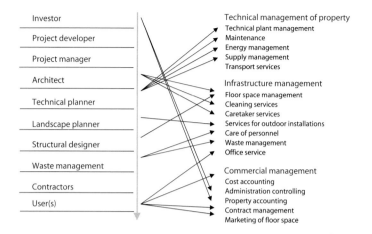

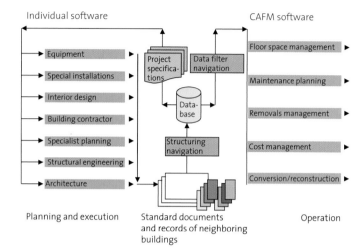

17.2 and 17.3 Documentation dependency from construction to building operation

17.3 Lifespan Documentation of a Building

Buyers are entitled to receive detailed documentation for every manufactured product, which enables them to quickly and reliably repair malfunctions or – if other operating conditions require – to undertake modifications on the basis of the building plans.

In the real estate market, this type of documentation has yet to become standard practice. The plan and script documentations for building systems and architecture are riddled with defects that limit the actions of the operator. The costs for such insufficiencies may account for 12 to 18 percent of service fees. Prior to the planning phase, it is therefore important to draft a project specification, with a focus not only on the construction phase but also on the subsequent operation.

Project Specification

Project specification is drawn up to create documentation structures in graphic and alphanumeric systems for architects, planners and contractors. It is an organizational manual that should be applicable for the entire life span of an object. To provide rapid and reliable access to information at all times, experts must be consulted to establish the nomenclature of documents and systems. Identification systems, which are commonly employed in industry (e.g. power plant construction or petrochemical installations), are

too labor- and cost-intensive for real estate management.

The specification must also factor in the subsequent operation of the building and consider the usefulness of the compiled data.

Data Management

In the age of electronic data processing, most documents are generated in electronic form. Paper documents are replaced by electronic files. Messages are sent via an Internet portal. This has already become standard practice, although generally without specific coordination. The result is that much information is only marginally useful and of poor documentation quality.

A central server on which data are stored should be set up to ensure that all participants are kept up to date during the construction phase. All information should be available in an updated version and redundancies should be avoided. To ensure that all participants in the building process can access the information in the form of documents, drawings or images, the necessary protocols for data management must be defined in the project specification. Priorities include:
– Granting access rights,
– granting write-only and read-only authority for data and documents,
– defining the file extension,
– defining the directory structures and
– controlling data transfer.

To this end it is necessary to describe the specific conditions for Internet communication. Suitable software is needed for documentation management, and it should be selected, purchased and made available to all participants at the beginning of the project.

Data Quality Control

Regulating documentation contents and data transfer improves the quality considerably by comparison to conventional procedures. This is achieved, in part, by regular control of the conditions set forth in the specification. The quality control should be carried out by the author of the specification owing to the depth of knowledge required. When supervision is in the hands of experienced facility management companies, plans and events, which might have an adverse effect on subsequent operation, are identified and corrected in a timely fashion. It is therefore both strategically sound and economically efficient to integrate qualified FM services into the construction phase.

The use of the specification must be a subject for negotiation when contracts are awarded to planners and contractors. This approach to prevents supplementary demands.

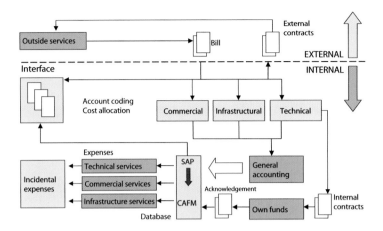

17.4 The product of successful project management from the transfer of data into the management cycle

17.4 Facility Management in the Construction Phase

During the construction phase, the FM planner is called upon to continually assess the plan and execution with a view to subsequent efficient operation and to solve any arising conflicts in consultation with investors and project partners.

Functionality of Building Automation Systems

When an operating and information system is being installed for building systems, a variety of different demands converge. While planners and contractors focus primarily on visualizing the processes and functions of the systems, future building managers and operators are also interested in obtaining information on operating times, consumption and long-term records of operating and temperature curves.

The interest is based in requirements relating to optimization potentials, which can be developed for each building once a given start-up phase has elapsed. As a person rendering services, the operator must deliver proof of such optimization measures in annual protocols and document the reasons for possible inefficiencies.

Another requirement linked to building information and communications systems are the service level agreements (SLAs). These are

parameters intended to trace possible deviations between the contractually established conditions and those that actually occur in operation, and to record the duration of such discrepancies. It is self-evident that such functions of the system can only be calibrated by facility management.

Wear and Tear of Technical Installations

The choice of building systems is closely linked to quality characteristics such as fail/breakdown safety, wear and tear projections and economic efficiency.
Given the multitude of products and the range in quality, testing the quality of the products offered by construction companies prior to installation and identifying potential weaknesses poses a daunting challenge.
It is vital to establish the maintenance requirements of the selected products, not only of building systems but also of building materials, to do so in an expert fashion, especially with regard to cleaning, and to present cost comparisons prior to installation as a basis for material selection.

Recording Operating Costs

In multitenant buildings, utility meters must be installed for individual tenants. They must be allocated in detail on the basis of methods of apportionment.

Defining allocations that reflect area use requires a high degree of detailed coordination between technology and marketing.

Security Concepts

Appropriate systems must be chosen to satisfy the increased security requirements within large building complexes, and security personnel must be deployed in appropriate locations in consultation with the FM planner to prevent unauthorized access. Building security issues also include constructional measures, which may go as far as individual admittance systems.

Energy Supply

Deregulation in the energy sector makes it imperative to invite competition between the individual local energy suppliers. Consumption cost analyses must be prepared early on and possibly compared to contracting models.

Waste Management

High-rises accommodate a great number of people, who generate business and domestic waste. Waste management has become highly competitive with municipal and private disposal companies bidding for the same contracts. This competitive, environment should be exploited, in combination with implementing optimum waste management concepts. Here, too, areas for storage of wet and dry waste and sufficient transportation routes for the waste streams must be taken into consideration in relation to the specific concepts.

17.5 Facility Management during the Handover

In the chronology of a building's lifespan, the construction phase is followed by the acceptance and delivery of the object, the handover. The service providers for the subsequent operation of the object should already be selected and assume their responsibilities at this point.

During the handover phase, the data from the document management system (Fig. 17.5)

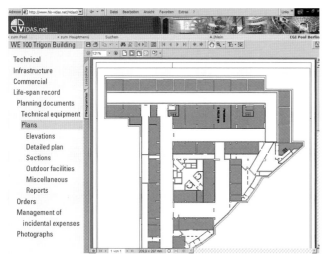

17.5 Document management system

must be updated and processed for operation. Modern documentation management systems can be transformed seamlessly into life-span systems for the duration of the building's operation. One prerequisite for smooth data transfer is adherence to the rules set forth in the specification. During the handover phase, which is also referred to as the implementation phase, the document management system is supplied with all relevant data and information pertaining to operation. This includes a complete report on the current condition of the property, consumption data and actions, which guarantees faultless operation and ensures user satisfaction.

17.6 Facility Management Options

There are several options for structuring the organizational aspect of facility management. Choosing the appropriate organizational structure is dependent on the facility use and the corporate structure of the investor.

Owner Management

When properties are erected for an investor who has the sufficient personnel and competency in his own organization, he or she will generally bring these factors to bear and assign the relevant tasks to his or her own employees.

Outsourced Management

Most new buildings are operated by external service providers. This is primarily because they have the necessary qualifications and personnel capacities. One key argument for outsourcing is the ease with which commissioned services can be called in. In performance-oriented contracts, service personnel are only available until the particular service has been delivered.

Owner Management – Outsourced Labor

In owner-operated organizations, services cannot be fully provided by internal personnel in an economically viable manner due to the variety of tasks to be performed. For this reason, such buildings are only staffed with owner management, while all repair and trade services are purchased through an outsourcing process.

Separate Purchase of Management and Labor Services

In Germany a service provider is awarded the management tasks and contractor responsibility in a general contracting package; the separation of management and contracting services is common, however, in other European countries. This approach has the advantage of tapping into the highest level of expertise within the organizational structure for each individual service task.

The separation automatically includes management in the controlling process and takes advantage of the neutrality this structure offers to objectively evaluate the quality of execution.

17.7 Service Tenders and Contracts

Figure 17.6 provides a comprehensive overview of the multitude of tasks that fall under facility management.

Available services must be analyzed for efficiency in relation to each relevant task. The selection of contractors chosen to serve as facility management service providers is made in three steps:
- Pre-qualification process
- Tender process – conventional
- Submission process – Internet

Pre-qualification Process

Identifying suitable companies requires a rating (Fig. 17.7). These processes are designed in a highly individual fashion because the relevant spectrum of tasks and location are key factors in the selection of suitable parties. A range of 30–50 evaluation criteria has been established. The analysis helps to narrow the field in terms of which parties should be invited to participate in the submissions phase.

Tender process – Conventional

Service tenders are critical because they consist of hard facts and soft facts, in contrast to product tenders. Hard facts are comparable or measurable services. Soft facts are qualitative and service-oriented criteria, which cannot be fully assessed when an offer is submitted.

The services and their allocation to properties should therefore be defined with the great clarity. The aforementioned documentation management system – and the property inventory defined in it – furnishes the density of information that enables the parties submitting for a tender to undertake sound calculations.
Tenders must contain at least a draft contract

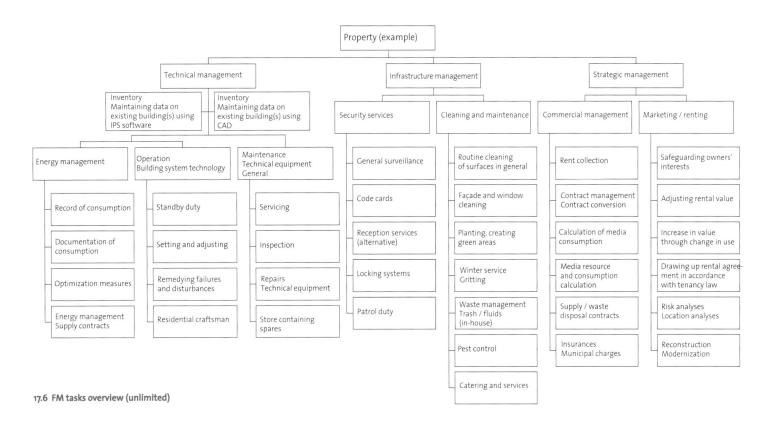

17.6 FM tasks overview (unlimited)

for the general contractor, the conditions and processes for operation documentation, the conditions and process for reporting on economic efficiency, the rules of service level agreements and an agreement to submit to regular service assessments carried out by the client.

Such contracts can be quite complex. Professional legal support is highly recommended in these matters.

Submission Process – Internet

In addition to conventional tenders (Fig. 17.8) services may be requested via an Internet platform.
The service directories from the document management system (lifespan file) are made password-accessible on the Internet platform. Tenders are posted online and are directly available for evaluation. Services can even be purchased in an auction-like process. In this case, every service provider has the opportunity to view the competitors' offers anonymously and to adjust his own offer within a set timeframe to the price range of the competition. **Figure 17.9** shows an example of

an electronic submission process with auction character.

Evaluating Offers

Thorough evaluation of the offers in terms of the price-service ratios is paramount in today's highly competitive market. Cost alone must never be the driving factor for a

decision. The service providers have acquired sufficient knowledge through a detailed tender description to plan and present their object organization and personnel profile to the jury that will award the contract.

Awarding the contract is based on the evaluation of the tender presentation, consideration of comparable references, and competitive price analysis.

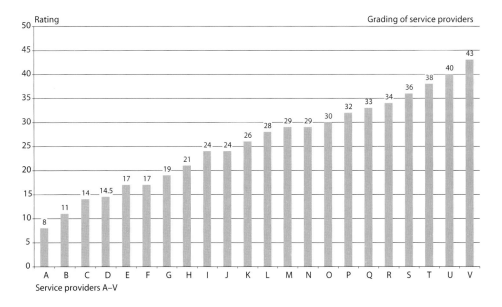

17.7 A practical example of rating

17.8 Sample contents of a complex tender for FM

17.8 Ensuring Functionality and Value Appreciation

High-rise objects are only economical for the investor if their value continues to appreciate over several decades. This means that a facility management concept would not be complete without extensive, periodic quality control. The controlling procedures are designed to ensure that all contractual obligations are met. This is especially relevant with regard to budget observance, user satisfaction and maintaining the value of building systems and of the building itself. By determining the performance quality the investor has implemented all measures to ensure the optimized economic operation of the property.

Prospects

Facility management and the services that fall under its umbrella are now considered as fixed components in a corporate organization. As the requirements in the individual areas and the process procedures continue to grow in complexity, the organizations concerned with this topic are in constant flux. Whereas in the past the focus was primarily on the traditional trades, qualified management has taken on greater importance in view of the growing integration of networks, data processing technology and organization. Such management must meet the growing demands of both users and investors. Universities and colleges are responding to this new range of abilities to meet the professional requirements of the future. The professional image of the facility manager has assumed an academic character and an educational background in business administration or engineering has become the norm. However, these foundations alone are no longer sufficient. Additional training in real estate is required, unless it is already integrated in a particular curriculum. The attractiveness of the property and the appreciation in value that goes hand in hand with it are the factors that will determine the success of the responsible individuals and organizations.

e-sub Electronic Submission for Facility Management Services

Price Comparison List	Date of last change	Date of last change	Date of last change	Date of last change	Date of last change
Property					
	Date/time	Date/time	Date/time	Date/time	Date/time
Name of bidder:	Bidder 1	Bidder 2	Bidder 3	Bidder 4	Bidder 5
Item 2.1 Technical services	50,680.00	68,796.00	63,789.00	55,000.00	66,467.00
Item 2.2 Technical services	21,542.00	14,776.00	16,789.00	20,010.00	16,872.00
Item 2.3 Technical services	10,299.00	6,709.00	6,045.00	7,800.00	6,135.00
Item 3.1 Infrastructure services	33,446.00	22,842.00	28,805.00	35,500.00	39,369.00
Item 3.2 Infrastructure services	133,446.00	61,434.00	117,597.00	130,890.00	107,371.00
Item 3.3 Infrastructure services	125,452.00	134,191.00	31,004.00	129,677.00	36,006.00
Item 3.4 Infrastructure services	29,116.00	30,880.00	26,719.00	30,097.00	22,654.00
Item 3.5 Infrastructure services	6,098.00	7,231.00	5,833.00	4,331.00	8,840.00
Item 3.6 Infrastructure services	6,237.00	3,894.00	6,028.00	7,626.00	3,961.00
Item 3.7 Infrastructure services	484.00	515.00	333.00	920.00	374.00
Item 4.1 Commercial services	14,258.00	29,677.00	14,677.00	18,447.00	35,000.00
Item 4.2 Commercial services	22,064.00	3,956.00	11,560.00	12,098.00	19,129.00
Item 5.1 Strategic services	677.00	5,967.00	3,580.00	9,503.00	6,376.00
Item 5.2 Strategic services	20,236.00	9,892.00	20,306.00	7,000.00	19,129.00
Total price	**477,035.00**	**400,760.00**	**353,065.00**	**468,899.00**	**387,683.00**
Deviation from lowest value	230,248.00	153,973.00	106,278.00	222,112.00	140,896.00
Deviation from highest value	59,546.60	-16,728.40	-64,426.40	51,410.60	-29,805.40
Ranking	**5**	**3**	**1**	**4**	**2**

17.9 Practical example of an electronic submission procedure

17.10 Criteria for evaluating successful QM as a basis for drawing up contracts

Appendix

Subject Index

Bibliography

[ ] source directly quoted
– secondary literature

01 Typology

[1] L. Sullivan: "Das große Bürogebäude, künstlerisch betrachtet" (1896). In: A. L. Huxtable. Zeit für Wolkenkratzer oder die Kunst, Hochhäuser zu bauen. German edition: Archibook Verlag, Berlin 1986.

[2] V. N. Lampugnani (ed): Lexikon der Architektur des 20. Jahrhunderts, Robert Maxwell p. 257, Hatje Cantz Verlag, Stuttgart 1983.

– W. Boesiger und H. Girsberger (ed.): Le Corbusier 1910–65. Zurich 1967

– M. Campi: Skyscrapers. An Architectural Type of Modern Urbanism. Birkhauser Publisher for Architecture, Basel 2000.

– J. Dupré: Skyscrapers. A History of the World's Most Famous and Important Skyscrapers. Black Dog & Leventhal Publishers, New York 1996.

– El Lissitzky – Maler, Architekt, Typograf, Fotograf. Ausstellungskatalog. Halle 1982

– B. Flierl: Hundert Jahre Hochhäuser. Hochhaus und Stadt im 20. Jahrhundert. Verlag Bauwesen, Berlin 2000.

– P. Goldberger: Der Wolkenkratzer. Das Hochhaus in der Geschichte und Gegenwart. Deutsche Verlags-Anstalt, Stuttgart 1984.

– C. Jencks: Die Postmoderne. Der neue Klassizismus in Kunst und Architektur. Klett Verlag, Stuttgart 1987.

– C. Jencks: Skyscrapers – Skycities. Academy Editions, London 1980.

– Jourdan & Müller Architekten: Hochhäuser für Frankfurt. Hochhausentwicklungsplan Frankfurt 2000. Architects brochure 1998.

– J. P. Kleihues, J. G. Becker-Schwering, P. Kahlfeld (ed.): Bauen in Berlin 1900–2000. Nicolaische Verlagsbuchhandlung Beuermann, Berlin 2000.

– S. Bradford Landau, C. W. Condit: Rise of the New York Skyscraper 1865–1913. Yale University Press, New Haven and London 1996.

– C. Mierop with G. Binder, Institute francais d'architecture: Skyscrapers Higher and Higher. NORMA Editions, Paris 1995.

– H. Müller-Vogg (ed.): Hochhäuser in Frankfurt. Wettlauf zu den Wolken. Societätsverlag, Frankfurt 1999.

– M. Rodenstein (ed.): Hochhäuser in Deutschland, Zukunft oder Ruin der Städte? Kohlhammer Verlag, Stuttgart 2000.

– StadtBauwelt 132 (Bauwelt 48) 1996: Kuala Lumpur

– StadtBauwelt 135 (Bauwelt 36) 1997: Hongkong

– StadtBauwelt 142 (Bauwelt 24) 1999: Shanghai

– R. Stommer (text), D. Mayer-Gürr (ills.): Hochhaus. Der Beginn in Deutschland. Jonas Verlag, Marburg 1990.

– A. Tacharnow und S. Kawtaradse: Die Stalinistische Architektur. München 1992

– B. Taut: Die Stadtkrone. Jena 1919

– C. Willis: Form Follows Finance. Skyscrapers and Skylines in New York and Chicago. Princeton Architectural Press, New York 1995.

– M. Wutzke, Starconcept GmbH, Darmstadt (ed.): Skyline Guide. Deutschland 2001/2002. Verlag Das Beispiel, Darmstadt 2001.

– J. Zukowsky (ed.): Chicago Architektur 1872–1922. Prestel Verlag, Munich 1987.

03 Organization of Office Towers

– B. Flierl: Hundert Jahre Hochhäuser. Verlag Bauwesen, Berlin 2000.

– W. Fuchs: Die Zukunft der Büroimmobilie. congena Texte 2/2 2001.

– R. Puell: Bürohausraster. congena Texte 1/2 2001.

– M. Rodenstein: Hochhäuser in Deutschland: Zukunft oder Ruin? Kohlhammer Verlag, Stuttgart 2000.

04 Site Operation

[1] E. Schubert, P. Racky: Abhängigkeit der Baukosten eines Gebäudes von seiner Höhe. BW Bauwirtschaft 6/96. Bauverlag, Berlin 1996.

[2] H. H. Schetter: Hochhausbau gestern (1976) – heute (2000) am Beispiel Dresdner Bank in Frankfurt. Article in conference publication: Tendenzen im Hochhausbau. International conference, Frankfurt 2001.

[3] T. James: The Empire State Building. Harper & Row, New York 1975.

[4] F. Conti: Weltwunder der Baukunst. Volume IV. Weltbild Verlag 1987.

[5] Philipp Holzmann AG: Hochhaus Maintower in Frankfurt/Main. Project report.

[6] OLG (Oberlandesgericht – Appeals Court) Düsseldorf, NRW-RR 89, 1421. OLG Karlsruhe, IBR 92, 362. OLG Zweibrücken, Decision of 24.06.1997 – 1W51/97, IBR 98, 207. OLG Düsseldorf, Verdict 17.07.2000 – 9U112/00, IBR 2001, 370.

[7] G. Drees, H. Sommer, G. Eckert: Untersuchungen des zweckmäßigen Einsatzes von Turmdrehkranen auf den Hochbaustellen insbesondere des Wohnungsbaues. Final report, Bundesministerium für Raumordnung (Ministry for Environmental Planning), Bauwesen und Städtebau 1980 (Building and Urban Development).

[8] V. Misch: Optimierung von Bauverfahren. Unpublished manuscript.

[9] E. Steinert, M. Weißschädel, D. v. Bernuth: Expertenbefragung 2001. Unpublished manuscript.

[10] F. K. Racky, H. Fröhner, G. Milbrecht, H. Bergner: Messeturm Frankfurt/Main – Bauausführung. Beton- und Stahlbetonbau, 86/1991. Verlag Ernst & Sohn, Berlin 1991.

[11] ACS Self-climbing formwork. PERI GmbH, 2000.

[12] R. Schmitt: Die Schalungstechnik. Verlag Ernst & Sohn, Berlin 2001.

[13] C. Motzko: Ein Verfahren zur ganzheitlichen Erfassung und rechnergestützten Einsatzplanung moderner Schalungssysteme. VDI Verlag, Düsseldorf 1990.

[14] G. Hilke: Herausforderung beim Bau hoher Häuser. Article in conference publication: Tendenzen im Hochhausbau. International conference, Frankfurt 2001.

[15] A. Bubenik: Die Fassade und ihr Einfluss auf die schlüsselfertige Bauausführung. Dissertation at the Institut für Baubetrieb, Technische Universität Darmstadt 2001.

[16] K. Silbe: Wirtschaftlichkeit kontrollierter Rückbauarbeiten. Dissertation at the Institut für Baubetrieb, Technische Universität Darmstadt. Mensch & Buch Verlag, Berlin 1999.

05   Geotechnics

[1] P. Amann, H. Breth and D. Stroh: Über den Einfluss des Verformungsverhaltens des Frankfurter Tons auf die Tiefenwirkung eines Hochhauses und die Form der Setzungsmulde. Report by the Versuchsanstalt für Bodenmechanik und Grundbau, TH Darmstadt, Issue 15, Darmstadt 1975.

[2] U. Arslan: Baugrund-Tragwerk-Interaktion. Report by the Institute and the Versuchsanstalt für Geotechnik, TU Darmstadt, Issue 33, pp. 29–49, Darmstadt 1994.

[3] U. Arslan, H. Quick, C. Moormann and O. Reul: Geotechnische insitu Messungen an Hochhausgründungen und baubegleitende Qualitätssicherungsmaßnahmen. Article in seminar publication: Hochhäuser. Darmstädter Statik Seminar 1999, TU Darmstadt, Institut für Statik, Report Nr. 16, XV.

[4] H. Breth: Das Tragverhalten des Frankfurter Tons bei im Tiefbau auftretenden Beanspruchungen. Report by the Versuchsanstalt für Bodenmechanik und Grundbau, TH Darmstadt, Issue 4, Darmstadt 1970.

[5] R. Katzenbach, U. Arslan, C. Moormann: Piled Raft Foundation Projects in Germany. Design Application of Raft Foundation, pp. 323–39, Hemsley, Telford, London 2000.

[6] R. Katzenbach, H. Quick, U. Arslan: Commerzbank-Hochhaus Frankfurt/Main: Kostenoptimierte und setzungsarme Gründung. Zeitschrift Bauingenieur 71/1996. Issue 9, pp. 345–354.

[7] R. Katzenbach, U. Arslan, C. Moormann and O. Reul: Möglichkeiten und Grenzen der Kombinierten Pfahl-Plattengründung (KPP), dargestellt am Beispiel aktueller Projekte. 4. Darmstädter Geotechnik-Kolloquium. Proceedings of the Institute and the Versuchsanstalt für Geotechnik TH Darmstadt 1997. Issue 37, pp. 89–116.

[8] P. Ripper, Y. El-Mossallamy: Hochhausgründungen in Frankfurt. Article in seminar publication: Hochhäuser. Darmstädter Statik Seminar 1999, TU Darmstadt, Institut für Statik, Report No. 16, XVI.

[9] P. Ripper, U. Adamietz, Y. El-Mossallamy, C. Loreck, J. Teschke, I. Martinoff: Neue Lösungen für wasserdichten Baugrubenverbau vorgeführt am Projekt UEC Frankfurt, 8. Darmstädter Geotechnik-Kolloqium. Proceedings of the Institute and the Versuchsanstalt für Geotechnik, TU Darmstadt 2001, Issue 55, pp. 21–43.

[10] H. Sommer: Konstruktive Möglichkeiten zur Vermeidung von Verkantungen bei Hochhausgründungen. European Conference on Structural Foundations, conference publication, Vienna 1975, pp. 237–239.

[11] H. Sommer, P. Wittmann, P. Ripper: Piled raft foundation of a tall building in Frankfurt Clay. 11th ICSMFE, San Francisco 1985. Vol. 4, pp. 2253–2257.

[12] P. Wittmann, P. Ripper: Unterschiedliche Konzepte für die Gründung und Baugrube von zwei Hochhäusern in der Frankfurter Innenstadt. Presentations at the Conference on Structural Foundations, Karlsruhe 1990. Conference publication pp. 381–397.

[13] M. Löffler, H. G. Reinke, N. Meyer: Hochhausgründung in Bonn durch eine modifizierte Pfahl-Plattengründung. Pile symposium, Braunschweig 2001.

06   Load-bearing Structures

[1] J. Zukowsky (ed.): Chicago Architektur: 1872–1922. Prestel Verlag, Munich 1987.

[2] P. Banavalkar, Parikh. Change in Trend of Structural Systems for High-Rise Building in Seismic Regions. Trends in Tall Building, International Conference, 5–7 September 2001, Frankfurt.

[3] A. Krebs, D. Constantinescu: Der Einfluss der Axialverformungen der vertikalen Tragglieder von Hochhäusern. Darmstadt Statics Seminar: Hochhäuser 1999, Report No. 16 – TU Darmstadt.

[4] J. Hegger: Hochhäuser aus Stahlbeton. Hochhäuser, Entwerfen – Planen – Konstruieren. Conference publication RWTH Aachen, 30–31.03.1995.

[5] G. König, R. Grimm, J. Meyer: Erläuterungen zur Richtlinie hochfester Beton. Bautechnik, 1997/4.

[6] H. Schulitz, W. Sobek, K. Habermann: Stahlbauatlas. Birkhäuser Verlag, Berlin 1999.

[7] H. Bode: Euro-Verbundbau, Konstruktion und Berechnung. Werner Verlag, Düsseldorf 1998.

[8] M. Taus: Millennium Tower Wien. Neue Wege in der Verbundtechnologie. Stahlbau-Rundschau No. 92, Vienna 1999.

[9] G. König, S. Liphardt: Hochhäuser aus Stahlbeton, Konstruktionen. Betonkalender 1990, Part 2. Verlag Ernst und Sohn, Berlin 1990

[10] J. Colaco: Steel and Steel Composite Structures for High Rise Buildings. Hochhäuser. Entwerfen – Planen – Konstruieren. Conference publication RWTH Aachen 1995.

[11] W. Sobek, W. Sundermann, N. Rehle, H.-G. Reinke: Tragwerke für transparente Hochhäuser. Bauingenieur Volume 76, July/August 2001.

[12] G. König, A. Berneiser: Tragwerkslösungen und Baustoffe im Hochhausbau. Hochhäuser. Entwerfen – Planen – Konstruieren. Conference publication RWTH, Aachen 1995.

[13] G. König, A. Laubach: Innovative Entwicklungen im Hochhausbau – Tragwerke, Konstruktion. Bauingenieur 76. pp. 309–313. Springer VDI Verlag, Düsseldorf 2001

[14] B. Taranath: Steel, Concrete, and Composite Design of Tall Buildings. Second Edition. The McGraw-Hill Companies Inc., Columbus OH (USA) 1997.

[15] M. Phocas: Tragwerke für den Hochhausbau. Verlag Ernst & Sohn, Berlin 2001.

[16] B. Stafford-Smith, A. Coull: Tall Buildings Structures, Analysis and Design. Wiley & Sons Inc., Toronto 1991.

[17] C. Mierop, Institute Francais d'Architecture: Skyscrapers. Higher and Higher. Edition Norma, Paris 1995.

[18] M. Schnellenbach-Held, K. Pfeffer: Tragverhalten zweiachsiger Hohlkörperdecken. Beton- und Stahlbeton, Issue 2001/9. Verlag Ernst & Sohn, Berlin 2001.

[19] S. Liphardt: Hochhaustragwerke – Stand der Entwicklung. Darmstädter Statik-Seminar: Hochhäuser, Report No. 16 – TU Darmstadt, Darmstadt 1999.

[20] M. Phocas: Tragwerke von Super-Hochhäusern. deutsche bauzeitung 2002/4, Stuttgart 2002.

07 Construction and Design

[1] Architektur Wettbewerbe 1792–1949. Taschen Verlag, Cologne 1994.

[2] A. L. Huxtable: Zeit für Wolkenkratzer. Archibook Verlagsgesellschaft, Berlin 1982.

[2b] L. H. Sullivan: The Tall Office Building Artistically Considered (1896). In: A. L. Huxtable. Zeit für Wolkenkratzer.

[3] H. Klotz (Ed.): Vision der Moderne – Das Prinzip Konstruktion. Including: J. Posener. Die moderne Architektur. Prestel Verlag, Munich 1986.

[4] S. Giedeon: Raum Zeit Architektur. Otto Mayer Verlag, Ravensburg 1965.

[5] W. Schirmer (ed.): Egon Eiermann, 1904–1970. Deutsche Verlags-Anstalt, Stuttgart 1984.

[6] K. Yeang: The Green Skyscraper. The Basis for Designing Sustainable Intensive Buildings. Prestel Verlag, Munich 1999.

08 Structural Dynamics

[1] E-DIN 4150, Erschütterungen im Bauwesen, Part 1: Vorermittlung von Schwingungsgrößen. Beuth Verlag, Berlin. Draft version February 1999.

[2] DIN 4150, Erschütterungen im Bauwesen, Part 2: Einwirkungen auf Menschen in Gebäuden. Beuth Verlag, Berlin June 1999.

[3] DIN 4150, Erschütterungen im Bauwesen, Part 3: Einwirkungen auf bauliche Anlagen. Beuth Verlag, Berlin February 1999.

[4] DIN 4149, Part 1, Bauten in Deutschen Erdbebengebieten. Lastannahmen, Bemessung und Ausführung üblicher Hochbauten. Beuth Verlag, Berlin Edition April 1981.

[5] E-DIN 4149, Part 1, Bauten in Deutschen Erdbebengebieten. Lastannahmen, Bemessung und Ausführung üblicher Hochbauten. Beuth Verlag, Berlin, Draft version July 2001.

[6] ISO 2631–1978, Guide for the Evaluation of Human Exposure to Whole-Body Vibration. Beuth Verlag, Berlin 1978.

[7] VDI Guideline 2057, Beurteilung der Einwirkung mechanischer Schwingungen auf den Menschen. Beuth Verlag, Berlin 1999.

[8] H. Bachmann, K. Moser: Erdbebensicherung von Bauwerken, Birkhäuser Verlag, Basel 1995.

[9] B. A. Bolt: Erdbeben – Schlüssel zur Geodynamik. Spektrum Akademischer Verlag, Heidelberg 1995.

[10] J. Eibl, U. Häussler-Combe: Baudynamik. Beton-Kalender, 1997, Part 2. Verlag Ernst & Sohn, Berlin 1997.

[11] GERB, Schwingungsisolierungen. Berlin 1992.

[12] A. Krebs, R. Kiefer, D. Constantinescu: Wasserbehälter zur Tilgung windinduzierter Schwingungen. Bauingenieur 68/1993, pp. 291–302.

[13] F. P. Müller: Baudynamik. Beton-Kalender 1978, Part 2. Verlag Ernst & Sohn, Berlin 1978.

[14] F. P. Müller, E. Keintzel: Erdbebensicherung von Hochbauten. Verlag Ernst & Sohn, Berlin 1984.

[15] H.-W. Nordhues: Entwicklung und Parallelisierung einer modalen Kapazitätsmethode zur Berechnung nichtlinearer Strukturen unter dynamischer Beanspruchung. VDI-Fortschrittsberichte, Series 4, Vol. 132, Darmstadt 1995.

[16] T. Paulay, H. Bachmann, K. Moser: Erdbebenbemessung von Stahlbetonhochbauten. Birkhauser Publishers, Basel 1990.

09 Effects of Wind

[1] A. G. Davenport: The Application of Statistical Concepts to the Wind Loading of Structures. Proc. Inst. of Civil Engineers 1961, 19, pp. 449–472.

[2] J. Gandemer, A. Guyot: La protection contre le vent. CSTB, Paris 1981.

[3] H. J. Gerhardt, O. Jung: Lagesicherheit mechanisch befestigter Dachabdichtungen bei Windbelastung. Bautechnik, Issue 11/1991, pp. 372–378.

[4] H. J. Gerhardt: Experimentelle Untersuchungen zur Entrauchung großer Räume unter besonderer Beachtung des Windeinflusses. vfdb-Zeitschrift Issue 2/2000, 49th Year, pp. 47–54.

[5] T. Lawson: Wind Effects on Buildings. Volume 1: Design Applications, Applied Science Publishers, London 1980.

[6] W. H. Melbourne: Criteria for Environmental Wind Conditions, J. Ind. Aerodyn. 3/1978, pp. 241–249.

[7] H. Müllejans: Möglichkeiten der Vorausberechnung von Strömungs- und Temperaturfeldern in großen Räumen. HLH 29, Nr. 8/1973, pp. 302.

10 Façade Structures

[1] S. Gronert: Die neue Geschichte der alten
     Materialien. Designzentrum München,
     Munich 1994
[2] P. Grübl, H. Weigler, S. Karl: Beton-Arten,
     Herstellung und Eigenschaften. Verlag
     Ernst & Sohn, Berlin 2001.

11   Façade Technologies

–   E. Oesterle, R.-D. Lieb, M. Lutz, W. Heusler:
     Doppelschalige Fassaden – ganzheitliche
     Planung. Callwey Verlag, Munich 1999.

12   Insolation and Shading

[1] P. Gössel, G. Leuthäuser: Architektur des
     20. Jahrhunderts. Taschen Verlag, Cologne
     1990.
[2] DIN 5034, Beuth Verlag, Berlin 1999.
[3] K. Daniels: The Technology of Ecological
     Building. Birkhauser Publishers,
     Basel 1994.
[4] H. F. O. Müller, C. Nolte, T. Pasquay:
     Klimagerechte Fassadentechnologie –
     II. Monitoring von Gebäuden Doppel-
     fassaden. Final report of AG Solar-funded
     research project "Klimagerechte
     Fassadentechnologie", Chair for
     Klimagerechte Architektur und Bauphysik,
     Universität Dortmund, Dusseldorf 2002.
[5] H. F. O. Müller, T. Pasquay: Klimagerechte
     Fassadentechnologie – Messungen an vier
     Gebäuden mit Doppelfassaden und deren
     Auswertung. In: Innovative Fassaden,
     VDI reports 1642.
[6] T. Pasquay: Natural Ventilation in Highrise
     Buildings with Double Façades. Saving or
     Waste of Energy. PLEA 2001 Proceedings,
     pp. 223–227.
[7] H. F. O. Müller, C. Nolte, T. Pasquay:
     Die Mittel aktiv zu sein. In: Die klimaaktive
     Fassade. AIT-Edition Intelligente Archi-
     tektur. Verlagsanstalt Alexander Koch,
     Leinfelden-Echterdingen 1999.

13   Building Systems

–   K. Daniels: Gebäudetechnik, 3rd Edition.
     Oldenburg Verlag, Munich 2000.

14   Integrated Conepts

–   H. F. O. Müller, C. Nolte, T. Pasquay:
     Die Mittel aktiv zu sein. In: Die klimaaktive
     Fassade. AIT-Edition Intelligente
     Architektur. Verlagsanstalt Alexander
     Koch, Leinfelden-Echterdingen 1999.
–   J. Wiley: Passive Solar Commercial
     Buildings. A Sourcebook of Examples and
     Design Insights.
–   K. Yeang: The Skyscaper Bioclimatically
     Considered. ACADEMY Editions, London
     1997.

15   Fire Protection

–   W. Klingsch: Brandschutztechnische
     Planung von Hochhäusern. In: Conference
     Proceedings: Trends in Tall Buildings.
     Frankfurt, 09/2001 (TU Darmstadt).
–   W. Klingsch: Hochhäuser: Brandschutz.
     In: bauzeitung 1–2/2002.
–   W. Klingsch: Ganzglasfassaden im
     Hochhausbau: Brandschutz.
     In: Bauingenieur 9 (1999),
     Springer VDI Verlag, Dusseldorf.
–   W. Klingsch: Building Services as
     integrated part of Fire Safety Concepts.
     In: REHVA Journal, 2003.
–   www.bpk-fire.de

16   Elevator Installations

[1] G. C. Barney, dos Santos: Lift Traffic
     Analysis Design and Control.
     Peter Peregrinus Ltd, London 1977.
[2] G. R. Strakosch: Vertical Transportation:
     Elevators and Escalators. Wiley 1967.
[3] H. M. Jappsen: Elevator Doors for
     Comfortable and Efficient Elevators.
     Presentation at ELEVCON '95, published
     in Elevator Technology 6.

List of Authors
(following order of chapters)

Dipl.-Ing. Ellen Kloft

Born 1966
Began architectural studies at the Darmstadt University of Technology in 1987. Awarded scholarship by the Studienstiftung des Deutschen Volkes. Freelance from 1995 to 1997, worked in architectural practices in Frankfurt and Darmstadt (Hoechstetter und Partner). Since 1997 scientific staff member for Construction and Experimental Design under Prof. Johann Eisele. Specialist research topic: "High-rises in the context of new technologies". Participant in exchange program GSE 2000 in São Paulo/ Brazil, organized by Rotary International. Own practice since 2001, prosa architektur & grafik.

Joachim Tenkhoff

Studied law in Münster, subsequently practiced as lawyer. 1989–1990 legal advisor und branch manager in Berlin with DIL (Deutsche Immobilien Leasing GmbH). 1992–1997 property developer and head of property development Berlin with ECE Projektmanagement G.m.b.H. 1998–2003 director at Tishman Speyer Properties Deutschland GmbH, one of the leading international property development firms, with headquarters in New York and offices in the USA, Europe and South America (among the best-known developments/investments are the Rockefeller Center, Chrysler Building, New York; Messeturm, Frankfurt; Sony Center, Potsdamer Platz Berlin). In April 2003 founded Tenkhoff Properties GmbH, with offices in Berlin.

Dipl.-Ing. Frank Spandl

Born 1963
Initial training as draughtsman, subsequent studies in architecture. Designer of diverse projects: administrative buildings, shopping centers, residential complexes, industrial buildings.
Since1995 project manager with HOMOLA AYH, also responsible for the company's information and quality management.
Appointed to Board of HOMOLA AYH in 2000.

Dipl.-Ing. Timo Brehme

Born 1966
Studied architecture at the Technische Universität Munich.
Professional experience gained at different architectural practices. Since 1996 working at congena.
Specialist areas: design of the work environment, CAD in consultation, organization of construction planning and office property consultation.

Dipl.-Ing. Frank Meitzner

Born 1961
Studied architecture in Aachen und Vienna Professional experience gained in architectural practices in Europe and the USA. Since 1991 working at congena.
Specialist areas: design of the work environment, organization of construction planning, user project management and office property consultation.

Prof. Dr.-Ing. Christoph Motzko

Born 1957
Studied civil engineering at the Darmstadt University of Technology. Production leader at a leading international producer of formwork systems. Promotion to construction manager, head of construction (airport construction). On the board of technical directors for a foreign concern of a large German construction company.
In 1996 appointed professor at the Darmstadt University of Technology, Institute for Site Operation.

Prof. Dr.-Ing. Ulvi Arslan

Born 1950
From 1968 studied civil engineering at the Technical Universities in Istanbul und Berlin, specialist area: geotechnics.
1974–1980 scientific staff member at the Institut für Bodenmechanik und Grundbau, Darmstadt University of Technology.
Doctorate 1980. 1980–1983 worked in engineering firms, 1983–1993 head engineer at the Versuchsanstalt für Geotechnik, since 1994 research and teaching at the Darmstadt University of Technology, faculty: civil engineering and geodesy (in geotechnics).

Dr.-Ing. Peter F. Ripper

Born 1947
From 1968–1974 studied civil engineering at the Darmstadt University of Technology. 1974–1975 consultant engineer at the Erdbaulaboratorium Dr. Erb. 1975–1979 scientific staff member at the Institut für Bodenmechanik und Grundbau, Darmstadt University of Technology, 1976–1979 head of the Bodenmechanische Labor. 1984 doctorate in geotechnics. 1981–1986 consultant engineer at the Grundbauinstitut Prof. Dr.-Ing. Sommer. 1986–2001 chief executive and co-owner of Baugrundinstitut Trischler & Partner in Darmstadt (since 1998 ARCADIS). Since April 2001 on the Board of AICON Amann Infutec Consult AG and CDM Consult AG – the engineer's network.

Prof. Dipl.-Ing. Manfred Grohmann

Born 1953
In 1973 began civil engineering studies at the Darmstadt University of Technology. 1979 technical office Fa. Wayss & Freytag. 1980 scientific staff member at the Darmstadt University of Technology, Institut für Grundbau. 1983 founded engineering firm Bollinger + Grohmann, structural design in all areas of high-rise construction. 1998 professor for building structure at the Universität Kassel, architectural faculty.

Prof. Dr.-Ing. Harald Kloft

Born 1963
1990 degree as structural engineer at the Darmstadt University of Technology. 1991–1993 worked in the area project management for the firm Strabag Bau AG. 1993–1998 scientific staff member and awarded doctorate at the Darmstadt University of Technology. 1998–2001 project leader at the offices of Bollinger + Grohmann in Frankfurt. 2000–2002 deputy professor for structural engineering at the Kaiserslautern University of Technology and visiting professor at the Staatliche Hochschule für Bildende Künste – Städelschule, Frankfurt. Since 2002 professor for structural design at the Kaiserslautern University of Technology. 2002 founded, together with Sigurdur Gunnarsson and Klaus Fäth, osd – office for structural design.

Prof. Dipl.-Ing. Johann Eisele

Born 1948
1970–71 studied civil engineering at the Technische Hochschule in Darmstadt (THD). 1971–78 degree in architecture at the Technische Hochschule Darmstadt. 1987 visiting professor at the Hochschule für Kunst und Musik in Bremen. 1988 visiting professor at the THD. 1989 visiting professor at the Technische Universität Braunschweig. Since 1990 professor at the Darmstadt University of Technology for Construction and Experimental Design. Architectural firms: from 1979 "eisele+fritz", 2000 founded "54f" Architektur/ Design/ Kunst.
Since 2002 executive director at the "Zentrum für Interdisziplinäre Technikforschung" (ZIT).

Prof. Dr.-Ing. Johann-Dietrich Wörner

Born 1954
1973–79 studied civil engineering in Berlin and Darmstadt. 1982–83 research residency in Japan. 1979–90 worked at engineering offices of König und Heunisch. 1985 doctorate from the Darmstadt University of Technology (with a dissertation on the realistic description of component structure interaction during earthquakes). 1991–95 research and teaching in massive construction at the Darmstadt

University of Technology. 1994 founded the engineering firm of Wörner und Partner. Since 1995 research and teaching in the area of statics at the Darmstadt University of Technology and president of the Darmstadt University of Technology.

Dr.-Ing. Hans-Werner Nordhues

Born 1965
1985–91 studied civil engineering in Dortmund and Darmstadt. 1991–94 scientific staff member of the Darmstadt University of Technology. 1995 doctorate from the Darmstadt University of Technology ("Entwicklung und Parallelisierung einer modalen Kapazitätsmethode"). Since 1994 executive partner in the engineering firm of Wörner und Partner.

Prof. Dr.-Ing. Hans Joachim Gerhardt

Born 1944
From 1963 studied mechanical engineering at the RWTH Aachen, specialist subject: heat engineering.
From 1968 studied mechanical engineering at Brown University, Providence, R.I., USA (M.Sc.). Since 1972 research and teaching at the Fachhochschule Aachen in the areas industrial and structural aerodynamics. 1998 doctorate from the TU Berlin ("Windeinwirkung auf Bedachungssysteme").

Dr.-Ing. Sigurdur Gunnarsson

Born 1968
1993 graduated as structural engineer from the University of Iceland. 1993–1998 scientific staff member and awarded doctorate from the Darmstadt University of Technology. 1998–2001 worked at Werner Sobek Ingenieure, Stuttgart (former deputy project leader for the new Generaldirektion der Deutschen Post AG in Bonn). Since 2001 deputy professor for structural engineering in the architectural faculty of the Kaiserslautern University of Technology. Since 2002 visiting professor at the Staatliche Hochschule für Bildende Künste – Städelschule, Frankfurt. 2002 founded, with Harald Kloft and Klaus Fäth, osd – office for structural design.

Dipl.-Ing. Martin Lutz

Executive partner at DS-Plan GmbH. Design and consultant engineer, with specialist areas: façade technology and building physics. Author and co-author of several books and numerous publications.

Prof. Dr.-Ing. Eberhard Oesterle

Chief executive DS-Plan GmbH, consultant engineer for energy optimization of buildings, specialist areas: façade and air-conditioning. Author and co-author of numerous books and publications.
Honorary professor at the Universität Stuttgart.

Prof. Dr.-Ing. Helmut F. O. Müller

Born 1943
1966–1972 architectural studies at the universities of Hanover and Stuttgart (degree) as well as at the School of Environment Studies, London University College. 1972–1982 design and research in the construction industry, an engineering practice and at the Universität Stuttgart (1979 Dissertation "Methodisches Vorgehen beim Konzipieren lichtdurchlässiger Aussenwandelemente"). 1982–1993 Professor in the architectural faculty of the Fachhochschule Cologne. Founder of the Institut für Licht- und Bautechnik at the FH Cologne (ILB). Since 1993 professor of the new chair for climate compatible architecture – since 2000 – and building physics at the faculty of civil engineering, Universität Dortmund. Since 1997 executive partner GLB, Gesellschaft für Licht und Bautechnik mbH Dortmund.

Dipl.-Ing. Hans Jürgen Schmitz

Born 1964
1986–1992 architectural studies at the Technische Hochschule Aachen. Lighting designer for office space, Cologne from 1992–1998. In 1997 began work on dissertation (Daylight conditions in atrium buildings) at the Technische Universität Dortmund. Since 1998 on the staff of the Gesellschaft für Licht- und Bautechnik in Dortmund.

Prof. Dipl.-Ing. Klaus Daniels

Born 1939
Studied general mechanical engineering at the Fachhochschule Cologne. 1964–1969 employed by diverse contractors: project engineer. 1969–2001 Board chairman at HL-Technik AG. Since 1990 professor at ETH (Swiss Federal Institute of Technology) Zurich, chair for building services. Since 2001 chairman of the supervisory board at HL-Technik AG.

Dipl.-Ing. Matthias Schuler

Born 1958
From 1979 studied mechanical engineering at the Universität Stuttgart, specialist area: technologies for a rational use of energy. 1987–1992 scientific staff member at the Universität Stuttgart, Institut für Thermodynamik und Wärmetechnik. 1992 founder and chief executive of the firm Transsolar, Schwäbisch Gmünd/Stuttgart, teaching responsibilities at the Fachhochschule Biberach and the Universität Stuttgart. Since 2001 visiting professor in the faculty of architecture, Graduate School of Design, Harvard University, Cambridge, MA.

Prof. Dr.-Ing. Wolfram Klingsch

Born 1944
1965–70 studied civil engineering at the Technische Universität Braunschweig. 1971–81 teaching and research, worked at various engineering firms, lecturer in fire protection at the Universität Essen. 1975 doctorate, 1981 appointed to the chair of materials technology and fire protection at the Bergische Universität Wuppertal. Official expert, surveyor, consultant engineer. Chief executive BPK Brandschutz Planung Klingsch Ing. Ges. mbH.

Ing. Hans M. Jappsen

Born 1937
1957–1961 Ingenieurschule Koblenz (today Fachhochschule Koblenz). Until 1962 assistant at the Ingenieurschule Koblenz in the discipline mechanical engineering and sound control. Until 1971 worked at MAN, elevator construction. Since 1972 freelance consultant engineer for elevator installations and building logistics with offices in Germany and Switzerland. Since 1972 designer of elevators in a large number of tall buildings in Germany, particularly in Frankfurt. Official expert for elevator systems and escalators. On the DIN standards committee for elevators and representative of DIN, member of ISO/TC178/WG6, Firefighters Lifts.

Dipl.-Ing. Siegfried Schilling

Born 1949
Studied electrical engineering. 1972–78 developer of measurement, operating and control installations. From 1978 departmental head for services, specialist areas: conception and implementation of economical and ecological management concepts for real estate, as well as the consultation and evaluation of services. Since 1993 executive partner of the engineering and services firm HL-Service Management GmbH in Siegen. 1995–2001 lecturer in Facility Management at the Universität Münster.

Picture Credits

A Brief History of the High-rise

"Tribute in Light", Light installation to remember the victims of September 11, New York, photo: AP

Typologies

Archiv FG Entwerfen und Baugestaltung, TU Darmstadt: Figs. 27, 30, 37, 39, all photos Peer Cassebaum
Bennett, David, Skyscrapers. Form & Function, London 1995, ill. 14: Fig. 4
Chicago Historical Society: Fig. 1
Commerzbank AG, Frankfurt: Fig. 40
Davidson, Hayes (Visualisation), Miller, Tom (Photographer): Fig. 35
ESTO, New York: Fig. 12, Photo: Ezra Stoller; Fig. 13, Photo: Ezra Stoller; Fig. 14, Photo: Wayne Andrews; Fig. 15, Photo: Peter Mauss; Fig. 16, Photo: Peter Aaron
Fessy, Georges: Figs. 28, 29
FLC / VG Bild-Kunst, Bonn 2003: Fig. 20
Gappoev, M.M., Universitätsprofessor, Moskau: Figs. 41, 42, 43, 44
Heil, Christine, London: Figs. 31, 32, 33, 34
Kloft, Harald, Berlin: Figs. 45, 46, 47
Landesarchiv Berlin: Fig. 26
La Ville, Art et Architecture en Europe 1870–1993, Paris 1994, ill. 135: Fig. 19
Library of Congress: Fig. 7
Meinel, Udo, Berlin: Fig. 25
Museum of the City of New York: Fig. 6
Philadelphia Saving Fund Society: Fig. 10
Smoothe (Visualisation): Fig. 36
Stiftung Archiv der Akademie der Künste, Berlin: Fig. 18
Tacharnow, Alexej and Kawtaradse, Sergej, Stalinistische Architektur, München 1992: Fig. 24
Thornten-Tomasetti Engineers, New York: Fig. 48
Tishman Speyer Properties, London, Photo Nick Wood: Fig. 8; Photo Sector Light Design, London: Figs. 11, 38
VG Bild-Kunst, Bonn 2003: Figs. 17, 22, 23
Viskochil, Larry A., Chicago at the Turn of the Century in Photographs, New York 1984, ill. 6: Fig. 2
Underhill: Fig. 5
Walter Gropius / bauhaus-archiv, Berlin: Fig. 21
Wurts Brothers: Fig. 9

Zukowsky, John, Chicago Architektur 1872–1922, München 1987, S. 62: Fig. 3

01 Project Development

Sony Berlin GmbH, photo Pierre Adenis: Fig. 1.1

03 Organization of Office Towers

congena (CAD Rights): Figs. 3.1–3.3, 3.5–3.9
congena Archive: Fig. 3.4

04 Site Operation

All drawings by the author
ACS Selbstkletterschalung PERI, Volume 1/2000, p. 22: Fig. 4.9
ACS Selbstkletterschalung PERI, Volume 1/2000, p. 58: Figs. 4.5, 4.6
Doka-Kletter-System, Doka Broschüre Edition 1998, p. 23: Figs. 4.7, 4.8
Philipp Holzmann AG, Hochhaus Maintower in Frankfurt, p. 4: Figs. 4.3, 4.4

05 Geotechnics

CDM Amann Infutec AG, Darmstadt: Figs. 5.1 a–c, 5.2, 5.5, 5.7 a–e, 5.8 b, c, 5.9, 5.10, 5.12 a–d, 5.14
CDM Grundbauinstitut Sommer, Darmstadt: Figs. 5.3 a, b, 5.4
CDM Jessberger, Bochum: Fig. 5.17
Gruber+Kleine-Kraneburg, Frankfurt (visualization): Fig. 5.18
Murphy/Jahn, Chicago, Deutsche Post AG (model photo): Fig. 5.16
Philipp Holzmann AG, Frankfurt: Fig. 5.13 a–e
Schneider & Schumacher, Frankfurt (model photo): Fig. 5.8 a
TU Darmstadt: Figs. 5.11, 5.15
Vivico Real Estate, Frankfurt: Fig. 5.6

06 Load-bearing Structures

All graphics by Kay Gänsler
Authors' archive, with photos by Manfred Grohmann, Harald Kloft, Arne Künstler, Kay Gänsler: Figs. 6.3 a, 6.6 a, b, 6.17 a, 6.18 a, 6.21, 6.22 a, b, 6.23 a, 6.25, 6.30, 6.32, 6.34, 6.36, 6.39, 6.41
Davies, Richard, Arch.: Foster and Partners, London: Fig. 6.42
Eisele, Johann, Darmstadt: Fig. 6.27 a
Flierl, Bruno: Fig. 6.26 a
Foster and Partners, London: Fig. 6.42 a, b
Gunnarsson, Sigurdur, Stuttgart: Figs. 6.29, 6.38
Pfeffer, Carsten, Fa. BubbleDeck: Fig. 6.37
Thornton-Tomasetti Engineers, New York: Fig. 6.26

07 Construction and Design

Author's archive: Figs. 7.4, 7.14, 7.25, 7.28, 7.35, 7.37
Archive FG Entwerfen und Baugestaltung, TU Darmstadt: Fig. 7.17, photo Peer Cassebaum, Darmstadt; Fig. 7.18, photo Thomas Spiegelhalter; Fig. 7.26; Fig. 7.32, photo Johann Eisele, Darmstadt; Fig. 7.39, photo Bettina Wirth, Darmstadt
Archive Kollhoff/Nemec, Berlin: Fig. 7.2
Behnisch, Behnisch + Partner, Stuttgart: Fig. 7.38
Buffalo and Erie County Historical Society: Fig. 7.7
Chicago Historical Society: Fig. 7.5
Commerzbank AG, Frankfurt: Fig. 7.41
Davies, Richard: Fig. 7.22
ESTO, New York: Fig. 7.1, photo: Peter Mauss; Fig. 7.8, photo: Ezra Stoller; Fig. 7.11, photo: Ezra Stoller; Fig. 7.12, photo: Ezra Stoller; Fig. 7.19, photo: David Sundberg; Fig. 7.20, photo: Ezra Stoller, Fig. 7.21, photo: Ezra Stoller; Fig. 7.24, photo: Peter Aaron; Fig. 7.27, photo: Wayne Andrews; Fig. 7.34, photo: Norman McGrath; Fig. 7.40, photo: Ezra Stoller
T.R. Hamzah & Yeang Sdn. Bhd., Selangor, Malaysia: Fig. 7.42
Hanisch, Manfred, Mettmann: Figs. 7.15, 7.30
Hedrich-Blessing courtesy of Rizzoli Urbanism, New York: Fig. 7.9
HPP Hentrich, Petschnigg & Partner, Düsseldorf: Fig. 7.15
Joedicke, Jürgen, Stuttgart: Fig. 7.29

Lambot, Ian, Surrey: Fig. 7.31
John Portman & Associates: Fig. 7.13
Santi Visalli: Fig. 7.16
Thornton-Tomasetti Engineers, New York,
  photo: Michael Goodman: Fig. 7.33
Viskochil, Larry A., Chicago at the Turn of the
  Century in Photographs, New York 1984,
  ill. 6: Fig. 7.6
Windstosser, Ludwig, Stuttgart: Fig. 7.36
Wurts Brothers: Fig. 7.3
Yeang, Ken, Kuala Lumpur: Fig. 7.43
Zimmer, Dirk, Berlin: Figs. 7.10, 7.23

08 Structural Dynamics

All drawings by the author
Bolt, Bruce A., Erdbeben, Schlüssel zur
  Geodynamik, Munich 1995, Fig. 3.12, p. 105:
  Fig. 8.1; Fig. 2.2, p. 27 and Fig. 2.10, p. 37:
  Fig. 8.2
DIN 1055, Part 4: Windlasten, Fig. 1: Fig. 8.15
DIN 4150, Part 3, Erschütterungen im Bau-
  wesen, Fig. 1, p. 4: Fig. 8.7
Eibl et al., Betonkalender 1997, part 2,
  Fig. 5.6, p. 839: Fig. 8.6
Ingenieurbüros Wörner und Partner:
  Figs. 8.3–8.5, 8.8, 8.11–8.14, 8.16a, b –8.22
Pauly et al.: Erdbebenbemessung von
  Stahlbetonhochbauten, Fig. 1.10, page 26:
  Fig. 8.9
Pauly et al.: Erdbebenbemessung von
  Stahlbetonhochbauten, Fig. 1.12, page 28:
  Fig. 8.10

09 Effects of Wind

All drawings by the author
Murphy/Jahn Arch., model photo Deutsche
  Post AG: Fig. 9.10
ECE Projektmanagement, visualization photo:
  Fig. 9.14
Gerhardt, Hans Joachim: Fig. 9.6

10 Façade Structures

All drawings by the author
Archive picture, Universität Darmstadt:
  Fig. 10.17 a
Archive picture, Universität Kaiserslautern:
  Fig. 10.22 a
Burgmer, Thorsten, Darmstadt: Figs. 10.3 b,
  10.10 b
ESTO, photo: Ezra Stoller: Figs. 10.10 a, 10.16 a
Gunnarsson, Sigurdur, Stuttgart: Figs. 10.1 a –c,
  10.9 a, b, 10.13, 10.15 b, c, 10.19 a,–d, 10.22 b,
  10.23 a,–c
Heuser, Jörg, Frankfurt: Fig. 10.4 d
Ishioka, Eiko, New York: Fig. 10.3 a
Kisling, Annette, Berlin: Fig. 10.16 b
Kloft, Harald, Darmstadt: Figs. 10.2, 10.12 b, c,
  10.17 b

11 Façade Technologies

All drawings by the authors
BUG AluTechnic AG, Kennelbach/Austria,
  Arch. Alsop architects, London: Fig. 11.33
DS-Plan GmbH: Figs. 11.1, 11.2
DS-Plan GmbH, Arch. Kollhoff und Timmer-
  mann, Berlin: Fig. 11.3
DS-Plan GmbH, Architektengemeinschaft
  Biefang, Nuremberg, Dürschinger, Fürth,
  Spengler, Nurem: Fig. 11.8
Esch, H. G., Hennef, for Arch. Ingenhoven
  Overdiek Kahlen und Partner, Dusseldorf:
  Figs. 11.10, 11.26
Josef Gartner & Co., Gundelfingen, Architek-
  tengemeinschaft Biefang, Nuremberg,
  Dürschinger, Fürth, Spengler, Nuremberg:
  Figs. 11.7, 11.27, 11.34
Knauf, Holger, Düsseldorf for Arch. RKW Rhode,
  Kellermann, Wawrowsky, Dusseldorf:
  Figs. 11.12, 11.13, 11.32
Kroll, Bernhard, für Arch. Schweger + Partner,
  Hamburg: Figs. 11.14, 11.15
Wäller, Jan-Frederik, Dusseldorf, Arch. Alsop
  architects, London: Figs. 11.5

12 Insolation and Shading

All drawings by the authors, computer
  graphics by the authors: Figs. 12.3–12.5
Archive Hans Jürgen Schmitz: Fig. 12.6
RWE-Energie-Bau-Handbuch, Volume 11/1995:
  Fig. 12.2
Schuster, Heide: Fig. 12.1
Interim report of "Testfassade" research project
  funded by AG Solar NRW for the faculty
  chair: Climate compatible architecture and
  building physics, Universität Dortmund:
  Fig. 12.15

13 Building Systems

Daniels, Klaus, Gebäudetechnik, Ein Leitfaden
  für Architekten und Ingenieure, Munich,
  3rd Edition: Figs. 13.1–13.8, 13.10–13.13
Project study by HL-Technik AG, Munich:
  Figs. 13.9, 13.14–13.35

14 Integrated Concepts

All drawings by the author
Author's archive: Figs. 14.1, 14.3, 14.4, 14.5, 14.7,
  14.24 a-c
Arch. Murphy/Jahn, Deutsche Post Berlin:
  Fig. 14.13
Kauffmann Theilig & Partner, design for a
  high-rise in Shanghai: Figs. 14.17, 14.18, 14.19
Pearce, Mike: Fig. 14.2

Every effort was made to acknowledge and
obtain permission for all pictures. The publishers apologize for any ommissions that may
have occured.

Acknowledgements

With contributions by 24 authors from diverse specialist disciplines, this High-rise Manual is the result of a highly motivated collaboration of all those involved, beginning with the different authors and their stimulating suggestions regarding content and form, to the production team working tirelessly in the background.

The authors must be thanked for their patience and forbearance during the many queries and correction runs.
The high-rise team at the Darmstadt University of Technology, including Eva Schwarz, Sabine Habicht, Martin Böttcher, Thorsten Burgmer and Sven Kling are thanked by the editors for their work. Particular mention goes to Sven Kling for his terrific support regarding content and organization.
Lastly, the Zentrum für Interdisziplinäre Technikforschung (ZIT) at the TU-Darmstadt must be mentioned for supporting the High-rise Manual with a research project on the topic of high-rise buildings.

The Editors

Translation into English:
Elizabeth Schwaiger, Toronto
Robin Benson, Berlin
Derek Henderson, Architext, Dresden

Graphic design:
Sven Kling, prosa architektur & grafik, Darmstadt
Continue AG, Basel

A CIP catalogue record for this book is available from the Library of
Congress, Washington D.C., USA

Bibliographic information published by Die Deutsche Bibliothek
Die Deutsche Bibliothek lists this publication in the Deutsche
Nationalbibliografie; detailed bibliographic data is available on the
Internet at http://dnb.ddb.de.

© German edition 2002 HochhausAtlas by Verlag Georg
    D. W. Callwey GmbH & Co. KG, München.
    2003 Licence granted to Birkhäuser – Publishers for
    Architecture, P.O. Box 133
    CH-4010 Basel, Switzerland
    Part of Springer Science + Business Media

Printed on acid-free paper produced from chlorine-free pulp. TCF ∞
Printed in Germany
ISBN 3-7643-0274-7

9 8 7 6 5 4 3 2 1
www.birkhauser.ch

BPK Brandschutz
Planung Klingsch

International Fire Safety Consulting

As consulting engineers with offices in Düsseldorf, Frankfurt/Main and Remscheid, BPK Brandschutz Planung Prof. Dr.-Ing. W. Klingsch IngenieurgesellschaftmbH lays claim to a special position in the area of fire safety. Proven expert knowledge makes the practice fully qualified to provide comprehensive services in fulfilling demanding commissions over the complete field of fire safety. Its staff of about 30 is able to point to years of international experience and comprehensive knowledge across the whole spectrum of fire safety. This does not only include sound knowledge of building materials, components and law but also specialist expertise in construction, building technology, fire detection, smoke venting, escape and rescue routes, management of fire safety on site etc. In addition to the company's role as a consulting engineer, it also offers services such as fire safety certification and expert reports. The main area of activity is drawing up of fire safety concepts, for buildings in particular, and the assessment of the likelihood of them being approved by the supervisory authorities where there is conflict between design requirements or use concepts and the requirements of the building regulations. In these circumstances BPK is able to devise tailormade fire safety solutions oriented towards the customer's objectives. Whether it is fully-glazed façades in high-rise buildings or dynamic fire control strategies for lifts, BPK has developed new safety concepts with the aid of new design processes. Many of these ideas have been adopted as guidelines and codes of practice for special buildings and some have been incorporated into European standards and regulations.

The special fire protection concepts developed by BPK are distinguished from others in that the individual fire protection components relating to construction, building technical services and organisation are interactive and not just cumulative in their effects. This interaction increases safety and leads to economic benefits, because the use of high quality calculation and design methods makes it pos-

sible to carry out essential installations more effectively. In order to be able to develop these solutions, one of the tools BPK uses is modern computer simulation software specially designed for fire engineering. In this way, customised special solutions are devised and the restrictions of a generalised approach or the legal requirements of the building regulations can be minimised without loss of fire safety. In addition to computer simulations, BPK can, where necessary, also provide experimental model simulations as well as full-size investigations, which include acceptance tests inside finished buildings.

High Rise Ensemble at Frankfurt a. M., Germany (from left to right): EUROTHEUM, MAIN TOWER, COMMERZBANK TOWER (tallest high rise building of europe), JAPAN CENTER fire design and engineering by BPK

BPK –
International Fire Safety Consulting
Brandschutz Planung
Prof. Dr.-Ing. W. Klingsch
Ingenieurgesellschaft mbH
Internet: www.bpk-fire.de

BPK Düsseldorf
Wahlerstr. 32
D-40472 Düsseldorf, Germany
Telefon: 0211/436183-0
Telefax: 0211/436183-83
E-Mail: office-dus@bpk-mail.de

BPK Frankfurt
Liebigstr. 20
D-60323 Frankfurt/Main, Germany
Telefon: 069/717136-0
Telefax: 069/717136-36
E-Mail: office-ffm@bpk-mail.de

BPK's competence in fire safety and protection is recognised internationally: The consultancy has been commissioned with high-quality projects in many European countries as well as in the USA, China, Japan and Egypt.

The company's experience over the whole field of fire safety engineering for multi-storey buildings is founded on over 50 high rises in Germany and further high-rise building projects abroad. The company has also worked on numerous high-profile and demanding fire safety design projects, including: airports at Frankfurt, Düsseldorf and Munich, trade fair centres in Frankfurt and Düsseldorf, the Reichstag in Berlin, underground rail stations, shopping centres, museums and public assembly facilities as well as large industrial plants, transportation tunnels etc.